Exploring the 46 Adirondack High Peaks

Also by James R. Burnside

The Selling of General Electric
(1990)

Letting Go:
The Self-Directed Work Force
(1992)

GE Field Engineering:
The First 100 Years
(1994)

Exploring the
46 Adirondack High Peaks

*With 282 photos, maps and mountain profiles,
excerpts from the author's journal,
and historical insights.*

James R. Burnside

High Peaks Press

Seventh Printing 2004

International Standard Book Number: 0-9624923-2-9

Library of Congress Catalog Card Number: 96-94033

High Peaks Press
2307 Cayuga Road
Schenectady, New York 12309
(518) 372-2605

Printed in the United States of America.

To my wife, Elizabeth

*who waved us off happily,
every time.*

CONTENTS

FOREWORD

This is a book of exploration and adventure in one of America's best loved yet least known wilderness areas: the Adirondack high peaks of upstate New York.

It also is the culmination of a quest — an attempt to reconcile the romanticism of the Adirondacks past with clinical reports coming out of the Adirondacks present.

The book is meant for four kinds of people.

First, those who want to climb and explore the 46 highest mountains of the Adirondacks, but don't know how to go about it.

Second, people who have climbed all or some of the peaks, and want to recapture those glory days.

Third, others who would love to climb and explore, but can't for whatever reason.

And fourth, those who have no interest in climbing, but love the Adirondacks and wonder what goes on up there.

The high peaks form the core of the Adirondack State Park, a Vermont-sized lodestone which each year attracts some 10 million people from all over the world.

Most are drawn not so much by the contours of the park's 2,000 mountains as by the ever-presence of water — 30,000 miles of brooks, creeks and rivers, nourished by 2,300 lakes and ponds. These visitors, like most year-round residents, are lowlanders, who view the mountains as mere dots on the map, a brooding backdrop for the action below.

They are not the first to feel that way. From the earliest days of American history to little more than 100 years ago, the Adirondack high peaks were not only ignored, but shunned.

Dutch settlers in Albany believed that unicorns roamed afield. Indians referred to the area as Couxsachrage — the "dismal wilderness." Colonists and the British skirmished on the lower slopes during the Revolution but never attempted to climb the heights.

A surveyor's map of the area in 1772 showed one lone mountain — Gore. It's still there, but Gore is 30 miles south of the true high peaks and 417 feet short of their status.*

---

*In 1937, the newly formed Adirondack Forty Sixers Club defined 46 Adirondack mountains as "high peaks" because they were at least 4,000 feet high. Later measurements showed that four of them did not reach that height, but they are still considered part of the group.

While the Adirondacks remained dormant, pioneers rushed west to climb Pike's Peak in Colorado, identify the headwaters of the Missouri River in Montana, and discover Mt. Hood in Oregon. It was more than 40 years after the latter when an explorer reconnoitering from an iron mine in the southern Adirondacks saw a "shining peak in the distance." He formed a group to climb it the following year, in 1837, and the mountain — the state's highest — was named for New York's governor, William Learned Marcy.

Historians suspect that Mt. Washington, New England's highest peak in neighboring New Hampshire, was sighted by the Italian explorer Verrazano when he skirted the coast in 1524. True or not, Mt. Washington was climbed in 1642, almost two centuries before Marcy was even discovered.

The renowned Adirondack historian, Alfred L. Donaldson, concluded, "Stanley had found Dr. Livingstone and familiarized the world with the depths of Africa before the average New Yorker knew anything definite about the wonderful wilderness lying almost at his back door."

Time confirmed that judgment. It would be almost another century after Marcy was first climbed before the last of the 46 high peaks was surmounted, in 1925.

Tales brought back by the first people to surmount all of the Adirondack high peaks — brothers Bob and George Marshall, with their guide, Herb Clark — stirred a trickle of interest. A half century later, it swelled to a torrent.

A recent state commission reported an exponential surge in Adirondack hikers — up 700 per cent in a little less than two decades. More than 100,000 now swarm to the peaks each year, many to try climbing the 46 highest.

I dipped my toe into the growing rivulet in 1967, enlisting sons James C. and later, Benjamin J. to see if we could join the elite group which had accomplished the feat. The challenge was intimidating: at that time, less than 400 climbers had managed to climb all 46, even though more than 50 million people lived within a day's drive of the park.

This book documents our conquest and exploration of the peaks — how we went about it, what we found, and some personal experiences as recorded in my journal, compiled from field notes.

Almost every step of our way unfolded a landscape littered both with the legacy of the past and the prospect of present danger. Surely no other wilderness region in the U.S. has released such an outpouring of emotion as the Adirondacks.

American historian Francis Parkman referred to it as "our dark, unstoried woods." He then proceeded to blaze some of the most moving literary trails ever to wind through a wilderness.

The philosopher William James, in a letter to his wife, put into words what so many Adirondack hikers have experienced but could never express. He had spent, he wrote, "a good deal of [the night] in the woods, where the streaming moonlight lit up things in a magical checkered play...It was one of the happiest lonesome nights of my existence, and I understand now what a poet is."

Robert Louis Stevenson, recuperating from chronic lung disease at Saranac Lake in 1887, described the Adirondacks as "a kind of insane mixture of Scotland and a touch of Switzerland and a dash of America and a thought of the British Channel in the skies." Stevenson must have lamented the latter; it reminded him of "drear October." Ruminating in a letter to William James' equally famous brother Henry, Stevenson avowed, "I like water." But, he added, "either running swiftly among stones, or else largely qualified with whiskey."

Most of the writers and artists of the era were, again, lowlanders. Today, those who venture to the Adirondack highlands find that harsh reality often diffuses romantic images. Exploration is not only difficult, it can be dangerous.

One reason is that almost half the Adirondack high peaks are trailless; all of the loftier White mountains in New Hampshire have marked trails linked to shelter huts. A member of the mountaineering support team on Mt. Everest in 1984, Forty Sixer Linda Nerwin, observed, "I learned after climbing in mud, rain and blowdown in our Adirondacks that other areas in the world are not so tough."

In fact, experts say the winter climate in the Adirondacks is more severe than that of the Himalayas. A major factor is latitude. The Adirondacks are only a sixth as high, but they're a thousand miles north of Mt. Everest, which soars upward from the latitude of Orlando, Florida.

Because of the northern exposure, Adirondack climbers face fearsome weather changes (one noted a drop of 60 degrees in a few hours). Such conditions, compounded by rain and snow (which occurs one of every three days), breed hypothermia, which causes the body to lose heat faster than it can generate it.

Climbers who wear cotton instead of wool and carry no high energy foods find body heat plummeting along with air temperature. If one gets lost (it happens to more than 250 people a year in the Adirondacks) or becomes disoriented in a remote area, the risks escalate. A hiker on Algonquin Peak who went to get help for a hypothermic partner returned less than an hour later to find him dead.

The chilling prospect was brought home twice to me during our explorations when I experienced the early stages of hypothermia. Its approach is swift and insidious. As a consequence, Joel White of the Appalachian Mountain Club warned that, "one of the hardest things to learn is how to turn around and come back."

Ben and I conquered the last of our 46 Adirondack high peaks, Skylight, in 1981, becoming Forty Sixers nos. 1695 and 1696. We still go back to climb and explore, often the same mountains but from different directions. Even old routes unfold new discoveries.

It reaffirms the obvious: no one can unlock all the glories of the Adirondack high peaks in a lifetime. The one who perhaps came closest, Verplanck Colvin, the indefatigable state surveyor who tromped over a good many of the mountains in the mid-19th century, concluded it was "a region of mystery, over which none can gaze without a strange thrill of interest and wonder at what might be hidden in that vast area..."

This enduring mystery is the force which draws so many people to the peaks. It is perhaps the only place on the crowded eastern seaboard where one can get away from the hordes — where one can explore for a full day without seeing a single person, or a single sign of civilization from a mountain top.

The Adirondack high peaks promise one of the last great ventures into the unknown that one can undertake in an area comprising 85 per cent of the remaining wilderness in the northeastern United States. For me, and certainly in the minds of my sons, it was high adventure, conjuring up the exploits of Lewis and Clark, Francis Parkman, Richard Halliburton, Amelia Earhart, Sir Edmund Hillary and Tenzig Norgay...whoever fires your imagination.

Some say the Age of Exploration in the Adirondacks is over, that there is nothing new to discover. The vastness of six million acres continues to prove them wrong.

Paul Schaefer, who has spent the better part of this century exploring and defending the integrity of the park, recently discovered a glacial lake high in the east central Adirondacks. Schaefer — a Schenectady contractor who added touches of the Adirondacks when he remodelled the interior of our family room — noted that New York state had owned the lake for more than a century but it had never appeared on U.S.G.S. topographic maps.

The same invitation to wander and wonder awaits the newcomer. Every climb, every turn of the way offers the same first-time thrill that it did to those who came before.

The lure of the Adirondacks is timeless. It's yours to experience — on your own or, if you prefer a surrogate climber, perhaps through these pages.

Schenectady, New York

BEHIND THE MAKING OF THIS BOOK

Any person who climbs just one of the 46 Adirondack high peaks comes down with a curious malady. It's called summit madness. The only known cure is to climb the other 45.

It was natural for me to get hooked on the fever, having been brought up in Iowa. There, of course, "brought up" did not mean climbing a mountain.

Iowa's highest point used to be the crest of a 1,631-foot mound in northwestern Osceola county. Now, the bar height has been notched up 44 feet to a hump nearby on which stands a cattle trough behind the barn on Merrill and Donna Sterler's farm. Both knolls look like all the others, which make up what used to be rolling prairie that blanketed the state.

Three things prompted me to try and climb the 46 high peaks after coming east.

The first came when my wife and I took our oldest daughter Judy to St. Lawrence University in Canton, New York in the spring of 1967, prior to her formal entrance in the fall. While browsing in the university bookshop, I picked up a copy of *The Adirondack Reader* by Paul Jamieson, another former Iowan who had been a Professor of English at the university. It opened the door to an exciting new world that was foreign to me.

The second was a back injury which prompted an outdoor regimen of walking to build up those muscles.

The third impetus came from my son Jim, 10 years old at the time, who convinced me to try our first peak later in 1967. We climbed 28 more in the next few years until he went off to college and discovered girls, and that was the end of that. Or so I thought.

A decade later, my younger son Benjamin, also 10 at the time, caught the fever by reading my journals. He begged me to administer the antidote — start all over again with him.

The old bones were pretty creaky by that time, but start over we did. It was as much a matter of surprise as relief when we finished.

It wasn't easy, since we live more than 100 miles away from the trail-heads, and favor day trips instead of camping overnight. According to my journal, to climb and complete the exploration of the 46 we drove 19,441 miles to and from the mountains, hiked 716 miles over trails and unmarked terrain, and climbed 178,360 feet.

Let me see if I can put that in context. The equivalent, assuming you could find a decent road, would be to drive from Schenectady, New York to Fairbanks, Alaska, then loop out across the Aleutians to Siberia, and make a bee line south through China for Katmandu, Nepal.

From there, you'd proceed west 50 miles to pitch your tent. Then you'd climb Mt. Everest, which is another 50 miles away, eight times, going back and forth from base camp.

Of course, then you'd still have to drive back to Schenectady by the same route.

Put another way, your climb up the mountains we explored would be roughly the same as ascending the highest Adirondack peak, Mt. Marcy, 56 times by the most popular route. Or, from sea level, climbing a single mountain nearly 34 miles high.

It took me 14 years to complete the conquest. In all that time, and since, little has changed. A few former trackless peaks now have trails — Phelps and Iroquois, for example. Even shy Esther mingles more with the crowds. There are now three major unmarked paths — stomped to half a foot deep in places — which converge on their tortuous way toward Esther from the marked Whiteface trail.

But the pleasures of the peaks have not changed: the wild game that's as skittish as you are when your paths cross; the ponds and springs missed by cartographers; the forests which ripple off toward the horizon; and, on your way to the trailheads, the townspeople who impart a sense of what things have been like over the past century.

Today's climber will likely see, as we did, the bear, deer, bobcat, otter, beaver, wild turkey, marten, loon, osprey, raven, trout, and coyote. And the state Environmental Conservation Department is doing its best to see that you spot species that were exterminated in the Adirondacks but are coming back — bald eagle, lynx, moose and more.

Climbers will also explore areas — my sons and I still find this hard to believe — that not much more than a half century ago had never been trod by civilized man. The Adirondack high peaks are the perfect prescription to fulfill that basic need which Thoreau called "the tonic of wildness."

You may wonder about the order in which the peaks are presented. It has nothing to do with preference; they're listed in the order I first climbed them.

Each chapter, or climb, is headed by data which may be useful. It includes a profile of the trek to and from the summit, the elevation and distance, a typical time for the round trip, and the degree of difficulty. You'll find the rationale for the latter on page xvii.

Take the typical times with a grain of salt. In our case, I often had to drag older son Jim up the slopes, while later on son Ben had to drag me.

We usually spent about an hour of the time shown for lunch or whatever on each summit.

Also keep in mind that a few people in superb condition have climbed all of the peaks in weeks instead of years. On the other end of the scale, Forty Sixer club member Anne Dennis made my pace look supersonic; she stretched her climbs over 62 years. Obviously, she shares my philosophy: What's the hurry?

You'll also find my view rating for each peak, updating the subjective judgment of the Marshall brothers and Herb Clark, rendered back in 1926. Anyone's view, of course, is colored by the weather, time of day, blisters, protective clothing, black flies, remaining trail snacks and water, the good or bad prospect of the descent, and so on.

As a partial palliative, I've included photos of what we saw during our explorations, and views which capture the mood of the peaks. With due deliberation, you can suit the data to your own purposes and then peg your own standards of view and degree of difficulty.

For those of you who are ready for the grand exploration, have a great time!

J.R.B.

THE 46 ADIRONDACK HIGH PEAKS

High peak	Rank in height	Elevation (feet)	View Rating	
			Original (1926)	Current (Author)
Algonquin Peak	2	5114	5	5
Allen Mtn.	26	4340 *	17	35
Armstrong Mtn.	22	4400 *	18	31
Basin Mtn.	9	4827	6	11
Big Slide Mtn.	27	4240 *	29	22
Blake	43	3960 *	37	28
Cascade Mtn.	36	4098	34	13
Cliff Mtn.	44	3960 *	42	43
Mt. Colden	11	4714	20	16
Mt. Colvin	39	4057	19	27
Couchsachraga Peak	46	3820	32	44
Dial Mtn.	41	4020	35	45
Dix Mtn.	6	4857	9	2
Mt. Donaldson	33	4140	28	40
East Dix	42	4012	39	38
Mt. Emmons	40	4040	41	41
Esther Mtn.	28	4240	43	36
Giant Mtn.	12	4627	22	7
Gothics	10	4736	14	1
Gray Peak	7	4840 *	21	29
Mt. Haystack	3	4960	1	6
Hough Peak	23	4400 *	31	42
Iroquois Peak	8	4840 *	4	18
Lower Wolfjaw Mtn.	30	4175	27	37
Macomb Mtn.	21	4405	15	15
Mt. Marcy	1	5344	8	3
Mt. Marshall	25	4360	12	20
Nippletop	13	4620 *	3	4
Nye Mtn.	45	3895	46	46
Panther Peak	18	4442	10	21
Phelps Mtn.	32	4161	38	26
Porter Mtn.	38	4059	40	30
Mt. Redfield	15	4606	7	25
Rocky Peak Ridge	20	4420 *	33	8
Saddleback Mtn.	17	4515	25	10
Santanoni Peak	14	4607	2	9
Sawteeth	35	4100 *	16	19
Seward Mtn.	24	4361	11	34
Seymour Mtn.	34	4120	30	23
Mt. Skylight	4	4926	13	12
South Dix	37	4060	44	32
Street Mtn.	31	4166	45	33
Tabletop Mtn.	19	4427	26	39
Upper Wolfjaw Mtn.	29	4185	36	24
Whiteface Mtn.	5	4867	23	14
Wright Peak	16	4580	24	17

* Elevation of highest map contour line.

About the View Ratings

View ratings were originally applied in 1926 by the Marshall brothers and Herb Clark, who first climbed all 46 Adirondack high peaks. My own objective ratings are tempered by conditions on the days of climb, plus changes wrought by the great hurricane of 1950 and the self-healing of the wilderness from that and other calamities — the great forest fires in the early part of this century, lumbering, etc.

All ratings, of course, are subjective. But all climbers agree on one: Nye Mtn. rates dead last.

On Names and Numbers

Over the years, heights and names of Adirondack mountains have been moving targets.

Gazeteers in the 19th century thought the Catskills were the highest mountains in the state. The Adirondacks' Whiteface, they said, was no more than 2,700 feet. In fact, it tops the Catskills' highest, Slide Mtn., by almost 700 feet.

By the mid-20th century, the accepted elevation and order of height of Adirondack peaks were dictated by the U.S. Geological Survey of 1950. Then, a year in advance of the 1980 Olympics at Lake Placid, the bureau published new maps in metric units instead of feet.

Both the Adirondack Mountain Club and the Adirondack Forty Sixers Club applied — or so it seems to the layman — arcane formulas for metric conversion, which yielded different elevations and orders of height for the peaks.

I've sided with the conclusions of the former; only 10 of their elevations differ from those of the 1950 survey, and none varies more than 10 feet. The constant in all rankings is Marcy. It's always been king of the hills.

In the early days of Adirondack exploration, one needed a scorecard to keep up with name changes. Originally, Algonquin was MacIntyre, or McIntyre. Marshall was known at various times as Clinton, Herbert and Iroquois. Marcy was referred to at one time as Tahawas, the Seneca Indians' term for "cloud splitter."

Even today, the spelling of the high peaks varies from maps to guidebooks — Tabletop vs. Table Top, Nippletop vs. Nipple Top, Wolfjaw vs. Wolf Jaw, etc. I've spelled them the way I think they best match contemporary usage. Take your choice.

The Degree of Difficulty

For those who may wish to explore on their own, the mountain profile at the head of each chapter includes a rating for the climb described.

The ratings are based upon the scale suggested by the Schenectady Chapter of the Adirondack Mountain Club:

C: Easy; under five miles. Moderate to slow rate of walking.
B: Moderate to difficult; five to nine miles. Some steepness.
A: Difficult; 10 to 15 miles. May have large vertical ascents.
AA: Very difficult. Only for the experienced hiker.

UNFAMILIAR TERMS

Lowlanders often have trouble with mountain talk. Here are a few of the most commonly-used terms, and their meanings.

ADK: Adirondack Mountain Club. Established in 1922, dedicated to the protection and responsible recreational use of the New York state Forest Preserve, parks and other wild lands and waters. 814 Goggins Rd., Lake George, NY 12845-4117. (518) 668-4447.

AMC: Appalachian Mountain Club. Formed in 1876 to promote hiking and mountain exploration in the northeastern U.S. 5 Joy St., Boston, MA 02108. (617) 523-0636.

AMR: Adirondack Mountain Reserve. Private preserve administered by the Ausable Club, located three miles south of Keene Valley in St. Huberts, NY 12943. (518) 576-4411.

ATIS: Adirondack Trail Improvement Society. Organized in 1897 to focus on the mountains around St. Huberts and the Ausable Lakes.

Bench mark: Surveyor's mark left on a stationary object to show position or elevation.

Blowdown: Trees blown down by high winds. Widespread damage caused by the hurricane of 1950 is a prime example.

Bushwhack: A trek through terrain which has no marked trails — i.e., which is trailless.

Cairn: Mound of stones to guide hikers, usually on bare rock surface.

Cirque: Huge, rounded hollow carved by glaciers in upper mountain reaches.

Cobble: Small, naturally-rounded mountainous formation.

Col: Pass between two mountains, or gap in a ridge.

Conifers: Cone-bearing trees — i.e., pine, fir, spruce.

Cripplebush: Entwined, stunted growth, such as mountain balsam, found at high elevations. Scientists call it krummholz; what most climbers call it is unprintable.

DEC: Department of Environmental Conservation (New York state). Also, see ENCON.

Duff: Decaying leaves and branches covering the forest floor.

ENCON: New York state's Department of Environmental Conservation. Also, see DEC.

Flag trees: Usually conifers, with branches growing only on sheltered side. Caused by severe winds at high elevations.

Flowed Land: Area south of Lake Colden, dammed in the last century to divert flow of Opalescent River to Calamity Brook, providing water for the iron mine at Tahawus.

Forty Sixers: Adirondack Forty Sixers, Inc. Club members have climbed the 46 highest peaks in the Adirondacks; "aspiring members" have climbed 30 or more. Mailing address: 279 Rand Hill Road, Morrisonville, NY, 12962.

Great Range: Spectacular array of high peaks leading some eight miles southwest from Keene Valley to Mt. Marcy.

Herd paths: Random routes tramped by climbers on trailless high peaks.

Lean-to: Log shelter with one open side, protected by an overhanging roof, facing a fireplace.

Loj: Diminutive name for lodge (Adirondak Loj) maintained by the ADK at Heart Lake, five miles south of Rt. 73 at the end of a turn-off between Lake Placid and Keene. (518) 523-3441.

Masting: Harvesting of nuts from forest trees.

Scat: Excrement of animals, especially game animals such as bears.

Slash: Residue on the forest floor from logging, or a result of fire, storms, etc.

Sweep: Person on group hike designated to round up stragglers.

Topo: Topographic map.

Tote roads: Routes through the forest used by loggers. Many were "paved" with corduroy, a surface formed by logs placed side-by-side against the grain of traffic.

Trailhead: Starting point for a foottrail.

Trap dike: Cleft in a cliff caused by erosion of material softer than the foundation rock.

U.S.G.S.: U. S. Geological Survey.

Cascade Mtn. from Pitchoff Mtn.

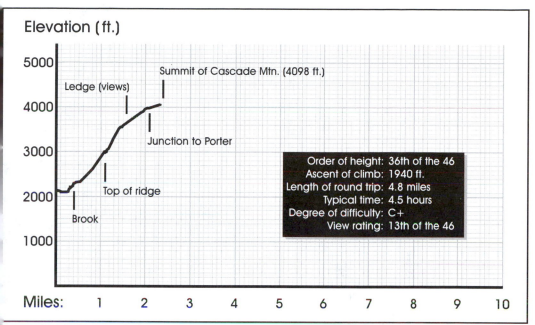

Elevation (ft.)

Summit of Cascade Mtn. (4098 ft.)

Ledge (views)

Junction to Porter

Top of ridge

Brook

Order of height:	36th of the 46
Ascent of climb:	1940 ft.
Length of round trip:	4.8 miles
Typical time:	4.5 hours
Degree of difficulty:	C+
View rating:	13th of the 46

Miles: 1 2 3 4 5 6 7 8 9 10

For contour trails, see U.S. Geological Survey map, pgs. 2-3.

1.
CASCADE

Those who want to explore the 46 Adirondack high peaks usually turn to hiking veterans for advice.

I posed the standard question to Dave Newhouse, a neighbor at the time, who later became president of the 22,000-member Adirondack Mountain Club: What's the best mountain to start with, one that's not too hard to climb, but gives a measure of the rest?

He answered without hesitation: "Cascade. There's no more exhilarating introduction to the Adirondack high peaks."

Newhouse was right on the mark. For starters, Cascade offers the shortest round trip. At a little more than four miles, it's about two thirds the distance of the second shortest circuit in the high peaks — the climb up Giant Mtn.

Many of the higher peaks pose risks because of difficulty, lack of direction, and distance. But Cascade is benign. It's not only the easiest of the 46 to climb, it has a trail.

As a result, Cascade is a magnet for people of all ages from spring through fall. Even during winter, the trail may be sprinkled with seasoned hikers.

"Easiest," of course, is relative.

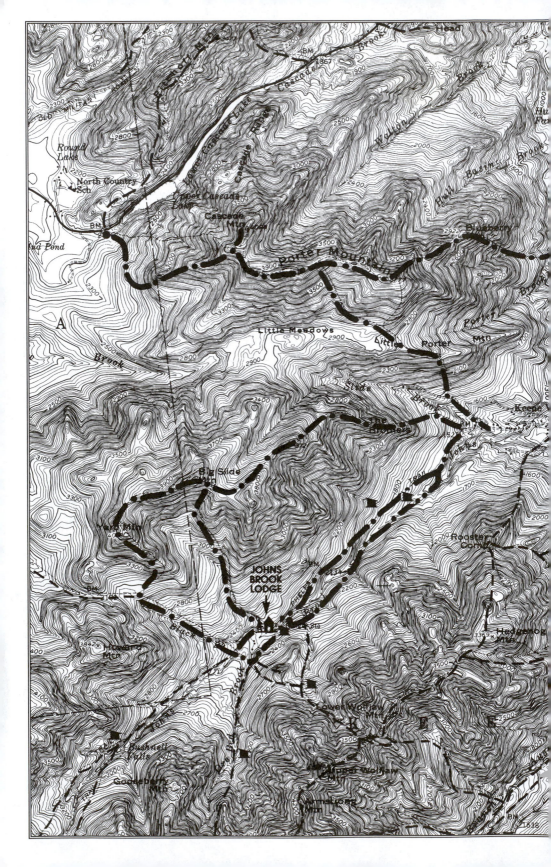

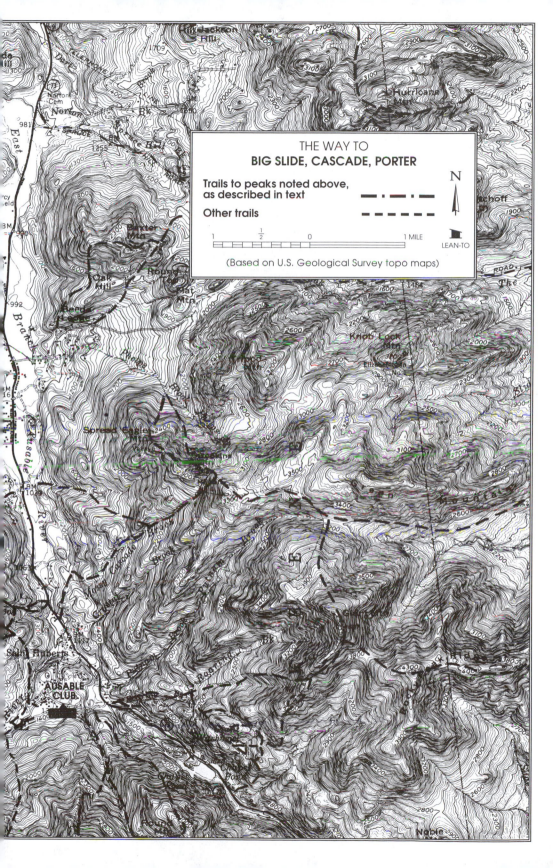

THE WAY TO
BIG SLIDE, CASCADE, PORTER

Trails to peaks noted above,
as described in text

Other trails

N

1   ½   0   1 MILE

LEAN-TO

(Based on U.S. Geological Survey topo maps)

Journal entry: Saturday, September 23, 1967. The profusion of birches is magnificent. But son Jim and I stare mostly at the outcroppings of rocks and roots that are the handholds for our next steps. The prospect is discouraging. A very long, steep rise is followed by an approach to another long, steep rise.

The promise of high adventure. *Spring on Cascade offers a glorious introduction to the highest peaks of the Adirondacks. The short hike is one of the most popular of the 46.*

The trail up Cascade was exceedingly steep until 1974, when it was re-routed. It is now so moderate (albeit a little over a mile longer) that Cascade just misses being the most popular peak to be climbed by first-timers in the Adirondacks. The all-time favorite, Mt. Marcy, edges it out by a narrow margin.

A major reason for Cascade's popularity is that, while rated a runt, it shares most of the genes of its big brothers and sisters.

One of these is a progression through different Adirondack forest zones. These range from mature maples, beeches and oaks in the lowlands through conifers and birches above, to a culmination near the summit of dwarf trees and alpine plants.

The glories of exploring the Adirondacks were described by a Boston minister named William H. H. Murray in the spring of 1869. His report was so exuberant it prompted a tourist influx that fall which came to be known as the "Murray Rush."

The Reverend cautioned, however, that the Adirondacks are not for everyone: "Many gentlemen leave their wives and children here (in hotels) while they are in the wilderness sporting."

Old Sport, times have changed.

Journal entry: Saturday, July 1, 1978. *A few hundred yards up the trail, Ben and I pass a young couple urging onward a child, perhaps three years old. They'll never make it, I predict. But it's a lovely day for them to take a short hike on the wooded slopes.*

Near the halfway mark, Ben and I stop in a cool glade and adjust the camera to automatically take a photo of us together. We are surprised to see the threesome nod pleasantly as they pass. Mortified, we snap up, pack up, and scoot around them.

One almost always meets groups with children on the trail in summer. They generate a high degree of enthusiasm for hiking. The Adirondack Forty Sixers Club newsletter reports that Bill Kozel and his wife-to-be, for example, liked climbing the highest Adirondack peaks so much they decided to get married on one, and chose Cascade. Their daughter, Cassy, is named for — you guessed it.

And the lure endures. Grace Hudowalski, the first woman to climb all of the 46 peaks, and only the ninth person to do so, felt the urge to re-climb them when she was 70 years old. Her doctor warned her, since she had just broken two ribs, that she shouldn't be climbing.

In 1986, said Grace, a different doctor "told me to walk with a cane, but he didn't tell me not to climb." So, at age 80, with the aid of the cane and four younger companions, Grace again climbed Cascade.

Cascade does not have a true alpine summit above treeline. The latter begins in the Adirondacks between 4,200 and 4,800 feet; only 17 of the high peaks thrust above that level. But while Cascade's bare cap was exposed by fire, it looks like an alpine summit, and to the climber that makes all the difference.

False hope. *Cascade's summit looms ahead, or so it seems. As on most peaks, the actual top is a bump or two beyond this beckoning knob.*

You can see the beginning of Cascade's rocky cap before you are upon it. On so many of the loftier Adirondack peaks the summit unfolds within the last 50 feet, almost as an anticlimax. Not here.

The senses quicken. Mountain juices pump strongly in the young as the summit cap begins to unfold.

A few hundred feet from the top, one emerges from a thick mantle of dwarf conifers to see Cascade's substantial summit. It juts just beyond the Adirondack climber's psychological sound barrier: the 4,000-foot level.

Of course, Cascade doesn't reach a hundred feet beyond that. But to the bone weary, novice explorer, even that generates joy.

Journal entry: Saturday, July 1, 1978. Son Ben is like one possessed. Some mysterious power thrusts him upward. As the summit unfolds for me, geared to a more sluggish pace, I see him standing on top, alone and alert. Every climber will remember the thrill of scaling that first Adirondack peak.

There may be people all around, but when the eye spots the weather-worn copper bolt, or benchmark, confirmed by the surveyor that this is indeed the end of the climb, there is no one else in sight. No early-day Iroquois warrior spotting an Algonquin enemy in the wilderness could feel a higher sense of triumph or accomplishment.

It is the rule rather than the exception to find a multitude on Cascade's summit. In climbing it a dozen times from early spring to late fall, this has always been the norm. On the first exploratory trip which Jim and I made in late September, swirling clouds blotted the view; rime ice on the trees encouraged snowballs. Yet there were still climbers on the trail as well as on top.

Hikers are disappointed to find crowds after struggling to climb even more difficult peaks such as Giant, Gothics, or Dix. But Cascade is different. Undulating rock hollows, warmed by the sun, offer welcome hideaways from the people as well as the wind. Many hollows prompt you to linger, because they're cushioned with a mixture of moss and a grass-like plant called Deer's Hair. But resist the temptation: alpine plants on the summit are protected species, many rare and endangered.

Conquest complete. *There's no feeling quite like it. Cascade may not be the biggest of the 46, but as the first to be surmounted, it can be the best.*

In good weather, the views from Cascade are outstanding. This is a matter of some contention, as noted by differing view ratings (see pg. xvi). I place Cascade 13th on my view rating scale for the 46 high peaks; climbing pioneer Robert Marshall rated it 34th.

It doesn't seem realistic to rank a peak 34th when its summit reveals 30 other high peaks, including the king of the hills, Marcy. Admittedly, the view from Cascade isn't front row center. But it's as good as that available from any other Adirondack balcony. And from Cascade, the view of the northern twins, Whiteface and Esther, is better than from any of the other 43.

There is one new view from Cascade, and for that matter

Benchmark fever. *No jewel was ever cradled more carefully than Cascade's summit bolt in the hands of an aspiring explorer.*

from many of the other high peaks, that's intrusive. It's a hangover from the 1980 Olympics at nearby Lake Placid — the 70- and 90-meter ski jumps, with strobe lights blinking away day and night. "Ski junk," says son Ben, who equates it with small sightseeing planes, also from Placid, which skitter around the mountaintops like pesky bugs.

Ben is like his older sister, Gretchen, both born on April 7 but a few years apart. They hate to see any development that's esthetically displeasing. Especially in the Adirondacks.

Three-tenths of a mile down from Cascade's summit is a trail junction with a sign pointing to nearby Porter Mtn. It prompts the standard dilemma for the hiker: How about doing Porter, too? On any decent day, it's clearly in view, topped by an enormous boulder a half mile off and a half hour away.

Porter Mtn. from Cascade. *The issue is: Shall we go on over today, too? Dix Mtn., right rear, seems to say: "Compared to me, it's easy." Ben suggests we give it a try.*

The answer borders on the philosophical.

If one ultimately plans to do a separate hike up Porter, climbing from its base on the side opposite from Cascade, the trek from Cascade will be worth the trip; it offers an extra measure of pleasure.

If the weather is poor, and the summits are socked in, then there's not much point in the crossover. Exploring a dark and foreboding col between the two peaks is not inspiring.

If hikers aim to climb all 46 in a hurry, then it doesn't make any difference when they do it, or how. But they'll miss a great deal of the joys of doing Porter a different way, along with all the others, if they do it just for the record book.

One of the best times to climb Cascade is early spring. Energy surges everywhere — in the bursting buds, the flash of birches, the profusion of trillium and wood sorrel and bunchberry, the cobalt of the sky, and of course in the frisky joy of young hikers.

At a critical moment, winter signals with a last gasp that it is loosening its grip on the Adirondacks. It will still be crisp and somewhat icy on the summit. But at the northwest edge,

Big wheel. *An Adirondack Mountain Club volunteer shows the only way to get an accurate measurement of trails in the high peaks region.*

the Cascade lakes 2,000 feet below will send up word that warmth and gladness are inexorably working their way back.

Journal entry: Saturday, March 26, 1983. Every ice break-up generates its own distinctive sound. Back home, the subsiding water level on the Mohawk River conjures up a haunted house. Stress on the ice mimics the creaks of a weakened floor. Then, huge sheets crash to the water, forcing out air in ghastly groans.

Here, the noise is not spasmodic, but continual. Cracks in the lake ice set off a forlorn moaning and booming that suggests a giant with a giant stomach ache.

The pass which separates Cascade from its northern neighbor, Pitchoff, is a U-shaped valley grooved by glaciers, as opposed to those cut in a V-shape by streams. Even now, from Cascade one can see remnants of the Ice Age — two of the best known Adirondack glacial boulders, called erratics, on the southwest shoulder of Pitchoff. Climbers hope for the return of golden eagles which were observed soaring over nearby cliffs in 1967.

Whatever the time of year, it's worth studying the precipitous, northwestern slopes that descend to the Cascade lakes. With a pinch of dreams, one can snare a glimpse of Adirondack past.

The two Cascade lakes form a skinny body of water originally known as Long Pond and Square Pond, which hugged the base of what was then called Long Pond Mountain. The lakes were later called Edmunds Ponds for a pioneering family in Keene. In 1878, an enterprising couple named Miller built a hotel on the intervening spit of land. The hotel fronted the cascade on the brook which traces down a vertical, natural fault creasing the cliff. The Millers, being romantics as well as entrepreneurs, renamed both the lakes and the mountain for the cascade.

Even on a diminutive mountain such as Cascade, it's sobering to consider the steepness of the path that used to rise from their hotel to the present summit overlook. The first group to climb all of the 46 high peaks, in the early part of this century — the Marshall brothers and their guide Herb Clark — followed the general course of this trail but found no trace of it. On the lower reaches, in particular, they lamented the loss: "We had to crawl and pull ourselves along the rocks."

There is little evidence today of the "slashes", or forest debris, they noted on Cascade and Porter. Fires had ravaged the slopes in 1903. But the barren rock summits of Cascade and Pitchoff still bear scars from that conflagration.

Before leaving the summit, those who are up on geology may want to explore the upper reaches of the slide. Watson's *Military and Civil History of the County of Essex, New York* refers to "rich mineral caves" in the area. To date, no one has admitted discovering their location.

Journal entry: Saturday July 1, 1978. As I record data in my notebook, I see that today is the birthday of Elizabeth, Ben's mother. I can only hope that when we get home she'll still admit to being my wife.

When Cascade is a first conquest, hikers will be shocked by the unexpected: going down can be harder than going up. The descent calls into play a different set of muscles on the back of the legs. The constant jolting to the heels is like that experienced by beginning joggers. It may seem an eternity until the sounds of the highway tell you the soft seat of your car is nearby.

Across from the trailhead, perhaps a hundred yards down the road, is another link to the past. A huge boulder bears an image of the stagecoach which horses pulled through the pass in the previous century.

Present-day hikers have trouble shifting mental gears to bring that into focus. And with good reason.

One can sense the challenge of traveling in the last century by exploring the trail which traces between Pitchoff and the Sentinel Range to the north. The path follows a six-mile, abandoned segment of the Old Military Road that coursed from Keene to North Elba. The latter was a tiny settlement at the junction on Rt. 73 where a road leads south to the ADK's Adirondak Loj.

Stagecoaches originally used that road until it became so bad it was changed to its present route beside the lakes through Cascade Pass. Adirondack chronicler Maitland De Sormo described it as "rutty, high-crowned, treacherous, pockmarked, and primitive." Historian Alfred Donaldson got right to the heart of the matter: Such roads, he said, are "passable in winter, impassable in spring and impossible in summer."

The stagecoach took six hours to negotiate the six miles now traced by the trail; it was so bad that passengers often were forced to walk to spare the horses. A trip by car today from Keene to the trailhead at Cascade Mtn. takes less than 15 minutes.

Memories of the old road nearby and the steep course of the former trail heading up from the lakes are reminders that the littlest of the 46 peaks, Cascade, has not always been as "easy" as it is considered today.

Journal entry: Thursday, August 8, 1991. Some say the Adirondacks, within the brief snapshot of time given to us, are immutable. I don't believe it — the Cascade trail gets steeper every year. And there is further confirmation of change — every time Jim and Ben and I climb the mountain, we discover things we've never seen before.

*"**The world** is so full of a number of things/I'm sure we should all be as happy as kings."* Son Ben was convinced Robert Louis Stevenson had this in mind when he wrote those lines while living in the Adirondacks.

Porter Mtn. from Little Crow Mtn.

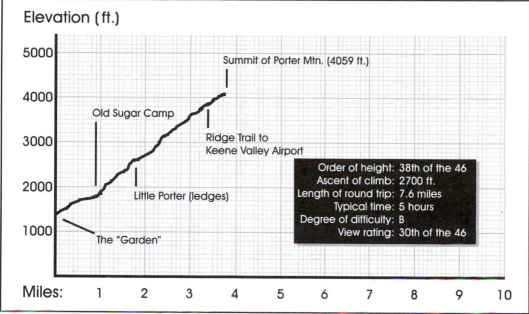

Elevation (ft.)

Summit of Porter Mtn. (4059 ft.)

Old Sugar Camp

Ridge Trail to
Keene Valley Airport

Little Porter (ledges)

Order of height: 38th of the 46
Ascent of climb: 2700 ft.
Length of round trip: 7.6 miles
Typical time: 5 hours
Degree of difficulty: B
View rating: 30th of the 46

The "Garden"

Miles: 1   2   3   4   5   6   7   8   9   10

For contour trails, see U.S. Geological Survey map, pgs. 2-3.

2.
PORTER

Porter is an enigma.

It looks dull. There's no point on top to give it the true shape of a mountain.

And, it's dull to climb. It reminds me, as a once-practicing journalist, of the advice given by Theodore Dreiser to an aspiring cub reporter. Dreiser was a newspaperman before he wrote the classic novel, *An American Tragedy*, which reached its climax on a lonely Adirondack lake.

The young apprentice had covered a story for him, but froze at the typewriter as the deadline neared. Advised editor Dreiser: "Son, there's nothing to it. Just put down one little word after another."

That's Porter — just one interminable step after another. An early edition of the Adirondack Mountain Club's guidebook series noted that its trail "is not difficult, but seems endless."

Yet Porter has some redeeming features.

Those who have never seen bears in the wild can, on the way to Porter, at least see where bears have been. The trail, which begins from a parking lot called the Garden, about a mile west of Keene Valley, passes through a stand of enormous beech trees. The vertical slashes on the smooth, blue-gray bark were made by bears during the masting season when they clawed their way up toward the beech nuts, one of their favorite foods.

There's also an old sugar camp a little less than a mile up the trail. The camp is engulfed in a grove of maple trees. When the leaves begin their color change in the fall, they transform the structure into a glorious rest stop.

Those coming from the gregarious east will appreciate a snug private cabin tucked away at trailside a bit farther on.

Journal entry: Monday, August 25, 1969. Obviously here is a hunter's jumping off station, or the retreat of a harried city dweller who wants to get away from it all. And he is prepared for anything, it would appear. Half a dozen signs warn of trespassing; neat stacks of firewood bulge from the porch and foundation crawl space.

From the trail, one will also see various dwellings in Adrian's Acres, a grouping of seasonal and year-round homes developed over several decades by Adrian Edmonds of Keene Valley.

At the mile and a half point is another cabin boasting an incredible view of the Great Range, along with other peaks to the south and west. Hikers on the Three Brothers across the valley who peer sharply back toward Porter will spot the cabin peeking at them from the edge of a cliff.

Little Porter, *viewed from the south on the first of the three Brothers, sprouts numerous exposed ledges. Ridge to the left leads up long slope to summit of big Porter.*

The Great Range, *rippling to the right toward Marcy, calls for a camera on Little Porter. First of the Brothers, right foreground, leads to Big Slide Mtn.*

From the Brothers, too, one can see the rocky ledges that culminate in an open prominence called Little Porter. This is roughly halfway up the trail; the exposed open faces are ideal for loafing and gazing.

Then the upward steps begin again for two miles, often coursing through grassy areas which gained the upper hand after forest cover was destroyed during the great fires early in this century. Farther on, the trail eases off on Porter's half mile ridge leading to the summit.

Journal entry: Friday, August 22, 1986. *There's nothing like hiking on the level near 4,000 feet. The high peaks offer only a few good opportunities, such as the saddle in Saddleback. Porter is another. The effect on me is as heady as having champagne in an unpressurized airplane.*

The chances are good that hikers reaching the top of Porter will be alone. On our four trips to Porter, only once have we met anyone there. And the two young men then were ADK Ridgerunners. Their duty, they said, was to "keep an eye on things and act like rangers. Except we don't carry guns."

Those who hanker for company can go on over to Cascade. An informal survey I made of license plates in the parking lot at the Cascade

Porter from col coming off Cascade. The journey is an easy half hour each way over the mile separating the two.

trailhead suggested that one third of the people came from Canada, one fourth from New Jersey, and the rest from all over.

Journal entry: Monday, August 25, 1969. Summit fever, that strange mixture of exhilaration and fatigue, grips us as we stand on the outcrop of Porter's crest. It seems like the world is spread out before us. Of course, the earth's more exotic places may be hidden behind the peaks that stab into the horizon. But Jim and I find with pleasure that some of the mountains are becoming familiar. That mass with the sweeping vertical stripes has to be Giant. And, of course, nearby is old friend Cascade.

A huge horizontal slab resting on Porter's summit offers a lordly throne for viewing the Great Range and Marcy. In front of them, and closer to Porter, is the clipped prominence of Big Slide. It's separated from Porter by Little Meadows, which nestles in a valley known during the last century as Railroad Notch. The latter gained its name because it once was surveyed as a potential railroad line.

The views from Porter are almost as good as from Cascade. One may ask, then, why it gets a view rating of only 30 when Cascade gets 13?

The answer, of course, is: It's all in the mind.

Even the Marshalls and Herb Clark ranked Porter 40th, trailing Cascade by six. Either way, Cascade gets the edge because it puts the climber a hair closer to the high ones than Porter, so more of them can be seen.

Journal entry: Monday, August 20, 1990. Ben says he's sure he can see Mount Royal in Montreal, 90 miles to the north. Even though that peak is less than 700 feet high, you're supposed to be able to spot it on a good day from Whiteface, which is 10 miles closer than from Porter. I'm sure it's possible today, because the air is as pristine as crystal. The image of Royal buoys Ben; he's been depressed because this will be his last Adirondack outing with me before he returns to college next Friday.

No benchmark *on Porter, but the view makes up for it. Marcy, right rear, finally comes into view beyond the snub tip of Big Slide Mtn. Great Range extends to the left.*

Porter suffers a psychological drawback from Cascade because not only does it have a less interesting shape, it lacks a benchmark. The one on Cascade, we discovered, had been burnished over more then a hundred years by the trampling of boots. Some pooh-pooh the distinction, saying it makes no difference. But to me, a benchmark gives a mountain a subtle touch of class.

That peripatetic promoter of the previous century, the Reverend William H. H. Murray, said of Adirondack summers in 1869, "...rain storms are unknown in this region, and the thunder showers which occur are a source of pleasure, and not of inconvenience, to a camper." Adirondack scholars aver that the preacher and author often overstated his case. They must also wonder if he ever ventured far from camp, let alone up on a long, exposed summit ridge like Porter's.

Journal entry: Monday, August 25, 1969. A dark, high cloud creeps through a notch in the mountains to the west, dragging a white curtain below. Rain. Daughter Judy and son Jim and I study it with detached curiosity. It moves in a straight line for Porter. Suddenly, a flash bursts on the crest of the mountain top, reinforced by a thunderclap. There is no time lapse between the two. We scatter to hide in the hollows.

Freshening sheets of rain coalesce into a downpour, which drenches us throughout our descent. Before we reach the car, Judy tells me: "One outing is enough. Thank you very much."

Years later, we gained sobering insight to our plight from an article entitled "Lightning in High Places", by then-ADK President Robert Ringlee and co-author John G. Anderson. They warned in the July-August 1992 edition of the club's *Adirondac* magazine: "A thundercloud is an electrostatic machine, a wind chimney whose updrafts can reach 200 miles per hour; it can hold 100,000 tons of water vapor or more along with raindrops, ice particles, hail and snow, even on a hot summer afternoon."

The authors also confirmed our judgment that day on Porter: "If you are on a high ridge...life can get a little dicey at times."

For diversion, a separate trail winds up Porter from Marcy Field, a sometime airstrip and miniature racetrack two miles north of Keene Valley on Rt. 73. This steep, roller coaster route joins the main trail to Porter a half mile below the summit. While it is three quarters of a mile longer, it has the dual attractions of Blueberry Mountain, a 2,922 ft. mini-peak, and its namesake fruit which is ready for the taking in late August and early September.

Porter Mountain was first climbed in 1875, fittingly by Dr. Noah Porter, then president of Yale University, for whom the mountain was named. At the time, the peak went by another name — West Mountain, probably because its bulk loomed to the northwest of Keene Valley, the favorite haunt of Dr. Porter.

There is no record of anyone climbing Porter before Porter. But, you never know. A few years back, a service station operator in Keene, which nestles on the north slope of Porter, told Trudy Healy, at the time the editor of the Forty Sixers' magazine *Adirondack Peaks:* "So there are 46 of them, are there? I haven't been on many of them yet. But I chased cows all over the hills when I was a boy. I'm tired of them."

If he chased them off the top of Porter, he surely would be tired.

Dr. Porter made the first ascent, according to the books, for all the usual climber's reasons: it was trailless, it had never been climbed, and it beckoned every time he came to Keene Valley.

This is hard to square with the psychological profile of Dr. Porter, sketched in 1974 by Yale historian Brookes Mather Kelley.

Yale "had lost, under Porter, its educational leadership," avowed Kelley. Yale's president was "never a great one for new procedures." In fact, the author said, "Porter was the scholarly type. Action was not his forte."

In his book, Kelley dropped a motivational clue. Four years prior to his appointment as president of Yale, "professors' salaries were less than $1,150 and had scarcely changed in thirty three years." As one result, a professional colleague noted that, "Mr. Porter with all his economy has exceeded his [salary] by $200 or $300, and has been obliged to use nearly half his available strength in eking out this deficiency."

Maybe the good doctor, like so many hikers, came to Keene Valley and climbed Porter not so much because it was there, but because it was an inexpensive outing. One of his contemporaries, Henry David Thoreau, put it succinctly in his journal: "That man is the richest whose pleasures are the cheapest."

Most climbers go up Porter today because it's one of the 46 high peaks.

Those who are moved neither by curiosity nor compulsion may want to give it a try for pleasure alone. A great way that's also inexpensive is to stay at one of the valley's growing number of Bed & Breakfast inns which offer superb morning views of Porter's southeastern flank. Then, when on the summit, climbers can close the loop by peering down to enjoy a splendid panorama of the hamlet.

They will soon come to know, as Dr. Porter surely did, that regardless of financial means, achieving that vantage point makes them rich indeed.

Whiteface Mtn. from the west branch of the Ausable River near Monument Falls.

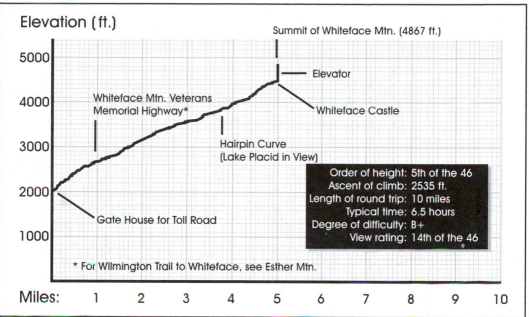

Elevation (ft.)

Summit of Whiteface Mtn. (4867 ft.)

5000

— Elevator

4000

Whiteface Mtn. Veterans
Memorial Highway*

Whiteface Castle

3000

Hairpin Curve
(Lake Placid in View)

Order of height: 5th of the 46
Ascent of climb: 2535 ft.
Length of round trip: 10 miles
Typical time: 6.5 hours
Degree of difficulty: B+
View rating: 14th of the 46

2000

Gate House for Toll Road

1000

* For Wilmington Trail to Whiteface, see Esther Mtn.

Miles: 1   2   3   4   5   6   7   8   9   10

For contour trails, see U.S. Geological Survey map, pgs. 22-23.

3.
WHITEFACE

There is an easy way and a hard way to climb Whiteface.

The easy way is to drive a car up the Whiteface Memorial Highway that snakes around the north side of the mountain. The eight-mile route has an average grade of eight per cent, never more than 10. It takes about 15 minutes.

The hard way is to climb by foot on one of the trails from the base. The shortest, beginning just west of Wilmington, ascends some 3,600 feet in a little more than five miles. An average round trip takes about seven hours.

Then there's the Whiteface Compromise: walk, the hard way, but take the road, which is easy.

The highway is open from May through mid-October. However, the weather may dictate otherwise. On any day, at any time, one may be rebuffed by a sign at the tollgate which warns: "Closed. Zero visibility."

Journal entry: Sunday, September 7, 1969. *"It's too dangerous,"* *the toll keeper tells son Jim and me as he denies us entry. "We don't* *want one of our service vehicles plowing into you on the road in this*

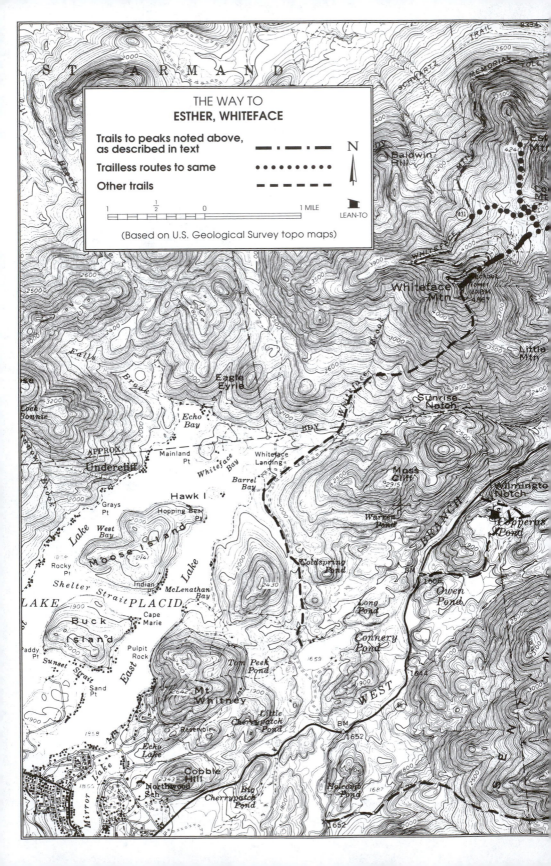

THE WAY TO
ESTHER, WHITEFACE

Trails to peaks noted above,
as described in text

Trailless routes to same

Other trails

N

1   ½   0   1 MILE

LEAN-TO

(Based on U.S. Geological Survey topo maps)

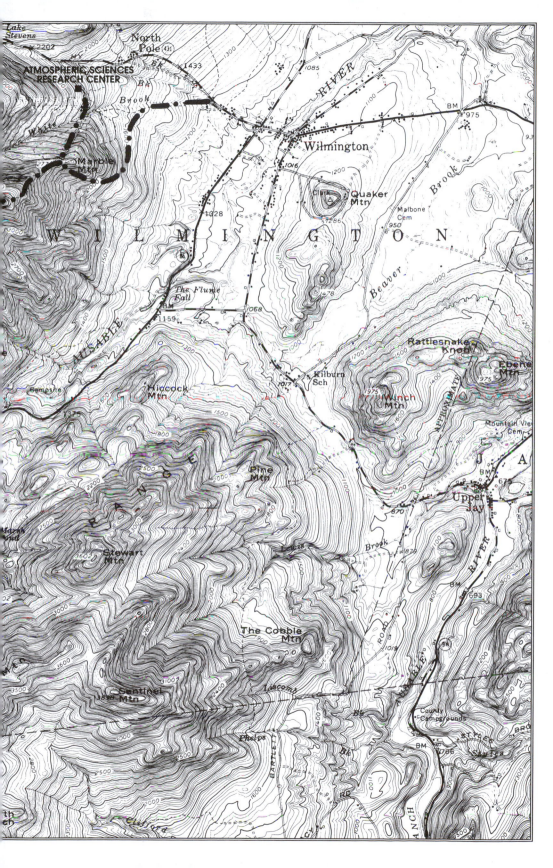

fog." After waiting three hours, we give up and decide to try again when the weather is clear.

Be advised that there is a Bureau of Forest Recreation in the New York State Department of Environmental Conservation (ENCON) in Albany which can run interference for you.

Journal entry: Sunday, September 14, 1969. Last week, I asked John Goerg, a friend and chief photographer on the staff of the department's Conservationist *magazine, to check out their policy.*

"The only restrictions on the highway are for bicycles and snowmobiles," he reported. "If you get any flak, have the gatekeeper call the Chief."

The title has a magic ring to it. While the top of the mountain is still shrouded in morning fog, we gain immediate clearance for our climb up the highway.

For the hiker, the transition from trail to toll road is easy. Benches with vertical backs replace the usual logs and boulders for rest stops. Overlooks offer a welcome change of scene from the close embrace of the woods. The views encompass a major portion of the Great Northern Forest, which the Adirondack Council calls "the largest intact remnant of the vast primeval forest that covered much of pre-Colonial eastern North America."

Trees stretch to the horizon on the north and west, dotted here and there with lakes and a structure or two. The highlands rise lordly to the left — first to some unknown pinnacle, then to 4,240-ft. Esther with a southern saddle curving down and then upward toward the summit of Whiteface.

Journal entry: Saturday, September 30, 1978. Ben and I have just started to climb when we hear what we think are children calling to each other, out of sight on the rise to our left. It's the honking of a ragged V of Canada geese. They confirm by avian roll call that all are present as they flap ponderously around the flanks of the mountain, heading south.

The first view of Whiteface comes a fourth of the way up. In clear weather, one can spot the Norman-style castle at the top of the road and, a short distance above it, the weather observatory on the summit.

The walker sees varied forms of life along the highway — the remains of salamanders and other small animals on the road, hawks high above, looping their lazy S-curves and, always, the busy flow of vehicles full of people, sealed in and staring.

Journal entry: Saturday, September 30, 1978. Two thirds of the way up, I count in a two-minute span a total of 22 cars and one bus.

Bulges on Whiteface *summit outline the weather station on the very top and tourist castle on right shoulder. View from this lookout is a fourth of the way up the Memorial Highway.*

Plus an airplane circling Whiteface's summit. If this rate continues, I calculate that during our ascent we will have been passed by nearly 2,000 cars and 83 buses. Plus a swarm of 90 airplanes.

Hairpin curves lead upward from the base of the final rise. It's only a few hundred yards straight up to the level of the highway's end, but to maintain its grade the road folds back and forth for almost two miles.

Lookouts along the way reveal their rewards: the Saranac River to the northwest; around the bend to the southwest the first view of that shining gem, Lake Placid, three thousand feet below; and the trail from Wilmington limping in at the end of the final hairpin, where ski trails formerly crisscrossed the northeastern slopes.

At the roadside parking lot where the highway ends, tourists disembark to stretch their legs and head into the castle for souvenirs and food. Since there is limited space, vehicles often are backed up on the hairpin curves until highway monitors with walkie-talkies give them a go-ahead as parking slots open up.

Journal entry: Sunday, September 14, 1969. *As a rule, Jim and I defer a trail lunch until we top off our peak. But at the castle near the parking lot, Whiteface's summit is still some 275 feet above us. We have hiked for three hours, it's getting chilly and we are ravenous. So we swallow our mountaineering pride, accept the onrush of civiliza-*

tion, and pitch into a steaming hot order at the cafe. Outside, the clouds found on most Adirondack peaks swirl by. But on this hike the window shields their silent passage, and a blanket of warmth and good kitchen smells enfolds us.

It's not unusual to see hikers who have climbed a trail from the base relaxing in the restaurant or on the summit. They're easy to spot, lugging trail packs covered with patches boosting their hiking clubs. Often they're in a triumphant mood, surrounded by groups of non-hikers.

The reason is that Whiteface is the most popular peak to be climbed last by those who aspire to become Adirondack Forty Sixers. That's the name of a small club whose hardy members have climbed all of the 46 high peaks. The scheduled final climb triggers in the minds of those who expect to complete it the call for a celebration, ideally with friends and family.

This is not easy to arrange on the 45 other Adirondack high peaks. On those, friends and family must go along on foot for the final arduous ascent. But not on Whiteface. Its highway, the only one to surmount any of the high peaks, eases the way for such group gatherings.

The cars, the crowds, and the buildings on Whiteface make environmental purists cringe. In their view they desecrate the original intent of the Forest Preserve article of the state constitution, enacted in 1894. It decreed that the Adirondacks and its forests should remain "forever wild", protected not only from lumbering but from the disruption of natural processes in the wilderness. This means, for example, that overnight campers are not allowed to cut down even small trees for firewood. In 1994, two cellular phone companies paid $10,000 to settle a dispute with ENCON which charged they had chopped down 47 trees near the top of Whiteface for their transmitters.

A pinch of environmental prescience might have forewarned that the encroachment which characterized Whiteface would forever erode the "wild" from its wilderness.

The process began in the middle of the last century when an enterprising guide from Wilmington cleared a way to the summit of Whiteface; it was the first formal mountain trail in the Adirondacks. This was followed in short order by three others, including the first and only bridle path to the top of any of the high peaks.

The die of permanent change at Whiteface was cast with the passage of various constitutional amendments: in 1927, for the Veterans Memorial Highway that leads to the base of the summit; in 1941, for "20 miles of ski trails 30 to 80 feet wide" that would transform it into a major ski center; and, in 1959, a move that would make it easy for the hordes to get to Whiteface — construction of the Northway, Interstate 87, from Albany to the Canadian border on the way to Montreal.

Journal entry: Monday, October 1, 1978. New noises add to the summit din — a helicopter swings by with components for the 1980 Winter Olympic complex being built on the eastern slopes. Dull booms from blasting echo from below.

The end product of construction and congestion at both summit and base causes Whiteface to teeter on the brink of honky-tonk. Yet there is one counterbalancing benefit.

A great many people who relish the high peaks either can't climb them on foot, or don't want to. The road to Whiteface's summit offers them their sole chance to share a vicarious thrill of the kind which on the other high peaks comes only to the plodding foot soldier.

People face two choices at the parking lot near the castle. They can ride an elevator to the summit, entering via a long, dank, horizontal tunnel carved 424 feet into solid rock. From there, the elevator bumps upward some 27 stories before disgorging its cargo at the top.

Or, they can clamber up a stone walkway that winds a fifth of a mile to the summit. In the doing, they will sense the emotional high that comes to hikers completing the climb from the base. Handholds along the way offer security from winds which blow even on the best of days.

The chill of the wind confirms that the summit of Whiteface is an alpine environment. With eyes closed, one can almost conjure up the musk oxen which roamed here long ago. The environment is cousin to the arctic tundra some 1,500 miles to the north. Both sides of the walkway reveal the harsh climate at work.

The gashes on Whiteface that are so prominent from a distance come into focus

Take your choice: From parking lot, climb the walkway a fifth of a mile to summit buildings, or ride elevator through tunnel in rock.

as scars from avalanches, common on many Adirondack peaks. One of the more recent ones, on Labor Day 1971, came after three days of rain and a four-inch downpour. It loosened the thin mantle of earth near Whiteface's summit and sent it plummeting downward with rocks and logs, bulldozing a clean swath on its way toward Lake Placid.

Such slides, according to Indian legend, prompted the Mohawks to call the peak Ou-no-war-lah, or "scalp mountain." Later explorers, however, rejected romanticism for realism: they named it Whiteface for the light gray streaks of rock exposed by the slides, which reflect light from the sun.

The walkway to the summit also offers a close-up of the handiwork of glaciers which covered the Adirondacks during the Ice Age. They cleaned not just random streaks but the whole mountain. Some of the glacial action in fact was so severe that it created on Whiteface the most distinctive alpine features of all the Adirondack high peaks.

On the sides of the mountain, the glaciers scoured out huge, rounded hollows called cirques. The trail to the summit skirts one of them, curving to the right along the upper rim, or headwall, that faces Lake Placid. The Whiteface ski center is plopped in the middle of another, on the opposite side.

Whiteface is a living example of how plant organisms gain a foothold on mountain slopes that have been laid waste by avalanches, fire and storms. The process is called ecological succession. Quick-starting trees such as aspen and paper birch, which thrive in the sun, gain a foothold first. Then, they're overshadowed by what are called the climax species — mature hardwoods and the red spruce and balsam fir.

During the ascent from the base, one notices that the trees become shorter and smaller the higher they grow. It's because the soil is thinner and more rocky at higher elevations; the climate becomes colder, more windy and more cloudy.

It's dramatic proof that the succession process works at a different pace at different levels. A 50-year-old balsam fir at the base, for example, may be 50 feet tall. Yet a fir of the same age near treeline will appear more like a coniferous Quasimodo.

Above treeline, on the bald surface traversed by the walkway, the succession process slows to a crawl.

Primitive lichens cling to rocks like so many colorful paint splotches. Over time, the lichens stimulate a slow chemical process that breaks down the rocks to create a thin layer of soil. This washes into the cracks and provides a base for mosses and such plants as the Mountain Sandwort to take hold. All summer long, the delicate, cup-shaped, white flowers of the latter bob feebly in the wind.

In the next stage of succession, the mosses and sandworts enrich the soil for low shrubs, herbs and true dwarf trees, such as bearberry, only inches tall. These now cover much of the flatter areas near the summit. But then the process chugs to a halt. The alpine climate stops any further progression cold.

An unknown climber in the last century carved on the summit rocks of Whiteface his verdict of the ascent, as related by Seneca Ray Stoddard in his book, *Old Times in the Adirondacks:* "Thanks be to God for the Mountains."

Most people who clamber up the last steps of the walkway will agree. But on busy days, they do so with mixed emotions.

Sweeping views on either side cry out for attention. But dead ahead, the visitor faces a jumble of weather station buildings, coin telescopes, information signs, and people. Often, one has to squeeze along the perimeter to find an unobstructed view.

Expect company *on any good day. The highway allows more people to visit Whiteface than any other high peak.*

Journal entry: Sunday September 14, 1969. To the west, the Saranacs and Placid now come into view more sharply. A glint to the east pulls Jim and me toward the shining sweep of Lake Champlain and, beyond, the rounded humps of Vermont's Green Mountains. To the south, in soft silhouette, we see the central and northern Adirondack high peaks. And to the north, we bring into focus the blip on the horizon that is Mount Royal in Montreal.

Whiteface was not only one of the first Adirondack high peaks to be climbed, but has been climbed by more people than any of the other 45. The highway gives it an easy edge, of course. But there are two other factors which add power to the pull.

The first is the way it looks to those on the lowlands. Russell M. L. Carson, who wrote the first definitive history of the 46 in his *Peaks and People of the Adirondacks* in 1928, called Whiteface "the most graceful of all Adirondack peaks." City people who view Whiteface for the first time tend to like what they see, too. Many conclude that if it looks that good from the street, it must be worth the effort to go up and sample the view from the cupola.

The second reason for its popularity relates to the highway. Since it's easy to climb, it gives you more time on the summit to muse. And the dreamer does not need one of the telescopes to gain a historical insight into Whiteface.

Gazing to the north, one can imagine, in reverse, the excitement the explorer Jacques Cartier must have felt when Canadian Indians took him to the top of Mount Royal in 1535. He became the first European of record to view the Adirondacks. Foremost in the parade of peaks 90 miles to the south were Esther and Whiteface.

It's hard to visualize that more than three centuries later, people still proclaimed that the high peaks in Essex County, including not only Whiteface but Marcy, were less than 1,200 feet high. And all, avowed one writer who most certainly never climbed any of them, were "susceptible to cultivation to their summits."

By poking around on top, you can see remnants of the most extensive, scientific survey of the high peaks conducted by Verplanck Colvin during the last century. Ring bolts in the rock show where he and his crew cleared the crests, as they did on many of the Adirondack high peaks, to secure signal towers for survey work. Colvin boasted, with typical hyperbole, that they were impervious to the onslaughts of nature. The tower on Marcy, he wrote, "withstood one earthquake, a dozen tornadoes, and the frosts of two winters, and is still fixed and firm."

The wear and tear of time, along with a lessened need for fire observers, brought down most of the towers in the high peaks. Along with them went many of the wild animals which roamed the Whiteface wilderness of that time — moose, lynx and mountain lions. The moose are straggling back from New England and Canada; it's estimated that some 20 to 30 are now in the Adirondacks. A few lynx have also been re-stocked, with not too much success, because they keep getting run over by cars. And the clouds of passenger pigeons which roosted on the north face of Whiteface in the 1800s are gone forever, along with what naturalist and poet John Burroughs called their "soft, childlike calls."

Olympic ski runs scar the eastern slopes, including Little Whiteface. Heavy rains caused the slide in 1971.

It's tempting for highway hikers to forgo the Whiteface road on the return, and take one of the two trails — the Wilmington trail, or the one that leads to Connery Pond, some five miles northeast of the village of Lake Placid. In either case, however, it poses the problem of getting back to one's car at the highway tollgate.

Again, a Whiteface Compromise may be in order.

You can circumvent the cars and crowds at the parking area below Whiteface's summit by following the trail 600 feet down to where it skirts the first hairpin turn on the road. From there, the walk back on the road is half again longer than the trail to the bottom. But, because of the grade, it is easier.

Journal entry: Friday, October 1, 1993: The highway up Whiteface closes a week from next Monday, which is Columbus Day in the U.S., Thanksgiving Day in Canada. Those who drove to the top today got a preview of why: a modest blanket of snow covers the upper slopes and sheets of ice cling to the cliffs bordering the summit parking lot.

The signs of impending winter must have been clear also to the wild turkey we saw in the median on the Northway near Schroon Lake, just before reaching the Blue Ridge exit. It is scratching for as much food as it can find before the short, bitter days close in.

While the highway may be convenient, the Wilmington trail is still a key factor in exploring the northern twins of the Adirondack 46. If one does not take the trail for the climb to Whiteface, it's still the logical route to take for the ascent of Esther.

Part way, at least. The uppermost portion of Esther is trailless.

Lake Placid shimmers *in the autumnal haze. The beautiful lake gave its name to the village which hides demurely at the far end of Mirror Lake, seven miles to the southwest.*

Esther Mtn. from Whiteface Mtn.

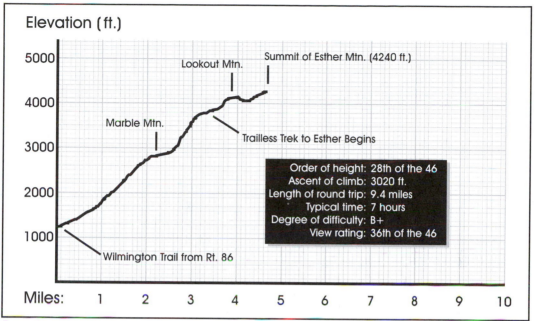

Elevation (ft.)

Lookout Mtn.

Summit of Esther Mtn. (4240 ft.)

Marble Mtn.

Trailless Trek to Esther Begins

Order of height: 28th of the 46
Ascent of climb: 3020 ft.
Length of round trip: 9.4 miles
Typical time: 7 hours
Degree of difficulty: B+
View rating: 36th of the 46

Wilmington Trail from Rt. 86

Miles: 1 2 3 4 5 6 7 8 9 10

For contour trails, see U.S. Geological Survey map, pgs. 22-23.

4.
ESTHER

At the beginning of the 20th century, explorers considered Esther a mountainous nobody.

They knew little about her, and cared less. With good reason — Esther had long been overshadowed by Whiteface, the big brother that towered beside her.

Then, people began to recognize that Esther had charms of her own. For a while, it seemed that she might catch up with and maybe even surpass Whiteface in popularity.

A modest ski center with T-bar lift rose a mile and a quarter to the east of Esther on a spur called Marble Mountain, some 1,500 ft. below. But a sporadic lack of snow forced skiers to higher elevations. So, more trails — along with two rope tows — began to trace an intricate pattern on the slopes leading to another spur called Lookout Mountain, three-quarters of a mile to the south of Esther.

As more people came, another ski lodge was built on the summit of Lookout, along with more trails on Esther. One trail, in fact, led all the way to Esther's summit.

Then in the 1950s, the romancing of Esther came to an end. Whiteface began to flourish while Esther floundered. The state transferred the ski center to Whiteface's east side, remote from Esther. New chairlifts, base lodge and trails were dedicated in 1957, and the area was expanded.

The lift up Marble and the lodge on Lookout were demolished, and the ski trails on Esther abandoned. The ski lodge at the base of Marble became a station for the state's Atmospheric Sciences Research Center.

Nature, in its thorough, methodical way, began the physical healing process. Today, Esther offers in narrow focus a mirror image in time of what Whiteface used to be like: Esther has reverted to wilderness.

Present-day explorers say, however, that as a result of her psychological snubbing, Esther acts like a woman scorned. The tales of her fury are legendary.

Esther was hard to manage even before she became popular. Those few climbers who ventured onto trailless Adirondack high peaks during the 1930s considered Esther the hardest of all to climb.

Her querulous reputation persisted. Bob Baldwin, a Forty Sixer whom son Jim and I met on an Adirondack expedition in 1975, told us that Esther was by far his most difficult challenge in the high peaks. "My son Mark and I failed on three previous attempts," he said. "But we finally made it yesterday." Jim and I were instantly convinced — at the time, the four of us were struggling to surmount trailless Nye Mountain, which high peak veterans had long described as "a nightmare."

A continuing barrier to success on Esther is a thick covering of prickly spruce trees, which stymies the invader at every step. It's the major reason why the Adirondack Forty Sixers Club calls Esther "as tough a piece of random scooting as a seasoned climber could ask for."

Another obstacle was created by the haphazard jumble of trees left from the hurricane which roared through the high peaks on November 25, 1950. The hurricane had veered far north of the usual path of tropical storms, but it retained enough power to uproot and toss trees about like so many jackstraws within almost a half million acres in the Adirondack Park.

One complication not as obvious to those on Esther as to visitors on Whiteface is the crescent-shaped open spaces on Esther's high slopes that are left when balsam firs succumb to the harsh prevailing winds. Scientists call these openings "fir waves" because they move slowly upward at a rate of about five feet per year. Old trees die along the upper edge, adding to the jumble on the ground, while dense new growth on the lower edge moves up to plug the resulting gaps.

Current-day climbers face other problems, some of their own making. A profusion of herd paths, for example, promises safe passage to Esther from the Wilmington trail, but many lead to dead ends. Unsure climbers tie colored tape or ribbons to branches for return escape routes, but the fluttering fragments cause more confusion than consolation.

As a result, the average explorer searching for a route to Esther faces a classic question not unlike that in the riddle posed a hundred years ago by author Frank Richard Stockton: "Which comes out of the opened door: The Lady or the Tiger?" — i.e., which herd path leads to Esther, and which to frustration?

If Esther and other trailless wilderness peaks are indeed so difficult to climb, why then do people make the attempt?

Robert Marshall, who climbed all of the unexplored Adirondack high peaks in the 1920s plus the others among the 46 with trails, gave us the reason: they offer, he said, "the exhilaration of that most glorious of all pastimes, setting foot where no human being has ever trod before."

The Adirondack Park is so big that one can still tread

Into the jumble. *Many of the multiple herd paths fanning out toward Esther from the Wilmington trail are dead ends. The only way to find out is to plunge in.*

unexplored territory. To the purist, tracking a herd path through the seemingly impenetrable maze on Esther may not be the ultimate quest. But to the climber who sprawls exhausted on Esther's summit, it's a pretty fair substitute.

Getting to the start of the herd paths is the easiest part of the journey to Esther. There are two ways that are conventional, plus a third that's not.

The most popular way, for those who want to explore, is to climb the long trail from Wilmington. The easy way, for sunshine patriots, is to drive up Whiteface to the summit parking lot and then hike down the trail a bit more than a mile to where jousting with the wilderness begins.

The hard way is to leave the Whiteface Memorial Highway some two thirds of the way up, and then strike off cross-country to the northeast to search for a way leading from Lookout Mountain toward the summit. Be forewarned: once off the highway, you will find, as the Forty Sixers noted in their 1970 edition of *The Adirondack High Peaks*, that you are "up to your eyeballs in windfalls and other impediments."

Two years before that first book of the Forty Sixers was published, son Jim and I plunged into the wilderness from the highway to search for Esther. Surprisingly, we made it to the summit on our first try. In retrospect, I think it was because we were lucky, exuberant and more than a bit naive.

We had been intrigued by the prospect of a short cut to Esther indicated on the U.S. Geological Survey's 1953 topographic map of the Lake Placid quadrangle. At the 3,700 ft. level, dotted lines showed ski trails wandering up to a junction near Lookout Mountain.

Today, it's hard to spot any trace of those old trails while traveling up the highway. But back then, at the turnoff where a definitive stream meets the toll road, one could find occasional boulders blazed with blue paint along the stream bed.

> *Journal entry: Saturday, September 20, 1969. It's too early to be up on this frosty morning; I'm still half asleep. Jim brushes a thin layer of snow off the roadside picnic table so we can pack our gear. Starting out, we discover that the snow-covered, velvety bulges on the ground hide clumps of moss, which are saturated with moisture. We go no more than a few yards before I sink into one and leap out with a shoe full of icy water. At least now I am awake.*

> *Luck on the mountain is fleeting, and so it is today. After going perhaps an eighth of a mile, the old ski trail breaks into two segments, neither of which continues the blue markings. We choose the right fork, because it heads more to the southeast, as indicated on the map, and climbs more sharply than the others. We trust in the first axiom of climbing: trails seek the steepest part of the mountain.*

That bushwack up the southwest flank of Esther led through a patchwork of obstacles stitched with threads from the past.

The route, overgrown with new evergreens and littered with fallen logs, was either an abandoned ski trail or an old logging road, or maybe both. In any event, walking was better than riding or skiing would have been, though somewhat risky. The stream cut back and forth, leaving limpid backwater pools along with potholes, drained of water but hidden by brush and as much as three feet deep.

Explorers of that era often came to junctions where the trail diverged into segments. Signs that once announced their intentions in bold letters creaked aimlessly in the wind, rendered meaningless by the relentless weather.

> *Journal entry: Saturday, September 20, 1969. For the first time we can see the summit of Whiteface looming to our right. But as we move along, we wonder if we are on the right track. According to the map, Whiteface should be almost behind us. What to do?*

There is nothing like a trek into the wilderness to convince the newcomer that one's mental compass needs calibration now and then.

Charles Dudley Warner, who crafted some entertaining essays on the Adirondacks of the last century, explained the problem in his book, *In The Wilderness:*

"I tried to keep my mind fixed upon the fact of man's superiority to nature; his ability to dominate and outwit her." But Warner had to admit, after finding he had wandered for hours in an endless circle near Keene Valley that, "My situation was an amusing satire on this theory."

Journal entry: Saturday, September 20, 1969. Bushwhacking Axiom No. 2 has become obvious to Jim and me: trust your compass. We haul it out, lay it on the map, and are distressed by what it tells us: we should be on a course to the north, not the easterly direction we have been taking.

All befuddled explorers will empathize with Warner, who concluded: "To my amazement, the compass, which was made near Greenwich, was wrong. Allowing for the natural variation of the needle, it was absurdly wrong. It made out that I was going south when I was going north. It intimated that, instead of turning to the left, I had been making a circuit to the right. According to the compass, the Lord only knew where I was."

Journal entry: Saturday, September 20, 1969. Jim and I manage to sort our way through the dense forest that rises steeply to Lookout Mountain. Where the slopes begin, we find a junction with signs which point to "Whiteface via the Wilmington trail" to the south, "Lookout Mountain" to the east, and "Mt. Esther" to the north.

Common sense dictates against trying this short cut to Esther today. The old complex of ski trails has been obliterated by tangled new growth, the signs are long gone, and the difficult passage is compounded by a maze of rotting trees. The route was discouraging but doable 25 years ago. It would be double the trouble now without an experienced guide.

The traditional trail from Wilmington is longer — some three and a half miles before one heads into wilderness toward Esther — but it is by far the more interesting. From the trailhead a little more than a half mile off the Whiteface Memorial Highway above Wilmington, it begins by meandering upward through magnificent stands of hardwood. Then, it completes a lazy loop around the southeast flank of Marble Mountain, positioned like a guardian at the gateway to Esther.

There is an option to the lower part of the Wilmington trail which cuts out about a mile and a half of hiking and 800 feet of climbing. A side trail starts from the parking lot at the Atmospheric Sciences Research Center — the site of the lodge at the original Whiteface Mountain Ski Center — just below the gatehouse on the toll road to

Whiteface. From a cluster of scientific instruments in the shallow valley below the main buildings, an unmarked path leads up a steep, rocky drainage trough, the path of the former T-bar ski lift.

Concrete supports from the old lift offer level and stable resting spots along the incline leading up Marble. Not that there's much to stop and look for — the trees on the mountainside are new growth, and uninspiring.

One type of tree, however, is worth noting. It reveals a reason why New York state's most northern ski center was moved from Marble to the east side of Whiteface.

The trees are conifers, and the specimens are called "flag" trees. Strong winds allow branches to grow only on their lee, or sheltered sides — hence the name for their shape. The winds in winter also on occasion clear the slopes of snow that can be skied — more often than promoters of the earlier ski area cared to admit, according to Tony Goodwin, editor of the ADK's current guidebook on the high peaks.

Hiker's best friend in black fly season: a mesh head net. From the summit of Marble, Esther looms two and half miles away and 1,500 feet up.

The segment of the Wilmington Trail from the summit of Marble to the junction where the bushwhack to Esther begins is one of the most enjoyable in all of the Adirondack high peaks. The trail is beautifully designed, with moderately steep but short stretches alternating with long, easy rises. Each graceful turn of the trail unfolds something of interest, including changing views of Esther's remote summit.

Journal entry: Saturday, May 30, 1981. Hikers are usually plagued from May through July by that scourge of the Adirondacks, the black fly. Today, however, the insect swarms are made up of butterflies, including the Mourning Cloak which Ben favors. As a collector, he is ecstatic. But he is also frustrated, for all he has is a mosquito head net, a poor substitute for a capturing net.

Journal entry: Saturday, May 17, 1986. *Black flies have displaced the butterflies. Neither Ben nor I mind because other things beckon. We decide that what we thought was a distant airplane must be a love-sick ruffed grouse, or maybe the more elusive spruce grouse, trying to drum up some action. The black mud of the trail traces a satiny trim around the colorful blankets of trillium on either side.*

Out of sight, we hear a heavy thrashing about in the brush; maybe a bear but most likely a deer. A hiking couple passes in a hurry, vowing to "give Esther a try, since we gave up on the Sewards." Ben and I proffer our sympathy. No one I know of who's ventured into the Cold River region where the peaks are located has referred to their conquest as a picnic.

Shortly before reaching the junction, the ridge slackens off and the trail passes a peculiar structure. It is shaped like a sentry box laid on its side, with one end open. It suggests an old-time survival shack, since there are many traces of overgrown ski trails nearby. But the ADK guidebook resolves the surmise: it is an old toboggan shelter.

Rescue shack? *This unusual structure, plopped in the midst of an overgrown network of old ski trails, is a toboggan shelter. It would look good to climbers in foul weather.*

Ten minutes later, the first of the herd paths to Esther appears. It's easy to miss because a weatherbeaten sign that marked the way in the mid-1980s is now missing — likely for firewood at one of the makeshift, blackened rock piles near the junction.

The third approach to the trackless paths leading to Esther is the segment of the Wilmington trail that descends from the summit of Whiteface. It's worth exploring for several reasons.

With little effort, you can savor superb mountaintop views. By driving to the top of the Memorial Highway and taking the elevator to the summit, the hiker can then descend the trail for about a third of a mile in the open, above treeline. On the right, to the east, one will see the chairlift ascending from the ski center, site of alpine events during the 1980 Winter Olympics. Beyond it is a closeup of where recent landslides slashed to the base. And all around are a good share of the other high peaks, including that lonesome 46er, Esther, dead ahead to the north.

One will notice, in a matter of minutes, the stark contrast between the busy world of tourists on the summit of Whiteface and the tranquil world of the wilderness as you descend to where the trees begin again.

This segment is also worth doing because it's short and easy, both coming down and going back up. In less than an hour, a descent of a thousand feet on a well-traveled trail arrives at the point where the trial-and-error search for Esther begins.

The first prominence on the way to Esther is Lookout Mountain, a short 15 minutes from the Wilmington trail. Those who study maps will wonder why it's not listed as one of the Adirondack high peaks, since it's clearly marked as 4,100 feet.

It's because of an arbitrary rule established by the Marshall brothers and their guide, Herb Clark, when they became the first to climb all 46 of the high peaks in 1924. To qualify as a part of that select group, they decided, a peak "should either rise at least 300 feet on all sides, or be at the end of a long ridge at least three quarters of a mile from the nearest peak."

The topographic, or topo, map gives the answer: the slopes of Lookout do not rise beyond 200 feet from the slopes of Whiteface, and even less from the bottom of the saddle on the way to Esther. Poor Lookout is a two-time loser — its summit is also littered with rubble from the ski lodge which once perched there.

In good weather, Esther will loom a mile away. On

On Lookout. *Remains of an old ski lodge litter the summit; flag trees confirm the severity of winds. Esther beckons from the end of an undulating ridge.*

one of those crisp days that bring such glory to the Adirondacks, she will appear more as a temptress than a tormenter. But on a bad day, the trek from Lookout to Esther can be depressing.

A quarter of a mile beyond Lookout, the path dips to the bottom of a swampy expanse, which in rainy weather becomes a morass. Back in Iowa, or down below in the Ausable River valley near Wilmington, the black soil would be called prime bottomland. Up here, it's treacherous ooze, the product of rotted vegetation and poor drainage — one more obstacle for the explorer.

Beyond the col, the approach to Esther begins to undulate upward like a moderate roller coaster, with the summit coming into view on some of the crests. Most of the time, however, the path moves through the clutches of fallen trees intermixed with dense undergrowth on either side.

Journal entry: Saturday, May 30, 1981. That spirited explorer of 70 years ago, T. Morris Longstreth, spoke for many of us when he said: "In the Adirondacks, no morning sky could foretell the evening. The weather was either a dazzling uncertainty or a drizzling certainty."

It was hot and humid when we started at the base of the Wilmington trail. Now, it's cold enough for jackets. We discover why the black flies were missing down below; they're all up here. A protruding branch of a fallen tree has punctured my cheek; the flies assemble on my Band Aid for a trail snack.

Ben and I are climbing with Tom Stanwood, a veteran Forty Sixer who's guided us on several explorations. "Count yourselves lucky," says Tom when he hears us complain about the close quarters. "If it starts to rain, as it looks like it may, this path will turn into a 'car wash.' The branches will be the brushes, and you will be the cars."

There is no record that Verplanck Colvin, superintendent of New York state's Adirondack survey during the last century, ever climbed Esther. But his report to the legislature in 1879 suggests that he might have.

In describing "the difficulties encountered, and obstacles to be constantly overcome in field-work," he enthused that "the wood-man...shrouded and shut in by the deep, wonderful forest, emerges at length from its darkness to the daylight of the clearings, like a man who has passed under a great river or arm of the sea through a tunnel, knowing little of the wonders that had surrounded him."

Esther is like that. One emerges from her wooded grasp to see the bulge of her summit at the end of a long, wooded ridge. In the midst of an open rock face is a benchmark and, next to it, a pile of stones which props up a metal cannister containing a notebook and pencil. The

Adirondack Forty Sixers maintain these on all of the 20 trailless high peaks. Climbers who wish to become "aspiring Forty Sixers" can jot down their names in the notebook, and send in the names recorded by the previous three climbers.

Journal entry: Saturday, May 30, 1981. One climber must have made it here on a day like ours — we have racing clouds, rain, wind, cold, the works. His scrawled entry: "Wish all my enemies could have the pleasure of dying on this rock."

Esther's summit clearing offers relief from blowdown and confusing herd paths. Even so, blowing clouds complicate the way and the view.

The summit rock also displays a bronze plaque attached by early-day Forty Sixers in 1939. They marked the centennial of Esther's first climb by a 15-year-old girl named Esther McComb who lived on a nearby farm. She had decided to climb Whiteface from the north, got lost and found herself atop her namesake instead.

Her climb through uncharted wilderness was remarkable. At the time, less than 10 of the other Adirondack high peaks had been climbed. Also, because her parents lived in a backwoods area that was remote from populated areas, they had forbidden Esther and her siblings to climb the surrounding mountains.

Today, in clear weather, climbers can enjoy many of the same views which unfolded for Esther. One can peer down the east slope and see the microscopic movement of people in Wilmington, 3,000 feet below. Farther on is lonely Hurricane Mountain. And still farther to the east is the sparkling ribbon of Lake Champlain sprawled in front of the jagged serrations of Vermont's Green Mountains.

Journal entry: Thursday, August 9, 1990. An otherwise clear sky is blemished by vapor trails of jet airplanes from nearby Plattsburgh Air Force Base. They crisscross the skies, no doubt because of the tensions aroused by Desert Storm, which erupted in the Middle East earlier this year. On our way driving up, we noticed that gas prices have jumped in the last few days from $1.00 to $1.43 per gallon.

Spaces between flag trees on the western edge of the summit reveal a panorama of the Saranacs, along with the Seward mountain chain to their left. Directly south of Esther, other Adirondack high peaks come into view: Colden, Dix, Giant, and many of the peaks in the Great Range.

Dominating everything, of course, is Whiteface, to the south of Esther and a bit west. When atmospheric conditions are just right, garbled voices float over from the tourist castle and the summit. Along with mixed emotions.

Whiteface, viewed from Esther, confirms why it is called the most elegant and majestic of the Adirondack mountains. But popularity is not the sole motivation for visiting the high peaks.

Joel Tyler Headley, a preacher and journalist who went to the Adirondacks in the mid-1800s for his health, revealed a compelling rationale for the explorer:

"I love the freedom of the wilderness and the absence of conventional forms there. I love the long stretch through the forest on foot, and the thrilling, glorious prospect from some hoary mountain top. I love it, and I know it is better for me than the thronged city."

Young Esther McComb must have shared that belief. Her impetuous journey inspires others to get acquainted with the other Esther today. They soon discover that while this least known of all Adirondack high peaks is difficult to get along with, she can still be attractive.

So that's how we did it, *muses Ben. The highway which laces the north side of Whiteface shows our climb up the highway more clearly than any of our contour maps.*

Giant Mtn. from the Ausable Club, at St. Huberts, N.Y.

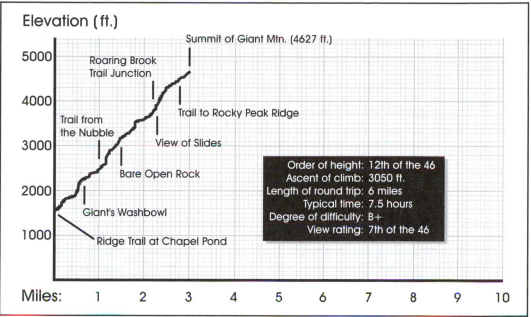

Elevation (ft.)

Summit of Giant Mtn. (4627 ft.)

Roaring Brook
Trail Junction

5000

4000

Trail from
the Nubble

Trail to Rocky Peak Ridge

3000

View of Slides

Bare Open Rock

2000

Giant's Washbowl

1000

Ridge Trail at Chapel Pond

Order of height: 12th of the 46
Ascent of climb: 3050 ft.
Length of round trip: 6 miles
Typical time: 7.5 hours
Degree of difficulty: B+
View rating: 7th of the 46

Miles: 1   2   3   4   5   6   7   8   9   10

For contour trails, see U.S. Geological Survey map, pgs. 46-47.

5.
GIANT

Each Adirondack mountain speaks to the explorer in its own way.

One of the first to greet you when coming from the south is a prominent ridge on the east side of the Northway about a mile before reaching the Chestertown exit. The ridge flaunts an artless welcome on a huge sign no doubt crafted by locals: "Hello."

The first high peaks, Macomb and Dix, peep from the north as the highway begins its descent past the rest stop overlooking Schroon Lake. But Macomb reveals only a serrated crest. It conjures up the comb of a bashful rooster, crouching low beyond intervening hills.

A mile past the rest area prior to the turnoff for Route 73, the trailless little Dixes — South Dix and East Dix — stare down from the west with a sullen arrogance. They know they can get away with it; the only way the climber can get at them, from any direction, is to plot a course through or over the mountains which wall them in.

Just before the Northway turnoff to Rt. 73, a long high horizontal ridge with a blip on the western end blots out the northern horizon like a dead end sign: Rocky Peak Ridge. A mile further west, another peak thrusts a sharp snout even higher: Giant Mountain.

Giant, to the casual observer, sends conflicting messages. When viewed as you approach from the east, Giant displays a kind of tired

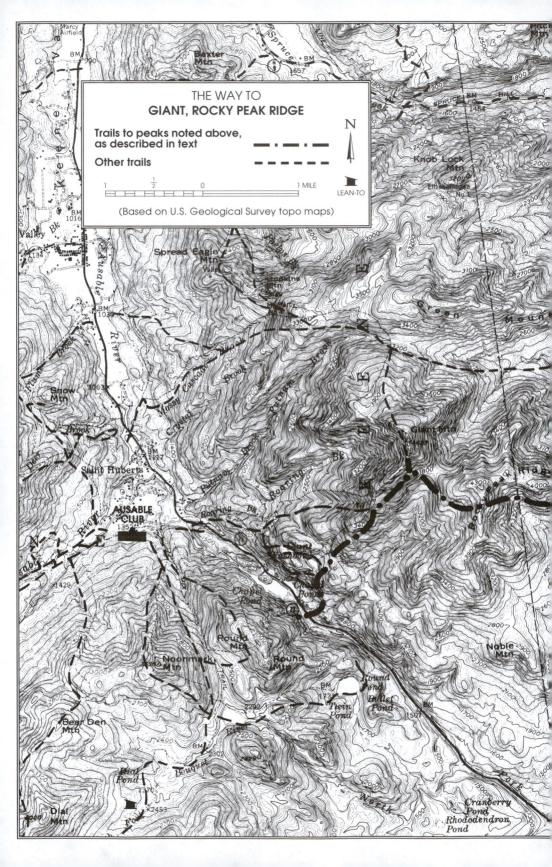

THE WAY TO
GIANT, ROCKY PEAK RIDGE

Trails to peaks noted above,
as described in text —·—·—·—

Other trails ——————

N

1 ½ 0 1 MILE

LEAN-TO

(Based on U.S. Geological Survey topo maps)

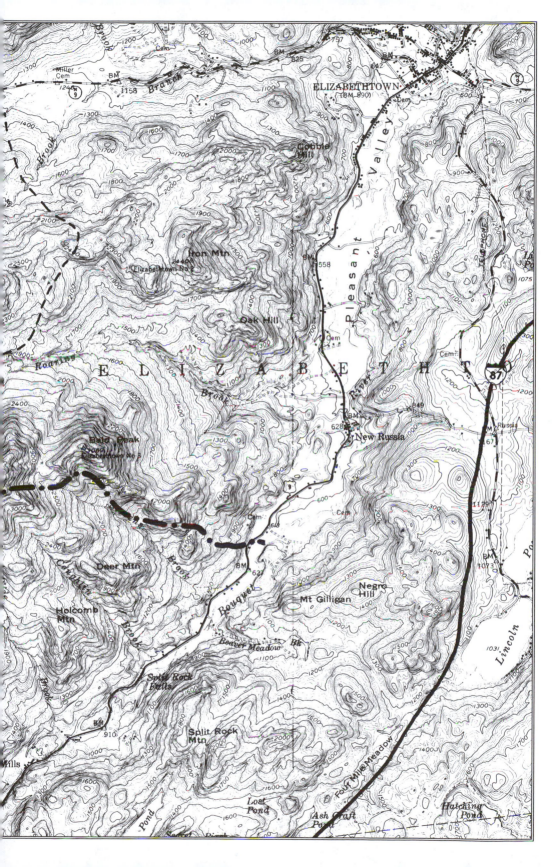

elegance. Its semi-barren slopes have been scarred by avalanches, by the tail end of the 1950 hurricane, and by forest fires which seared the eastern and southern slopes early in the century. Plants and trees have begun the long struggle to regain their virgin vigor.

The west face of Giant, viewed from the Ausable Club in St. Huberts, has been disfigured even more by periodic landslides. It is as if a gigantic scouring pad had swept from summit to base, again and again, leaving vertical stripes down to gleaming bedrock.

But the core message imparted by Giant during the 10-mile trip from the Northway to Keene Valley is that of an overpowering presence. It's no wonder the residents of Elizabethtown, from where both Giant and Rocky Peak Ridge obliterate views of high peaks to the west, applied the formal name of Giant of the Valley.

> *Journal entry: Sunday, September 28, 1969. Every time we drive by on Rt. 73, I crane my neck to look for a summit above the mountainous bulk on our right. At one opening through the trees, a lofty prominence comes into view, poking its head into the clouds. It can only be Giant. Son Jim is anxious to go up and get acquainted. To me, the prospect is more intimidating than enticing.*

Early incursions to Giant were made from the north and east via a trail from Hopkins Mountain, two miles east of Keene Valley, and on the east from Elizabethtown and New Russia on Rt. 9. The latter two trails disappeared, but another penetrated to the south and west from Rt. 9N, converging with the Hopkins trail on Green Mountain for the final, rugged, one-mile assault of Giant's summit.

The two trails are still there, but they're not used much anymore. The Hopkins' route offers little in the way of views, and the other — in spite of an "interesting outlook" mentioned in the current ADK guidebook — is a mile and a half longer and more than twice the distance of the approaches from the southern side of the mountain.

In 1968, the state cut a new trail to Giant from the west, beginning at Rt. 9 near New Russia. It traces all the way over Rocky Peak Ridge, replacing a long-gone trail from decades earlier. If Giant is your goal, this is doing it the hard way. It's longer than any of the other trails, and requires a mile of vertical climbing, plus another 20 feet piled on for good measure.

The two most popular routes to Giant are the Ridge trail, starting on the opposite side of Rt. 73 near Chapel Pond, and the Roaring Brook trail, which begins near the first turnoff to the Ausable Club from the highway, some three miles before coming to Keene Valley when driving north.

Roaring Brook is an Adirondack name which Murray Heller, in his book *Call me Adirondack*, files under the "Phenomenon of Ditto." In short, the body of water is not unique.

The category, says Heller, includes some 43 Mud Ponds, 16 called Clear Pond, and 14 named Lost Pond. In the same way, the name Roaring Brook is not unique to Giant Mountain.

There is another Roaring Brook on the south flank of Street Mountain, flowing south to Duck Hole from — this should come as no surprise — Lost Pond. And there are other Roaring Brooks in the Adirondacks, including a second one on Giant, on the opposite, or east side of the mountain.

But the Roaring Brook at the trailhead on the southwest base of Giant is not ubiquitous. It promotes its presence with a 325-foot waterfall that prompts people to stop and stare from the highway. During most of the year, excluding the spring run-off, the flow is slim and wispy.

On June 29, 1963, however, it lived up to the full meaning of its name, and then some.

The southwest wall of Giant is a cirque, similar to those on Whiteface — carved by glaciers in the form of an amphitheatre. During midafternoon on that sultry summer day, thermal updrafts began building clouds above Giant. Shortly before five p.m., the angry, blackened mass towered six miles high.

Some speculate that the hollowed-out side of Giant helped shape and trap the formation in place by acting as a funnel. Those on or near Giant must have believed it, because something triggered the release of six inches of rain in just 90 minutes (Keene Valley, three miles away, received only one quarter of an inch).

The torrent was too much for the shallow soil on Giant's steep upper reaches. With clay as a lubricant, the soil slipped loose in strips a few feet wide at the summit. But in the 3,400-foot rush to the base, it gathered not only speed but everything in its way until the swath above the falls of Roaring Brook was 200 feet wide.

Rubble and debris swept over the falls and covered portions of Rt. 73 to a depth of 10 to 15 feet. The landslide overran several cars passing by and others parked in the lot at Roaring Brook meadow. Fortunately, none

Roaring Brook Falls *tumbles down toward base of the Roaring Brook trail to Giant. View is from Rt. 73, a mile northwest of Chapel Pond.*

of the two dozen people in them were harmed. One of the most vivid recollections of those on site was a strong, sour stench from the organic material exposed and brought down by the slides.

Today, those who climb Roaring Brook trail can see traces of the cataclysm. The trail skirts the falls, where a ledge halfway up was sheared off. There are also traces of the widened streambed above the falls, although the views of Giant's slides from areas which had been laid bare are now being blotted out by the born-again forest.

A bit more than a mile from the base, the Roaring Brook trail splits to head in two different directions to hook up with the Ridge trail from Chapel Pond. The more direct route heads due west for two miles to its junction. The other heads southeast for a mile, passing two interesting sidelights: the Giant's Nubble, a rocky prominence that offers fine views of the slides and Chapel Pond Pass, and the Giant's Washbowl, a peaceful, bashful mountainside pond.

Journal entry: Monday, August 21, 1978. As we alight at Chapel Pond, son Ben, who is 10 years old, suggests: "Let's climb the Thumb Mountains next." I bite, of course, and he explains: "When I put my thumb on the map over Elk Lake, it's circled by the Dixes, Dials, Nippletop, Colvin and Blake. What do you say?"

First things first.

Chapel Pond Pass, the jumping off point for the Ridge trail, is the U-shaped valley traced by Rt. 73 between Giant and Round mountains. It was ground down by the same glacial action that formed the saucer-shaped depression on Giant's west side.

It would appear that Chapel Pond is aptly named. The fluted columns of the cliffs on either side soar like organ pipes in a natural cathedral. In fact, Chapel Pond was named not from religious fervor, but for a corruption of the word Chapelle. That was the name of a French Canadian guide who served with British General John Burgoyne during the early years of the American Revolution.

Chapelle helped Burgoyne and his men hack a road through the torturous wilderness on their way from Ausable Forks to the Schroon valley. It was one of the first of the many Military Roads in the Adirondacks. Obviously, it was designed not for pleasure but, depending on Burgoyne's persuasion, for advance or retreat.

Today, not only pleasure but ease of access make the pass one of the most popular areas in the high peaks. In 1990, one of every eight people registering for hikes did so at trailheads entering the Giant Mountain Wilderness.

Not everyone comes to explore, of course. One can often spot rock climbers across from Giant on the Chapel Pond Slab, one of the east's longest rock climbs. Others find pleasure in discovering that Chapel

Pond has been spared the ravages of acid rain. Campers report it has plenty of trout to supplement store-bought rations.

Wildlife at Chapel Pond Pass thrives in spite of the people. Golden eagles have been noted, although less often than a few decades ago. And more and more, thanks to efforts of the state Department of Environmental Conservation, one can spot peregrine falcons as well as northern goshawks. The latter, in fact, will let you know if they feel their young are threatened, by diving at you.

Journal entry: Monday, August 21, 1978. The Ridge trail register brings to mind the advice offered hikers by Ralph Waldo Emerson. He was an occasional visitor at Putnam Camp, located just below the Roaring Brook trailhead at the base of Giant.

Warned Ralph:
"Few people know how to take a walk. The qualifications...are endurance...an eye for nature, good humor, vast curiosity, good speech, good silence and nothing too much."

I look at the near-vertical cliffs that will be our first challenge, and wonder what he would consider "too much"?

A good design, coupled with numerous switchbacks, dissolves any concern about the steep beginnings of the Ridge trail. In a little more than half a mile, it eases to a bare rock ledge that provides a choice seat for viewing the splendor on the west.

Chapel Pond appears almost directly below. Beyond is the first good view of Sawteeth, Gothics, Armstrong and the two Wolfjaws. And just across the valley, to the southwest, is a mountain the neophyte would expect to be Nippletop, because of its profile.

But the map shows it is Noonmark, which "marks noon" for the people in nearby Keene Valley when the sun arcs to a vertical position over the mountain's summit. In front of Noonmark is Round Mountain, which never makes a sharp impression from the road because it has no well-defined peak to distinguish it from its neighbors.

Journal entry: Sunday, September 28, 1969. Jim is intrigued with a dead tree whose top is about the same height as the lip of the rock overhang we are on, but five or six feet out. He flops down to look over the edge and speculates that it would be a great way to get down the cliff in a hurry. Uh, huh. The tree is not only rotten but 50 to 60 feet high. I get nervous and suggest we push on.

A hundred yards beyond the ledge, the trail dips slightly to the south rim of the Giant's "Washbowl," which is a glacial pond. It's maybe an eighth of a mile long, considerably less than when it was first measured

Giant's Washbowl, *a lovely, lonely, glacial pond, tempts the climber to defer for awhile the remaining two-mile ascent.*

by the state's survey chief, Verplanck Colvin, in the last century. And, it'll probably shrink further, like other shallow Adirondack lakes at high elevations, as grass and weeds crowd in from the shores. Eventually, one guesses, it will become a swamp.

The trail skirts the Washbowl on the east. A bridge lends a hand to the hiker for crossing the pond's outlet, where beavers have been at work. Climbing becomes easier and in the next half mile, the trail meets two spurs, including the one over the Nubble, from the Roaring Brook trail.

As the trail winds through a grove of large conifers, one notices an abrupt change to white birch at the beginning of a steep rise. This is the perimeter of a massive forest fire which in 1903 burned nearly a half million acres on Giant and other Adirondack peaks, spurring the state to institute a fire control system.

As the trail moves onto bare rock, the climbing becomes easier.

Journal entry: Saturday, June 26, 1981. We barely reach the first cairn, a pile of rocks to mark the way in bad weather, when Ben spots a squirrel poking its head from the hollow of a dead tree. But this is no ordinary squirrel.

We must have startled it because it leaps outward, spreads its four legs, and soars by as a furry airfoil — buffy gray on top, creamy white below, with two beady black eyes to guide it while a flattened tail steers from behind.

What luck! Flying squirrels are mostly nocturnal, but this one displays the right stuff in broad daylight.

The roadway, while not in view, is at the bottom of the narrow valley far below. The full range of Adirondack peaks sprawls beyond it to the west — the first view of Dix and the trailless peaks to the southwest; the

Dials and Nippletop; and the chain of mountains in the Great Range that leads from Lower Wolfjaw to the highest peak in the distance that can only be Marcy. As one climbs higher, the MacIntyre Range will come into view with the snub peak of Algonquin barely visible.

The open area over which the trail leads for some half a mile is a gigantic sheet of Appalachian bedrock, crisscrossed with interesting patterns of fractures. Geologists call these dark joints "dikes," which were formed by molten rock which sought out cracks in the bedrock and pushed to the surface from great depths. Because this rock is normally softer than bedrock, erosion and weathering have left the fractures as indentations which are a darker color than the grayish slabs surrounding them.

First open ledge, *scoured clean by a forest fire in 1913, offers splendid views of the rock-climbing cliffs at Chapel Pond, at base of Round Mtn.*

Journal entry: Sunday, September 28, 1969. Some of the Adirondack dikes are supposed to be imbedded with dark red garnets, but I can't see any. It's probably because I'm red-green color blind. It causes the same problem for me with four-leaf clovers — I've looked for years, and have yet to spot one.

Beyond the bare rock face, the trail winds through scrub conifers, with a choice of routes — one up and over a high knob, and a pass-around which leads down to a short level stretch before starting upward again. It is easy going, in the open for a while, then through larger trees until the trail joins the one from Roaring Brook coming in from the west.

A couple of times, the climber will think the summit of Giant is in sight. But as on so many Adirondack trails, it will be only a prominence along the way. Suddenly, on reaching the top of one more ridge, the summit will emerge, full flower.

One can now see in close-up how Giant's towering dome cradles the huge depression on its west face, and how the whitish paths on the face mark the stupendous earthflows which ripped their way to the bottom.

The trail levels off briefly, then begins the final steep climb through gnarled, dwarfed trees along the ridge leading to the summit. Off to the right, on the southeast, is Rocky Peak Ridge, angled like a monstrous boomerang.

The summit of Rocky Peak Ridge is only a little more than a mile away, but unfortunately this is by air. To reach it, a climber has to descend 850 feet into the col between the two mountains, then climb another 660 feet to the summit of Rocky Peak Ridge. And, of course, reverse the process on coming back to Giant.

Journal entry: Saturday, June 26, 1981. At the first overlook on the way up, I noted a bus parked at Chapel Pond. Not rock climbers, I hoped. This past week, two climbers fell to their deaths from the Shawangunks, an escarpment in the Catskills in southern New York state, and five were killed in a 2,000-foot ice-fall on Mt. Hood in Oregon. That news makes me nervous.

Shortly after leaving the Giant's Washbowl, Ben and I learned that the bus did not transport rock climbers — we were passed on the trail and almost over-whelmed by passengers who came from Montreal, chattering in French. Now, nearing the top, a descending couple warns us: "It's like a convention up there." They are right. So much so, there is no room for Ben and me to have lunch at the summit overlook. We relax in a sheltered hollow 50 yards back down the trail.

Giant is second only to Marcy as the place to see the most high peaks. From Marcy, one can spot all but two — low-slung Couchsachraga far to the west, and East Dix which is blocked by nearby Hough.

Giant presents a panorama of 38 — all but Cliff, Couchsachraga, Emmons, Gray, Redfield and Santanoni, with two questionables, Blake and Panther. From Giant, Marcy is unmistakable — it thrusts

Spectacular slides point the way to Giant's summit, a mile away and 700 feet higher. First comes a brief respite, a level trail segment through cool woods.

above the rest to the west like the inverted edge of a blunt meat cleaver.

The great viewing is due in large part to the work of Verplanck Colvin. He recognized that Giant would provide great sight lines to the other peaks for his state survey work if Giant's

Cowlicks of the world, unite! From Giant, Ben and I can't decide which is more refreshing — the breeze, or the view of the Great Range which leads to Marcy and other great adventures.

summit were cleared of trees. Which he promptly ordered his crew to do. And that close crop has kept the peak bald ever since.

Harold Weston, an Adirondack artist from Keene Valley, reported on the view from Giant in his book *Freedom in the Wilds*: "If the weather is exceptionally clear, the rising sun silhouettes Mount Washington of the White Mountains in New Hampshire [150 miles away]. Even on good days, one normally cannot see beyond the Green Mountains in Vermont."

Weston also confirmed that there used to be at least one lean-to just north of Giant's summit, but it has long since disappeared.

Journal entry: Saturday, June 26, 1981. I'm too tired to explore for the site of any lean-tos.

The Giant's conquered, the stomach's full, and the mind wanders. Mine does, at least, away from the crowds.

One thinks of Colvin and his signal party on Giant — as usual in his summit climbing, he was hours late and a few thousand feet short. He and his group didn't catch up with his advance party on the summit until 6:45 p.m. They finished their work, then began the first of a series of perilous descents which read, in Colvin's reports to the state legislature, more like fiction than fact:

"Too late to descend," his guides advised. But an overwhelming thirst, no water, and Colvin's resolve to the task dictated otherwise. He and his crew reached the base at 1 a.m.

One also thinks of Archibald Campbell, who must have wandered near here when he took some Mohawk Indian Chiefs with him in 1772 to view the site of the Old Military Tract he proposed to buy from them. This was a plot of nearly three quarters of a million acres in Essex, Franklin, and Clinton counties which the state legislature had determined to protect "from frequent pillage by the Indians." The chiefs gave a cursory look to the north and west and said they were satisfied and were ready to go home. It was not only late in the season and late in the day, they indicated, but more important, their rum had run out — never mind the water.

And one thinks of Charles Broadhead, considered the first to climb any Adirondack high peak; he surmounted Giant on a surveying excursion in 1797. Bushwhacking without a trail on any of the 46 is bad enough today. It must have been a formidable challenge then. He recorded facing not only the usual, nearly impenetrable "Timber Balsam and Spruce" but — this was on June 2 — "snow 24 inches deep."

But mostly one thinks of the oldtime Adirondack guides, and speculates what it would be like to be one of them, the better to hike and explore.

Probably not Elijah Simonds of nearby Elizabethtown. He was known as a great hunter during his 79 years. But in later years he left New York state to hunt and trap in the middle west, including my home state of Iowa. It's nice to go back there for visits, but for heavens sake, it doesn't have any mountains.

A better choice of guide would be John Cheney, who was on the expedition that discovered Marcy. A noted magazine editor and writer of that day, Charles Fenno Hoffman, concluded that Cheney came as close as any of the Adirondack guides to James Fenimore Cooper's Natty Bumppo (he was the scout called Hawkeye in The Last of the Mohicans*).*

That's wishful thinking, of course, even if Marcy were waiting to be discovered today. Most of us present-day explorers have spent too much time at home or in the office to gain the strength, stamina and skills needed to be a guide.

Of course, we can still voice our opinions about it. But even Cheney the guide has the edge there. Listen to what he told Hoffman about the view to the east from the summit of Marcy: "Old Champlain, though fifty miles away, glistens below you like a strip of white birch when slicked up by the moon on a frosty night, and the Green Mountains of Vermont beyond it fade and fade away until they disappear as gradually as a cold scent when the dew rises."

Can you believe that a non-writer like this rough-hewn backwoodsman could come up with something like that? It's awesome.

The midsummer afternoon *urges one to dawdle for a last look at Giant's Washbowl and Chapel Pond. They sparkle in the sun, in John Burroughs' words, "as beautiful as a dream."*

While Giant has more people clambering over it than many of the other high peaks, it still nurtures an abundance of Adirondack fowl and fauna. To find them, climbers say, all you have to do is look and listen.

Journal entry: Monday, August 21, 1978. Ben and I see no one on our way down. Strange to say, neither do we see any wildlife.

Last week, in the Nature Conservancy's Lisha Kill Preserve near our home in Schenectady, I startled a ruffed grouse. On previous solitary stalks there with my wife, we've run across deer, possums, raccoons, Canada geese, skunks, Great Horned owls, ground hogs, squirrels, chipmunks, etc. Yet I've rarely seen any of them on hikes in the high peaks with either Jim or Ben, though all of the creatures are relatively common.

Then I recall the phrase in Emerson's prescription for a walk: "good silence." Ben's incessant, conjunctive chatter, which is just like Jim's, is the antithesis: the boys make too much noise — they talk all the time.

But in the midst of his commentary, Ben says: "I just love hiking."

Which answers the obvious question: Which is more important, to commune with nature, or to keep the lines of communication open with the younger generation?

Rocky Peak Ridge from Ridge trail junction below summit of Giant Mtn.

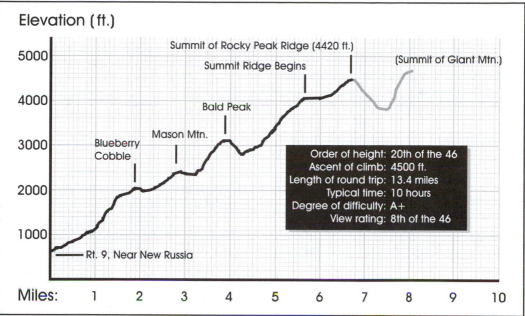

Elevation (ft.)

Summit of Rocky Peak Ridge (4420 ft.)

Summit Ridge Begins

(Summit of Giant Mtn.)

5000

Bald Peak

4000

Mason Mtn.

3000

Blueberry
Cobble

Order of height: 20th of the 46
Ascent of climb: 4500 ft.
Length of round trip: 13.4 miles
Typical time: 10 hours
Degree of difficulty: A+
View rating: 8th of the 46

2000

1000

Rt. 9, Near New Russia

Miles: 1   2   3   4   5   6   7   8   9   10

For contour trails, see U.S. Geological Survey map, pgs. 46-47.

6.
ROCKY PEAK RIDGE

Adirondack hikers who have explored this mountain seem to be as polarized as the characters in Dickens' *A Tale of Two Cities*. They say their experience was not only "the best of times" but "the worst of times."

Tony Goodwin, editor of the current Adirondack Mountain Club high peaks guidebook, promises that the exploration, coupled with a climb of Giant on a cool day when fall colors are at their height, "is probably the best hike in all of the Adirondacks."

To hear others, you would think they were talking about an entirely different mountain.

Robert Marshall, one of the trio which first climbed the 46 high peaks, described Rocky Peak Ridge in 1922 as, "burned completely over and around...hardly worth the trouble." He condemned it with a view rating of 33rd.

Russell M. L. Carson, the renowned Adirondack mountain biographer of the '20s, called it "all ugly and bare...a trailless mountain that is seldom climbed."

In 1971, the Adirondack Forty Sixers' first book said of the Giant's Wife — an alternative name for Rocky Peak Ridge — "she can hardly be called a fitting consort for her companion of the west." An advisory from the Schenectady ADK chapter added the admonition: "Bring plenty of water. You won't find any on this trail."

Neal S. Burdick, editor of *A Century Wild* and the ADK's *Adirondac* magazine, opined in 1985: "Trekking along this bare spine reminds me of hiking the Scottish Highlands." Depending on your lineage, that could be a compliment or a complaint.

Complaints, in fact, were well founded. The fires that blackened Rocky Peak Ridge in the early 1900s were so fierce they consumed much of the mountain's duff, the decaying matter on the forest floor. In the 1991 Outdoor Guide of *Adirondack Life*, Goodwin noted that "road engineers thoughtfully planted a thick stand of Scotch pines along the newly improved Chapel Pond Pass road so that motorists would be spared having to look at the fire-scarred slopes."

Rocky Peak Ridge, concluded Carson, is "a conspicuous example of the evil that forest fires can do."

Today, Rocky Peak Ridge is a conspicuous example of the rejuvenating that time can do. New growth is thriving but it has not sprouted enough to block the view from many areas. As a result, the Adirondack Forty Sixers' newest book, *Of the Summits, Of the Forests*, described it in 1991 as "one of the most spectacular trips in the mountains."

Neal Burdick, again referring to Rocky Peak Ridge, made clear his affinity for Scotland when he said, "this may be as close to heaven as I'll ever get."

Journal entry: Monday, October 6, 1969. Jim and I have no peak in mind for climbing until just before we head north, when my wife overhears us mention Rocky Peak Ridge. "Wasn't there an article in the paper about that?"

A quick search through back issues of the Schenectady Gazette *brings it to light: "Trail Blazers Carve Path to Rocky Peak."*

The new trail from the east was cut by the state in 1968. Prior to that, there had been only a herd path from Giant and an end-of-the-century trail from a mile or so south of New Russia on Rt. 9. The latter headed west as far as the eastern summit of Rocky Peak Ridge. Both were obliterated by the forest fires.

The little hamlet of New Russia, incidentally, is not peopled by Russian immigrants. It was named more than two centuries ago for a smelting process. It's hard to visualize now, but the town was once a thriving, iron-producing hub.

Journal entry: Monday, December 13, 1993. I called the town clerk to ask for the population of New Russia. The woman who answered didn't know, but volunteered to ask a resident who happened to be in the office. "He says it's about 40 people, tops," she reported. "If that's good enough for you, he says it's okay with him." And, she added, "It's sure good enough for me."

The climb by the new trail from New Russia is longer — a little over 13 miles round trip, vs. a circuit of some nine miles by way of Giant. It also calls for more climbing — 4,810 ft. vs. 3,800 over Giant. But the rewards of Rocky Peak Ridge are more revealing, and prolonged.

From the trailhead at Rt. 9, old corduroy-log tote roads lead through new-growth willow and birch, amid much evidence of logging. Gradually the trail winds through larger stands of mature hardwoods, then around a series of rocky ledges that reveal the valley, receding below.

Journal entry: Monday, October 6, 1969. We have gone perhaps a mile when Jim and I see our first sign. New York State's Department of Environmental Conservation has waxed descriptive with the single word, "Trail."

A cutoff leads to scenic Blueberry Cobble, which in season offers wild raspberries as well as blueberries. Beyond, the climber will spot a stark and rocky prominence that appears to be the summit. But it's only Bald Peak, a thousand feet up at a stiff angle, and roughly halfway to the ultimate goal.

The actual climbing is not as bad as it appears from afar. On a good day it can be memorable.

Journal entry: Monday, October 6, 1969. The promise of Indian Summer has been fulfilled; it is pure delight to stroll through the woods around the Cobble. The sun has finally broken through the fading mist, which has acted like ground glass filtering the brilliance of the foliage. Later in the morning, the sun's full rays set the leaves ablaze, only to have them extinguished again and again by the passing shadows of trees.

What a joy to be hiking in the woods! I wonder what the poor people are doing — poor, that is, in the sense they have never climbed an Adirondack peak in autumnal splendor.

Eventually, the climb up Bald Peak becomes challenging. One must scramble up and around rocky outcroppings spotted with stubby trees and alpine growth.

The summit of Bald Peak reveals an interesting shoulder of Rocky Peak Ridge to the southwest. It is strewn with debris left by glaciers; one gigantic boulder balances on end, seemingly ready to topple at the first whisper of the wind. The shoulder of the long, narrow ridge points west toward the summit. From there, another shoulder veers off to the south.

The compleat climber. *Son Jim, age 13, is prepared for anything: red hat to warn October hunters, plenty of snacks in an old army knapsack and, for comfort, a shirttail out.*

In front of the ridge, however, is a valley reminiscent of the yawning gap between Giant and Rocky Peak Ridge. Even when the nearest high crest across the valley from Bald Peak is reached, one still faces a long trek before completing the conquest of Rocky Peak Ridge.

Among the many streams feeding Lake Champlain, some 20 miles to the east, is the Boquet River, now seen coursing eastward through Pleasant Valley to pass the distant trailhead. Two branches of the Boquet spring to life in the high Adirondack peaks which form a vertical wall to the west. The soft outlines of the Dix Range nurture the headwaters of the south fork; Nippletop, hidden from here by Giant and Rocky Peak Ridge, collects the waters which form the north fork.

Journal entry: Monday, October 6, 1969. *They say if you look in the haze of Indian Summer long enough, you can make out dim figures from the past. Jim and I try to conjure up the Indians who used the Lake Champlain-Lake George corridor between the mountains long before Europeans encroached.*

We squint, too, to see if Rogers and his Rangers will again creep through the pass to be ambushed by the Indians. And we strain to see if we can spot the mouth of the Boquet on Lake Champlain where Gentleman Johnny Burgoyne and his British officers may be holding another council of war to fret about the Colonial upstarts.

The swirling mists close in; we give up and head onward.

From Bald Peak, the trail descends some 400 feet into the valley; understory trees and their roots offer emergency handholds. The bottom of the valley levels off momentarily, then the trail begins another steep climb to the top of the ridge.

The short, stubby trees thin out, then disappear as the trail winds through a grassy plateau. This is in sharp contrast to the usual jungle thickness on Adirondack peaks. The climbing becomes easy and, on a good day, the views are said to be grand all the way to the summit. Assuming you can find it.

Antidote *for a lost mountaintop: a sheltered rock, a quick lunch, and the surety that Indian summer beckons below.*

Journal entry: Monday, October 6, 1969. *Folds of fog whipped by the wind wrap us in bitter cold. We are somewhere on the ridge but can locate no cannister in a cairn to record our names. We guess that with the new trail it is no longer needed, and has been removed. We hate to go without leaving proof of our ascent. But after a quick lunch under a sheltering ledge, and with no break in the clouds, we head for the warmth below.*

A hundred yards or so to the south of the trailhead at Rt. 9 is a tiny cemetery, neatly fenced in. Two large-lettered headstones mark the passing of a husband and wife in the early part of the last century. He was born five years before the American Revolution and, per a secondary marker, was a veteran of the War of 1812. The two smaller stones are undoubtedly for children who died in infancy.

It is clear they were pioneers. And it seems fitting that they are passed regularly by latter-day hiking pioneers on their way to and from Rocky Peak Ridge.

Journal entry: Monday, October 6, 1969. *Jim and I count ourselves among the pioneers. During our eight and one half hours on the mountain, covering some 13 and one half miles, we have seen no one.*

Climbing Rocky Peak Ridge from the west is relatively straightforward.

A fifth of a mile before reaching Giant's summit by the Ridge trail from Chapel Pond, a side trail heads east a mile and a third to Rocky Peak Ridge. The col between the two mountains is deep and steep. As the *Gazette* noted, the descent from Giant to the col is the equivalent of clambering down a 70-story building. The article could have added that the climber is then faced with an ascent up Rocky Peak Ridge which is the same as climbing another 55-story building.

The only problem is that before you can do either, you must first climb Giant. If you do it via the Roaring Brook trail, the total ascent to Rocky Peak Ridge is the equivalent of climbing a building 400 stories high. Or, in more familiar terms, it's about the same as climbing the Empire State Building four times. Without, of course, the smooth steps and flat landings that would help slow the puffing.

Journal entry: Saturday, June 27, 1981. I'm out of shape and have made only a couple of climbs this year — one up snub-nosed Mt. Jo near Adirondak Loj in the heart of the high peaks, and another up Hunter Mountain in the Catskills with Ben and his Boy Scout troop. So to prep for more, I've ignored the elevator in our office building and climbed the five stories of stairs morning, noon and night. It hasn't helped much.

There were no cars when we parked to begin the Ridge trail up Giant on our way to Rocky Peak Ridge, so we assumed we had the mountains to ourselves. Wrong.

During the first half mile, we've been passed by three hikers, including one I know: Dave Vermilyea, an avid climber who authored the chapter on winter hiking in the Forty Sixers' 1970 book. Ben quickens at the name because Dave's wife was Ben's former teacher.

Dave tells us he's out to set no records today. "Just a stroll," he smiles. "I can't stay long." And he disappears up the trail.

Unlike us, he takes Giant strides.

The descent into the col from Giant is more moderate than one would expect from the view on high. And the gradual climb up the slope toward Rocky Peak Ridge borders on being a pleasant stroll. It's in marked contrast to the final approach on most Adirondack summits.

Philip G. Terrie, Jr., in his update of Carson's *Peaks and People of the Adirondacks*, hints at how the major attraction of Rocky Peak Ridge — its views — came about: "Nature has many ways of healing the scars left by careless and arrogant men."

The scars came from forest fires. Some were ignited by lightning, others by sparks from old-time steam locomotives. As Edith Pilcher noted in *Up the Lake Road*, some also may have been set by "arsonists, seeking jobs as fire fighters." The latter earned two dollars a day, high wages for Adirondackers in the old times.

During the first years of the healing process, Rocky Peak Ridge yielded no more than grass. Then enough soil developed to nurture a modest forest of poplars and birches. Conifers took over on the upper slopes, but have not made much progress on the summit itself. In the face of unrelenting stiff breezes, the conifers win a battle here and there, but they'll never win the war.

The expansive open ridge invites the explorer to sprawl and enjoy the sights.

Looking west, one can almost believe that the backside of Giant has been smeared by Christo, the Bulgarian-American artist who threw an orange curtain across a mountain valley in Colorado, cast pink plastic around Florida islands, and most recently draped the German Reichstag in shimmering, aluminum-coated fabric.

Looking east, the trail meanders along Rocky Peak Ridge to the huge, balanced boulder, dips into the defile, then climbs over Bald Peak, and snakes its way down to New Russia.

Battered but unbowed: *the eastern backside of Giant as seen from the summit of Rocky Peak Ridge.*

Journal entry: Saturday, June 27, 1981. *Looking south from our position on the broad summit ridge, Ben and I discover we are not alone.*

Two young women, shielded from the wind by the summit cairn, nap in the sun under the watchful eye of a German Shepherd. They greet us sleepily; the dog merely rolls his eyes in our direction. Otherwise, the summit is flat, empty and forlorn, almost forbidding.

One of the most memorable sights on this climb is a tiny glacial body of water called Marie Louise Pond. It nestles precariously on the side of a saddle between Rocky Peak, a lower sibling on the ridge, and Rocky Peak Ridge itself. The pond was named for the daughter of a man named Thomas P. Wickes, who hired a couple of Keene Valley guides to cut a trail from Giant to Rocky Peak Ridge at the turn of the century.

From the barren summit, *Lake Champlain and the Green Mountains come into soft focus to the east.*

First-time climbers are often convinced they have discovered a "lost pond" when they break through to the shores of Marie Louise Pond. But the archives show that it was known a quarter of a century before Wickes and his daughter came on scene. In fact, local residents had stocked the water with trout and fished there with elevated zest.

Journal entry: Saturday, June 27, 1981. *Ben and I are convinced that it's feasible to make a trailless climb of Rocky Peak Ridge from the south.*

The potential route is a brookbed which wanders down to the highway a quarter of a mile to the east of the Giant trailhead at Chapel Pond. The route looks doable on the map since the stream begins its downward flow as it crosses the trail at the low point of the col between Giant and Rocky Peak Ridge.

From the road below, though, dense woods line both banks of the stream. We've had trouble determining the main stream branch that leads up other trailless peaks, so we decide to scout it out from the infant stream above. The way should be easier coming down.

At the trail junction near Giant's summit, we again meet Dave Vermilyea who has just returned from Rocky Peak Ridge. He reports the trip across took him 35 minutes. Some "stroll." We had estimated it would take us an hour each way.

We ask him what he thinks of our plan to descend via the brook bed. "Personally," he says, "I'd never do it. If something happened, they might never find you."

He is very convincing.

Journal entry: Wednesday, August 7, 1991. *Tucked away in the corner of our sports closet in the basement at home is the pack I used 22 years ago on that first Rocky Peak Ridge climb with son Jim. It's made of canvas, with leather-reinforced edges and, believe it or not,* has a strap to loop over one shoulder. Like most other hikers of that era, I bought our gear from the local Army-Navy surplus store.

I intend to file away that old relic along with memories of other neophytes we've met during our explorations:

The lanky, pale, young man in a dark business suit and tennis shoes who queried us in October 1971 as he hopped from rock to rock in mid-stream near Bushnell Falls: "How far is it to the top of Mt. Marcy?" (Answer: Five and one half miles, with a climb of 3,500 feet. And it'll take four and a half hours. In daylight.)

Trail to New Russia descends to skirt the north side of Marie Louise Pond, at left below. It then climbs Rocky Peak, right, and Bald Peak, to the rear.

And the young couple who trudged in a downpour along Marcy Brook toward Lake Colden, heads and arms poked through holes in inverted, black plastic garbage bags. (Sorry to tell you, guys, but the lean-tos are full.)

Or, the red-faced youngster who wheezed his way to the top of Blue Mountain on a scorching day in June, 1986, then asked us anxiously: "Where's the water fountain?" (Answer: 1,600 feet below — an hour or so away, at the Adirondack Museum, just up the road from the trailhead.)

Most explorers survive their early tests, as did we. It's fortunate, because the Adirondack high peaks can be stern and unforgiving teachers.

Algonquin Peak, center, Wright Peak, left, and Iroquois Peak, right, from entry road to Adirondak Loj.

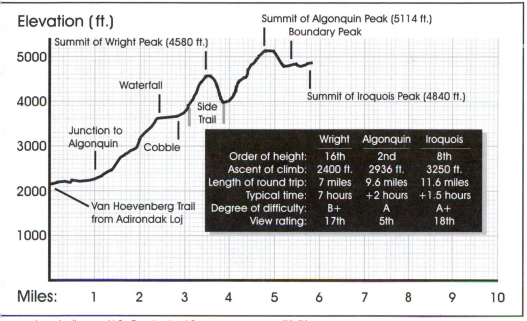

Elevation (ft.)

Summit of Algonquin Peak (5114 ft.)
Boundary Peak

Summit of Wright Peak (4580 ft.)

5000

Waterfall

4000

Summit of Iroquois Peak (4840 ft.)

Side
Trail

Junction to
Algonquin

3000

Cobble

	Wright	Algonquin	Iroquois
Order of height:	16th	2nd	8th
Ascent of climb:	2400 ft.	2936 ft.	3250 ft.
Length of round trip:	7 miles	9.6 miles	11.6 miles
Typical time:	7 hours	+2 hours	+1.5 hours
Degree of difficulty:	B+	A	A+
View rating:	17th	5th	18th

2000

Van Hoevenberg Trail
from Adirondak Loj

1000

Miles: 1   2   3   4   5   6   7   8   9   10

or contour trails, see U.S. Geological Survey map, pgs. 70-71.

7, 8, 9.
WRIGHT, ALGONQUIN, IROQUOIS

A few years ago, near the end of October, a 22-year-old hiker from Montreal named Alain Dufresne became separated from his group on the substantial summit of Algonquin Peak, the second highest mountain in the Adirondacks.

It was late in the day and as he hurried downward to catch up, he missed a crucial turn in the trail. Alone in the growing darkness, he managed to grope his way to the northern base of the mountain. As related in the *Lake Placid News*, he then crossed Indian Pass Brook and entered a jumble of swamps and stream tributaries bordering another high peak, Nye Mtn.

After a struggle of some five miles, Dufresne collapsed, totally exhausted. He was, ironically, within a mile and a half of Last Chance Ranch, which connects to the road leading to Adirondak Loj at Heart Lake. His frozen body was found in the snow by hikers next spring.

That same fall, on Thanksgiving Day, two backpackers — Steven L. Collier and Patrick J. Eagan — were surprised by a snowstorm as they surmounted the pass between two other high peaks, Iroquois Peak and Mt. Marshall, on their way to Lake Colden. In the increasing cold, their cotton clothing began to take its toll as they trudged through a foot and a half of snow in fading light.

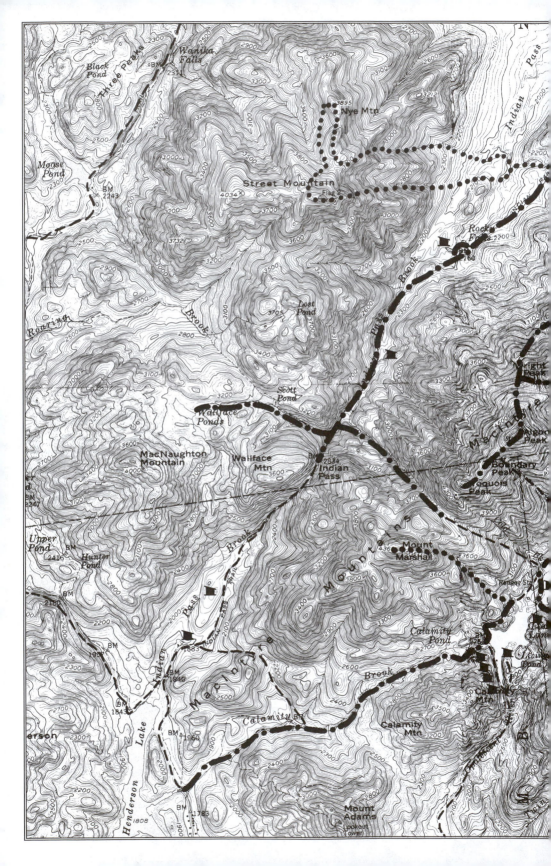

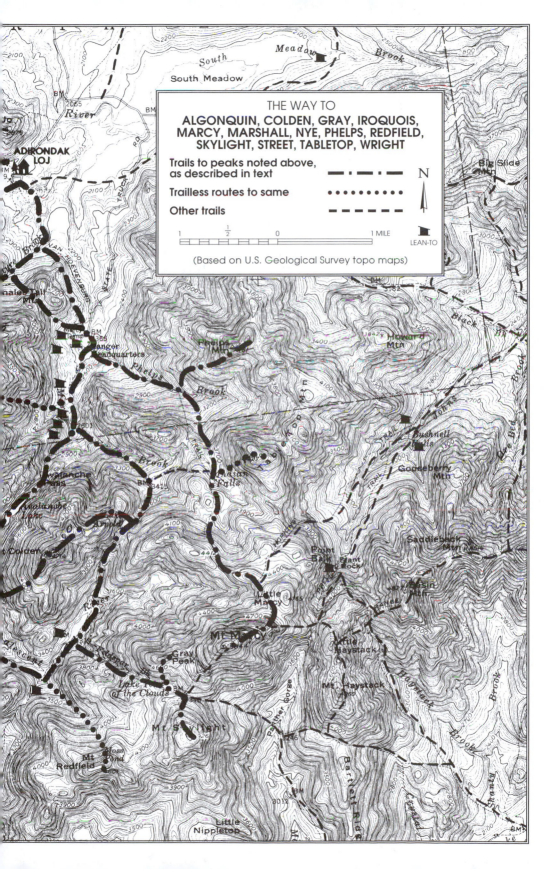

THE WAY TO
ALGONQUIN, COLDEN, GRAY, IROQUOIS, MARCY, MARSHALL, NYE, PHELPS, REDFIELD, SKYLIGHT, STREET, TABLETOP, WRIGHT

Trails to peaks noted above, as described in text ——·——·——·——

Trailless routes to same ··············

Other trails —— —— —— ——

N

1   ½   0   1 MILE

LEAN-TO

(Based on U.S. Geological Survey topo maps)

Hypothermia slowed Collier until he was unable to walk. Eagan dashed a half mile down to the ranger's station at Lake Colden and returned with a rescue party. It was too late; his companion, weakened by a dramatic lowering of body temperature, died before he could be moved to a shelter for treatment.

Three years later, again in late October, two men on Wright, the high peak adjoining Algonquin, came close to putting their names on the lengthening roster of hikers who never made it back. John Hughes and Clint LeBrecht lost track of time as they explored the summit, and had descended less than a mile when pitch blackness stopped them. Neither had a flashlight. "My partner," reported Hughes to the Albany, N.Y. *Times-Union*, "was wearing white pants and shirt and I couldn't see him standing beside me."

The pair managed to stumble and crawl the remaining two and a half miles to the trailhead with the aid of flame from a butane lighter, camp stove and waterproof matches. They reached the parking lot after midnight, just as a light tempo of freezing rain elevated to that of a deadly tattoo.

These incidents — on just one mountain range, covering only a brief span of time — illustrate the risks hikers face in exploring the Adirondack high peaks.

They also underscore why the National Safety Council calls mountain hiking "a dangerous sport." Measured by deaths, it is outranked only by mountain climbing, hang gliding, parachuting and snowmobiling. In fact, mountain hiking is more than twice as dangerous as scuba diving and alpine ski racing. It is 64 times more dangerous than downhill skiing.

Along with the risks, the challenge of the MacIntyre Range brings a bonus to explorers: an introduction to Adirondak Loj, the high peaks hideaway of the Adirondack Mountain Club. The Loj is at the end of the road which leads some five miles to the south from Rt. 73 between Keene and Lake Placid.

The Loj is open to anyone. For the hiker, it is a comforting base camp near the trailhead that leads to the MacIntyres and other high peaks. It offers meals and accomodations in the main building, or space in cabins, lean-tos and tent sites.

For others, the Loj is a great place to laze on the shore of Heart Lake and contemplate the beckoning benevolence of Marcy as well as the MacIntyre Range.

Whatever one's intent, the Loj extends a bridge back in time to a poignant love story, and to an early form of artificial intelligence that never caught on.

The present Loj was preceded by a huge log structure, built in 1880 by a young man named Henry Van Hoevenberg. Three years earlier, he had come to the mountains for his health. He found that and more: an attractive young visitor named Josephine Schofield, from Brooklyn, New York.

Van Hoevenberg did what many young romantics would like to do today. He took Josephine to the top of Mt. Marcy, expanded her vision to match his own, and persuaded her to become engaged. From the mountaintop, they vowed to

Adirondak Loj *is an ideal base camp for the high peaks. Heart Lake, left, offers swimming and no-motor boating.*

build a tourist lodge in the wilderness. They chose as its location a small lake that glistened some five miles to the northwest, and talked of pioneering a fresh and meaningful life in the wilderness.

Josephine's parents, unfortunately, had never climbed Marcy and did not share such youthful vision. They insisted that their daughter come home with them, along with her dreams.

Henry Van Hoevenberg kept the lovers' dream alive, if not their alliance. He built a three-story lodge which at the time was the largest log building in the U.S. He named a 2,876-ft. rounded peak at the backdoor of his lodge Mt. Jo, for his lost love. And, he bestowed on the little lake that had enchanted him and his fiancée from the top of Mt. Marcy a new name — Heart Lake, instead of the prosaic Clear Pond.

The greater part of Van Hoevenberg's vision endures. Mt. Jo and Heart Lake are well-known landmarks for hikers intent on the high peaks. A neighboring mountain to the northeast, site of bobsled and other alpine events during the 1932 and 1980 winter Olympics, is named Mt. Van Hoevenberg. The major trail to Marcy is also named for him, while many other trails, including the one to Algonquin, were cut under his direction.

Van Hoevenberg called his original structure Adirondack Lodge. However, that changed when it was taken over for a period of years by the Lake Placid Club, then headed by Melville Dewey.

Dewey, as you may remember, was known as "the father of modern library science" because of such innovations as his Dewey Decimal System for classifying books. He also promoted a simplified spelling system. The latter, in the main, gained him more points for eccentricity than intelligence.

Consider his argument for an amendment that would permit the state to build permanent lodges in the Forest Preserve: "Shal NY use as

wel as own 1 of the world's finest recreation parks? I hav been studying
this problem ever since I came here 1st 41 years ago. Wel-meaning but
unintelligent fanatiks tyed our hands completeli."

The change to Adirondak Loj was another product of that artificial
world conceived by Dewey.

Journal entry: Tuesday, September 4, 1990. *It's a perfect day,
cool, with only two bothersome bugs during the mile hike from the
Loj to the Van Hoevenberg Trail cutoff that leads to Algonquin.*

*The place may have been crawling with people yesterday, which was
Labor Day, but not today. So far, we have seen only three on the trail:
a couple who seem to be preoccupied with thoughts of Van
Hoevenberg's era, and a college-age girl in such a rush she surely
must be late for orientation.*

From the junction, the trail to Algonquin moves erratically upward.
After about a half mile, it crosses an old ski trail which turns to the
southwest between Wright and a lesser spur called the Whale's Tail.
The rationale for the latter name becomes clear when one views it from
the ski trail at Marcy Dam.

Within minutes of leaving the ski trail junction, the Algonquin hiker
passes a side trail on the left that leads to an official camping site. Just
beyond, the curve of a protruding rock wall amplifies the sound of a
stairstep waterfall coming into view.

Journal entry: Friday, May 8, 1981. *Two men at the cascade warn
that Ben and I will be climbing through snow in the hollows of the
upper reaches of the Algonquin trail. They grumble because the black
flies have begun their forays earlier than usual this year, and the only
place they could find to pitch their tent last night at the campsite near
here was on snow and rotten ice.*

*I am tempted to suggest they try day-tripping, but I do not believe they
are in a receptive mood.*

The trail becomes steeper, moves up a rocky gully, levels off to climb
through a stand of white birches, then climbs through a restful stand of
firs. The trail soon moves through a notch in the north shoulder of
Wright Peak where a cobble on the outside rises a hundred feet to provide the first view of Algonquin.

From the cobble, the trail turns south to begin a short, steep climb to
the side trail leading due east to Wright. The scramble to the top is only
four-tenths of a mile long. The latter half goes beyond timberline, with
the grade easing as the trail crosses the fractured rock dome via cairns
which lead to the summit of Wright.

Journal entry: Sunday, October 12, 1969. *A half mile to the southwest, Algonquin thrusts skyward like a bull-necked wrestler trying to break the grip of the clouds. Tiny figures laboring up the trail which follows the wrinkle on its side tell us there is much climbing to come.*

Two miles to the southeast is Mt. Colden, unmistakable because of the great slides which slash down its west face to Lake Colden, and to Avalanche Lake nearby.

Many hikers climb Wright for more than its views. They come to search the summit for remnants of an Air Force B-47 jet bomber which crashed during a routine training mission in 1962. The site of the mid-winter accident was so remote and the disintegration of the plane so complete that its location was not discovered for five days.

Journal entry: Sunday, October 12, 1969. *Teen-age boys in a group which passed us earlier are crossing back and forth on the summit, and Jim knows what they are looking for. Another hiker tells us most of the pieces are on the steep eastern slopes; he saw the glint of sun on large metal fragments as he hiked over from Algonquin.*

For a time, Jim finds nothing. Then over the lip of a summit cliff he spots a large chunk of a circular aluminum rib attached to jagged sheets of metal skin. It is too large to take whole, so we fold the excess pieces back and forth until they break off with a short segment of the rib frame.

Wright has been buffeted by more than a jet bomber. It's plopped in the midst of a tectonically active region on the eastern flank of the high peaks. As a result, scientists say, the earth's crust in that area arched up three and one half inches between 1955 and 1973. That arching led to earthquakes.

The earthquakes, in turn, created a sudden increase in sheer stress which acted like a

Souvenir of Wright. Jim retrieves remnant of B-47 Air Force bomber which crashed near the summit in 1962. Algonquin looms to rear.

trigger in producing landslides. These were especially severe in the spring of 1971, not only on Wright but on other high peaks such as Gothics, Macomb, Marcy and Whiteface.

The combination of these and earlier slides on the southeast slope of Wright acted like a magnet on some Adirondack explorers. The Adirondack Forty Sixers observed, in describing Wright in 1971, that "those in search of a thrill and some added exertion go up the slide."

The route up the big slide on Wright's east side is easy to find: take the Avalanche Pass Trail south from Marcy Dam to where an old log flume comes in on the right. Cross Marcy Brook and then follow the first tributary on the right until you come to the base of the slide.

Journal entry: Sunday, May 30, 1982. All we have to do now is go straight up. Or so it seems.

Ben and I are with four strong, experienced climbers — our friend and sometime guide, Tom Stanwood, and his friends Phil Corell, Wally Herrod and Tom Ellis. All are Forty Sixers; Corell and Herrod are past

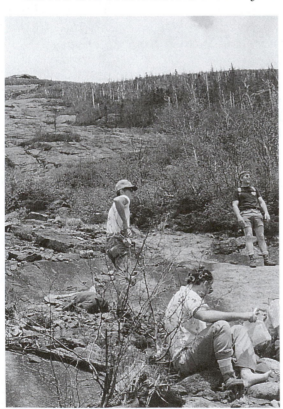

presidents of the club. Fortunately, they know the way. Also, fortunately, they and Ben are willing to wait while I trace back and forth up the steep slopes, the only way I have a chance of climbing the slide.

The top of the slide brings another challenge: a thicket of dwarf balsams and black spruce which forms a seemingly impenetrable barrier to the summit.

Its name has been contorted as much as the trees. Botanists and plant ecologists refer to it as krummholz. "Cripplebrush" was what Bob Marshall's guide, Herb Clark, called it. And, added Marshall, "anyone who has had his shins and arms battered by half an hour's tussle with it will appreciate the appropriateness of the nomenclature."

Sliding up. *Forty Sixer veterans Wally Herrod, foreground, Tom Ellis, left, and Phil Corell retrace path of landslide which ravaged Wright in 1971.*

It's also called cripplebush, puckerbrush, and other names which are unprintable.

From the Wright Peak junction, the trail to Algonquin climbs due north, ascending 1,200 feet in less than a mile. The first half mile follows a wash that leads steeply over several smooth, vertical, rock ledges. To the rear, one gains a measure of progress by noting the rate at which Whiteface sinks into the horizon.

The stiff climb, bad enough by itself, is often complicated by perverse weather. And it doesn't always show up as hypothermia.

Journal entry: Saturday, June 25, 1983. The forecast calls for the best day of the year. It's about time — we've had rain in Schenectady the last 14 weekends in a row.

After three and one half hours of climbing in cloudy, very cool weather, Ben and I top off Algonquin. And what do we see? Nothing. It's frigid and the summit is completely socked in.

We hurry down to the Loj in just two hours. And what do we see? Everything. The air is clear and beautiful.

Journal entry: Sunday, July 3, 1983. It's a beautiful day, but beastly hot. Also, it seems to Ben and me, there are more hikers than black flies, if that's possible.

As we go up the long, dusty section of the trail leading from the Wright junction to the timberline on Algonquin, my pace slows noticeably. I suggest to Ben that we stop because I feel weak and dizzy. I guess I've tried too hard to conserve the water in my plastic carrier (there is no water on the upper trail) and have generated a mild case of heat exhaustion.

I heed the advice in an article by the ADK's Tony Goodwin: "Lie down, raise the feet, and drink liquids." For good measure, I take a salt pill. In 15 minutes, I'm ready to go again.

Goodwin added a warning: "It's all right to continue to hike, albeit at a reduced pace, but probably best to go back down the mountain." Which we do. Good thing; on the way down Ben tells me he's not feeling so good, either, for the same reason.

If there is a stairway to hikers' heaven in the Adirondacks, it is on Algonquin.

The trail itself, from treeline to summit cap, is enticing in its own way. Like the track of some mindless beetle, it winds up and around and over the wrinkled rock face, leaving hints as to where it went by depositing occasional yellow paint blazes and cairns.

Near the summit, the grade moderates and the trail metamorphoses. It becomes a series of orderly placed steppingstones which beckon the hiker upward. Trailside signs reinforce the implied message from the tundra and plants surrounding the stones: Don't step on me.

It is obvious that someone has gone to a great deal of trouble to keep hikers from harming the fragile growth in this arctic environment. That someone is largely Edwin Herbert Ketchledge, retired forester and botany professor who brings an ecological conscience to the Adirondack high peaks.

Ketchledge, along with a couple of colleagues from the state's College of Forestry at Syracuse, noted in the mid-'60s that alpine vegetation on 16 high peak summits was deteriorating under the pounding of hikers' boots. Of the six million acres which make up the Adirondack Park, only about 85 acres were home to this unique kind of summit growth. Almost half of that total was on Algonquin and its companion peaks of the MacIntyre Range.

This was an ecological red flag for Ketchledge. The alpine gardens had endured since the last ice age in the Adirondacks, but were now on the brink of devastation. If they disappeared, one would have to go to Newfoundland, Alaska or the Arctic for the closest view of such specimens.

What Ketchledge set out to do, in effect, was to recreate

Lofty steps protect alpine meadow on Algonquin's summit. Wallface rears beyond, with MacNaughton at right. Santanonis veer to left, Sewards to right rear.

and protect the legacy of the Pleistocene Epoch on Algonquin and other Adirondack high peaks.

He envisioned a two-pronged plan of attack. The first would establish single, marked routes through endangered areas to protect the plants and control erosion. And the second would spruce up the summits of selected peaks, including Algonquin, by way of environmental hair transplants.

Summit reseeding became Ketchledge's passion, with Algonquin the prime focus of his devotion. As of last count, in 1992, he had climbed it 168 times to conduct his experiments.

Obviously, Ketchledge needed help in achieving his lofty goals. And he got plenty of it, through a partnership program of The Nature Conservancy, the Adirondack Mountain Club, the Adirondack Forty Sixers, and the landowner, the state of New York.

As a result, hikers topping off Algonquin during the warmer months begin the final ascent on steppingstones which wind through bright green tundra meadows. These, together with patches of soil in various rock crevices on the summit, are beautified with a hundred or so rare alpine plants.

As a part of the program initiated by Ketchledge, uniformed Summit Stewards greet hikers on not only Algonquin but Marcy, Haystack and Colden. They serve as surrogates for the plants, explaining to visitors why they should stay on the rocks and off the plants.

Algonquin's stone stairway may not lead to heaven, but for the dedicated hiker it comes pretty close.

The views are much like those on Wright but the extra 500 feet of elevation boosts the viewer above everything in sight except Marcy. Trailless Gray Peak and Mt. Skylight huddle close on Marcy's right side, while the peaks of the Great Range ripple off to its left, toward the east. To the north, almost directly in line with the return trail, is Heart Lake and, far beyond, Whiteface. To the northeast, those ominous twins, Street and Nye, crouch in silence.

To the southwest is something new and intriguing that is not visible from Wright. The rocky cap of Algonquin drops off sharply to a deep col, where a shrub-covered slope ascends gradually to Boundary Peak. Supposedly, this was so named because it marked the dividing line between the ancient beaver hunting grounds of the Algonquin Indians on the north and the tribes of the Iroquois nation to the south.

Beyond it, perched like a pyramid at the end of a rocky, scrubby ridge that dips slightly and then rises again to its base, is Iroquois. Behind it, to the right slightly, is the tip of Mt. Marshall.

To complete the spectacle, the trail veterans who study such things say that on a clear day you can see 135 lakes from the summit of Algonquin.

Panorama from Algonquin. *Colden (stripes) is overshadowed by Marcy, right center, and the Great Range, to its left. Giant is far left, Dix at center rear.*

Journal entry: Friday, May 8, 1981. At first, Ben and I share the summit with only one couple. Then, two young men under full pack heave up and announce they will camp here overnight.

Ben and I tell them it's prohibited because of the damage that could result. We point to the fragile flowers quivering in the breeze. "Good enough for me," says one. "I just joined the Botanical Garden Society on Long Island where we live, so I can understand the concern."

The urge to camp out on Algonquin's summit comes as no surprise; the setting is as spectacular as the views. But if you're tempted, don't be seduced by the siren call of the romantics.

Since the beginning of the 1980s, the state's Department of Environmental Conservation has posted signs at all trailheads stating that no one may camp in the Adirondacks above 4,000 feet except in an emergency or in midwinter — from December through April.

It could be, from the earliest times on, that people have been entranced to the point of confusion by Algonquin and its immediate neighbors.

The peaks make up the MacIntyre Range, which was originally named for Archibald McIntyre, one of the chief owners of the old iron mine at Tahawus, some seven miles to the south. Yet somewhere along the line, somebody — no one seems to know for sure who or when — added an "a" to give it the present spelling.

Algonquin got its name from Verplanck Colvin in 1873 when the state surveyor placed copper bolt No. 12 on its summit. But on the benchmark, Colvin spelled it "Algonqin."

Boundary Peak, halfway over to Iroquois, was referred to in all of the ADK guidebooks before 1945 as "Boundry."

And Mt. Marshall, just beyond Iroquois, has at various times been named Clinton, in honor of Gov. DeWitt Clinton, best known for his Erie Canal; Herbert, in honor of Herb Clark, the Marshall's guide on their pioneering circuit of the 46 high peaks; and the present name, in honor of the late Bob Marshall, nationally known conservationist and brother of George.

Journal entry: Saturday, August 1, 1981. When Ben and I climbed Algonquin three months ago, I suggested that we go on over to Iroquois. "It's three o'clock," I told him. "We could make the round trip in a couple of hours, and hike back to the Loj in another three. The forecast is for great weather all day, so we should have no problem."

"I don't know," said Ben. "It's getting late. Why can't we just stay here for a while and enjoy it?" Which we did.

Today, however, Ben is chafing to go. He's read about Iroquois and he's heard me and his older brother Jim talk about it. Now, he wants to see for himself. Ben knows that while the path to Iroquois has never been marked, the mountain is no longer considered

On to Iroquois. *Col below Algonquin leads to Boundary Peak, center, then to the Adirondack's eighth highest. Marshall peers over Iroquois' right shoulder.*

trailless. But he wants to see if the notorious "hog wallow" near Boundary — actually a unique alpine bog — and the acres of cripplebush are still as bad as he's heard.

Ben also wants to check out Robert Marshall's claim that Iroquois is "the wildest mountain in the Adirondacks."

Marshall's writings suggest that he was influenced by a journey from Marshall to Iroquois, including the steep climb from Algonquin Pass over a rocky knob named the Wart — sometimes called the Shepherd's Tooth — on the south slope of Iroquois.

Ben also wants to see if he can spot from Iroquois the wreckage of another airplane, this one just off the center of Algonquin Pass on the Marshall side. In August 1969, just two months before son Jim and I explored Iroquois, a single-engine propeller craft was caught in a downdraft at night while flying toward Lake Placid. Fortunately, the pilot was able to walk away from the wreck unharmed.

But most of all, Ben wants to come back safely from Iroquois. He's read my journal of the earlier trip which Jim and I made.

Journal entry: Sunday, October 12, 1969. *According to the map, Iroquois lies a mile away. But from our perch on Algonquin, it appears to be no more than a few hundred yards. Jim and I change our minds, however, when we see that the half dozen hikers between us and Iroquois show up as tiny specks.*

The weather is still holding — it's balmy with the same white clouds scudding out of the west. We decide to leave our packs, as we did when we scaled Wright, so we can travel light and fast.

It's relatively simple to scramble down the steep, southern exposure of Algonquin by following the cairns, then pick up the path that leads into the small trees at the first col. The path soon brings us to Boundary. Beyond this rocky peak, we again enter scrub growth but now find great difficulty in following the path. There are no markers and various paths branch off from the main one, no one more distinct than the others. We did notice that two people had climbed Iroquois from its left shoulder, so we bushwhack generally to the left toward their route.

Jim and I thought we had trouble on Esther, but it was nothing compared with the jumbled mass of cripplebush here. We make some progress by stepping from branch to branch, but move carefully because we don't want to slip and either sprain or break a limb so far from help.

Finally the cripplebush thins and we move up steep ledges encrusted with moss. We're delighted to see on a nearby summit the youth with a green pixie hat we saw with two older men on the lower Algonquin trail, and again on Wright. He shouts that we should circle east and proceed up a narrow rock defile. It takes us no more than five minutes to reach Iroquois' summit.

By now Jim and I are exhausted, but happy to record our names in the tablet that's in the cannister hanging from a pole anchored by a rockpile*. The three previous climbers to register are Chris and Norm Reynolds of Westbrook, Maine, and Gotz Von Berglichingen of Augsburg, Germany.

The two older companions of the youth labor up the route we ascended, and register their names in the cannister. Then together the five of us chat while we catch our breath.

We assume that Gotz is the pixie.

We can tell from their conversation that they are experienced climbers. They have been on Iroquois before and are among the few who have made the trailless trek of a little more than a mile beyond to Marshall. They discuss alternative return routes and finally decide to bushwhack down the eastern slopes of Iroquois to the valley and then follow Indian Pass Brook trail north to Adirondak Loj.

They tell us that we missed the main trail from Boundary to Iroquois; we should have kept to our right, along the west edge of the ridge on the way over. While the trail is neither marked nor maintained, they say it should not be too difficult to follow on our return.

Jim and I are sorry we cannot join these veterans on their return to the Loj. But our packs await us on Algonquin.

As they move away through the thicket to the west, there is a more compelling reason we are sorry to see them go. Algonquin is no longer in view. Nor, for that matter, is Boundary. Without our noticing it, a thick mantle of fast-moving fog has replaced the fluffy clouds and obliterated our line of sight beyond a few feet. From where we stand we know in which direction to go, but that's about all.

It is now four o'clock in the afternoon in the middle of October, and we face a stiff, five-mile hike back over Algonquin and down the long trail to our car. We are the last hikers to reach Iroquois and now are alone in the midst of a vast wilderness.

One forgets that this can happen in populous New York state. But we are well aware of it now. The nearest safe haven is a ranger station at

---

*The cannister on Iroquois was removed in 1977.

Time to go. *Clouds roll in as we sign in, then admire the view from Iroquois. Lake Colden is below right.*

Marcy Dam or another at Lake Colden. Both are miles away and in areas where we have never been. But even if we were to go for one, we would first have to track back over Boundary to the base of Algonquin and then tackle an unknown trail. And we are tired.

More important, I am aware that I have violated one of the cardinal rules of mountain exploration: never trade security for comfort. Our compass, map and single flashlight are in my pack on Algonquin. The enveloping fog is sure to make our return to regain them tricky and, if we lose our bearings, dangerous.

The only water we have is a small amount in the canteen in my pack; Jim's was long gone before we stopped for lunch on Algonquin. I have a bit of chocolate in my pocket for quick energy, but it's almost useless because it will only make us more thirsty.

We have no choice but to start back. And it appears the sooner we get going the better. Dusk will come in just two hours, at six o'clock. And the swirling mist is thickening. At least it's not blowing hard; an ADK guidebook warns that summit winds often become "so violent that shouting to one another is of no avail."

I'm also a bit concerned because of anxious glances from Jim, and because he pauses to rest even more than I do. But I think I can find our way back. I've always had a fair sense of direction, and should know in a hurry if we move too far down the slope on either side of the ridge. But I've heard many tales of experienced woodsmen losing their way because of carelessness.

Mostly, I'm mad at myself for getting us into this predicament.

Jim and I hurry down the rock slope of Iroquois into the cripplebush. This time, we check each fork when the path splinters in different directions. Our luck holds; we pass through the maze that includes the shallow, soggy valley we skirted on the way over, then follow a herd path which moves up a gentle slope.

The path soon emerges on a rock expanse which juts upward. It has to be Boundary. While we can't see it, it is the only landmark of this sort that could be here. A stiff, 10-minute climb to the summit confirms it. We stretch out and peer beyond on the other side. The ledges fall away and disappear in a swirling wall of mist.

We don't rest for long. The path seems easier to track now than on the way over, but we take great care because we can't see beyond the twisted trees that slow us down.

The path makes a steep descent, as we know it should, toward the bottom of the col. But it bothers me that it edges more and more down the eastern slope. I'm wary that we may have taken a wrong turn; neither Jim nor I remember making the twists and turns on this path.

A moment of decision arrives: a well-marked trail with yellow markers rises from a drop-off to our right. We are pretty sure we should not be going downward any more. To follow it the other way means we must make a sharp left. Yet we made no such abrupt turn when coming the other way. I suspect it may lead back to Boundary. But in any event, it's a well-used trail so we decide to follow it.

It doesn't take long to conclude that we are safely on our way...if our energy holds. The trail has to be the one cut by Verplanck Colvin on his Adirondack survey during the last century. The trail leads up from Lake Colden through the col between Boundary and Algonquin. As we follow it, the trail veers to the right and begins a precipitous climb up a rocky slope to disappear in the mist. There could only be one mountain with this contour — Algonquin.

We find it hard to believe that the breezy jaunt we undertook in descending the peak could become such a tedious climb in reverse. It's an ascent of only some 300 feet in less than a half mile, but it's so steep that we stop and rest every 10 yards or so. With

Tough road ahead: *It's five p.m. on Algonquin, with zero visibility, an hour of daylight, and four miles to go.*

relief, we see that no one has disturbed our packs on the lip of the summit. I dig for my canteen and we each take a small sip. We leave the remainder for our return trip.

The clouds now rush by with a vengeance. But Jim and I don't care. Our climbing for the day is behind us; it's downhill all the way. I see no point in telling Jim, however, that it's now five p.m., the sun sets in an hour, and we must still descend 3,000 feet and hike nearly four miles to reach our car at the Loj.

At times like this, Jim and I have always enjoyed being on our own private mountain. But it's different this time; the only thing to greet us are the lonely cairns which mark the trail leading off the crown of Algonquin. It's ghostly quiet as we continue down the steep path leading to the junction to Wright. The mood is compounded as the trees emerge briefly from their shrouds of fog, then disappear as the fog again enfolds them when we pass.

Near the Wright junction, the fog begins to lift — or, more to the point, we begin to descend below it. Jim's spirits brighten when he retrieves the piece of plane wreck he had hidden at the junction. We search for a spring that's supposed to be in the area, but find no clear flow, and move on.

The trail darkens as we thread past the cobble and begin the long descent around the base of Wright and the Whale's Tail. We stumble often and our one flashlight becomes essential. We know we won't be able to spot the waterfall that is ahead of us on the trail, so we listen for the sound.

It's pitch dark when we finally fill our canteens at the waterfall, drain them and fill them again for the remaining leg of our journey. We move slowly, for the rocks and logs we casually walked around in the daylight must each now be highlighted as we move single-file down the narrow trail. It is slow going.

We see nothing. But this two-hour walk makes us aware as no guidebook could that we are not the only ones in the wilderness. The hoot of an owl startles us when we first hear it. A rustle in the leaves beyond our beam of light tells us that some small animal is as jumpy as we are. But except for these sporadic sounds, the silence is a fitting companion to the blackness — both are enveloping, brooding, complete.

Jim keeps up a steady chatter as we swing along the trail. As we start to cross MacIntyre Brook on the big boulders which dot the waters, the light from the flashlight in his hand jumps wildly, and he scurries to my side. "I almost stepped on something," he says. We point the beam and see a misshapen log that vaguely resembles a reclining body. Jim is visibly nervous and says he hopes we'll make it out of the woods soon.

So do I. It's a relief that the flashlight beam can still pick up the trail coming in from Marcy Dam. That tells me we have less than a mile to go before reaching the Loj. Our spirits rise as we hear voices and soon see the rosy pinpoints of campfires reflecting on Heart Lake.

Jim and I have never been happy to see crowds on our explorations, but we make an exception tonight. We offer a cheery hello and our profound sympathy to a woman and two children looking for a stray dog. And we smile as we see groups clustered about their fires — young people softly singing their folk songs, a family group cleaning up the dinner dishes, others sitting in a circle as they enjoy the comforts of camp and of dreams flickering up in the flames.

There's a biting chill to the night air, and Jim and I agree it would be wonderful if we could join one of the fireside groups and tell them of our adventures. We would spin a fine yarn about how we bested the elements for a triple conquest. Of course, we would leave out those things we did, or did not do, which were foolish.

In a typical year, New York forest rangers conduct some 250 search and rescue missions within the state. Seventy per cent of them are in the Adirondacks, with another 10 to 15 per cent in the Catskills.

According to the rangers, "At least 50 per cent of these missions are caused by lack of flashlights."

This would suggest that to avoid becoming a statistic, those who intend to explore the Adirondack high peaks should do two things:

First, check with and abide by the safety guidelines which are posted at most access points to the high peaks by the Department of Environmental Conservation, and are listed in the guidebooks of the Adirondack Mountain Club. The guidelines relate to proper clothing (wool vs. cotton, for example), equipment and supplies, destination vs. time, emergency procedures, camping locations, drinking water precautions, etc.

Bear in mind that in the journal entry noted above, it was considered safe in 1969 to drink from any water source separate from campsites. Now, however, one must take precautions because Adirondack waters are sometimes contaminated by a water-borne, intestinal parasite called Giardiasis, or "Beaver Fever."

By now, the second major caution should be obvious: carry not just one flashlight, but an emergency spare, along with extra batteries and bulbs.

Big Slide Mtn. from the third Brother.

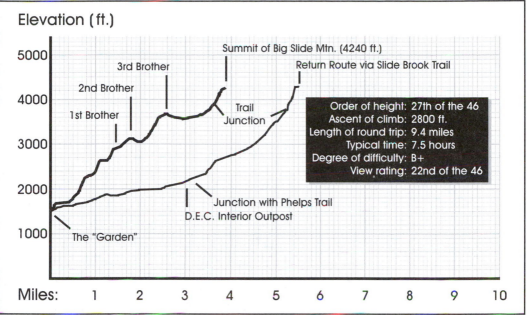

Elevation (ft.)

Summit of Big Slide Mtn. (4240 ft.)

Return Route via Slide Brook Trail

3rd Brother

2nd Brother

Trail
Junction

1st Brother

Order of height: 27th of the 46
Ascent of climb: 2800 ft.
Length of round trip: 9.4 miles
Typical time: 7.5 hours
Degree of difficulty: B+
View rating: 22nd of the 46

Junction with Phelps Trail

D.E.C. Interior Outpost

The "Garden"

Miles: 1   2   3   4   5   6   7   8   9   10

For contour trails, see U.S. Geological Survey map, pgs. 2-3.

10.
BIG SLIDE

Every Adirondack high peak harbors a wilderness image of its own.

With Allen, for example, it's remoteness; Dix, a summit ridge honed to knife sharpness. Nye bludgeons the senses with blowdown; Marcy, with a massif that thrusts higher than anything in sight.

Big Slide's image was shaped by an avalanche. In fact, there were two of them.

The more recent, in 1856, swept down the north side of the mountain to the upper reaches of South Meadow Brook. At the time, a trail kept pace with the brook from South Meadows to Keene Valley. It followed an old logging road which climbed through Railroad Notch between Porter and Big Slide. But it would be a half century more before a trail to Big Slide was cut from the Notch. The slide was little noted and soon forgotten.

An earlier avalanche, in 1830, was bigger and harder to ignore. It killed three men in an earth slide which peeled everything off the surface of the southeast face, from crest to base. Three hundred and fifty feet of near-vertical bedrock stretching to the summit stared down on those who ventured up Johns Brook from Keene Valley, some three miles to the east, to see what had happened.

It was almost three decades before one of the earliest settlers of the hamlet, Otis Estes, got around to giving the mountain its present name. That was about the middle of the last century, before the surge of summer visitors to Keene Valley began.

It was just as well.

More and more outsiders came to look at and enjoy the high peaks described by such explorers as Ebenezer Emmons and Verplanck Colvin, by romantic writers like William H. H. Murray and Charles Dudley Warner, by such well-known artists as Winslow Homer and Thomas Cole, and by guidebook pioneers such as E. R. Wallace and J. R. Stoddard. If Estes had not acted when he did, one of them would surely have suggested that the mountain be called what it had come to look like from Johns Brook Valley — a Big Thumb.

The early trails to Big Slide have disappeared. The first was cut from the south at the turn of the century by the proprietor of a hotel, also long gone, on Johns Brook. Another was cut a decade later on the opposite side of the mountain, beginning at the top of Railroad Notch.

A second trail from Johns Brook, the one used most often today, was opened in 1927. It begins at Slide Mountain Brook, about a third of a mile before reaching the ADK's Johns Brook Lodge when hiking in from Keene Valley.

Another trail was cut a few years later, wending to the northwest from Johns Brook Lodge before turning north to go over Yard Mtn. on the way to Big Slide. This route has never caught on much because it's a mile and a half longer, calls for a bit more climbing, and offers little in the way of views.

In 1951, hikers gained a scenic route — the trail from Keene Valley to Big Slide via a stairstep chain of small peaks called the three Brothers.

From Keene Valley, the trailhead for all three routes begins at the Garden where Johns Brook Road ends, three-tenths of a mile beyond the turnoff to Porter Mtn. First-time visitors are surprised to find that the Garden is a parking lot. For years it was in fact the garden site for a nearby private home, whose owners in mid-century gave the state permission to transform it for use by hikers and campers.

Journal entry: Saturday, May 23, 1970. Son Jim and I plan to go up Big Slide by the Brothers' route since it's almost two miles shorter than the climb up Slide Mtn. Brook from near Johns Brook Lodge.

We rest on the first convenient log after leaving the Garden, looking and listening. The man at the grocery store in Keene Valley told us the black flies are beginning to flex their wings. So we've tightened our pant legs and sleeves with rubber bands and lathered insect repellant over all exposed skin. A few of the pests buzz in to size us up, so we move on.

The trail from the Garden begins steeply, then moderates and dips to the left, as if lured by Juliet Brook below. Across the stream, the trail begins a moderate climb through maples and birches, sweeping upward at a sharp angle. A little over a half mile from the Garden, the pitch of the trail becomes very steep.

Journal entry: Saturday, May 23, 1970. This time, Jim and I are careful to avoid fading paint blazes on trees which on previous trips had led us to dead ends. The blazes were leftovers, we discovered, from an abandoned trail that used to lead from the Garden to South Meadows and on to Adirondak Loj.

Abruptly, the trail eases onto an open rock ledge. Here, the Johns Brook Valley unfolds from the northeast to the south and southwest in a breath-taking, panoramic half circle.

To the east is Giant, looking as if its massive slides might continue their downward sweep from the summit to engulf the tiny buildings below in Keene Valley. Some six miles to the north of Giant is Hurricane Mtn., not one of the 46 but impressive in its own way because of its solitary thrust to almost 3,700 feet.

Across Johns Brook Valley, the Great Range begins a tortuous climb from Keene Valley to the southwest. It first asserts its intentions in a series of hesitant thrusts — the mountainous blips known as Rooster Comb and Hedgehog Mtn. It then soars skyward to trace a majestic profile that ripples across the skyline for 10 miles.

The first mountains beyond Hedgehog are Lower Wolfjaw and Upper Wolfjaw. Lower vaguely resembles a snarling muzzle, but those who named the peak did so when sizing it up on Noonmark Mountain, to the south of St. Huberts.

Next comes Armstrong and beyond it, without a doubt, Gothics. The latter's awesome slides on the north face mimic flying buttresses soaring up to support the cathedral formed by the triple crests of its summit.

Beyond is Saddleback, easy to spot because of its shape. The mountains leading on to Marcy tend to blend together, but the first mass is Basin and the bruiser beyond is Haystack, with Little Haystack perched on its north flank.

Journal entry: Tuesday, June 26, 1979. It's almost balmy on the first ledge of the Brothers, but the peaks of the Great Range glisten with new snow.

It makes them look like a group of stout children, scrubbed to brilliance and dressed in their starchy, formal best, lined up and ready to march off to church.

There's no horseplay because Marcy, at the far end of the valley looms over them like a protective governess, a lacy mantle draped over her

The Great Range *unfolds from the first of the three Brothers. At left is Saddleback, with Basin to its right. The climber will soon gain a full view of Marcy, far center rear.*

massive superstructure. It is hard to tell if she's stern or smiling, because her head is wreathed in clouds.

From the ledge on the slope of the first Brother, the upward going is easy. The trail meanders back and forth through trees to more bare rock ledges; in fact, a quarter of the climb is in the open. A final, steep rise brings the climber to a flat rock clearing.

Journal entry: Saturday, May 23, 1970. *Jim and I throw our gear on the ground to take a breather.*

Suddenly, raucous shouts precede a group of scruffy young people racing up the trail. "Hippies," I predict to Jim. Like most people, I've been conditioned by newspaper stories in the '60s of campus demonstrations and riots. I suggest to Jim that we stay ahead of them.

The trail makes a brief climb before easing off on the open summit of the first Brother, a mile and a half from the Garden. Just beyond and below the summit, a house-sized lump of rock leans close to an exposed cliff to form a snug shelter. We're not the first to visit; someone has stacked dry logs next to the charred remains of a campfire.

The day remains gorgeous. There must be some Adirondack maxim which affirms that it never rains when you're next to the perfect shelter. And vice versa.

The trail then moves some fifth of a mile and a couple of hundred feet higher to a false summit on the second Brother. As we pause to catch our breath, I make a distressing discovery: I've lost my camera. I think I know where — it has to be next to a boulder where we rested after leaving the first lookout above Johns Brook Valley.

What to do: Descend nearly a mile to see if it's there, or take a chance and hope to find it on the way back?

My thoughts are interrupted by another ruckus raised by the hikers coming up from below. As they top the first Brother, we see them and wonder. Two boys with long hair and flapping bell-bottoms shout and gesture to us. Close behind, a college-age boy and girl prance upward following a huge dog which looks like a German shepherd.

Trouble?

Jim tugs at me: "Those are words, not shouts." He strains to hear, and says they've found my camera. I cup my lips to tell them I'll come down for it. "Stay there," they reassure me. "We'll bring it to you."

As they clamber up the cliffs, I wonder if they have subconsciously come to the mountains to identify with a simpler time and a simpler people. Their youthful grace and headbands are a match for those of the Indians who once roamed the area. But their smiles and schoolroom pallor belie any warlike intent.

They move on to view Porter from the true summit of the second Brother, just off the trail to the right, then hurry into the woods on the southwest toward the third peak.

The second Brother's false summit is not the only one on this trip. Two other peaks kindle the hopes of hikers: One is Yard, soaring high but not quite high enough to the southwest; the other is the third Brother, which from the first sibling looks huge, looming a mile away to the northwest.

But the climb up the third Brother is actually a pleasant stroll. The trail leads through white birches which accent scattered patches of evergreens and ferns.

Journal entry: Saturday, May 23, 1970. *Halfway up the slope, I tell Jim to stop and sniff the air. Skunk, I say, and Jim's face blends interest with anxiety. Then I realize my mistake — it's skunk cabbage, a pungent reminder that nature displays foibles along with its fineries.*

The third Brother's summit lets the climber regain bearings and breath. To the south, the profile of the Great Range moderates and behind it, for the first time, Dix and Nippletop come into view.

Nearby to the south and west, Yard assumes a proper, subservient role. Its northern shoulder slopes down, then points upward toward the first open view of Big Slide. Anyone who has been to Yosemite in California will equate it in an instant with the rock monoliths of that national park.

Journal entry: Saturday, May 23, 1970. Big Slide is a dead ringer for one landmark in Yosemite, but with a big difference: this is Half Dome with hair.

Jim nudges me and points at two climbers sprawled on the ledge below ours. They are our hippie friends, who appear exhausted. No wonder: one wears sandals, the other battered tennis shoes. They have neither packs nor supplies.

One of them waves and, haltingly, asks if we have any aspirin. I do and give him some, which he starts to take without water. I insist he use mine, but he takes only a short swallow and refuses more.

The trail through the deep valley which separates the third Brother from Big Slide is soggy. Jim's water is gone and since the trickles along the trail are turgid, he purifies it by popping a water purification tablet in his canteen.

We round a bend in the trail and there, tucked under the spruce and balsam is — a snowbank! Spring may be full blown back home, but it's struggling for life in the Adirondacks. And Jim discovers why his water is murky: it's spring run-off, not spring-fed.

A short distance beyond, we're startled to come upon two college boys who are humming away as they simmer stew over a campfire. They've spread their gear on trees to dry, and it's easy to see why. Their bivouac is in the worst possible location: a steep gully amidst heavy blowdown.

They were on their way to Big Slide last night, they say, when a blinding rainstorm forced them to camp on the trail. They joke about it and say it was great fun. Uh huh.

On leaving them, we cross the stream at the bottom of the col, then cross and re-cross it while moving up the side of Big Slide through conifers and more snowbanks, some good-sized. We turn at the junction of the trail coming up from Johns Brook and head steeply north.

Big Slide is a part of a huge mountainous formation which stretches all the way from Cascade down to Mt. Marcy. Adirondack guide Orson "Old Mountain" Phelps says that toward the end of the last century, it was "a wild group but little known even by hunters and trappers." Those who climb it from the south will understand why: Big Slide's upper trail is one of the steepest in the Adirondack high peaks.

It is so steep, in fact, that in 1993 ropes were installed for the final ascent. However, the state took them down the following year because of liability concerns.

Journal entry: Saturday, May 23, 1970. *A boy about Jim's age, wearing a Robin Hood hat, slithers down the wet, slippery trail toward us. "The top is only 500 feet up," he says.*

Jim and I have learned the logarithm of this land, and conclude: the boy is coming down and we're going up, so we probably have twice that distance to go.

In climbing, we rely on trees for leverage more than the rocks underfoot. I rest often, and Jim disappears above. The summit confronts me abruptly when the trail levels in a short, twisting turn. I find Jim lying flat, peering over the edge of a broad, rocky outcropping, and join him to see what's so interesting below.

It's really nothing — nothing, that is, but a steep drop-off that seems to go down forever. Somewhere below, the base flares outward and the slide continues a thousand feet or so toward Johns Brook.

Rock climbers call the bald face on Big Slide, "an outstanding wilderness route." The 1993 Annual Guide of *Adirondack Life* notes that, "Since the face is too high for a top rope, the route must be led from the bottom." Almost as an afterthought it adds, "the climb leader must be ready to make a commitment."

Anyone who sees that bare, vertical face of Big Slide up close — whether a rock specialist or not — will recognize that the commitment is not voluntary.

Surrounding peaks *frame the deep chasm plunging from Big Slide. Yard Mtn. is in center foreground, with Phelps beyond. Colden is at left rear, the MacIntyre Range to right.*

From the summit, the peaks of the Great Range now appear in close-up. Gothics' stark scars punctuate the middle of them, dead across the valley from Big Slide. From Giant on the east, the peaks lie scattered along the southern horizon, culminating on the west with Marcy, Colden and the MacIntyres.

Journal entry: Saturday, May 23, 1970. The prospect of returning by the bouncy route of the Brothers is disheartening. So Jim and I decide to descend the trail south to Johns Brook, then follow it east to the Garden.

Going down beats going up. The lower trail helps out, too, by following the open slide on occasion along with traces of old lumber roads. In an hour we cover more than half the distance and two thirds of the elevation that took us four hours in coming up the Brothers.

Shortly after turning east at the junction with the Phelps trail along Johns Brook, we meet a New York state ranger, Spencer Cram, whistling in the backyard of his station. Beyond the clearing where his cabin stands, more young people on both banks of the river are preparing dinner, singing, and lolling around. Without exception, they have long hair — the place is infested with hippies!

The ranger suggests that we hike out by an exit route which follows the south bank of the river. It's shorter, he says, and he can't understand why the Adirondack Mountain Club had to build a trail of their own on the north bank. We thank him and follow it out.

Slide Brook *accompanies the trail from Big Slide's summit to Johns Brook valley. Slides of Gothics loom at right rear; Armstrong is at left.*

It doesn't take us long to find out why the ADK built a new trail: the ranger's recommended route is rough, wet and rocky. The going is far slower than any trail should be.

About a half mile from the Garden, the trail leads north to the streambed. It follows the river briefly, then crosses to the other side via huge rocks marked with paint blazes.

The river is noisy with its load of spring run-off, and as we approach to cross, we startle an old gentleman who has not heard us. He seems to be retracing, if not recreating, the joys of a leisurely stroll from another era. He wears a suede touring cap and a belted English hunting jacket with matching knickers. My guess is he's at least 80 years old.

Nice day, we observe. "Yes," he says. Then he adds with a twinkle in his eyes as he sees us edge toward the rushing waters, "but I don't feel like swimming today." He braces his chin, unlimbers his walking stick, and ambles on.

We search to find a better line-up of boulders to cross than those marked which are wet and slippery, but decide to give them a try. It's tricky, but we make it and move on to the Garden.

It's almost dark and the parking lot is deserted except for a girl on the opposite side. As we come closer we see that she also is dressed like a hippie. But, I note, she is tenderly tucking a baby into a carriage.

It occurs to me I should stop labelling these exuberant young people "hippies." After all, I have a daughter in college, another in high school and son Jim in the eighth grade; they're not exactly fashion plates, but they're not hippies. Who am I to judge what their peers are like because of the way they dress?

I glance once more at the young mother as she rocks her baby in the carriage and it reminds me of Ben, our two-year-old. Talk about demonstrators! Within our household, little Ben is a willful destroyer, a rioter in rompers. Yet he's also a good boy, especially when he's asleep.

On the spot, I resolve to judge these young people in the mountains as good kids, until they prove otherwise.

Keene Valley has long been a threshold for those who want to explore the central and eastern Adirondack high peaks. Considering the flood of people who have poured in over the years, it's a wonder that Johns Brook Valley hasn't been trashed in the process.

Johns Brook, as far as anyone knows, was named for one of Keene Valley's 18th century farmers, John Gibbs. No one knows for sure either why there's no apostrophe in his name when used in conjunction with the river or the valley.

Most likely, it's due to U.S. government mapmakers. As *The Wall Street Journal* reported a while back, "The federal name men are death on possessive apostrophes." Hence, in the high peaks we find on U.S. Geological Survey maps not only Johns Brook but St. Huberts. And out west, the rendering of what you would expect to be Pike's Peak, named for the explorer whose first name was Zebulon, is officially Pikes Peak.

People came to Johns Brook Valley in several waves.

The first was formed by Adirondack guides who in the 1830s began to exploit the Johns Brook wilderness for storybook hunting and fishing. Those were glory days for the guides and their clients because they had the area pretty much to themselves.

Others were drawn by the exciting reports that began to filter out from the Colvin surveys of the '60s and '70s and by the writings of romanticists. That interest also stimulated trail building. Orson Phelps, who along with his son Ed served at different times as Chief Guide for Colvin, cut an embryonic trail via Johns Brook to Panther Gorge, between Marcy and Haystack. But it wasn't maintained and therefore wasn't much used.

The turn of the century brought lumbermen. Traces of their tote roads can still be seen throughout the valley, including the southside trail which leads from Keene Valley to Johns Brook Lodge. Along with lumbermen came more people. Guides began to cut feeder trails up the mountain ranges on both sides of the old Phelps trail, which had been re-established as a major route to Marcy. A few private camps also sprouted on the lower reaches of Johns Brook. And by the 1920s a hotel called the Interbrook Lodge was thriving in an area about half way from Keene Valley to the Garden.

The onrush of civilization was put on hold in 1925 when the Adirondack Mountain Club built the Johns Brook Lodge some five miles to the southwest of Keene Valley. It represented a watershed for wilderness hiking in several ways.

First, the land was purchased from a lumber company, which had completed its work; logging was no longer allowed in the locality. Again, in the process of building the lodge, the ADK evicted a hermit from his cabin

Ranger cabin, *or Interior Outpost, is near junction of Slide Brook trail and Phelps trail from Marcy.*

on the land. That spelled the end of the old-time mountain guides because the squatter, Mel Hathaway, was one of the last survivors.

And finally, with the completion of Johns Brook Lodge, the ADK called a halt to further building in the area. The club bought a plot adjacent to the lodge and converted two small existing buildings for limited housing, naming them Grace Camp and Camp Peggy O'Brien.

Other than the ranger station below the lodge, which the state's Department of Environmental Conservation now calls an Interior Outpost, there are no more enclosed structures in the interior of Johns Brook. The only other shelters are Adirondack open-air lean-tos.

Nature's ally, time, has healed most of the scars from man's encroachment into Johns Brook Valley.

And, fortunately, the wilderness on the surrounding high peaks is still unscathed. Big Slide mountain is one of the most accessible and most rewarding. Explorers who have climbed it are enticed to try again.

And again. With mixed results.

Journal entry: Tuesday, June 26, 1979. It's a chilly 44 degrees in Schenectady, but the prospect is for a day of the kind son Jim and I were blessed with nine years ago on Big Slide: cloudless, pure.

Jim is in college, and my hiking partner now is son Ben, who was two years old when Jim and I last came here. The reluctant toddler is now a lusty 11-year-old who wants to retrace Jim's steps on every peak.

The lot at the Garden has only a smattering of cars. Could it be the gas shortage? Or that we are hiking mid-week? Or that we are a few days up on July Fourth, which traditionally ushers the summer crowd in and the black flies out?

Wrong on the latter: They've headed for the hills. Swarms of them join us as we rest on the second Brother. We jam on our Adirondack crushers, hats made of red wool felt which is supposed to repel insects. But it's obvious the flies have not been schooled in such niceties, and bore in on us. All along the approach route to the summit, it's clammy and oppressive — fly heaven.

We've met no one on the trail, and on the summit there is no one in sight. Except, as I note with my binoculars, three hikers on Gothics and seven moving specks on distant Marcy.

Plus hundreds of moving specks around us. Lunch is a sparring match to see who gets the most bites — us on our sandwiches, or the flies on us. It's no contest.

Ben refuses to put on repellent. Consequently, his performance is as maddening as that of the bugs. He squirms when he sits, then dances around the blunt rock summit, swatting and protesting.

I squint out from a thick layer of Cutter's Lotion, and prepare to tell Ben about the mountain challenges that face us on every side. "Dad!" says Ben, with great agitation, "I know all about them. Let's get out of here. I'm being eaten alive!"

We may have conquered Big Slide, but we've been bested by the beasties.

Journal entry: Saturday, April 17, 1982. *Ben and I remember the good images of the Brothers' route, so we decide to try again. We think we're early enough this year to beat the black flies.*

Wrong. We spot one on the trunk of our car in the Garden.

Ranger Peter Fish has posted a note detailing the death of a hiker in this area two months ago. It merely stiffens our resolve: We're always doubly cautious when hiking on the fringes of winter, either early or late.

We get no farther than the first of the Brothers when we face up to the fact that we won't reach our target today because of clouds, sprinkles, pockets of cold and warm air, and lots of snow. In places, we sink up to our knees.

Big Slide will have to await another day.

Journal entry: Saturday, May 22, 1982. *Big Slide has become an alternate to Cascade, drawing Ben and me back for a warm-up hike to start the new year.*

We've explored two of the three routes to Big Slide so today we decide to investigate the third. It would have been appropriate to do so a month ago in the snow — the first leg heading northwest from Johns Brook Lodge is called the Klondike Notch trail.

The Klondike trail convinces us we have made the right decision; we are alone except for a few, scattered black flies. It's an interesting route, but there are almost no views.

Yard itself, at 4,018 feet, is high enough to provide extensive viewing, but it's treed in. It's another also-ran among the Adirondack peaks: too close to Big Slide to be one of the 46.

Big Slide doesn't show its face until we surmount its summit. It offers the same lovely views, while the Brothers unfold a different perspective to the peaks on the reverse route we are taking over them.

The weather, as usual, changes constantly. The sky was a beautiful blue when we began. It became cold on top of Big Slide, then hot and cloudy during the roller coaster return to the Garden.

Journal entry: Saturday, July 31, 1982. *Hiking friends Tom Stanwood and John Winkler have invited Ben and me to join them in*

Deep pockets of snow *on the first of the Brothers tell Ben and me that we are not equipped to climb Big Slide today. Even so, warm pockets of air prompt Ben to cool his heels.*

a bushwhack up the backside of Big Slide. I can't make it, but Ben jumps at the chance, for two reasons.

First, he'll be exploring with two seasoned climbers. And second, he'll be able to see if the observation Bob Marshall made in the early 1920s, when he and his two friends pioneered that route to Big Slide, still holds: "We climbed it through a primeval forest from the head of South Meadow Brook. Even if there had been no view, the woods alone were worth the trip."

Ben reports they followed the course of the brook and the old trail from South Meadows, then began to work their way up the slide from the north. Since they couldn't see the summit, they took a compass bearing and headed up through the woods. They topped off on the ridge between Yard and Big Slide, and followed the trail to the summit of the latter.

Ben sensed the weather was telling them it was not a good idea to be on the peaks. "Off and on," he says, "we had clouds, thunder, lightning, and lots of rain."

And what about Marshall's comment, I ask?

Ben sighs and shakes his head. "Instead of what he predicted, I mostly saw mud flying from the boots of the two guys plowing on ahead of me. It wasn't exactly what I had in mind."

Mt. Marcy from Mt. Skylight.

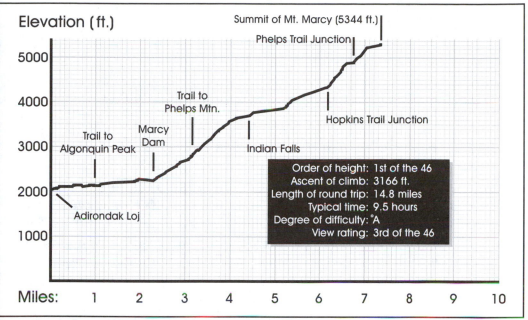

Elevation (ft.)

Summit of Mt. Marcy (5344 ft.)
Phelps Trail Junction
Trail to Phelps Mtn.
Hopkins Trail Junction
Marcy Dam
Trail to Algonquin Peak
Indian Falls
Adirondak Loj

Order of height: 1st of the 46
Ascent of climb: 3166 ft.
Length of round trip: 14.8 miles
Typical time: 9.5 hours
Degree of difficulty: °A
View rating: 3rd of the 46

Miles: 1 2 3 4 5 6 7 8 9 10

For contour trails, see U.S. Geological Survey map, pgs. 70-71.

11.
MARCY

What can you say about Marcy that hasn't already been said, even though you've climbed it several times?

Impressions, perhaps, from your initial foray onto this majestic mountain:

Journal entry, Friday, May 29, 1970. *"Marcy?" Jim asks. The prospect of high adventure brightens his smile.*

Yes, Marcy, I tell him. Up until now, we have targeted the outlying peaks on the assumption that, from the map at least, they look easier. Since none of them have been pushovers, it occurs to me that this is as good a time as any to go right to the heart of the action.

"Mercy!" says Jim. He knows this will put me in a good mood. Mercy is the name that Old Mountain Phelps, the most colorful of the early Adirondack guides, gave to his favorite peak.

There is some doubt as to whether this is a good day to explore Marcy. Hiking veterans tell us we can expect the trail to be busy on any decent day from spring to fall, and this is the Friday before Memorial Day weekend. But the forecast is for near-perfect weather so we decide to give it a try.

At Keene Valley we overhear an intriguing conversation between two townsfolk at the general store. It was 22 degrees in the village last night, they say, and a marauding bear was killed at the town dump. They glance at us outsiders as we strain to listen, but they do not smile. Are they putting us on?

Any nervousness is forgotten as we turn off Route 73 on the road that leads south to Adirondak Loj. The day is cloudless with a crisp bite to the air, enhanced by pinpoints of sun reflecting in the dew on the grass.

There they all are before us — Marcy, Colden, Algonquin, and to the southwest a vivid wedge of blue that identifies Indian Pass between the MacIntyres and Wallface.

How do you describe the breathtaking beauty of such a view? I decide to heed the advice for young writers in my daughter's high school English text: "Above all, refrain from the beauties of nature: the realities of tree structure and starlight can hardly be got into words, and you will not, of course, wish to display your own delicate nature moods to an audience which, not being in love with you, may find them tiresome."

Anyway, the prospect is gorgeous. And I know that if Jim and I could somehow compress the glory of this vista into a scenic postcard, we would at least scribble on the back: "Wish you were here."

We have second thoughts as we enter the parking lot at Adirondak Loj. It appears as if a great many people have been sending come-hither postcards. The lot is jammed with cars, so we waste no time in moving out on the Van Hoevenberg trail. At about a third of a mile, it leaves ADK property to continue on state land.

We had travelled the first mile before on our hike to the MacIntyre Range. So the winding, undulating path is familiar until we reach the trail junction and head southeast toward Marcy Dam. It's a pleasant surprise to find that the trail continues over gently rolling hills with hardly any ascent. The trail is well maintained, and corduroy logs make it easy to manage the wet spots caused by the spring run-off.

We strain to hear the sounds of Marcy Brook to the left but are befuddled by the wind in the trees. About a mile beyond the junction, there is no mistaking the roaring water below. The rush of the brook is amplified, then silenced as the trail traces near and away from its course.

Jim leads the way over a nasty, soggy stretch of corduroy when all of a sudden he leaps as if in pain and shouts, "Watch out, the third log is a floater!" Sure enough, I gingerly test it with my toe and it bobs up and down in the black water. There's no need to ask about his startled cry. In the distance, I can see through the delicate leaves a large patch of snow on some peak as yet unknown to us. Jim's yelp was not from pain but from the shock of icy water that came from the high country.

Soon we hear a puzzling sound for a mountain wilderness. It is a regular thump-thump-thump which we judge to be an engine of some sort. Could it be a sawmill? This area is not pristine wilderness, we know — there is much second growth timber along the early stretches of the trail. But can the state be so blind as to allow lumbering in this beautiful area? Such a natural resource is not only a fast-vanishing asset but, considering the mounting pressures of urban living, an urgent necessity.

It is with great relief that we reach Marcy Dam and discover that the thumping does not come from an engine. It is the result of a peculiar blending of man and nature working in harmony. Marcy Dam is a well-worn structure of logs and stone with a wooden plank spillway in the middle. Due to an unusual admixture of wind, water flow, and angle of fall — am I on target, oh engineers? — the heavy run-off slaps the spillway in a regular beat that lends a jarring note to the placid beauty on every side.

From the sagging plank bridge that crosses the brink of the dam, Jim and I view for the first time the jeweled lake mirroring a clearing that is the jumping-off point for so many trails in this popular, high peak country.

Our map shows that a trail to the south leads through Avalanche Pass to Lake Colden and the

At Marcy Dam. Camping areas with seven lean-tos surround this beautiful lake in the midst of the high peaks. Mt. Colden, in background, is some two miles to the south. Slope of Wright Peak is at right.

Flowed Land...whatever that is. The area also is the launching pad for trail trajectories soaring up to other peaks which Jim and I hope to explore — Colden, Cliff, Redfield, Gray and Skylight, and who knows what else.

Today we will continue southeast on the Van Hoevenberg trail to Marcy. From the map, it appears we will be returning here again to confront Phelps, Tabletop and others. There are a few peaks in the middle, like Haystack and Basin, which are about as remote from this location as from any other; we will worry about them in due time.

We assume the sizeable peak some two miles to the south is Colden; but there is a strange one even closer to the southeast. A check of the map shows that it is a loser. And it lucked out the hard way — its main summit just misses being listed among the exalted 46 by about a hundred feet.

I speculate about the plight of this also-ran. It's not even named on any map that I have. Without doubt, it's bypassed by hundreds of aspiring Forty Sixers every year who have eyes only for the stars of this mountain melodrama. And there are more than 50 Adirondack peaks just like this one which range above 3,500 but below 4,000 feet.

What fun it would be to set off through the tangled woods and finally peep out from the top of Old Nameless. There you could snicker at the tedious procession of ants on the trails all around as they struggle upward toward the glory of the summit registers. Great! I hereby resolve — Jim doesn't know this yet, and I hope he isn't taken up too much by football and girls by then — that after we surmount the 46, we will return and climb this peaked peak and cheer it up. It will be challenging, too, to chart new ground that may never have been scouted before.

Jim nudges me with impatience and breaks the spell. He hurries on because hikers are approaching from both sides to cross the bridge. Onward, ants. And wait for me, Jim!

We don't mind leaving the Marcy Dam area because it is almost too civilized. In addition to a ranger station there are several lean-tos, all occupied, the remains of campfires near picnic benches, and — ah, vanishing wilderness — an outhouse.

A short distance on, we note a trail branching right, to the south, for Colden. Our grade straight ahead is still easy; it follows an old tote road that lazes high above Phelps Brook to the right. Ahead are more signs of encroaching civilization: huge sawed logs have been placed over spongy areas to ease the passage. And as the trail veers toward the brook, we cross on a sturdy, well-constructed bridge. At this rate, I would not be surprised to find an elevator ready to lift us the final steep haul to Marcy's summit, as on Whiteface.

We are somewhat confused to find the trail splitting about a mile beyond Marcy Dam. However, the map indicates the two segments rejoin at Indian Falls, so for no good reason we choose the easterly route.

Just beyond, we are glad that we came this way because of a new sign indicating a "Trail to Phelps." Good. We can chalk off one more trail-less trek; our 1962 ADK guidebook does not record any such path.

Or is it an advantage? It's an invitation to more people, and that's not necessarily good, as we are finding.

Our way now follows an old, wide, logging road which looks like it would be ideal for skiing. The trail crosses from the left to the right bank of a branch of Marcy Brook and as we climb more steeply, my hunch is confirmed. At first we thought the sign for those descending was a practical joke: "Slow to 5 mph." But I conclude that it can only be to warn skiers of the bridged rock cut we have just traversed.

We have paid little attention to hikers who have passed. But I study closely two young people who wave cheerily as they go around us and stride up the trail. Both are blonde and sturdy and are dressed in similar outdoor garb. Jim insists they are both boys, but I'm not so sure. The close-cropped hair of one wreathes a face that is a bit more cherubic than the other. In any event, they look alike; if they are different, they must be brother and sister.

The guidebook describes Indian Falls as "one of the finest views in the mountains," and it is true. Here, Marcy Brook sweeps down through a widening clearing and, at the brink of a small precipice, cascades over the chiselled lip of a huge, rounded, rock ledge. We sprawl on it to enjoy another postcard setting. The entire length of the MacIntyre Range, including Marshall, Iroquois, Algonquin and Wright, etches a dark silhouette against a brilliant sky.

In some respects, it is like trying to enjoy the sights of New York City while sitting in the middle of Times Square. Hikers in groups stroll back and forth, blocking our view. A frizzie-haired hiker and girl friend call their dog, which splashes in the brook above a young man filling his canteen. The mutt comes joyfully, leaving muddy paw prints and a spray of water as he romps across our legs. The shattering blast of a bugle echoes from the depths of a valley below.

Behind us, at the nearby lean-to, two young matrons in drab uniforms flutter about to help their young charges clean up from an overnight stay and prepare to move out. "Girl scouts," says Jim. "Ugh."

Dimly through the foliage we see a second lean-to perhaps a hundred yards up the trail; it is crowded with college-age boys. The bustling noise of people filters through the woods from either side. The ants are very busy today.

From Indian Falls, the MacIntyre Range dominates the western sky. Algonquin is at center, surrounded by Wright, on right, and Iroquois, left. Marshall is out of view on left.

It is a relief to leave the tumult behind and follow the leisurely grade of the trail above Marcy Brook. We have gone no more than a quarter of a mile when we first hear giggles and shouts below, then see the scout troop chugging toward us, as if in full pursuit. While they are under full packs, we are astounded to find they are gaining on us. Chagrined is a better word — Jim is not about to let a gaggle of girls go round him, so we pour on the steam and soon lose them.

The hike so far has covered at least two thirds of the distance to our target, yet we have seen no sight of Marcy. Suddenly, between the trees ahead where the trail tops a small rise, we see it. Only the rocky crest is visible and, in a way, it looks just like the summit of the other high peaks that sport a bald dome. Marcy's distinguishing characteristic from a distance is its tremendously broad base. Of course, it is not in evidence now because we are on it.

The climb soon moderates as the trail winds through some very wet sections. The Hopkins trail from Bushnell Falls in Johns Brook Valley enters from the left; beyond, we descend a bit to pass the Hopkins lean-to and cross a broad expanse of black quagmire — more corduroy floaters! After a quarter of a mile, we pass the Plateau lean-to perched near the base of Marcy's monolithic summit. Both lean-tos are occupied.

On the far side of the latter we pause and are amazed at the monstrous topping of this "high peak of Essex," as its discoverer, the noted meteorologist William C. Redfield, called it. It has the same appearance of a gigantic speckled egg that we saw when approaching Algonquin, but the girth is at least two-fold. And, although the warm breath of June is pulling at the calendar page two days in advance, an enormous collection of snow still slumps in a hollow on the lofty east slope. No wonder the brooks are running and the trails gushing on the approaches to Marcy.

As we begin a steep climb through stunted spruces, we are again bothered by trail-doggers. This time it's a father with three children younger than Jim who keep pressing us to move along or let them pass. We decide they couldn't be this fresh unless they camped out here overnight. But we are determined not to be done in by this cradle crew, so we keep climbing.

The need for frequent, short rests tells us more forcefully than signs that we have come a long way — well over six miles — and that we are gaining altitude. "We're getting up in the world," I tell Jim. He winces — I know he means that my standard remark about reaching the high country is going stale.

At the junction of the Phelps trail coming in from Slant Rock, we pause to chat with two young men who casually squat against their full packs. Their water froze last night on Marcy, they say, so they are heading out on the Range trail. They will go as far as they please and camp out again.

It is beginning to dawn on Jim and me that we are members of a minority group. There must be some enchantment about parking out on the peaks that appeals to everybody but us. The urge to join them, however, is moderated by the size of their bedrolls.

A short climb through a checkerboard of scrub trees and snow patches brings us to an expanse of bare rock leading into a level area made mushy from melting snow. Beyond, there is no doubt that the final assault is about to begin. The trail forms a sharp, upward angle toward the forbidding summit.

It always seems to me that at the timberline, the receding trees release magic juices which act as a powerful propellant on the younger set. Jim urges me on, still farther away each time I rest until finally, with solicitous exasperation, he shouts, "I'll wait for you at the top."

It's all right with me. I lean against a rocky slab to get the breathing back to an even puffing and relish the view. If it were a high peak explorer's privilege to order the sights set before him, like the choicest delicacies on a menu, this would be the visual banquet.

Brief respite comes at site of former Plateau lean-to; Marcy's summit looms a mile away. At timberline, rocky trail follows cairns and paint blazes.

Before me to the north are the appetizers: Tabletop and Phelps, with those scenic side dishes Big Slide, Cascade and Porter tempting to the northeast. Whiteface, like a high caloric sweet deliberately placed out of reach, beckons from the northern border of the tableau.

To the east is the entree — Algonquin, garnished by the generous helpings of its sister peaks, with a random sprinkling beyond of such spicy pleasures as MacNaughton and the Santanonis.

Below me, unfortunately, are the ever louder yelps of the children. They have found that the mysterious propellant of the peaks is an antidote to the admonitions of their father. It is time for me to turn and hack away at the real meat of this mountain meal.

The summit of Marcy makes an abrupt appearance. It is almost an anticlimax, for the antics of the multitudes milling about compete with the scenic splendors. Some 30 hikers are resting, eating, strolling, romping and sighting. Beneath a rocky knoll to the south, two fellow nature-lovers are oblivious to the views; rather, they are closely exploring each other. As I walk past, they answer two questions that were posed earlier. They are the two blond athletes who passed Jim and me on the lower trail. And, it is obvious they are not both boys, and they are not brother and sister.

I join Jim on a vacant ledge and we spread our lunch on the rock surface. As on most Adirondack peaks, the wind is chilly and, finishing, Jim dons our new plastic emergency blanket. It is pocket size but paper thin and quickly tears when Jim settles down. This is no emergency so the test is worth the investment. We resolve to find a stronger substitute for the forthcoming trailless hikes where we may really need it.

Mt. Skylight, *center left, beckons from Marcy, with Allen Mtn. at left behind Skylight. Mt. Redfield is behind author; North River Mountains are in center, six miles to the southwest.*

How tempting it is to forge on to the other target peaks which tantalize us nearby. Gray is within spitting distance to the southwest and just beyond are Skylight and Redfield. The awesome Panther Gorge separates us from Haystack, which looks just like what its name implies, along with its not-so-little brother on its north shoulder. They appear to be so close — and then we discern the busy antics of two hikers laboring with their heavy loads across the saddle between the youngster and the elder. More ants!

A strapping, hearty hiker packing a monstrous load has been pacing the promenade and stops to share his enthusiasm for the challenges. "That's Gray," he says, pointing to Skylight. "But I'm on my way to Haystack, and who knows how many more today?"

He's got the right spirit, I think. And with that kind of restless energy, he just might set a record of some sort, even though the peaks recorded may not match those on the map.

I wonder if he's fired up by the feat of Adirondack Mountain Club member H. L. Malcolm, who in 1933 at the age of 49 set a record for that era. Starting from Adirondak Loj at one minute after midnight on October seven, Malcolm traversed Giant, Noonmark and the two Wolfjaws, then Armstrong, Gothics, Saddleback, Basin, Haystack, Marcy, Skylight, Colden and Algonquin, returning over Mt. Jo to the Loj.

Panther Gorge *plunges to dizzying depths on the west; Mt. Haystack rims its far border. Dix Mtn. looms beyond Nippletop, right center; Macomb is at their left.*

Since it was still an hour before midnight — of the same day, that is — he climbed Mt. Jo a second time to rack up a total ascent of more than 20,000 ft., covering a distance of just over 40 miles. As William Chapman White noted in Adirondack Country, *"there is no report on what Mr. Malcolm did the next day, or, in fact, when he got to his feet again."*

Our voluble hiking friend strides intently down the trail. I can't help thinking he will have more trouble getting out of bed than Mr. Malcolm if he plans to haul that heavy pack across the range.

The high pressure area seems to be stuck, for the clear, pure air holds. It is nice to see that one well-known maxim of the mountains is not inviolate. On descending, it seems to Jim and me, the elements usually drench the hiker, dim the view or darken the way. Not today.

In spite of the length of this hike, we agree that it has not been especially tiring, except for the final, steep assault (and for all that, I'm still glad it has no elevator as on Whiteface). This is a well-designed trail.

One thing the trail designer cannot compensate for — and I'm sure Van Hoevenberg would never have predicted — is the deleterious effect of countless pounding feet during the hiking season. As we descend, Jim and I see the result of this in the destruction of corduroy walk-

Great Range *surges toward slide-slashed Giant. In order from right, peaks include Basin, Saddleback, Gothics with scarred slopes, Armstrong, Upper and Lower Wolfjaw.*

ways, in the soil literally stomped to bedrock on the slopes, and in the deterioration of trail shoulders where hikers have skirted wet spots.

Below the Plateau lean-to, the full impact of the flood of humanity rushing up Marcy hits home. A young man and his wife under full packs hurry toward us, asking, "Are the lean-to's full?" Close behind them are four more young people, then a pack of rambunctious boys followed by their outing leader, puffing but game. They pose the same question.

Indian Falls by now is a small community full of the bustling sounds and sights of people who may only stay a night but have paraphernalia for the long pull. Beyond, we rarely move more than a hundred yards without greeting other out-of-breath newcomers who ask the standard query. Since we hate to hobble their hopes, we let it go with, "There's a lot of people, but a lot of space." We hope they take it the right way and have fun.

Dusk is deepening as we return to Adirondak Loj for our car. It is a bit tricky maneuvering through the jammed lot and the first quarter mile out the road; cars and campers line the ditches on either side.

Now this is a switch. We are leaving the woods to return to the city to be alone. The trail veterans are right: Avoid the popular haunts and, above all, holiday weekends. Well, we missed the holiday, but not by much. And I have mixed feelings about whether this is the wrong time to be on Marcy.

Without some exposure to the other more remote peaks, this trip might have curbed our urge to go on. But Jim and I know this is not typical of the average Adirondack peak or of a spring day in the mountains. Maybe it would have been better to wait for another day, or even another year.

Still I can't help but think this was the right time to be here. Suppose we had delayed this trip and found in a couple of years that Marcy had become the Mt. Whitney of the east? The trail up Whitney in California is twice as long and there are far fewer people within easy access of that peak than here. Yet last year the Park Service reported that 10,000 hardy hikers made the trip to the summit; the Forest Service even put the estimate at 20,000, including more than a thousand on Labor Day alone. If that happens to Marcy at some early date, then our timing is faulty only because we are already late.

As it is, Jim and I have learned two important and revealing lessons.

First, Marcy is a treasure of nature that should be available to anyone who makes the effort to see it; the fine system of trails and shelters makes that possible.

Second, because it is such a treasure of nature, Marcy should be cared for with intelligence.

With this in mind, Jim and I will gladly be counted among the ants. But we resolve to emulate some of their more industrious traits, rather than just follow the crowd.

How has Marcy fared since then? To those who have explored this major peak over time, it has become something of an anachronism.

The state has moved to accommodate the increasing number of hikers who come to do homage. At the same time, the state has improved Marcy's mountain environment in ways which fulfill the eloquent intent of the constitution to keep the Adirondacks "forever wild."

Basic improvements confirm that much trail work has been done. Logs and planks and boulders now ease the way for hikers in more swampy areas and on eroded slopes.

The old log-cribbed structure at Marcy Dam which stuttered at passing hikers is gone; it had been built to float down logs cleared from the interior after the fires of 1903. A new dam, plumbed to perfection, forfeits the springiness of the old one but gives more assurance to those who lean on side rails while admiring the views.

New York state has also taken steps to heighten the feeling of wilderness for those drawn to Marcy.

The lean-tos above Indian Falls were removed in 1976. The views from there are better than ever, if that's possible. Two huge garbage pits which fouled the scene near the waterfall have been filled in.

Both the Hopkins and Plateau lean-tos farther up the trail also are gone, bowing to regulations which prohibit lean-to camping above 3,500 feet. Hikers who enjoyed the Plateau lean-to will shed tears; it offered a million dollar view of Marcy for the pittance of climbing six and a half miles with a gain of 2,300 feet in elevation.

Early hikers who continued onward found an even better view from a small stone shelter contructed in 1928 on the lip of Marcy's summit. Forty years later, the Department of Environmental Conservation destroyed it. Too many people, the state concluded, stayed overnight and flirted with the danger of violent consequences from Marcy's unpredictable weather.

Hiking and environmental groups have reinforced the state's goals through their work in stabilizing trails and conducting summit seeding and environmental stewardship, as they do on Algonquin. As a result, the fragile vegetation that's a holdover from the Ice Age has been stabilized.

The work came too late for five species, lost since 1949. But the glory of 19 of New York's rare, threatened and endangered species, found only on Marcy's summit and the highest concentration in the state, has been preserved.

The splendors of Marcy's summit beckon from all sides. One can see more of the 46 high peaks than from any of the others. Only Couchsachraga, the lowest of them all, and East Dix, barely a hundred feet higher, are out of sight. The former crouches behind the Santanoni Range to the west; the latter, on the east, is a hostage of Hough.

It seemed inevitable that Marcy would become a victim of its magnetic attractions. Ranger Peter Fish estimates that some 10,000 people now climb New York state's highest peak each year. That matches the number who surmounted California's Mt. Whitney in 1970, the year son Jim and I first climbed Marcy. It's unlikely, however, that Marcy will catch up with Whitney's current total or that of Marcy's neighbor in the White Mountains of New Hampshire, Mt. Washington.

The summit of the latter has certain "advantages" over Marcy: an observatory with a cafeteria, museum, gift shops and even a post office. It also has, as Suzanne Lance noted in the 1990-91 fall/winter edition of *Adirondack Peeks*, "the cog railway bringing carloads of tourists dressed in their white shorts and sandals, despite the 57 degree summit temperatures."

She noted wryly, prior to embarking on a four-day traverse of the Presidential Range in New Hampshire, "What an odd way to plan for a hiking trip: making reservations at huts which would feed us breakfast and dinner, and reserving spots on a shuttle bus to drop us off at our choice of trailheads. This wasn't a hiking vacation. It was more like a travel agency-sponsored tour."

There may be people around when you reach Marcy's summit, and it's as hard to climb as ever. But the lure of the wilderness which urged you on is still there to reward you.

Journal entry: Saturday, September 17, 1979. A week ago, my younger son left a scrawled note on my desk:

> *I'm feeling*
> *to bad*
> *to con-*
> *tinue*
> *moun-*
> *tain cl-*
> *imbing. Ben*

Only 11 years old, and already a sorehead. I had said no to something he wanted.

Fortunately, he's like his older sibling, Jim: resilient and ebullient. I mention Marcy, and Ben is ready to go.

As it was when Jim and I were here before, the trail is loaded; at least 50 hikers mill about at Marcy Dam. On the way to Indian Falls, ranger Gary Tyler herds a dozen "pilgrims," as Old Mountain Phelps would call them, conversing in a foreign language — German, I think.

At the trail junction which leads to Phelps, we meet a vigorous young engineer under full pack. He's here on vacation from Buffalo, venturing into the Adirondacks for the first time. He has twisted his ankle and wonders if he will make it to the top, or should even try. "Last year," he sighs, "I completed a 400-mile bicycle tour from Buffalo to Montreal. It was a breeze compared to this."

And so it goes to the summit, where numerous hikers vie to tread on the topmost rocky bump.

I had often tried to describe the sensation of being there for Ben, but it defies description. When he finally secures a place, his stare is mute confirmation; he's oblivious to everyone around him.

Journal entry: Saturday, August 16, 1986. It's hot, humid and buggy. There's no view at Indian Falls, and the summit is fogged in.

West from Marcy. *Nineteenth century guide John Cheney visualized "mountains that seem shouldering each other to boost the one whereon you stand, up and away Heaven knows where."*

Which explains why, on reaching the summit at 3:30 in the afternoon, Ben and I see just three young men who soon leave. Two more people arrive, but depart within five minutes.

Which also explains why my field notes record: "Great! It's our mountain. Marcy tops them all."

Verplanck Colvin knew what he was doing in 1872 when he selected the number of the Adirondack Survey copper bolt to be implanted on Marcy's summit.

It was Number One.

Lower Wolfjaw Mtn. from the first of The Brothers.

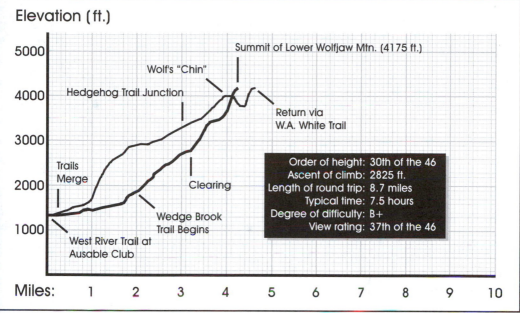

Elevation (ft.)

- Summit of Lower Wolfjaw Mtn. (4175 ft.)
- Wolf's "Chin"
- Hedgehog Trail Junction
- Return via W.A. White Trail
- Trails Merge
- Clearing
- Wedge Brook Trail Begins
- West River Trail at Ausable Club

Order of height: 30th of the 46
Ascent of climb: 2825 ft.
Length of round trip: 8.7 miles
Typical time: 7.5 hours
Degree of difficulty: B+
View rating: 37th of the 46

Miles: 1 2 3 4 5 6 7 8 9 10

or contour trails, see U.S. Geological Survey map, pgs. 120-121.

12.
LOWER WOLFJAW

Journal entry: Sunday, June 7, 1970. Jim and I are not sure how to approach our next major challenge in the Adirondack high country: the Great Range.

It's one of several monumental ridges which act on the high peaks like magnets to metal, lining them up generally in north to south order. The ranges include Dix to the southeast, Colvin and Nippletop to the south, and the MacIntyres, Santanonis and Sewards to the west. The Great Range, enshrined in the center, is the most spectacular of them all.

Big Slide gave us a side view of the Great Range, which surges erratically to the southwest from Keene Valley. And Marcy provided the perfect observation post to check out the length and girth of the peaks which make up the chain. They're formidable from any viewpoint.

The best way to conquer an army of mountains like this, I decide, is with caution. And, one at a time.

As you might expect, Jim and I look for the easy mark. And there's no contest — Lower Wolfjaw. It's the little guy at the end of the column, the least imposing as to defenses, and vulnerable to a flanking maneuver. We formulate a strategic plan of attack by scouting our options.

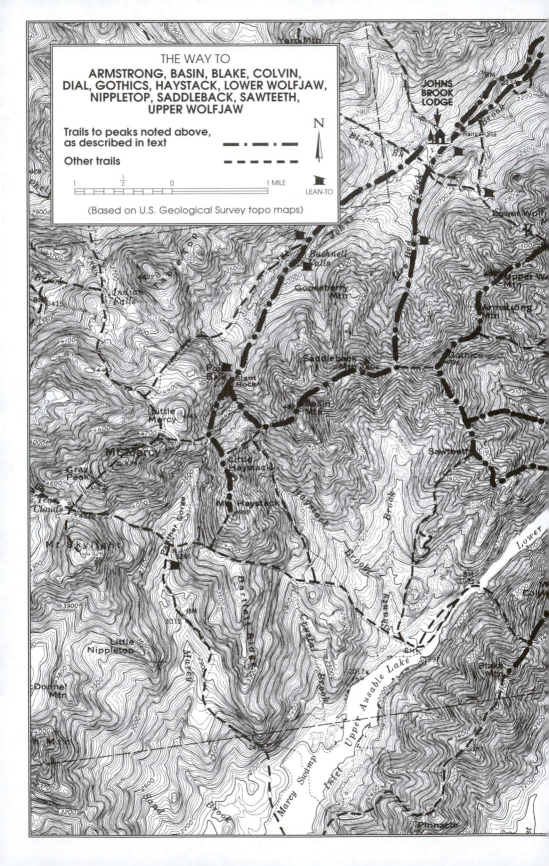

THE WAY TO
ARMSTRONG, BASIN, BLAKE, COLVIN, DIAL, GOTHICS, HAYSTACK, LOWER WOLFJAW, NIPPLETOP, SADDLEBACK, SAWTEETH, UPPER WOLFJAW

Trails to peaks noted above, as described in text

Other trails

N

1   ½   0   1 MILE

LEAN-TO

(Based on U.S. Geological Survey topo maps)

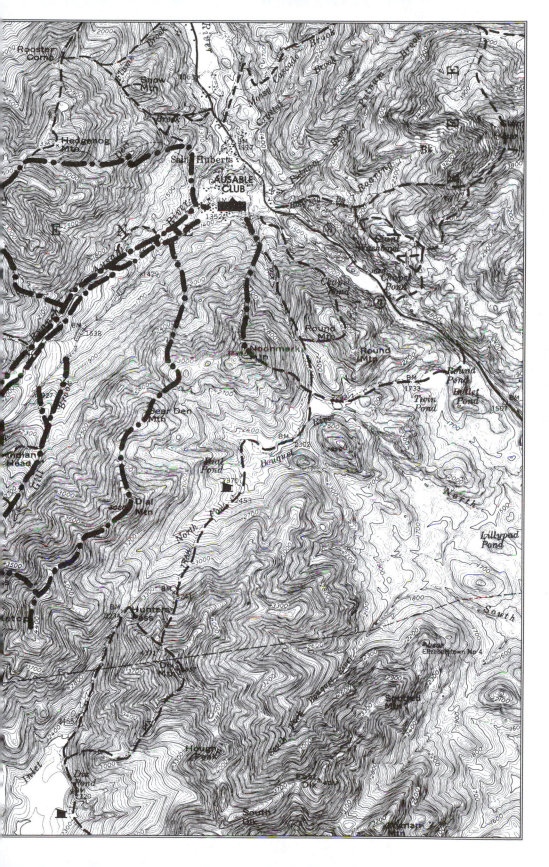

The direct way is by the Great Range trail, which heads south from Keene Valley over the Rooster Comb and Hedgehog Mtn., then turns southwest along the crest of the ridge toward the summits of the two Wolfjaws. Or, we can do battle from either side: head southeast from a junction off the Johns Brook trail near the lodge, or follow the east branch of the Ausable River toward Lower Ausable Lake for about a mile before angling to the northwest at a trail junction.

The latter route adds a couple of hundred feet more climbing than the trail up Johns Brook Valley, but it's almost two miles shorter. And it looks more doable than the Range trail, which is three quarters of a mile longer, with a good many ups and downs.

But there's an even more compelling reason why I want to climb Lower Wolfjaw by way of the valley leading toward Lower Ausable Lake: it'll bring us past one of the last of the fabled institutions frequented by the Adirondack gentry, the Ausable Club.

Most people going to or from Keene Valley on Rt. 73 don't realize they've come within a half mile of the Ausable Club when they pass the little settlement of St. Huberts, some two miles south of Keene Valley. A discreet sign at the intersection points up the road to the southwest; there, the clubhouse nestles primly off the highway in Victorian splendor.

Pioneers coming from the south in the early 1800s bypassed the area, too. They favored plots which looked more inviting for farming in Keene Flats, as Keene Valley was then called. Some of the pioneers were war veterans with big hopes for exploiting land grants. Others came from Vermont and scattered sites in New England, urged on by the new-country conviction that a better life lay somewhere west.

But the early settlers soon came to a discouraging conclusion: Adirondack farming, with a growing season of barely a hundred days, offered perilous security. The artist Harold Weston, whose father was one of the founders of the Ausable Club, noted sadly that, "Bears killed the sheep, fox stole the chickens, raccoons ransacked the corn."

Most of the settlers, therefore, supplemented their incomes by hunting and trapping in the Adirondack wilderness which beckoned at their backdoor. The bounties to be had, coupled with the area's natural beauty — Keene Valley has been called "the Switzerland of America" — spawned two new streams of income: catering to summer visitors, and serving as Adirondack guides.

One of the original settlers of the Keene Valley area, Smith Beede, did make the turn at the St. Huberts intersection and established a sizeable farm. He was also among the first to recognize that there were more opportunities in pilgrims — Old Mountain Phelps' term for tourists — than in plowing. He first tested the water by taking in summer visitors at his farmhouse, the present-day site of Putnam Camp. It nestles just north of Roaring Brook Falls at the western base of Giant Mountain.

The response was so overwhelming that he decided to build a hotel a half mile to the west, naming it Beede's Heights for that segment of his farm on which it was located. The hotel became not only an instant success but the genesis, in site if not in name, for today's Ausable Club.

But in the mid-'80s it became apparent that not just Smith Beede had eyes on the Ausable valley. An ad in *Wallace's Guide* shouted, "20,000 acres! Good Timber Lands for Sale, Situated in the Adirondack Wilderness...No finer opportunity has ever been offered to lumbermen or manufacturers."

This was the trigger that prompted a group of wealthy Philadelphians to begin buying some 30,000 acres of land in the Ausable Valley area, including a portion of the advertised property. The purchase included both the lower and upper Ausable lakes and all or part of 13 of the 46 high peaks. The lands extended to the summit of Mt. Marcy, to Lake Arnold on Mt. Colden, to the present site of Johns Brook Lodge, and to the lower slopes of Dix Mtn.

The purchase was made in the name of the Adirondack Mountain Reserve (AMR), which stated its intention to preserve the "masterpieces of nature" which the purchasers had come to know and cherish. Some of the "masterpieces" were rude camps which they had long enjoyed on Upper Ausable Lake.

While the AMR founders were fond of the wilderness, they soon decided they needed lodgings that were more extensive and accessible for their families and guests. So in 1890 they bought Beede's hotel. It later burned to the ground and was replaced by a new, three-story hotel called St. Huberts Inn. It was re-named the Ausable Club in 1906, when it merged with the AMR. Over the years, the AMR/Ausable Club increased its holdings until by 1910 they totalled some 45,000 acres.

But the original goals of the Adirondack Mountain Reserve ranged beyond summer quarters and preservation. It was organized as a business, not a nonprofit institution. As such, it aimed to become self-sustaining by reinforcing membership fees with the sale of lots near the club and timber from the outer fringes of the property.

Over time, even this revenue fell short of maintaining financial equilibrium. The clubhouse itself is only open during July and August — avoiding the earlier height of the black fly season — and provides only limited accomodations from the end of May until mid-October. Also, few of the residences are maintained year-round.

So in 1921 the club initiated a series of land sales to New York state, culminating with a final transaction in 1978. The sales reduced AMR's holdings to some 7,000 acres and brought down the elevation of the outer boundary of its property to about 2,500 ft. One result of the purchases was that the state's Forest Preserve fulfilled one of its long-time goals: ownership of all Adirondack high peaks of 4,000 ft. or more. The purchases also ended any threat of encroachment by loggers.

Most important, through its stewardship over more than a century, the AMR helped preserve the heart of the Adirondack State Park, including the high peaks surrounding the Ausable Club.

The Ausable clubhouse is a long, rambling, three-story structure with dormers snuggled between huge chimneys on the roof. A large cupola at the front caps viewing porches, stacked one atop the other at succeeding floor levels.

Cottages are sprinkled about, some in the surrounding woods. The clearing reveals a golf course, putting green, tennis courts, swimming pool, and lanes for lawn bowling — all the requirements for gracious recreation.

And there is a gorgeous backdrop for the elegant setting. To the east, Giant looms in striped splendor like a domineering doorman. To the west, partially hidden by trees, is an ascending succession of peaks that promises allure and adventure.

Journal entry: Sunday, June 7, 1970. This is our first foray into the seemingly sacrosanct Ausable Club area. Jim and I have driven in a few times before, but have never hiked through for a close look.

It is like stepping back in time. The Ausable Club is a part of the fabric woven by the carriage trade. The clubhouse is a reincarnation of the Grand Hotel, but this time it is in the Adirondacks, not Saratoga.

Ausable Club *lies a half mile from St. Huberts, some two miles south of Keene Valley. Victorian clubhouse is one of last vestiges of such oldtime Adirondack institutions.*

Through the morning mist that cradles the ancient structure, one can almost see the young ladies of an earlier era promenading along the covered veranda. The taffeta of their long skirts crackles as they swish past their approving elders. The latter loll in high-backed rockers, enjoying the quiet chat which follows a sumptuous breakfast.

The young swains, resplendent in white flannels and flaming argyles, ignore the young ladies with studied casualness. However, their performance on the close-clipped lawn betrays their true intentions. They cast laughing glances to the porch again and again as they romp with each other in heroic horseplay, endure the children with exaggerated indulgence, and toss sticks to the poodles which leap wildly in the enveloping fog.

But there is no such tableau at the Ausable Club today. There is fog but no one comes into view, not even a solitary dog. Jim and I are alone as we head in to explore what for us is brand new hiking territory.

The trail to Lower Wolfjaw turns right from the road leading to Lower Ausable Lake about a quarter of a mile beyond the clubhouse, descending to cross the East Branch of the Ausable River. There, a junction offers a choice of the West River trail along the west bank of the Ausable, or the W. A. White trail which loops north and then west to join the Range trail.

Journal entry: Sunday, June 7, 1970. *Jim and I choose the West River trail. It moves gently up and down along the river bank, leading us straight into this storybook world of the Adirondacks.*

Below, to our left, the Ausable River shoots shimmering sheets of green over rounded rocks of all sizes. They gleam from polishing caused by countless journeys downstream during flood season.

At this early hour, the trail is damp and fresh. Patches of it are speared by beams of sunlight which manage to break through the forest canopy. The trail, tracing a graceful pattern on swatches of black soil, softens as it winds through huge, virgin trees, then disappears in the enveloping mist.

Looking overhead, one can see why early ship builders came to the Adirondacks for pine trees to make masts and beams for their sailing vessels. Some grew to six feet in diameter and soared 250 feet high.

The noble trees bring to my mind a series of Adirondack forest etchings my oldest daughter Judy prepared for a college art class. I asked her later to run off a few sets of the prints because several hiking friends had admired my framed copies and wondered if they could buy some from her.

But Judy was the typical starving artist. "Sorry, Dad. I sold the copper and zinc plates I drew them on so I could eat."

The ADK guidebook calls this route leading to Lower Ausable Lake a "lovely woodland walk" with little steep climbing. And so it is. It moves easily to an overlook above the babble of the river, then to an even higher lookout which offers views of the Colvin and Nippletop ranges. It then meanders to the junction with the Wedge Brook trail, which ascends westward toward Lower Wolfjaw.

The trail follows the upward track of the brook for a while, then angles to the west. After a little more than a mile, it passes through a clearing choked with nettles.

Journal entry: Sunday, May 25, 1986. Each time I come to this clearing on Lower Wolfjaw — this is my third — it reminds me of the Catskills.

The Adirondack clearing is at about 2,800 feet. If this were in the Catskills, such an opening would be a common sight, even at higher elevations. Some of the slopes I've explored on the Catskills' Windham High Peak, for example, are dotted with clearings. They're easy to spot because they're squared off by stone fences which served as repositories for nineteenth century farmers as they cleared their fields.

Windham or any number of neighboring peaks could be called Heartbreak Ridge; almost all of the farms are now abandoned. So much toil and so little to show. The legacy, other than stone fences, is an occasional plot with a

Ausable River *tumbles through gorge as it heads east from Lower Ausable Lake. Overlook is about a mile and a half from the Ausable Club on the West River trail.*

neglected apple tree or lilac bush crouched in mourning over a crumbling foundation.

Not so in the Adirondack highlands. This is cold, hard, wild country. There was never a thought of farming on the upper slopes of the peaks, so this clearing has to be a leftover from lumbering, not farming.

Beyond the clearing, the trail rises steeply. Through gaps in the trees, Ben and I can see where rock slides have ripped the southern flanks of Lower Wolfjaw.

As we near the trail junction where we will veer northward toward the summit, Ben draws near and whispers, "We'd better watch out; this is bear country." Tom Stanwood, our veteran hiking friend, told us he spooked a bear on this spot while descending from Lower Wolfjaw.

I tell Ben to relax. A recent TV nature show reported that you're 300 times more likely to die in a car accident than to be killed by a bear. I don't mention that, after the fact, this would be of small comfort.

Anyway, there are no bears in sight today. But another animal has left its calling card: a sign pointing to Lower Wolfjaw has been chewed in half by a porcupine. Again, it reminds me of the Catskills.

In the early '60s, before Ben was born, I led the rest of our family up the Catskills' highest peak, 4,180-ft. Slide Mtn. During that innocent age, the state's old Conservation Department had installed an outhouse on the summit. When son Jim opened the door, he found himself staring into the beady eyes of a porcupine.

These animals generally eat bark and twigs, but they like to top it off with the salt found in objects handled by humans, including not only signs but canoe paddles, axe handles and the like. And, they go to unusual lengths to get them. As one can plainly see. Or smell. Or hear. A hiker reported he was awakened one night on an Adirondack mountaintop by the "horrendous grating noise" of a porcupine gnawing on the paint of a nearby steel fire tower.

Some references say that in a pinch you can eat porcupine flesh. However, the World Book Encyclopedia *warns, "Most persons do not consider it tasty." Robert Marshall, one of the trio who first climbed the 46 Adirondack high peaks, refuted that notion. As Alton P. Dieffenbach reported in the ADK's* Adirondac *magazine, Marshall secured this recipe from an Alaskan Koyukuk Indian:*

> *"Place the porcupine and a rock in boiling water. Cook until you can shove a fork into the rock. Then throw out the porcupine and eat the rock."*

The left fork at the junction is a cutoff trail that leads a little more than a quarter mile to the Range trail, where the trail then dips to the notch between the two Wolfjaws. The right fork also joins the Range trail in short order, heading up the sharp, western ridge which leads to Lower Wolfjaw's summit.

The final climb, while only a bit more than a half mile, seems to go straight up.

Journal entry: Sunday, June 7, 1970. I'm winded, and not buoyed by the mountain air, which is heavy and humid. But now there is an added burden — a throbbing pain in my left knee, a king-sized Charlie Horse.

I favor it as I strain to keep up with Jim, but the wet slope is very steep and exhausting. It's also been four hours since we left the Ausable Club.

Jim is exuberant and plunges ahead. At first, he waits for me to catch up. Then, impatiently, he dashes off and disappears in the milky white that shrouds the peak. Conifers stab through the fog; the black flies seem maddened by the prospect of the wounded: me.

But it's amazing what a short rest can do for a wheezing mortal. I struggle up a scraggly ridge and glory in seeing Jim on a rock ledge. His mouth is agape as he watches the scattered clouds reluctantly share their views while they scurry on to some urgent rendezvous.

Jim and I are ravenous, so we break out lunch. We start to eat...and so do swarms of black flies. I've read that newly-hatched flies are the favorite food of trout, and this is the height of the fishing season. But there is something wrong with this picture. These flies are not on the streams below; they are here, and they are feasting on us.

We cover our sandwiches, swab on a new insect repellent, and tighten our pantlegs. The new lotion is effective. But the problem is that the flies have to come close to find out they don't like it. We eat very carefully.

We note there is no benchmark on Lower Wolfjaw. I'm not surprised — there has never been a consensus on just how to spell it.

Mapmakers have been ambivalent about the mountain's name for years. Some of the old maps used two words — Wolf Jaw. The old USGS topo map lumped the upper and lower peaks together, overprinting them as the Wolf Jaws. A later Marcy quadrangle calls each the Wolfjaw.

Either way, the term was applied by an artist who was composing a landscape on nearby Noonmark Mtn. during the 1860s. The two major humps in that segment of the Great Range, he concluded, looked just like the jaws of a wolf. Hence the name.

Journal entry: Saturday, April 24, 1982. Ben and I have just climbed Noonmark to check out the painter's view of the Wolfjaws. We confirm what I had suspected: it's a bit of a stretch to visualize a wolf's jaws in either one or both of the peaks. In fact, you gain a much better perspective of Lower Wolfjaw on the other side of the Great Range, from the first Brother on the way to Big Slide.

I imagine the artist was just one more romantic from the last century. Like Wordsworth, maybe, wandering "lonely as a cloud."

Romanticism is hard to come by on Noonmark today. Even though it's early spring, Ben and I are up to our knees in snow. A snowshoe rabbit, still in winter white, cocks a long, quizzical ear at us before bounding away on outsized feet.

On a good day, there are fine views from Lower Wolfjaw even though it is at the tail end of the Great Range. One of the best is the panorama to the west over the Great Range leading to Marcy. Other peaks in sight from the summit and from the trails on the approaches include Noonmark, Giant, the Nippletop range, Big Slide, and the Dix range. Robert Marshall considered the latter, "one of the great individual views of the Adirondacks."

Journal entry: Sunday, June 7, 1970. Since we've made it this far, Jim and I decide to head to the northeast and make a great circle by descending via the W. A. White trail. White was an early leader of the

From Lower Wolfjaw, Great Range climbs toward Upper Wolfjaw and Armstrong to Gothics, far left, then Basin, right center, and Marcy, right rear. Haystack is at center rear.

Ausable Club who designed not only this trail but the portion of the Great Range trail from Gothics to Haystack. His hiking credentials are legendary: He was still climbing Marcy when he was 80 years old.

I decide not to tell Jim about my sore leg, but do suggest we take it easy. The map is encouraging: it indicates we will swing around an easy arc on the descent.

Wrong. The trail seems to go straight down and is very slick; the only safe descent is to hold on to protruding roots. After an unexpected col, the trail moves up steeply to another summit, the "Wolf's Chin," then moderates briefly.

One would hope that on occasion the trail designer would ease the way with tricks of the trade — switchbacks, detours, lazy loops, and so on. Not Mr. White. His course for the descent looks like the product of linear logic: a straight line.

The trail leads down a long, steep, mile and a half to the turnoff near Hedgehog Mtn., then another mile to a lookout with a lordly view of Keene Valley and the surrounding peaks. It then veers past a turnoff to Snow Mtn., and moderates in grade at the Maghee Clearing. This was a garden plot, known as a "Follow," owned by one of the founders of the Ausable Club. Less than a mile will bring us to the West River trail near the clubhouse.

It seems an eternity, but I finally limp into the parking lot and throw my gear into the car. In the distance, we hear the loud cry of a hawk. It could be one of the graceful birds we saw today, soaring high above the summit of Lower Wolfjaw, free and full of life.

For me, this day has added a new dimension. I've been winded and tired on other hikes, but today I'm so stiff and sore I can hardly walk. Am I coming unglued? How can I hope to keep up with a 13-year old in exploring 34 other high peaks, most of them more difficult than this one?

Jim breaks my train of thought: "Dad, we're alone." I look around and see nothing but buildings and grounds. There is no one in sight, and again no barking dog. Whereas I seemed to glimpse a gracious past in the eerie quiet this morning, the reality of the empty clubhouse answers my question now with startling clarity.

Of course, I'll be back, regardless of aches and pains. Where else can you find such solitude? Certainly not in our teeming cities, nor at the office and, with a growing family, only rarely at home.

The Adirondack high peaks are the perfect place to get away from it all — discounting the flies — as Jim and I did today for seven hours, and to cover so much ground both in hiking kinship and in our thoughts.

Journal entry: Saturday, July 7, 1979. What a difference a month makes. The Ausable Club, stark and ghostly when we were last here during its 10-month period of hibernation, has come to life.

The people milling around pay no attention to Ben and me, except for a cheerful young father who smiles as he and his wife round up their brood, and a florid-faced gentleman plopped in a deck chair on the porch of the clubhouse, puffing away at his cigar. I gather from the approving glance of the older gentleman that he has concluded, too late, the area offers enticements other than the sedentary arts.

We decide to reverse the course Jim and I took, and ascend Lower Wolfjaw by the W. A. White trail. The initial section is still a visual feast — gradual, restful and inviting. Then the trail leads toward the same tedious procession of summits; each promises to be one of the wolf's jaws, but disappoints because it is not.

As if to provide consolation, a tiny wren at the Hedgehog junction cocks its tail at us, then splatters a song in harmony with the jagged tree tops. We think of the wren as a domestic bird; it's surprising therefore to welcome the "winter" variety at 3,300 feet.

Finally, on the mountain's northern summit, we meet the first of various club members who have ventured from the porch to make the

Big Slide *offers a head-on view of its scars from the north. Lower Wolfjaw's summit also rewards the hiker with premier views of Giant and the Nippletop and Dix ranges.*

climb in the other direction. The cheerful young father we saw below smiles at us. But not his wife; she sprawls at trailside, almost prone, breathing hard. Their two sons, about Ben's age at 11, stand bright-eyed and expectant near their grandfather. He gestures expansively at the main summit, a much larger, green hump which looms beyond the deep chasm they have just traversed.

On the precipitous trail leading down from the top of Lower Wolfjaw, we say hello to a friendly lady on her way up. She is the picture of hiking vitality, and tells us she has made the climb from the club before. "I hope to get a good nap on top," she says, smiling. From previous experience she should know better: it's lunch time up there, and the black flies are famished, as usual.

There are no bears this time at the Wedge Brook trail junction. But we are greeted by a couple who have stopped there for a break. He is fifty-ish and gung-ho. Jogging shorts serve as a planter for the vigorous crop of gray hair on his chest; huge hiking boots complete his outfit. She is dressed down in quiet T-shirt and slacks, and is obviously content to follow her leader.

"We're staying at the club for the summer," he says. They have just come off Upper Wolfjaw and he points in the direction from which we have come: "We'll finish up with the little one." Hmm. He does not say, and we do not ask, why they detoured down here instead of going directly across the notch between the two Wolfjaws.

Ben has long since finished his water and is very thirsty. We stop at a broad expanse of the slide on Wedge Brook and fill our canteens. But our water purification tablets turn the water a murky brown. They must have gone bad, so we do not drink.

For a change, we cross the Ausable River at the base of Lower Wolfjaw and begin the last mile to the clubhouse on the road from Lower Ausable Lake. Suddenly, Ben grabs my arm and whispers: "A deer."

Sure enough, a mature doe browses on tender tree shoots a few yards from the edge of the road. We

Grazing doe *ignores hikers. It has learned that hunting is forbidden in the Adirondack Mountain Reserve.*

freeze, expecting any minute that the normally shy creature will flag its departure with white, uplifted tail. But the doe is unperturbed, noting our passing with only an occasional quiver of its tail along with a soulful look from liquid eyes.

We suddenly realize why there is so much wildlife in the area. The Adirondack Mountain Reserve has been closed for so long to hunting and even to some fishing by members that most have lost their fear of humans. They have not had to worry about guns and fishhooks for decades.

The Ausable Club area has been transformed for a Saturday night ritual. The dimming of multiple light globes in the clubhouse dining room sends the signal to members in surrounding cottages that dinner is served. But on screened porches of nearby dwellings, the muffled murmurs coming from ladies in long evening gowns and gentlemen in formal jackets do not abate, indicating that dinner will have to wait a bit.

On the golf course, a baby sitter delights at the gentle gamboling of her young charges. Nearby, an elegantly coiffured woman strides purposefully across a picture-perfect green toward one of the porch parties. She could be transported bodily to Fifth Avenue in New York City, and would feel no need to change a thing.

On the roadway leading to the hikers' lower parking lot, we pass three boys and a girl, all about Ben's age, chatting in the exuberant language of youth. The girl is dressed in a modish Mother Hubbard — good idea in this land of bugs, although that may not have been the intent. The boys are resplendent in blazers and regimental ties. Before long, you can bet, they will dress down. Way down.

Ben is more interested in slaking his thirst than in dining. So we backtrack to Keene Valley for our own kind of social hour, and enjoy cold cans of pop on a bench at the deserted gas station. Happily, it has an outdoor vending machine.

We then head south for a late dinner in the cavernous cafeteria* at Frontier Town. Only two other diners are there, which equates to fewer patrons than providers.

I have often wondered if the girl behind the counter, who has taken our order so many times, will ever recognize that we are de facto members of this club. This time, she provides the right answer: a faint smile.

How nice it is to have a "home" in the high peaks.

---

* *Prior to its conversion to a McDonald's restaurant.*

Sawteeth from the Ausable Club.

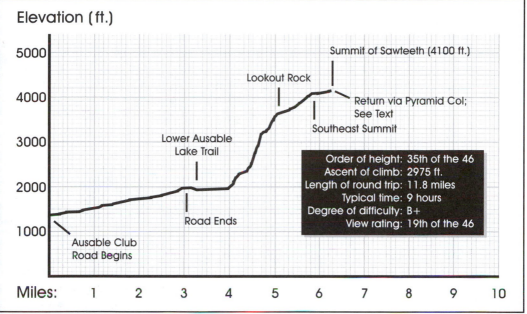

Elevation (ft.)

5000

4000 — Summit of Sawteeth (4100 ft.)

Lookout Rock

4000

Return via Pyramid Col;
See Text

Southeast Summit

3000

Lower Ausable
Lake Trail

Order of height: 35th of the 46
Ascent of climb: 2975 ft.
Length of round trip: 11.8 miles
Typical time: 9 hours
Degree of difficulty: B+
View rating: 19th of the 46

2000

Road Ends

1000

Ausable Club
Road Begins

Miles: 1   2   3   4   5   6   7   8   9   10

For contour trails, see U.S. Geological Survey map, pgs. 120-121.

13.
SAWTEETH

The first Adirondack high peak to cry for attention from the driveway circling the front of the Ausable Club is Giant. It blots out a good portion of the sky to the east.

Yet on turning toward the clubhouse, one immediately sees in the southwest the jagged profile of another peak, about twice as far away. It looks lonely out there, and the map confirms why: the peak is divorced from its neighbors in the Great Range by a deep valley, and perches precariously close to Lower Ausable Lake, across from Colvin and Blake.

Early Geological Survey maps labelled the mountain Sawtooth. But a glance at the stairstep slopes and sharp notches in its silhouette is proof that it has to be plural.

Serious climbing on Sawteeth does not begin until the hiker has gained a gradual rise in elevation of 700 feet by following the road which leads from the Ausable Club to Lower Ausable Lake. One drawback is that the lake is three and one half miles from the clubhouse.

Journal entry: Saturday, August 1, 1970. *The challenge of this isolated little peak has long bothered me. It's tucked away in a place that almost dictates you tackle it alone.*

Now Jim and I discover that the Ausable Club has a small bus which makes nine round trips a day from the clubhouse to the lower lake, in season. If there's room after club members board, outsiders can go along at 50 cents for adults and 25 cents for children.

A bus in the wilderness! I'm sure Adirondack Mountain Club purists would howl, but for us it's the answer to the dilemma of Sawteeth. Off to the bus stop!

No one else was here on our last visit in early June. Today, it seems that everyone is and they're all waiting for the bus. Jim and I enter the lobby of the clubhouse to purchase our tickets. I pocket a club folder from the counter.

A nattily dressed young man behind the massive, cluttered, front desk would look out of place anywhere but here at his assigned post. He stands next to a large, wall-mounted key rack, busily sorting mail into Victorian pigeonholes. The buzz of an ancient, plug-in phone system summons him to the opposite wall.

With our tickets, we turn and pick our way through the bulbous easy chairs and couches scattered about the main lobby. Through an archway to the left, tiers of dining tables dot a long hall, their starchy, white covers doing their best to cheer up the dark interior. A few gray heads bob over their plates at the tables.

There is no one else in the lobby, not even before the inviting fireplace which sprawls to the left of the screened front door.

I suppose it is the lack of people that reminds me why this rustic old remnant was put here in the first place. It was not for Jim or me, nor really for the people staying here today. Rather, it was for the philanthropists and philosophers, and for the painters and writers who flocked to the Adirondacks in the last century and early in this one to savor the solitude of the woods.

The Ausable Club was host to Woodrow Wilson before he moved from the presidency of Princeton University to that of the United States; to the pioneering aviator, Charles Lindbergh; to philosophers such as William James and Felix Adler; and to one of the presidents of Harvard University, James Conant.

Dr. Conant may have been enticed by summer visitors at nearby Putnam Camp. As Laura and Guy Waterman noted when they chronicled it in Forest and Crag, *"some sixty-nine Putnams had received degrees from Harvard."*

Many surely walked on these same boards. Other visitors trod carbon copies at Paul Smiths on St. Regis Lake, at the Prospect House on Blue Mountain Lake, and at other great Adirondack way stations of the past.

As Jim and I move outside, I am reminded of a comment made by Newell Martin, a spirited climber who graduated from surmounting the steeples and towers at Yale University to make the first recorded ascent of Sawteeth in 1875. He reminisced in 1931 that, "The philosophers are gone. The only important animals that now infest the wilderness are plutocrats."

Well, that was more than 60 years ago. Mingling today with the nondescript crew boarding our bus, one would be hard put to sort out the plutocrats from the pensioners.

There are backpackers old and young, an expectant angler with a smile as radiant as that of his pregnant wife, a swarm of excited children and, in the midst, their resigned but resolute parents.

Those who plan to explore the valley and the Ausable lakes, or the high peaks surrounding them, will find recurring references in guidebooks to the "Gate." It is, in fact, a wooden, swinging barrier controlled by a club gatekeeper who regulates traffic from the clubhouse to outlying territory of the Adirondack Mountain Reserve.

At first, the bus heads toward the southwest along a hardpacked, gravel road paralleling the gentle curves of the East Branch of the Ausable. In about a mile, it crosses a plank bridge over Gill Brook, one of the river's feeder streams, then snakes a torturous route up the steep, densely wooded valley.

At various junctions, the bus lurches to a stop to debark passengers. Trail signs beckon through the windows: Lower Wolfjaw. Upper Wolfjaw. Armstrong. Gothics.

Journal entry: Saturday, August 1, 1970. At the crest of the last high rise on the road, Jim and I note a sign on the right that points to our destination: "Sawteeth." But it is too late to get off. The bus grinds slowly down to a boathouse perched on the shore of Lower Ausable Lake. It will be only a short walk back, and we are glad to have a closer look at this beautiful lake.

From the boathouse, the lower Ausable stretches to the southwest in the shape of a long, skinny balloon between steeply wooded slopes on either side. Rock cliffs notch the greenery in random order. At the far end, there is a mile-long "carry" leading from the south end of Lower Ausable Lake to a Warden's Camp at the north end of Upper Ausable Lake.

As the bus sputters back on its return trip, the dozen or so end-of-the-liners scatter from the boathouse. Many launch their canoes and stab away at the waters that become increasingly choppy down the lake.

Some of the canoers, according to the club's centennial book, likely will head for a productive fishing hole near the mouth of a cave along the eastern shore. It's the entrance to a deep cavity formed years ago by a rockslide from Mt. Colvin. The jumbled boulders act like an old-style icebox in preserving the snows of past winters.

During the summer, this yields a double benefit to fishermen who come to try their luck at the cave's entrance: they're refreshed by cool breezes from the interior, and they're exhilarated by trout drawn to the site by the noticeably cooler water.

But hikers should not cast thoughts of this kind. The lake is open only to members, and only for fly fishing at the site.

The trail to Sawteeth skirting the northwestern side of the lower lake, however, offers attractions of its own; the ADK guidebook calls it the scenic trail. An alternate route to Sawteeth branches south from the trail to Gothics, about a mile and three quarters up from the dam.

The first half mile of the lakeshore trail provides good close-up views of Colvin and Blake, the two high peaks in the Colvin Range across the lake. The trail then leads up a series of gigantic, stone stairsteps which form the teeth of the mountain. Fortunately, from time to time the stairsteps come to landings — overlooks which offer breathtaking views of Lower Ausable Lake.

> ***Journal entry: Sunday, July 16, 1978.*** *"Is that where the pluto-crats used to go?" asks Ben, as he strains to see if he can spot Upper Ausable Lake. This is my second climb of Sawteeth, and I have guided Ben to the first good overlook, 250 feet above the lower lake.*
>
> *That was one of their favorite spots, I tell him. But I also suggest he stop searching for Upper Ausable Lake. We're not high enough to see much over the dense woods shrouding the "carry." And, even if our view to the south were clear, we would not see the upper lake today. Low, grayish-white clouds are moving in.*

Upper Ausable Lake was a favorite base camp for local Adirondack guides in the latter half of the past century. In fact, many of them built lean-tos and cabins there at the urging of the owner, a lumber company, which in turn expected them to protect its property.

Best known of the guides was Old Mountain Phelps, whose homestead was in Keene Valley. He was concerned with guarding more than just his cabin at the upper lake, one of the first to be located there.

Adirondack writer Charles Dudley Warner recalls that when Phelps guided him and his companions to the area, they asked the guide to build a shelter on the south side of the lake, since it offered the best view — including "that loveliest of mountain contours," Gothics.

But according to Warner, Phelps would have none of it. He favored the north side, which was in fact a fine camping site but had no special view. Phelps voiced his reason, which revealed a deep, sentimental attachment to the high peaks: "Waal, now, them Gothics ain't the kinder scenery you want ter *hog down*!"

Lower Ausable Lake *looks inviting even in murky weather. Boathouse is to left of swimming float, behind point of land. Scenic trail begins along right shore toward southwest.*

First overlook, *a mile along the trail, offers lordly view of Lower Ausable Lake. Steep flanks of Colvin-Pinnacle Ridge, left, diminish as the climb progresses.*

When the area was later purchased to form a part of the Adirondack Mountain Reserve, its founders and early members began to move in on Upper Ausable Lake, eventually owning and enhancing the campsites. Few of them fit the dictionary definition of plutocrats: "Members of a governing, wealthy class." One exception: a visitor early in this century, Theodore Roosevelt.

Nor did most other visitors in those days fit the definition. Among those who stayed at Upper Ausable Lake were such political innocents as Mark Twain and the renowned naturalist, John Burroughs.

One camp owner brought his family most summers to the isolated lake site, but saw no reason to deprive them of the pleasant style of living to which they had become accustomed. So, as Edith Pilcher reported in her book, *Up the Lake Road*, they brought along "a railroad chef (from their private railroad car) and maids and servants from their New York City residence. The camp received daily deliveries of fruits and vegetables from their farm on Long Island, via relays of employees who picked and packed them, and transported them by train, boat, carriage, buckboard, packbasket, and guide boat."

The Upper Ausable Lake area is closed to the public, with the exception of certain trails which provide access to the high peaks. Therefore, hikers passing through are rarely aware of camp activities.

The major reason, one would suspect, is that club members with camps on Upper Ausable Lake today do what most people do who have camps in the Adirondacks — they quietly relish their own special piece of the wilderness.

Journal entry: Saturday, August 1, 1970. The trail from the first lookout heads west and begins climbing Sawteeth in earnest.

Our view of the clouds has been objective; now it's personal. They are with us and around us. They are wet and so are we, as the rain begins to pelt us with force. It's warm, and friction from the wet straps of our packs is a constant reminder that the grade up Sawteeth is very steep.

The trail whipsaws back and forth as we pass a vertical rock face on the right, followed by another, and then a third, with a ladder which provides a boost at one deep gully. Obviously, these are the formations which from a distance give the mountain its name.

Journal entry: Monday, July 5, 1982. This is my third trip up Sawteeth, and the rock ledges always promote the same image: they would make a great home for snakes.

Yet the only one I've ever seen in the Adirondacks was a little garter snake which slithered off the trail on Buck Mountain on the eastern side of Lake George some 20 years ago. I know there are rattlesnakes on the other side of Lake George on Tongue Mtn. And Barney Fowler, the late Adirondack raconteur, affirmed in Volume Two of his Adirondack Album *that six years ago, a fisherman rock-hopping the south fork of the Boquet River where it crosses under Rt. 73 was bitten by a four-foot long timber rattlesnake.*

Journal entry, Saturday, August 1, 1970. *Another rock face has a sheltered overhang, so Jim and I stop to try on our new, hooded rain jackets. They were made in the Far East and are cheap. Less than a hundred yards beyond we find out why — the plastic material traps humid air, which acts as a suffocating blanket.*

Mixed emotions: we're unhappy the new material tears easily as we scrape past tree branches. But we're relieved to get air circulating on the inside.

Teeth of the saw. *Climbers must surmount four major rock ledges which give Sawteeth its name. A shaky log ladder helps at one deep gully.*

At slightly less than two miles from the boathouse, a side trail leads to Lookout Rock. In good weather, it offers a remarkable view of Lower Ausable Lake, 1,300 ft. below, plus other high peaks from Giant and Rocky Peak Ridge to those in the Colvin and Nippletop ranges.

The main trail then crosses a low ridge and ascends moderately through a conifer forest. Shortly, it confronts a col and a series of cliffs on the right, where the climbing seems to become almost vertical.

Journal entry: Saturday, August 1, 1970. *The faint thunder which we have been hearing in the distance has escalated into thunderclaps. The only shelter comes from the taller trees, but they seem too much like gigantic lightning rods to suit me. Jim and I splash through the trail rivulets at top speed. Soon we are exhausted. It is the moment of truth.*

I've often wondered how anyone really knows if you've climbed an Adirondack high peak, except for a trailless one where you leave proof by signing the summit register. Today it's tempting to head home and say we did it anyway.

"Jim," I say, "the guidebook says there are two summits on this mountain. I'm all tuckered out, so we're going to do the first and then float back to the car. If it doesn't count, that's too bad."

Jim looks as if he doesn't believe me, but grins happily. He's the one who usually grouses all the way to the summit while I wheedle him onward. The tables are turned, and he likes it.

We skirt a few more crags and with the help of another shaky ladder find the going easier. Suddenly, the trail slants sharply downward. The dense woods and fast-moving clouds blur our view, but there can be no mistake: we are on the southeastern summit.

Jim is ready to go back, but for me a nagging question tugs at my thoughts. The real summit should be less than a half mile ahead, and the col before us can be no more than 150 feet down. Why turn back now?

I confess to Jim that I want to correct a decision made under duress, and suggest that we go on. He throws me a look of betrayed honor, mutters something unintelligible (which is actually intelligent in the presence of his father), and stomps into the col.

He has no interest in my last bit of intelligence about Sawteeth: the col we are heading into is the so-called "Rifle Notch." That's the most pronounced of the serrations one sees from the Ausable Club.

The descent is muddy but easy and, except for a short steep pitch coming out of it, we move easily. Jim is like a juggernaut; his mission now is to get it over with. Head down, he marches ahead and soon disappears. In a few minutes, I hear his shout: "We're out of it. Boy!"

At the real, northwest summit, I can't help but say, "Boy!" too. The words might be different, but I'm sure Moses voiced something like that when he found he could roll back the waters of the Red Sea to let the Israelites flee from the pursuing Egyptians.

Beyond the small, open rock table that nestles in the summit foliage, the oppressive cloud covering has been miraculously rolled back. Only wispy remnants race by to catch up with the receding main body.

Marcy and its lofty neighbors sparkle in the welcome sunlight to the west. The good soldiers of the Great Range line up at attention toward the northeast all the way to Upper Wolfjaw, which has not yet emerged from the retreating cloud cover.

Directly before us is Gothics; it presents a different face than we have seen before. Its slashing slides are partially hidden by another mountain

Top of Sawteeth*. When the rain stops and the sun breaks through, hikers feel as if they are floating on clouds in the midst of the high peaks. Saddleback Mtn. is on the left, Gothics at right.*

nearly as high. This has to be a 4,000-plus footer, but I don't recall one there. The topographic map provides the answer: it's a spur of Gothics with a deep col separating it from the main summit.

The guidebook identifies the spur as Pyramid, and its shape confirms it. It's another loser — a couple of million more years of glacial action on the col, or a slightly different set of rules by the Adirondack Forty Sixers, and this one would have made it on its own.

After lunch, Jim and I loll on the ledge. He plots the peaks against the map while I segue into my favorite summit pastime — musing about mountains.

Our family has just returned from a three-week tour of Colorado. The spectacular peaks there are overwhelming — Long's Peak, Mt. Evans, the San Juan Mountains, the Sangre de Cristo Range, Pike's Peak, etc. The list seems endless.

The 30-plus mountains in Colorado which are 14,000 feet or higher make a comparison with the Adirondacks seem irrelevant. But it's not. That inveterate Adirondack enthusiast, Trudy Healy, who's conquered mountains in various parts of the world, had it right when she wrote in Adirondack Life *earlier this summer: "The satisfaction of climbing a mountain is not relative to its elevation."*

*"**The most beautiful** single view in the Adirondacks" is hiking pioneer Robert Marshall's verdict on Sawteeth. Foremost is Gothics, center; Pyramid Peak, a southern spur of Gothic, is at right.*

***Journal entry: Thursday, August 8, 1991.** The longer I climb, the more I think Trudy Healy must have meant you can be satisfied if you just make it to the top of an Adirondack high peak.*

Ten years ago, when Ben and I were near the cobble on Algonquin on our way to Wright, we stopped to chat with two different hiking couples who had climbed a great deal in Colorado. Both said the same: hiking the Adirondacks is much more difficult than the mountains in Colorado, even the more than 100 peaks which range above 11,000 feet. Their climb up Algonquin, they said, was steeper than anything they had encountered.

Ken Nicolai of Ft. Collins, Colorado, confirms that verdict in the current issue of the Forty Sixers periodical: "Mountaineering out West is quite a bit different than the Adirondacks. In many ways, it's probably easier climbing here than in the high peaks. The problem is they don't put much air in the air."

The latest U.S. Geological Survey hasn't helped make the climb up Sawteeth any easier. Between my first hike in 1970 and my climb in 1982, the topo map was changed to show that the peak had gained 40 feet in height.

The half-mile descent to the col between Sawteeth and Pyramid is steep but easy. From there, the trail from Gothics traces a long, sloping mile and a half to the boathouse on Lower Ausable Lake.

Shortly before reaching the lake, the rush of water on the left advertises Rainbow Falls, which even in midsummer dry periods spills shimmering sheets to a pool 150 feet below. The flow begins over an overhanging rock so that on occasion the space behind creates a prism of colors in the morning sunlight; hence the name.

In August 1993, a hiker was tempted to climb the falls from the base, but slipped halfway up and fell to his death. He had grabbed a rock which dislodged and fell on him. Side trails off the main route to Gothics offer safe access at both the base and the top of the falls.

Journal entry: Saturday, August 1, 1970. Jim and I find at the boathouse that we have just missed the 3:15 p.m. bus; the next one isn't due until a quarter after five. We toy with the idea of walking back the three miles but since the brightening day has improved the prospect of the lake, we decide to lounge and look.

Rainbow Falls shoots shimmering sprays 150 feet into narrow gorge, a quarter of a mile from the lake road near the boathouse. Trail to Gothics via Pyramid Peak passes a short distance nearby on the south.

The scene is idyllic. On the porch of the boathouse, two young couples chat quietly; they keep an eye on the happy cherubs who splash in the clear, emerald waters just beyond their sand castles on shore. A few yards out, a balding, mustachioed gent with a protruding midsection floats on his back like a walrus who glories in wallowing.

Two college-age attendants chat at graceful ease on the sloping ramp of the canoe shelter. Every so often, they shield their eyes to peer past the glint of the wavetops to check the progress of approaching canoes. As they come closer, we see that they are not shaped like ordinary canoes. Instead of the conventional rounding at front and rear, these have knife edges which arch sharply inward toward the occupants. Adirondack guideboats!

The guideboat is unique to the Adirondacks — "a canoe built like a boat." It was developed by guides who often had to portage a boat along with equipment over a considerable distance between lakes — over the "carry" between the lower and upper Ausable lakes, for example. At the same time, the boats had to be sturdy enough to provide a stable ride in rough Adirondack waters.

In the final, refined design, a 16 footer could weigh 75 pounds or less. A nine-foot specimen in the Adirondack Museum at Blue Mountain Lake, called the *Sairy Gamp*, weighed in at a hard-to-believe 10 and a half pounds.

The guideboats at Lower Ausable Lake — glistening in the reflection of the water and stacked inside the boathouse — are truly handsome. The side planking of most is pine or cedar, about three-tenths of an inch thick, and laid flush, not overlapping. Brass screws and copper tacks fasten them together. Thousands of them gleam through the clear varnish.

Journal entry: Saturday, August 1, 1970. This area would be great for summer vacations. So to kill time while waiting at the lower lake for the bus, I thumb through the brochure I picked up this morning to compare the cost of the club with that of an area motel.

It's a bit more expensive.

First of all, there are initiation fees and annual dues. Our family of six would need a suite, so that would add a substantial charge for room and meals each day, plus a 15 per cent service charge. Then there are greens fees for golf, per-day boat rental fees on the lower lake, slightly more for the upper lake, and so on.

I do like the basic intent of the A.M.R. as stated in the brochure: it recognizes the priceless quality of this wilderness tract, and intends to protect it. Yet I keep coming back to one sentence in the brochure: "The numerous trails maintained on the Reserve have always been freely open to public hikers, subject only to the restrictions against camping, hunting, fishing and entry during periods of exceptional fire hazard."

That does it. I think I'll pass on membership. Our sights are not set on the facilities, but on the mountains.

Journal entry: Sunday, July 16, 1978. Last month, the Adirondack Mountain Reserve completed the sale of 9,100 acres of its property to New York State. As part of the deal, hikers no longer can park at the clubhouse but now must start from the lot across Rt. 73 from the Roaring Brook trail to Giant. That adds a mile for each round trip when hiking past the clubhouse.

There's no accounting for the way people price land. In addition to its purchase from the A.M.R., the state is in the process of buying another 660 acres, including six miles of undeveloped shoreland on Tupper Lake, for $845,000. That works out to $1,280 per acre, compared to $85 per acre for the A.M.R. land.

The rationale for the price differential, according to the state's Department of Environmental Conservation, is that the Tupper Lake property includes "developable lake shore frontage compared to the relatively inaccessible land in the high peaks."

That means that the frontage on only one of some 2,000 lakes in the Adirondacks is valued at almost 15 times that of the A.M.R.'s wilderness property, which includes 11 of the Adirondack high peaks. And there are only 46 of them.

Incredible.

The club must have tried to soften the financial hit because it's jacked up the rates for the bus. One-way tickets are now a dollar for adults and 50 cents for children under 12. That's double what it was for Jim and me eight years ago.

Journal entry: Friday, August 22, 1986. *More problems? Bus tickets have ballooned again, to two dollars for adults and a dollar and a half for kids.*

We're tempted to walk.

Journal entry: Thursday, July 28, 1994. *According to the ADK's Adirondac magazine, the Ausable Club has "reluctantly decided to discontinue public use of the Lake Road bus as of the 1995 season," because of increasing use.*

I suppose the hiking missionaries will applaud. But I thought it was a lot of fun while it lasted.

Adirondack guideboat *docks at Lower Ausable Lake boathouse. Guides developed the handsome craft — "a canoe built like a boat" — for easier "carries" between lakes.*

Left to right: Gothics, Armstrong Mtn. and Upper Wolfjaw Mtn., from Nippletop.

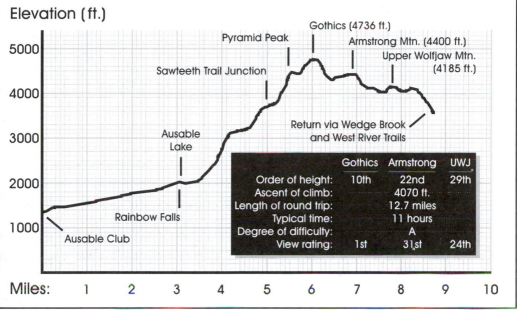

Elevation (ft.)

Gothics (4736 ft.)
Pyramid Peak
Armstrong Mtn. (4400 ft.)
Sawteeth Trail Junction
Upper Wolfjaw Mtn. (4185 ft.)
Ausable Lake
Return via Wedge Brook and West River Trails
Rainbow Falls
Ausable Club

	Gothics	Armstrong	UWJ
Order of height:	10th	22nd	29th
Ascent of climb:		4070 ft.	
Length of round trip:		12.7 miles	
Typical time:		11 hours	
Degree of difficulty:		A	
View rating:	1st	31st	24th

Miles: 1 2 3 4 5 6 7 8 9 10

or contour trails, see U.S. Geological Survey map, pgs. 120-121.

14, 15, 16.
GOTHICS, ARMSTRONG, UPPER WOLFJAW

Journal entry: Wednesday, July 15, 1981. The Adirondack Park Agency begins a three-day session today at Elk Lake Lodge, where son Ben and his mother and I are staying. I'm tempted to skip hiking and catch up on the doings of the A.P.A.

What interests me most are the two Adirondack writers who are supposed to attend: Anne LaBastille and Barbara McMartin.

I have just finished reading LaBastille's first book, Woodswoman, *published in 1976. She described how she came to the Adirondacks as a young waitress at a summer lodge, fell in love with the region, and constructed a log cabin in a remote area where she lives year-round. She was appointed a commissioner of the A.P.A. in 1975.*

I don't know much about McMartin except that bookstores feature her Adirondack trail guides, none of which I've yet read. The biog in her books indicates she's a consultant for the A.P.A.

Any friend of the Adirondacks is a friend of mine.

My first order of business today, however, is to fulfill a promise to Ben to do the triple crown of hiking in the Adirondack Great Range — Gothics, Armstrong and Upper Wolfjaw. He's been begging me to repeat the hike I made with son Jim back in 1970.

I think it's just as well that Ben and I steer clear of the A.P.A. anyway. I don't know much about the organization, but my impression is that it's a bunch of outsiders coming in to tell the locals what to do. That may not be accurate, but I sometimes feel that all outsiders who come to the high peaks are intruders — not just A.P.A. members, but us, too.

At the Ausable Club Ben and I join five people on the bus for the ride to Lower Ausable Lake. One asks where I got my hiking pants with the extra pockets on the outside in front. From Ben, I tell him. They're "hand-me-ups"; Ben ordered them, but they were too big so I took them over.

A short distance beyond the Gate, the driver jolts to a stop when a pick-up truck from the club meets and passes us on its way back to the main buildings. A young passenger in the bus comments to our driver: "I've never seen that man in the truck smile. He seems to be carrying the weight of the world with him."

The bus driver, who has been jovial up until now, turns solemn: "You'd understand if you lived here year-round."

Both locals, no doubt, who know that living in the Adirondacks can be hard. The club functions full-time only in July and August, so employees need other income. But the seasonal vagaries of fishing, hunting and winter sports do not guarantee steady work.

It was ever thus, in the words of Ralph Waldo Emerson. In 1872 he urged naturalist John Muir to leave the wilds of Yosemite and live in Massachusetts. "Solitude is a sublime mistress," he warned, "but an intolerable wife."

Gothics, according to Verplanck Colvin, who surveyed most of the high peaks in a state of pristine wilderness, is "the wildest and most rugged of the Adirondacks."

Not any more. It's been tamed by trails from all directions: from the north via Johns Brook Valley; from the south via two trails from the Ausable Valley; and from the east and west via segments of the Great Range trail. Gothics is formidable from any vantage point.

Journal entry: Saturday, August 29, 1970. *Son Jim and I are off to try Gothics and, if we feel up to it, maybe a couple more of the big ones in the Great Range. Jim is 13, that wonderful age when boys are ebullient by nature, optimistic in outlook, and resilient in distress: the perfect hiking partner.*

At Lower Ausable Lake, we are joined by two others from the bus for the initial leg of the trail from the lake toward Gothics. One is Fred

Fraser, State Editor of the Schenectady Gazette, *who's written various articles about the high peaks. The other is Dick MacAdams, a former Schenectady resident from Pennsylvania who's visiting Fraser. At the first junction, they will head south for Sawteeth.*

They exchange pleasantries about the merits of hiking gear: L. L. Bean, Eddie Bauer, R. E. I. and so on are fine outfitters, but outdoor gear from the local Army-Navy store is almost as good, and cheaper. Etc.

MacAdams confirms one of my observations about the high peaks. In the more than 20 years he's climbed the Adirondacks, he's hardly ever seen a snake. Yet on a recent Appalachian Trail outing in Pennsylvania, he says, he almost stepped on an eight-foot-long rattlesnake.

From Lower Ausable Lake, *Gothics, center, looms nearly three miles away and 2,870 feet above. Trail first climbs Pyramid, left.*

I'm glad that was not the kind of snake my wife nearly stepped on when we were climbing in the Catskills in early spring a few years back. The snake was five feet long and lethargic, but that was enough to convince her to stop hiking with me in that area. If it had been a rattlesnake, I doubt if I could have pried her out of the car near any trail, even in the lowlands.

Beyond the cutoff to Sawteeth, the Gothics trail begins at a moderate rise, then slants upward as if it were the slope of a pyramid. But the rewards of reaching the summit of the peak bearing that name are enormous.

Technically, Pyramid is a southern blip of Gothics, which beckons in benign splendor a half mile beyond an intervening col. But because it is plopped in the middle of the high peaks and is some 4,500 feet high in its own right, Pyramid proffers one of the best panoramic views in the Adirondacks.

From Pyramid, *soaring slides on south side of Gothics' western summit look as if they were supports for the outside of a medieval cathedral. Many consider Pyramid to be the best place in the Adirondacks to view the high peaks.*

Behind it to the south is Sawteeth, its sharp indentations now no more than a motley collections of bumps. Beyond it are noble Nippletop and the Dix Mountain range.

Pyramid is the proper place to see Saddleback, which would tempt Paul Bunyan to settle down on its nearby summit. Behind it, the breathtaking big ones line up in random order: Basin, with the neighboring Colvin Range cradling Upper Ausable Lake and Marcy Swamp, and Haystack, Skylight, and Redfield; even the elusive Allen peeks for position. In the background far to the west, various silhouettes strive for attention — with the MacIntyres at the head of the line.

Journal entry: Wednesday, July 15, 1981. Ben and I have just completed the stiff climb to Pyramid which Jim and I made in 1970.

It's too bad Pyramid isn't one of the 46 high peaks. If it were, I'd give it the number one view rating. Gothics, a close neighbor and a bit higher, gets the nod instead. Its only problem is self-imposed. As noted in the Forty Sixers' Of the Summits, of the Forests, "no view (in the Adirondacks) is truly complete unless it includes in its sweep the awe-inspiring Gothics itself."

Ben and I are startled to see two heads pop up from the trail which threads its way through the scrub trees onto Pyramid's summit. They belong to a healthy, happy young couple who second our feelings as they admire the view.

A tiny towhead peers from his father's back, where he is firmly anchored. "Cameron has been asleep most of the way up," says the proud parent. "We won't stay long because he may start to fuss." At the moment the solemn youngster seems content to scan the contours of our faces, never mind the peaks.

They have climbed this far, the father reports, in an hour and a half.

That is astounding. Ben and I have struggled two and a half hours to make it this far. And, the young man's beaming wife is noticeably pregnant.

It makes me feel like a windup toy whose spring has sprung. Oh, well, I make reasonable progress when the climb slacks off. Which leads me to suggest to Ben that we head for Gothics' main summit; it looks like an easy haul past the intervening col.

We are disturbed to find, on topping the main ridge of Gothics, a bivouac of two tents and a large amount of gear suspended from nearby trees. We hope a patrolling ranger will send the campers packing to a proper site below.

A contingent of 20 Boy Scouts has commandeered the broad summit rock. So Ben and I settle for second choice at a spot some 50 feet below. Ben is disappointed since it's his first time here, but he perks up while eating lunch. Gothics is as gorgeous from the bleachers in the end zone as it is from the 50-yard line.

Old Mountain Phelps, the Adirondack guide, not only revered the view of Gothics from Upper Ausable Lake, but for once in his quotable life fell short in trying to put his feelings into words. As Bill Healy relates in *The High Peaks of Essex*, Phelps could only manage to stammer out, "It has so many fantastic features about it that it's impossible to describe."

Superlatives about Gothics are justified. The glories of 30 major mountains are spread before the observer on every side. From Gothics' summit, one can spot eight of the 10 highest Adirondack peaks: Marcy (1), Algonquin (2), Haystack (3), Skylight (4), Whiteface (5), Dix (6), Iroquois (8), and Basin (9).

Marcy breaks the progression because, like a mother hen, it folds the protective, covering wing formed by its southwest shoulder around Gray (7). And, of course, the last on the list is Gothics (10) itself.

Gothics' summit is often crowded on weekends and holidays during the summer. But by climbing on an off-day when the crowds are gone and the frosty breath of fall warns that the conventional hiking season is coming to an end, one can sense the challenge that Colvin and his crew faced when they first climbed Gothics in early October of 1875. In his

From Gothics, *Saddleback, right foreground, and Basin lead to Marcy, center rear. Skylight is at left of Marcy, and Haystack on far left. Trail leads toward west peak of Gothics.*

Seventh Report to the New York Assembly, Colvin supplemented his voluminous data and maps with this narrative:

"Before us an irregular cone of granite, capped with ice and snow, rose against a wintry sky. The dwarf timber crept timidly upward upon it in a few places, not too steep to find a foothold, and on either side the icy slopes leaped at once down into gloomy valleys.

"Beyond, irregularly grouped, the great peaks, grizzly with frost and snow, were gathered in grand magnificence, all strange and new — in wild sublimity. No sound save the shuddering hiss of the chilly blast as it swept over the fearful ridge of ice that must be our pathway."

Colvin, as was his wont, completed the summit survey so late in the day that he and his men were forced to begin their descent after dark. In the process, Colvin almost lost one of his veteran guides. As related in his narrative, "We started along the icy ridges" when the elder guide slipped and, "was suddenly suspended over the edge of a cliff — where, a thousand feet below, the clouds were drifting — and rescued himself by the sheer strength of his muscular arms."

Over the years, trailblazers have helped hikers overcome the hazards of Gothics with ladders and the like. The best known aids are two cables affixed on the trail which leads up the western, exposed, rocky face of Gothics from the col separating it from Saddleback. But even these aids are not always enough.

Upper Ausable Lake shines to the south from Gothics; Boreas Ponds lie beyond, at right. The Colvin-Pinnacle Ridge thrusts in soft outline at left.

During the summer of 1992, according to the ADK's *Adirondac* magazine, a hiker slid 75 feet on the rock face, then spilled over a seven-foot ledge. His partner tried to help him make the descent to Lower Ausable Lake but the injuries sustained were so severe they could only reach the col between Gothics and Pyramid — the same spot traversed by Colvin on his escape route to the upper lake from his survey trip.

The injured hiker's partner realized he would have to descend to get help. But when the rescue party returned, deteriorating weather delayed evacuation by helicopter until the next morning.

Journal entry: Wednesday, July 15, 1981. When son Jim and I were on Gothics a decade ago, we felt a touch of wild kinship with Colvin and company. Over a period of almost 10 hours, we met only three people.

Today, on moving north from Gothics' summit, Ben and I again are alone, leaving the crowd on top. It appears to be no more than a pleasant stroll to reach Armstrong and Upper Wolfjaw. As if to affirm the judgment, Giant beckons with benevolence in the distance.

The descent to the col before Armstrong is no problem. There are some steep pitches downward, but on balance the way is easy, through scrub spruce and balsam.

Armstrong, right, and Upper Wolfjaw, spotted by clouds, appear to be but a pleasant stroll from Gothics. Near-vertical pitches call for caution along the way.

Beyond the col, the trail ascends a little more than 100 feet to Armstrong's heavily-wooded, south summit. The trail descends once more, then races up another hundred feet or so to the main summit.

Members of the Adirondack Forty Sixers' club have a compulsion about statistics that approaches those of baseball fanatics. They can tell you, for example, which of the 46 high peaks is most popular to be climbed first (Marcy) and which is most likely to be climbed last (Whiteface).

They also report that Armstrong has *never* been last on anybody's list of peaks climbed. One finds this hard to believe when emerging from the scrub balsam trees which smother Armstrong's summit. A generous rock ledge provides a stunning overview of the surrounding major peaks.

The reason Armstrong is never climbed last is that it's a way station. You may feel as if you're Chairman of the Board when you sit on Armstrong's rock ledge, with the mountains lined around you like a horseshoe-shaped conference table. But you won't dally long to preside: you're due for another meeting on one of the other high peaks, going either up or down the range.

Even so, it would be a mistake not to spend a minute looking back toward Gothics. It's one of the premier sights in the Adirondacks — a jumble of crags, slides and gorges, stretching to the horizon.

The only other compelling reason to make Armstrong a last stop on the circuit might be to search for a legendary lost mine. The son of one

*A **wild jumble** of crags and gorges greets the hiker on Armstrong. Gothics is at left; Haystack, center rear; at right, Saddleback and Basin. Marcy is at far right.*

of the early owners of the tract, for whom the peak was named, looked in vain for the site on the Ausable Valley side where it was supposed to be. The actual location was known only to the Indians.

On second thought, it might not be worth the bother. The mine tapped veins of lead, not precious metal.

Journal entry: Wednesday, July 15, 1981. The Range trail, as I remember, is easy as it bounces down and up on its way from Armstrong to the Wolfjaws.

Oops. I had forgotten an extremely steep drop over a series of ledges on the descent from Armstrong. It is part of the "aerial promenade" which Laura and Guy Waterman say in Forest and Crag *is "as rugged as any Northeastern trails."*

In High Spots, *an ADK magazine published in the early part of this century, Robert Marshall vowed that the route "violates almost every proper trail standard and is delightful for this very quality. It shoots straight up cliffs, stumbles over all sorts of tree roots, and skirts through narrow crevices among the rocks."*

As Ben and I struggle down the slope, I recall that this is the place where a ranger told us he helped evacuate a lady injured on Armstrong. The records show that she was not the first.

Tim Tefft of the Forty Sixers reports that he was lucky on the peak. Sort of. "On a descent off Armstrong, soon after a rain, we slid along through the muck and mire heading for Upper Wolfjaw. With one false step on an angled root, I slipped, spun, fell, and landed with my head well below my feet, one of which was ensnared in another root which saved me from plummeting down a precipitous ledge."

In the col at the base of Armstrong, Upper Wolfjaw looks easily climbable, and it is. The summit has a small ledge; the overview, while not up to Armstrong, is respectable.

More interesting to me are deer tracks on the soft summit trail. Why would a deer be up here when there's bountiful grazing below? It's possible, I suppose. The legendary Adirondack guide, John Cheney, told of shooting a large bull moose that had yarded down near the top of Seward Mtn., which is almost 200 feet higher than Upper Wolfjaw.

There's no way of knowing for sure, so Ben and I begin the steep descent of 700 feet — it's the fourth time for me — that will bring us to the junction with the Wedge Brook trail, which leads to the Ausable Club.

Journal entry: Wednesday, June 16, 1979. *Ben and I are late in getting underway for our first hike of this season. We choose an easy, warm-up hike — 2,876-foot Mt. Jo, which nestles just to the north of Adirondak Loj.*

On decending, we explore the ADK's new Hikers' Hut. Ben is fascinated by clippings which relate to mishaps on the peaks.

There are two accounts of deaths due to hypothermia, and another of a young hiker who disappeared two years ago on Marcy. There is yet another of a middle-aged man who collapsed and died while trying to complete his 40th high peak conquest, Dix Mtn.

Outside the door we are greeted by a voluble, young ranger who seems anxious to talk. Ben, who has made up his mind to be a ranger when he grows up, hangs on every word.

The ranger returned at 11 o'clock this morning from a rescue mission on the Great Range. A call had come in the previous night at 6 p.m. A woman, while attempting to conquer Gothics, Armstrong and the two Wolfjaws in one day, had tumbled off a shallow ledge and injured her leg.

"Armstrong is bad for a rescue mission," the ranger tells us. "The trail is excessively steep in each direction." The rescuers elected to make a one-mile bushwhack to the Ore Bed Brook trail on the west, and then follow it down to Johns Brook Lodge, leaving only three miles that are mostly on the level to Keene Valley.

The ranger tells us he is exhausted, and he looks it. Yet he loiters; he seems hungry to talk with others who share his interest in the high peaks. Like us.

I ask how often he's called on for this kind of mission. "A couple or three times a year," he replies.

I tell him about my come-uppance descending from Algonquin, when son Jim and I spent two hours in total darkness with but one flashlight. And, I add, I don't intend to be caught like that again.

"I know what you mean," says the ranger. "In 1968, my father and I ran out of daylight returning to Lake Colden after a hike over Marcy and Haystack. We made it to Uphill Lean-to but had to stop because we had no flashlight.

"We had only a candy bar between us, along with a discarded sheet of plastic with a rip down the middle. It was a poor substitute for a blanket. The night was bitterly cold, and we were miserable.

"The Adirondacks are so unpredictable," he continues. "An inch of snow fell here last Monday. Hard to believe in mid-June, when it's as hot as it is today." He smiles and shakes his head: "That's the high peaks for you."

His comments reconfirm the warnings implicit in the clippings. Maybe Ben and I are not so late after all in getting underway this hiking season.

It's traditional when we finish a hike in this area to stop on our return at the general store in Keene and enjoy a soft drink on the bench in front, courtesy of the Kiwanis Club. As we do so today, Ben initiates a rescue mission of his own .

The cheerful proprietress comes out through the open door to check on the condition of a butterfly on the window sill behind us. Its wings are tattered.

"Maybe we could move it to your garden," suggests Ben, our family's butterfly expert.

"I'm afraid there's not much we can do for it," she replies. "Poor thing."

Ben brightens up and points to a display inside the window. "There's another butterfly, in good shape. If we're careful, maybe we can take it outside so it can go home."

"Oh, no," the proprietress says, with a warm smile in her eyes. "I'm not sure but this is where it wants to be. It comes to visit me every day."

Journal entry: Thursday, July 16, 1981. *The Adirondack Park Agency is about to begin its second-day session, and it's a apparent that Anne LaBastille will attend. There was no mistaking that blonde woodswoman who canoed across the glass of Elk Lake early this morning with her big German shepherd in the bow.*

Right now, the dog cocks a suspicious eye at everyone who approaches the main building where the sessions are to be held; on occasion, it spits out a nervous bark. LaBastille must have received a dispensation, for lodge rules clearly state: "Please! No pets!" We learn that the dog is not Pitzi, the one mentioned in LaBastille's first book, but a look-alike called Condor.

Barbara McMartin, I am told, will not attend.

The afternoon sessions of the A.P.A. are open to the public, so Ben and I decide to attend. On our way, we spot the young couple we saw on Pyramid yesterday with Cameron, the towhead. The father tells us they are using Elk Lake as a base camp for more hiking in the high peaks. He scoops up his toddler when Condor barks at them.

The association's public relations representative asks us to sign in and identify our business in the column headed, "Representing." Ben whispers the proper response. I put it down: "Hikers."

When the A.P.A. was formed in 1971, the state legislature tried to balance conflicting Adirondack interests by appointing both local residents and outsiders to the agency. It was then charged with developing a master plan and policy for all state lands within the Park, along with a land use and development plan for private lands. The agency was also given review power over major development proposals.

The conduct of A.P.A. members at this meeting generates my sympathy for a couple of reasons.

For one, I'm surprised to see that they devote full time to business; the Adirondacks do their best to distract them from outside every window. And second, the A.P.A.'s agenda suggests that its members are waging a no-win war. Whatever they do, the outsiders will think they're not doing enough, while the locals will think they're doing too much.

This also generates sympathy for people who live near the high peaks. The challenges they face have to be the same ones faced by residents since Colvin's time.

People who don't live here see this as the good life. But for some, like the driver of the pick-up at the Ausable Club, it can be a hardscrabble existence. Essex, the "Home of the high peaks," is one of the most depressed counties in New York state. And a major industry, logging, is one of the most dangerous occupations.

For those who are able to manage the risks, of course, there are real rewards.

Adirondackers living near the high peaks never have to worry, as city dwellers do, about being crammed into cubicles. Their backyards spill out onto six million acres of wild country.

This puts them in harmony with nature, in an almost symbiotic relationship. There's fuel for the taking in the woodlots, maple syrup for the bottling, fish and game for the eating, and so on.

In Colvin's time, the latter was considered a limitless goal. In his essay, Gateways to the Wilderness, *published in* A Century Wild, *J. Robert Williams recounted the cry of both guides and gentry: "Trout and venison, venison and trout — those were the watchwords in all the hotels."*

Today's residents have a more enlightened view, although admittedly it's reinforced by regulations: the resources are not infinite. Perhaps the proprietress at Keene expressed it best in her unspoken admonition to Ben about butterflies: live and let live.

The Adirondackers I've gotten to know well are hardy and resolute, much like others who live in small-town America and in rural areas. They lead a simple, sometimes lonely life, and they like it that way. They're also solid citizens who put the flag up on more than just Memorial Day. You'd feel comfortable having them by your side if you were called upon to defend your country.

The small towns they cluster in near the high peaks don't have police forces. They rely upon the state police because their crime rates are low. The rate in Tinconderoga, a typical town near the high peaks which does have its own police force, is less than half the state average and less than a quarter that of New York City.

Up until the late '70s, you could phone anybody in small Adirondack villages by dialing just four digits. The last holdout, Blue Mountain Lake, didn't join the digital revolution until 1994.

Diners and restaurants near the high peaks still serve plain fare at fair prices. At one of our favorites, the Spread Eagle Inn* in Keene Valley, the sole waitress — daughter-in-law to the owners, the Auers — often serves while doing double duty, with her baby crooked in one arm.

And you don't need a street map to find your way around most towns. Before the Bashful Bear Bookstore moved to Keene Valley, it advertised that its store in Elizabethtown was "near the blinking light" — the crossroads that mark the center of town.

Above all, Adirondackers who live near the high peaks are blessed with an abundance of two rare qualities — peace and quiet. Because of this, they don't want outsiders coming in to turn things upside down. Residents believe they have earned the right to develop their areas in ways they think are best for them.

O, for the wisdom of Solomon! The Adirondack Park Agency has its work cut out for it.

---

* Now named the Ausable Inn.

Mt. Colvin, center, and Blake, left, from Elk Lake.

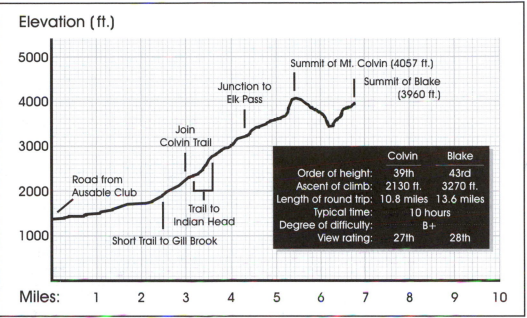

Elevation (ft.)

Summit of Mt. Colvin (4057 ft.)

Summit of Blake (3960 ft.)

Junction to Elk Pass

Join Colvin Trail

Road from Ausable Club

Trail to Indian Head

Short Trail to Gill Brook

	Colvin	Blake
Order of height:	39th	43rd
Ascent of climb:	2130 ft.	3270 ft.
Length of round trip:	10.8 miles	13.6 miles
Typical time:	10 hours	
Degree of difficulty:	B+	
View rating:	27th	28th

Miles: 1 2 3 4 5 6 7 8 9 10

For contour trails, see U.S. Geological Survey map, pgs. 120-121.

17, 18.
COLVIN, BLAKE

It's fitting that the two men most responsible for creating the Adirondack State Park and Forest Preserve should have high peaks named after them. However, there's some question as to whether they confer the proper recognition on Verplanck Colvin and Mills Blake.

Mt. Colvin is no great shakes when compared to its lofty neighbors. Its soft profile slopes up from the northern end of Lower Ausable Lake to culminate on a nondescript plateau. This is somewhat compensated for by views which crowd in on a small, open ledge near its pipsqueak summit.

The mountain is pretty bland for the mercurial man who spent 28 years doing the only thing he ever wanted to do in his lifetime: explore and document the dimensions of the high peaks. As superintendent of the Adirondack topographical survey, Verplanck Colvin criss-crossed the mountains, pushed himself as hard as he did his men, and submitted reports which skittered round and round like electrons trying to decide whether scientific fact or rosy prose was the more attractive nucleus to be its home.

Blake Peak is easier to accept because the mountain, like its namesake, plays a subordinate role in most respects. It ranks 43rd in height among the 46 Adirondack high peaks. It ranks near the bottom on anyone's list of view ratings. And when seen from Elk Lake, a lesser peak to the south of Blake on the Colvin Range appears to be higher.

Mills Blake wore the same badge of ignominy as the peak named after him. He was Colvin's field assistant for 20 years, but received little mention in the latter's formal reports and even less credit. As a final irony, the 1954 revision of the U.S. topographic map of the Adirondacks demoted Blake Peak along with three others — Cliff, Couchsachraga and Nye — from the list of mountains which reach 4,000 feet or higher. Blake, like the others, is still grouped among the 46 high peaks originally thought to be at least 4,000 feet, but it has clearly been relegated to second-class citizenship.

Verplanck Colvin pursued a single-minded commitment for almost two decades. As Philip G. Terrie observed in *Forever Wild*, "Colvin's obsession with knowing every detail about the Adirondacks led him to climb the high peaks again and again, from every conceivable direction, in every kind of weather."

Present-day explorers who consider following Colvin's lead on the two mountains will find this hard to do by trail.

There's no problem with the conventional route — the Gill Brook trail — which branches to the left, or south, off the road leading from the Ausable Club to Lower Ausable Lake. There's also a path from the upper end of that lake which leads up to the trail crossing the col between Colvin and Blake. However, access by that route is denied, because the lake areas are closed to the public.

Those who like to do things the hard way can follow the Marcy trail from Elk Lake to Pinnacle Ridge, where a side trail branches north along the Colvin Range to the summits of Blake and Colvin. Be advised, though, that this route is half again as long as the trail from the lake road and piles on another 400 feet of climbing.

The sensible solution for those who want to emulate Colvin and his assistant is to climb the two peaks by the conventional route, but do it more than once. You'll gain a different perspective each time if you separate the outings with a decent time interval, try them under different weather conditions, and choose a different partner for each climb.

Journal entry: Saturday, September 5, 1970. Verplanck Colvin had one advantage when he and Blake prowled the peaks: there weren't as many people around. This is the first day of the Labor Day weekend, and son Jim and I hope to avoid the crowds which descend on the Adirondacks during the holidays.

We have two factors in our favor.

The first is that on the map at least, Colvin appears to be a nice, nondescript, remote peak — a duty climb, if you will, which volatile hikers should bypass because it looks like a drag. That ought to cancel out Blake, too, because it tapers off on the far side of Colvin like an afterthought.

The second factor is the weather: it's foggy and chilly with rain threatening. As we get our bus tickets in the lobby of the Ausable Club, I buy a rain-proofed topographic map of the area prepared by the Adirondack Trail Improvement Society. Aha — this accounts for the "ATIS" trail markers we've seen in the area. The group is obviously associated with the Adirondack Mountain Reserve.

The glow from the fireplace in the lounge feels good on the fingers.

We wonder how smart our choice is as we board the bus. It's jammed with jovial riders, and we have to stand with the overflow. There is constant chatter about the peaks some will climb today, and the fish others will catch. Jim and I find with relief that we are the only ones to get off and begin the trail from the road.

The short cut to the Gill Brook trail covers a quarter of a mile at an easy grade. At the junction, we stop at a gorgeous, 10-foot waterfall which has hollowed out a tiny, idyllic swimming hole. This, Colvin observed in his Seventh Report, is Artist's Falls, "where the water pours in a clear sheet over a sloping rock...to glide brightly away amid the great boulders below." It's too chilly for swimming, and the trees confirm that cooler weather is on its way — the leaves are turning.

Again at an easy grade, we head southwest up the main Colvin trail. In no time, we cross a trail junction to Indian Head and the Fish Hawk Cliffs. These are renowned overlooks which are easy to reach and reward climbers with fine panoramas of the two Ausables. Fog blocked our view when Jim and I were on Sawteeth, but we gained a telescopic glimpse of the prominences from Gothics.

Everything is damp and it's sprinkling, so we keep moving and pass the other end of the trail which loops back from Indian Head and Fish Hawk Cliffs. It's gloomy and lonely, with no sign of a soul. Great! We made the right decision today.

It begins to rain hard, but we acknowledge a brighter side: proof of the value of our floppy, Adirondack, wool "crusher" hats, which can be squashed down in our backpacks. When we need them, they shield us from rain or sun, and provide warmth when it's windy and cold. When we don't need to wear them, they make great cushions for sitting on wet rocks and logs.

Gill Brook, now far below on our left, disappears from sight and sound. But as we pass a steep rock ledge, I note holes from erosion on the edge of the trail above the brook, and pull Jim back. The view through the holes is straight down for at least a hundred feet. Suggestion to ATIS: re-route this trail segment before you lose some friends.

The trail to Nippletop comes in from the south, telling us per the map that we are two thirds of the way to Colvin. Our trail, which parallels a long ridge on the right, becomes much steeper and wetter.

My hunch was right: few hikers tackle this mountain, because it is a drag. The trail traces an arching crescent along a ridge, with one undulating rise succeeded by another. Jim and I are wet and tired, and don't stop for rests as much as we did below, for we are anxious to top out. I don't think we have ever been so exasperated by a mountain, except perhaps by the boredom of Porter.

Finally, after a brief, twisting turn to the right, we mount a bare boulder with a pipe imbedded in the top — a souvenir from Colvin's surveying trip, no doubt — and it's downhill all the way.

Below us to the north and west are the Ausables, soft and gray like pools of molten lead. Sawteeth scrapes the skyline to the northwest. Beyond, through agitated clouds, we see a portion of the Great Range, from Saddleback and Gothics on the north, to the Wolfjaws, plus the lower reaches of Giant farther to the northeast. To the south, Blake is blanked by the woods.

Almost before our first bite of lunch, most of the view is gone, although a portion of Lower Ausable Lake remains in sight. We study three mov-

From Colvin's summit, *the Great Range offers an expansive view, including from left to right, Saddleback, Gothics and Armstrong. Clouds and rain, however, are moving in fast.*

ing flecks on the surface. Canoes. Foggy clouds move in fast from the southwest.

Jim tells me he hears voices, either from the lake, from the mountains across from it, or from the trail we have just ascended. I suspect the first two sources are out of

Lower Ausable Lake is soon the only thing in sight. Son Jim dons rain gear for the one-mile trek to Blake.

hearing range, and as we finish lunch Jim confirms it by matching figures to the voices. They are moving up from the trail below.

The "they" are a man with his son and daughter, both in their middle teens. As they pause to rest, the girl says to the boy, "Congratulations! You're halfway there." It's obvious he has completed climbing 23 of the 46 high peaks. The boy lights up with a proud smile. So does his father. An amiable, solid fellow — I would bet he's a General Electric engineer from back home in Schenectady.

The rain is now a slanting torrent worthy of a woodcut by Hiroshige. The threesome are in a hurry: on to Blake, they affirm. We grin wearily, and Jim adds, "Us, too. We don't want to do this one again."

In a few minutes, we follow them, and discover their packs hanging on a tree. Great idea! We can move fast with only a canteen and a knife. It's a well-marked trail so we don't have to worry about a compass as we did on our foggy, trailless return trip from Iroquois.

The trail makes another long, looping crescent over the south edge of the Colvin ridge, then plunges downward. We move fast and light, somewhat in the manner of a soggy feather. In fact, Jim and I slither down so fast that soon we are right behind the party of three.

Jim wants to go around them, but I point to Blake through a break in the clouds, and the col before us. It seems to go straight down and then straight up, so I suggest we take it easy. Considering the way we normally move going up — slow — they'll pass us right after we pass them. Besides, I don't want to prompt a flare-up of the knee troubles we had on our recent hikes. We sit to rest and they are gone.

We meet the three descending as we near the top of Blake, and ask about the view. It is just ahead, they say, but there is no view. A real *blah. Now, they are more relaxed with their conquests of the day on the record. As they start to leave, I offer the boy: good luck on the 46.*

"I'll need it," he says. "Most of the rest are trailless." Wearily, his father adds, "It's a race between when he leaves for school and how long I can last."

I know just what he means.

They gave an accurate description of the top, which is a few yards beyond. The blending of the dense woods with the mist marks a low point in our summit viewing. Through the scrub trees to the south there is a shimmering polka dot pattern that suggests Elk Lake; the sun that etches it is hidden in the lowering fog.

We search for a benchmark but find none. Per the map, Colvin, Blake and Pinnacle Peak are the highest blips on the five-mile ridge, and Colvin — the highest of the three — wins the gold. I'd give Blake a bronze at best. Back to the packs.

By studying the topographical map, one can make a reasonable case that the easiest return route is to take the trail in the col between Colvin and Blake down to Lower Ausable Lake, then walk along the south shore of the lake to the boathouse at the foot of the lake. Don't. There is a reason more compelling than the club warning that the area is off limits.

The executive secretary-treasurer of the Forty Sixers, A. G. Dittmar, recounted in the group's publication, *Adirondack Peeks*, how he tried this route before he became aware of the rules of the club and the facts of the terrain.

"The col descent was almost straight down and the route around the lake was nothing but steep cliffs which dropped off right into the water. After about an hour of up and down, rock after rock, I considered swimming but thought better."

By nightfall, Dittmar said he had only gone a fifth of the way and realized that for safety he would have to stop. "I spread my topographical maps around me and put my jacket on over them. This helped to keep out some of the cold. After an uneasy night perched on a 60-degree incline, I started out again." It took him until noon to reach the Ausable Club boathouse. His conclusion: "I had learned the hard way."

Journal entry: Saturday, September 5, 1970. *Sheets of rain are now blowing hard through the col from the northwest. Jim and I button up and push on.*

Halfway up the steep slopes of Colvin, we find an ADK guidebook on the trail; it had to be lost by one of the three. I put it in my pocket for protection from the rain. We will return it if we catch up with them.

As we retrieve our packs, I find a business card tucked under one of the flaps on mine. I assume it will tell us where to send the missing guidebook, so I put it in my pocket, out of the rain. We push on again.

The rain now has lazed to a drizzle so we make good time in spite of the slimy footing, and reach the waterfall at Gill Brook in an hour and a half. I note a much higher flow.

Dilemma: we cannot remember if the bus comes from the boathouse at five or 5:30 p.m. Should we wait at the cut-off trail, or walk? The returning rain answers our question; we huddle under a towering maple.

When the bus does come, we board and are greeted by the familiar father plus two. "Did you find my guidebook?" he asks. Yes, it's damp but intact, I say. A good thing, I tell him. You can't buy one in Schenectady. It's out of print and won't be available until next year. He is profuse in his thanks.

He asks about our return route, and recounts their struggle in climbing over Indian Head to reach the boathouse at Lower Ausable Lake. In good weather it would have been beautiful but today, he says, it was like lugging the last block to the summit of a pyramid.

Jim and I sit back and enjoy the ride almost as much as our new friend. The other passengers chuckle at our conversation, and then assume the standard transportation trance.

Who are they, I wonder, and what do they do when they're away from here? It's fun to speculate. From the listing in the Ausable Club brochure, many come from comfortable communities: Greenwich, Connecticut; Basking Ridge, New Jersey; South Londonderry, Vermont; Germantown and Philadelphia, Pennsylvania; Morristown and Princeton, New Jersey; Boynton Beach, Florida and Saratoga, California; Concord, Massachusetts and Beacon Street, Boston — plus a few esoteric mail drops like Prattling Pond Road in Farmington, Connecticut.

It's a human failing, I suppose, to try and match up people with livelihoods. In the woods, it's difficult. Most of our mountain associates dress as we do — like losers.

When we get off the bus, the images we award to vivid characters vanish with a puff. The suave young couple and the cute baby, who obviously are staying at the club for a break in the social whirl, pile into a flower-bedecked Volkswagen bus and rattle away. The elderly gent who is a shoo-in for a derelict saunters up to the club veranda, waves to assorted rockers, and heads inside.

I wonder, for that matter, what the man with the teens whom we met on Colvin does for a living. I pull out his business card, which identifies him: "Harry E. Colwell, III, Vice President, The Chase Manhattan Bank, New York City."

What do you know. I still think he would have made a good engineer.

Journal entry: Saturday, July 21, 1979. *Today, Ben is anxious to add Colvin and Blake to his list of conquests.*

I'm not so sure it's a good idea because it's hazy, hot and humid in Schenectady. But Ben doesn't care. "I just love it up there," he says. Verplanck Colvin would have been proud of him.

The air in Keene Valley affirms Ben's judgment — it's transparent, etching the high peaks against a cloudless, blue sky.

I had toyed with the thought that we might surmount the two peaks by the long ridge which leads north from 3,776-ft. Boreas Mtn. But Ben talked me out of it; he wants to retrace the route taken by his older brother Jim and me, by beginning on the Ausable Club road.

There's another reason why the Boreas route is not a good idea. In March of 1984, a Canadian pilot and his plane disappeared without a trace in the Adirondack wilderness. In spite of an extensive aerial search, six years passed before a hiker discovered the wreckage, a hundred feet below the summit of Boreas Mtn., some three miles to the southwest of Elk Lake. All those who climbed Boreas between 1984 and 1990 were unaware that they had passed near the hidden wreckage. A fire tower which stood on the summit has been removed, and the trail is now closed.

Journal entry: Monday, August 19, 1985. *Ben and his mother and I have just completed our second climb to the summit of Boreas Mtn. We came by the trail which heads west from the outlet of Clear Pond on the road to Elk Lake.*

The locals pronouce Boreas as "Boris," which relates no doubt to a variant spelling of an earlier era. It also adds a vague but ominous quality to the peak. Several other factors reinforce this, and convince me that I made the right decision in 1979 that Ben and I should not go for Colvin and Blake from "Boris."

My field notes from our first climb of Boreas in July of 1982, for example, were brief and to the point: "Clear, beautiful. Bugs awful."

Today, a month later, the black flies are supposed to be on the wane, but they're still out in force. One sure reason: Boreas' summit is filthy. It would have been disastrous for Ben and me to be dogged by these voracious pests if we had tried to make the 15-mile round trip from Boreas to Blake and Colvin. My field notes for today record another possible problem after reaching only the summit of Boreas: "Legs tremble."

As it is, we faced a mini-crisis on our climb up here. One of my wife's contact lenses became dislodged and we searched in vain for any surface — an old tin can, watch crystal, eye glass, whatever — that would serve as a mirror so she could reposition the lens.

We finally solved the problem with a broken piece of windowpane from the abandoned observer's hut near the summit of Boreas. But there are no man-made structures along the ridge to provide help if Ben should have trouble with his contacts. The ridge, like the mountain, is not only remote but densely forested.

Journal entry: Saturday, July 21, 1979. *Ben is so excited about our exploration of Colvin and Blake that he has prepared a menu headed: "Food for our hike":*

DAD	*BEN*
Spam with mustard on natural wheat bread.	*Meatloaf with mayonnaise on natural wheat bread.*
Coffee to drink.	*Iced tea to drink.*
Celery for a snack (salt).	*M & M's for snack.*

I get kidded by fellow climbers about my passion for Spam. I became addicted in the Army, because Spam tasted like ambrosia compared to the field food issued by the Infantry in its alphabet packages — C Rations, D Rations, and so on.

Spam brings an added bonus in the Adirondacks: it repels black flies. I don't know why.

Memories of my hike with Jim return as Ben and I reach Gill Brook. Today, it's in sharper focus because of the better weather.

The deep pool at the base of the waterfall lies cool and inviting. As the trail begins its relentless rise, first Bear Den, then the Dials appear on the ridge leading to Nippletop on our left.

Beyond the second junction to the Fish Hawk Cliffs, we pass a couple with two children, plodding upward. In turn, we are passed by a raucous tribe of five teenage boys, whose leader strives to maintain a precarious measure of control.

Ben and I have been hitting the water bottle heavily due to the heat of climbing, so as a substitute I break out a package of moist celery. Sprinkles of salt help replenish what we've been losing in perspira-

tion, and things begin to look up — or down, depending on your mountain viewpoint.

I had warned Ben that the final mile before reaching the summit would seem never-ending. So it is, and that combined with the heat of the climb wears me down. Ben yells from ahead for me to speed my pace. Since noise from above tells me he will not be alone, I tell him to go on.

At least, I am not the last to surmount the summit. As I haul off my pack, the family foursome staggers up behind me. The father looks more worn out than I think I do.

The black flies are gone, but the constricted space on the summit overlook is crawling with hikers...oohing and aahing, eating, and talking loudly. The voluble leader of the group with the five teenage boys outdoes them all, delivering what I suspect is a soliloquy for the benefit of the rest of us.

"Yes, I've been here before," he proclaims, "in the winter as well as the summer." He ticks off most of the recognizable peaks for his charges, and makes an obscure reference to "Indian Head Falls," which I've never heard of.

I am reminded of a maxim by son Ben's namesake, Benjamin Franklin: "There stands the orator with his flood of words and a drop of reason."

My favorite Ben whispers to me: "He hasn't told us one thing we don't already know."

Better day, better view. *White beaches mark boathouse on right side of north end of Lower Ausable Lake. Above and at right are Fish Hawk Cliffs and, beyond, Indian Head.*

Except one thing. Several in the group, including the orator, acknowledge that shortly before reaching the top they heard what sounded like a landslide. A close look at the west slope of Nippletop reveals fresh debris of a darker shade coursing into the face of an old slide about halfway up.

Good timing. Adventurers viewed the original slide which swept down in 1973 as a new challenge and a few climbed to the summit of Nippletop by this route. The Schenectady Chapter of ADK scheduled a bushwack up the slide two weeks

Fresh debris *from halfway up Nippletop confirms that its west face is acting up again. Other climbers also heard the rumbling of the landslide as they ascended the Colvin trail.*

ago, on the same day Ben and I climbed Lower Wolfjaw. It's a good thing the slide did not occur on their way up.

Today, unlike my last time here with son Jim, Ben and I gain a clean shot of Blake as we reach the far end of the Colvin plateau. We hang our packs on a tree stump, taking only our canteens. In half an hour we reach the col, which is dry except for damp spots — ideal home sites for the bugs.

One thing about Blake has not changed: it has no good view. But Ben is not convinced we are on the true summit, so he follows the trail leading to Pinnacle Ridge, a hundred yards or so. His excited shout tells me he is right.

Blake from Colvin indicates the challenge ahead: a descent of 700 feet from Colvin to the intervening col, then a haul up 610 feet to the wooded summit. And, of course, back again.

I find him standing on a small rock ledge with an unobstructed view of Elk Lake. It transforms my perspective of Blake. Here we are, alone, on a beautiful day, with our own private panorama. Blake has suddenly become one of my favorite mountains.

The Assistant has surpassed the Superintendent for at least one day.

Our main adversary today has been the flies, this time not the tiny black ones but big deer flies which delight in buzzing around your hair. Unintentionally, we liven their lives as we grasp branches to climb both down and up. In the process, we coat our hands with tree sap; then, slapping the pests, we transfer the goo to our hair, which rouses them to a frenzy.

A lone, plump hiker sprawls on the Colvin summit, simmering in the four o'clock heat. "I'm exhausted," he says. "I just got here even though I left the road at nine this morning. Do you have any water?"

Unfortunately, no, we tell him. It's why Ben and I intend to hurry down to Gill Brook, the first source of water. All three of us face a long time between swigs.

Before leaving the summit, Ben and I relish a last look around at the peaks, which appear to be cloaked in seamless folds of virgin spruce and balsam. Some 12 miles to the northeast, we spot Hurricane Mtn., where members of a group accompanying Colvin on a survey trip in 1873 decided to name the peak, where we now stand, in his honor.

Five minutes before Ben and I reach the falls at Gill Brook, we see a deer that is a carbon copy of the doe we saw along the Ausable Club road two weeks ago. It ignores us while browsing at trailside on saplings of sugar maple and yellow birch.

Tame deer like this one must be a prime target for the Ausable Club bus when it makes its run through the valley. I hope there's no collision, for the sake of both the deer and the bus.

Back home, in a driving rainstorm one night, a deer hit our car, almost totaling it. Twice before, I barely managed to avoid encounters between our car and a bull moose, once in Yellowstone National Park and another time near Mt. Washington in the White Mountains of New Hampshire. I shudder to think of the damage to our car, let alone us, if we had run into one of them. Moose pack such a knobby mass of intimidation that they make deer look like blown-glass knickknacks.

Tonight, Ben and I have no concern about the bus running into deer. We have missed the last one returning from Lower Ausable Lake.

From Blake, a small clearing reveals the sprawling waters of Elk Lake, with Clear Pond the sliver beyond. Trail to Pinnacle Ridge crosses the slope on the right.

Our only other wildlife encounter, heard but not seen, comes from the liquid loveliness of a hermit thrush. John Burroughs admired its flute-like call, and observed on one of his Adirondack visits, "how much he brought with him of the wild grace and harmony of nature."

And that is why, the noted naturalist added, "the people in the Adirondacks call it the Swamp Angel."

A newspaper reporter observed in 1993 that present-day hikers are, "by and large, a mystical crowd, who are drawn to the trail by its powerful and ultimately inexplicable allure." He quoted one addict as saying, "when you get near the end of the trail, you realize the main thing isn't putting in your miles. It's being on the trail, and once you're off it, you can't wait to get back on."

The reporter could have been quoting Verplanck Colvin, except for two things.

First, there weren't many trails on the Adirondack peaks when Colvin conducted his survey. And second, Colvin seemed to hate getting *off* the mountains even more than wanting to get back on. The nocturnal descents he and his crew made so often were vivid testimony.

Colvin's checkered career makes it hard to be precise about his legacy. Most acknowledge that there might never have been an Adirondack state park if he had not armed the public early on with the key reasons why there should be one: to preserve the scenic pleasures and natural resources of the area, to prevent erosion, to conserve its water supply, and so on.

But others render harsh judgment.

For example, cynics pooh-pooh the proposal Colvin made in 1873 to build a system of canals to transmit the waters of Adirondack lakes and rivers to the lower Hudson valley. This, he suggested, would make good use of "agriculturally worthless" land. And, as he predicted in a free-falling flight of hyperbole, it would serve as the long-sought Northwest Passage.

One could make a good case that this scheme was a product of youthful enthusiasm. Colvin was 26 years old at the time, and had just begun his duties as superintendent of the survey the previous year. His salary for this rigorous, dangerous work was $2,500 per year.

New York state legislators were among Colvin's contemporary critics. His arguments with them became so explosive and frequent that in 1890 he resigned. But he continued to feud with them and submitted proposals for such outlandish ventures as railroading and mining in the midst of the wilderness. Both of these were in direct opposition to his early, preservationist instincts.

Colvin lost his battles with the legislature, and spent his last years wandering the streets of Albany. He died in 1920.

Colvin can be faulted for one major failure. After almost three decades of scouting the peaks, he did not produce the central element of his survey: an Adirondack map. All Colvin left behind, according to his detractors, other than an office jumbled with notes and surveying equipment, were the reports he had submitted to the legislature.

One has only to read "all he left behind" to appreciate the true legacy of Verplanck Colvin. His reports, by almost any comparison, are equal to those of other American explorers, including the exhilarating journals of Lewis and Clark.

In 1873, Colvin climbed to the summit of a peak in the Ausable lake area which was, "unascended, unmeasured and — prominent as it was — unknown to any map." The final assault, he said, was a "cliff almost impregnable."

But Colvin's report did not just record clinical details such as the time of topping off, the elevation, temperature and so on. He had achieved, Colvin said, "a seat upon a throne that seemed the central seat of the mountain amphitheatre."

Many people, both then and now, have called this kind of writing flowery and overblown. But anyone who has ever slumped down on a summit overlook after a difficult mountain climb will thank Colvin for putting into words what he or she felt but could not express.

Colvin wasn't the only Adirondack explorer of his time to be accused of flowery writing. One of the first was Joel T. Headley, whose *The Adirondack: Or Life in the Woods* could, according to Neil S. Burdick, "stir a lethargic populace to action with rousing tales of wilderness derring-do." In a somewhat different vein, Edgar Allan Poe referred to Headley as "the autocrat of all quacks."

But one can almost believe that Headley had the noble purpose of Colvin in mind, along with his ignoble end, when he wrote: "How solemn it is to move all day through a majestic columnade of trees and feel that you are in a boundless cathedral whose organ notes swell and die away with the passing wind like some grand requiem."

It's comforting to remember, too, that while a requiem may be sad, it can also be spiritually uplifting.

Tabletop Mtn. and Phelps Mtn., left, from Van Hoevenberg trail to Mt. Marcy.

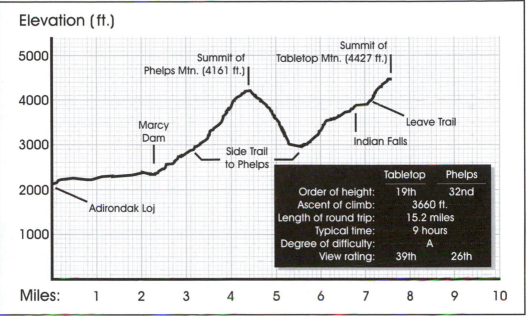

Elevation (ft.)

Summit of Phelps Mtn. (4161 ft.)

Summit of Tabletop Mtn. (4427 ft.)

Marcy Dam

Side Trail to Phelps

Leave Trail

Indian Falls

Adirondak Loj

	Tabletop	Phelps
Order of height:	19th	32nd
Ascent of climb:	3660 ft.	
Length of round trip:	15.2 miles	
Typical time:	9 hours	
Degree of difficulty:	A	
View rating:	39th	26th

Miles: 1 2 3 4 5 6 7 8 9 10

For contour trails, see U.S. Geological Survey map, pgs. 70-71.

19, 20.
TABLETOP, PHELPS

The Adirondack high peaks are a pleasant antidote to the stress of modern business.

In the city, you can communicate for days on end without seeing the people you communicate with, thanks to the Internet, telephone answering machines, voice mail, faxes, PCs, E-mail, cellular phones, and so on. But when you come to the small towns of the Adirondacks, right away you begin relating to people in the general store or the gas station or the diner on a one-on-one basis.

It doesn't take long to discover that Adirondack people have a different perspective than those who live in the city. You sense that business is not the most important thing in their lives.

One reason is that jobs are often only a means to a more important end: being able to live in the Adirondacks. In the case of a lucky few, their jobs call upon them to do what they really want to do: work in the Adirondack wilderness.

The Adirondack guide personifies that role better than anyone else.

As of 1994, the Department of Environmental Conservation had licensed 1,398 guides in New York state. Of that total, 546 were in the

Adirondacks. By coincidence, the latter was the exact number listed in Wallace's 1881 *Guide to the Adirondacks* at the height of their popularity in the last century.

But numbers are about the only thing the two eras have in common.

In the middle and late 1800s, Adirondack guides could do pretty much what they wanted in the wilderness. They invited the gentry to hunt and fish at will, and used the forest for camps and firewood as they saw fit.

That changed in 1919 when the state's old Conservation Commission began to require that guides be registered. Today, guides are tested to ensure they are proficient in CPR, in standard first aid and basic water safety, and are "sound in body."

The license numbers stamped on their metal badges certify that guides have paid the $100 fee for a five-year period, along with another $20 for each of their designated specialties: fishing, camping, hunting, rock and ice climbing, canoeing and rafting, and hiking.

Paul Jamieson observes in *The Adirondack Reader* that they are seldom asked to guide hikers. "On a summer weekend," he says, "they may, if they can bear it, lead a party of picnicking schoolteachers to a pond where water lilies grow." But, as he notes, most of them have other jobs and only go out with parties during the hunting season.

Anyone who has explored the high peaks will recall trailless times when an experienced guide would have come in handy. If they were free to choose, many presentday hikers would select a nineteenth century guide over a modern-day one. Back in the old days, there were few trails and maps. As a result, guides kept things interesting by pathfinding out of necessity.

Again, if a choice were possible, hikers would most likely choose the best known of nineteenth century guides, Orson Schofield "Old Mountain" Phelps.

Phelps the guide was popular with many of the influential people who summered in the Adirondacks. This came about not only from his love for the mountains but from his quaint opinions and appearance. The latter is preserved for us in Winslow Homer's large oil entitled "The Two Guides," which hangs in the Sterling and Francine Clark Art Institute at Williamstown, Massachusetts.

The larger man on the left, standing ramrod-straight with axe in hand, is Monroe Holt, a Keene Valley guide and town official. Phelps is his diminutive companion, gesturing at some unknown peak. Both are outlined against Beaver Mtn., not far from the farm near Minerva, New York where Homer the artist summered. The face of Phelps is almost obliterated by a beard run amok.

One of Phelps' admiring clients, the writer Charles Dudley Warner, painted a word picture of Phelps that matched the painting in his 1878 essay, *A Character Study.**** Phelps was, said Warner, "a sturdy figure, with long body and short legs, clad in a woolen shirt and butternut-colored trousers repaired to the point of picturesqueness, his head surmounted by a limp, light-brown felt hat, frayed away at the top, so that his yellowish hair grew out of it like some nameless fern out of a pot." His clothes, said Warner, "seemed to have been put on him once for all, like the bark of a tree, a long time ago."

Orson Phelps may have been one of the best known of the early Adirondack guides because of such artistic accolades, but he was not the best liked by his peers. Many of the 27 other Keene Valley guides considered him shiftless and lazy.

Warner analyzed not only this problem but the reason why Phelps endeared himself so much to both contemporary clients and modern-day hikers: "In all that country," wrote Warner, "he alone had noticed the sunsets, and observed the delightful processes of the seasons, taken pleasure in the woods for themselves, and climbed mountains solely for the sake of the prospect."

Warner concluded, "One does not think of Old Phelps so much as a lover of nature...as a part of nature itself."

Some complain that the modest Adirondack high peak named after Phelps is a poor tribute to the memory of the famous guide. In fact, there is no record that he ever climbed it. Yet the choice is highly appropriate in one respect: its summit overlook offers the hiker a marvelous broadside of Old Mountain Phelps' beloved "Mercy," the highest Adirondack peak of them all.

Phelps Mtn. is easy to climb via a spur trail which leads to the northeast from the Van Hoevenberg trail about a mile beyond Marcy Dam. Hikers often combine the trip with a climb of a neighboring peak, trailless Tabletop Mtn., which the old guide referred to as Flattop.

The pairing again is appropriate because it combines the two types of hikes in the Adirondacks which Phelps identified in his colorful vocabulary: "reg'lar walks" (on trails), and "random scoots" (in the trailless wilderness).

The dual outing can be more than an antidote for stress. Those who intend to explore all 46 of the highest Adirondack high peaks soon lock onto the attitude of Old Mountain Phelps. It becomes, in the words of Adirondack historian Alfred Donaldson, "something akin to questing for the Holy Grail."

---

* From Warner's *In The Wilderness*. The frontispiece reveals that Adirondack writing had been elevated to the forefront of American literature. Warner's book was "Prescribed by the Regents of the University of the State of New York for the examination for the preliminary certificate in English."

Journal entry: Sunday, September 13, 1970. Son Jim and I noted on our hike up Marcy that Phelps Mtn., while listed in the ADK guidebook as trailless, now has a marked path. We choose it as our target for today.

Campers on occasion have noted beavers at Marcy Dam, but there are none today. A trail detour leads across Marcy Brook just below the dam, because the middle section of the dam has been removed. What has been a beautiful lake is now a mud hole. ENCON is administering to the aches and pains of the dam in its old age, no doubt.

As we register near the ranger station, our "Hi's" are not acknowledged by a trio nearby. We hope it is not the mood of the mountains today.

But we suspect it may be as we move up the trail toward Indian Falls. Heavily-laden hikers are leaving early; they walk like their feet hurt or their joints ache, or both. One explains why: last night brought 40 degrees and a high wind. With lean-tos full, many slept in the open.

A few paces beyond, two college-age couples stumble down the trail. One grim-faced boy carries two full packs and is followed by his consort, limping with a makeshift cane and muttering dark oaths to anyone within range. The Women's Liberation Movement, it would appear, has imploded for her.

Jim studies the map to spot the Phelps trail junction, and suggests: Why not do two peaks today? First, Tabletop, which is trailless but less than two miles beyond the turnoff to Phelps, and then back to Phelps, which is safely marked. Why not, indeed? We head upward.

Indian Falls is the same, busy, wilderness city we remembered. We ask several hikers if they know the way to Tabletop. Negative. All are going up or down Marcy. Mainliners.

On the east side of the Marcy Brook branch, Jim and I find a profusion of faint trails in the general direction of Tabletop. Each of us follows a parallel path until Jim's peters out. To be safe, we mark my trail with small blazes since the footpath is indistinct and twisting. The compass tells us we are heading in the right direction at least — to the northeast.

The route to Tabletop from Indian Falls calls for about 700 feet of climbing. The early grade is easy and the path becomes more distinct, though it winds through dense woods. Jim wonders if it is an animal trail, but faint footprints in the damp soil tell me it is not.

There are no steep pitches on this trail. Before we expect it, we top off on a flat ridge, which shows why the peak is called Tabletop. We are on the southwestern edge of a rolling, wrinkled plateau that forms an imperfect triangle about a quarter of a mile on each side. A shallow depression lies before us while the indistinct points of the plateau lie beyond a hundred feet or higher. The two points are roughly the same elevation but we guess the one to the northwest is higher.

The trail plunges foreward and disappears into — cripplebush! This is Iroquois all over again, only worse. Jim and I blaze with a vengeance, until we detect the faint traces of another trail, and stick to it. Side trails flare out like the underground structure of a tree; we hope we are following the tap root.

Jim is impatient when I pause at a confusing trail junction; he plunges ahead on his own. Almost at once, he shouts back, "I found it!" Jim has located the cannister on the true summit.

The log book in the cannister is in tatters. We document our feat in a page from my pocket notebook, and leave a couple of spare pages for other climbers.

When viewed from Indian Falls, one can see why Tabletop was given its name. But when exploring its top, it soon becomes clear that it is more like a shag rug than a polished surface. In fact, the only way to tell that you have reached the summit it to locate the cannister holding the register.

Finding your way is complicated by two factors. The first is a jungle of jackstraws formed by virgin trees blown down during the infamous hurricane of 1950. The second is a thick blanket of young balsam and spruce trees which smother the intermediate spaces.

The *Gazette's* Fred Fraser told of one climber who left this lament in the register: "To think these trees look so good at Christmas." Vowed another, "I hereby rename this mountain Hellenback." Still

Top of the table. *Jim deciphers the tangled trails and heads straight for the summit cannister. Many hikers search for hours before conquering Tabletop.*

another echoed a common complaint of summer climbers: "Bugs all over the place, and I tore my pants."

Probably the earliest traverse of Tabletop, by surveyor Charles Broadhead, indicates that conditions were no better two centuries ago. He recorded in 1797: "Top the mountain — very rough, chief of the timber fallen down by the wind — the greatest part of this mountain is covered with snow 12 inches deep."

That was in early June. So you can imagine the depth of snow in winter. In fact, more and more people now come to the Adirondacks during that season to climb and explore. On Tabletop, they discover that trees bring a mixed blessing. The trees shield them from the strong, bitter winds, which can literally bowl people over on the open summits of higher Adirondack peaks. But the trees also snag unwary hikers in spruce traps, hidden air spaces formed below branches covered by deep snow.

The Forty Sixers' journal reports, as one example, that two winter climbers on Colden rescued a lone skier, separated from his group and well off the trail, trapped 12 feet down in a spruce hole.

The views are sparse near Tabletop's summit cannister, unless you climb one of the sturdier conifers nearby, or locate one of the lookouts a hundred yards or so to the south of the summit, where there are clear views of Marcy and the Great Range.

Journal entry: Sunday, September 13, 1970. Jim and I hear a wild thrashing in the northeast corner of the tangled Tabletop triangle. It occurs to me that Jim may be right about animal trails. On second thought, this animal is on no path.

A voice calls out: "Are you on a trail?" Yes, we shout back; we're at the summit. More wild thrashing, nearer and nearer. The confident hiker who strides toward us over the fallen timber matches the hearty voice. We meet Fred Hunt who hails from Paul Smiths, which is some 15 miles north of Saranac Lake. He tells us his mission is to check the condition of the summit cannisters for the Adirondack Forty Sixers.

Yes, he is a Forty Sixer — four times this year, in fact, he says. And where has he been today? Well, he started early from Adirondak Loj, and so far has climbed five high peaks.

Uh huh. This guy must be putting us on. But in keeping with the spirit of the mountains, we ask him if he would like us to wait so he can follow our marked trail to Indian Falls. "No, thanks," he says jovially. "I'm off to Phelps. He points in that direction. "I'm going straight across."

He's got to be kidding. The clouds are much lower now and we can see the rain moving toward us; the Great Range is indistinct and Marcy is blotted from sight. Jim and I will have enough trouble following our tiny blazes through this morass, yet this man says he intends to follow the course of the crow. Unbelievable.

Jim and I make slow progress in following our blazes. I'm not sure we would have made it back to the Marcy trail without them.

Indian Falls is now a deserted village. The two lean-tos are both occupied, but just barely. In one, a lone hiker wearily assembles his soggy gear. In the other nearest the falls, a young man and woman munch sandwiches and suck on a long-necked bottle. Four's a crowd, I decide, so Jim and I perch atop a huge boulder on the far side of the stream and break out lunch. The light drizzle which began on the descent has now blossomed into a full blown rain. From the shelter, the couple waves us over, so we join them.

They are from Vermont, and say they thoroughly enjoy our mountains. Again and again, they marvel at how we keep them so clean. Here, there is none of the litter they say is so prevalent in the Green Mountains. We tell them that most serious Adirondack hikers volunteer for trail clearing crews, and also pick up litter as they hike. The latter practice is second nature with Forty Sixers.

The depressing weather makes our return trip to the Phelps trail junction seem longer going down than up. As Jim and I begin to ascend the new trail, as yet unmarked, we sag to the side after a hundred yards. We are both tired, and I'm about ready to quit. As we commiserate, a cheerful figure comes bounding down the trail. Fred Hunt.

I aim to find him out: What were those peaks you climbed today? "Cliff, Redfield, Gray, Marcy, Tabletop and Phelps," he allows. However, he admits, "this is enough. I'm a bit tired."

He may be tired but he's not pessimistic. He outlines an ambitious plan for subduing the high peaks: he will climb all 46 during each month of the year. It should be no problem, he suggests, except maybe in December when the snow is too soft for quick traverse. Early spring on snowshoes is best, he informs us.

It dawns on me that this man may be for real. He didn't pass us on our way down from Tabletop. He could have crossed over directly from Tabletop. And if a man can do that, it's conceivable that Fred Hunt can do what he plans to do.

Fred Hunt does not sit as he talks. He gives us a smile and a Goodbye, and hurries downward.

Jim and I again leave our packs on a tree to speed our ascent. But the trail to Phelps is steeper, wetter, and almost twice as long as the trek up Tabletop. We know there is one good overlook two thirds of the way up. But today it offers only the opportunity to study the anatomy of clouds, close up.

It is almost five p.m. when the welcome alpine moss and scrub trees announce that we are near the summit. Painted arrows lead us around and over a series of rocky ledges and here, opposite a broad overlook, is the cannister. The names of two previous hikers from New York City are illegible in the scruffy notebook. But there is no mistaking the bold signature of the last visitor — Fred M. Hunt of Paul Smiths.

He's for real.

We will not see Old Mountain Phelps' "great view of Marcy" today. From the edge of the overlook there is no sense of height at all. We face only brooding fog, and since it has lost much of its brightness we do not linger.

There is only one group in the lean-tos at the Marcy Dam clearing. Through the front picture window of the ranger's cabin, we see him poring over some papers on the kitchen table. Some day when we have more time, it would be nice to chat with him.

"Great view" *is what the ADK guidebook promises from Phelps. But not today. Clouds blot out everthing one can normally see, from Big Slide to Marcy, Colden and Algonquin.*

What tales we could hear from him and his predecessors — of Henry Van Hoevenberg, who laid out this trail and built the original Loj; of Old Mountain Phelps, who led parties to Marcy so many times; and of the hordes of people who have hiked past this lovely spot over the years.

Many were hapless, like a few we saw today. Others were helpless, and the presence of the ranger spelled the difference between life and death for them.

The ranger could also tell of loneliness — or of the joys of solitude, depending on his viewpoint. It must be the latter, or he wouldn't have chosen this profession.

This also must be the mindset of Fred Hunt. Alone, he strode out at 2:30 this morning and before sundown surmounted four trailless peaks and two others, often not bothering to follow trails. He faced blowdown with disdain, as on his approach to Tabletop from Marcy and on the direct route he took to Phelps. The ADK guidebook says the latter is "not recommended."

The enormity of Fred Hunt's grand design sinks home. He has conquered all 46 high peaks four times in the past 12 months. Now he plans to make a circuit of them during each month of the year. And he expects to have only "a little trouble in December."

Trouble in December? How about January and February, when the howling winds and plunging temperatures lock up the lakes with several feet of ice and smother the Adirondack high peaks with even more snow?

A few years ago, my wife and I went hiking during a heavy snowstorm in the Lisha Kill Nature Preserve near our home in Schenectady. Shortly after losing the trail in the deepening drifts, we discovered we had been traveling in circles within the plot, which covers little more than a hundred acres. Yet Fred Hunt talks of plunging by himself into an area made up of more than a million, isolated, wilderness acres where he'll be miles from help. And not once, but again and again during every season.

He must love the serenity of the peaks. Of course, it could be that he has to travel alone — I never heard of anyone who could keep up with that pace.

More and more, as Jim and I sense the rhythm of climbing the 46 Adirondack high peaks, we are gaining a better understanding of the powerful attraction they have on people. For one thing, the climbing during our exploration has made us stronger. In the clean air, we breathe more easily and attempt more than we would have dreamed a year ago.

But there is more to the lure of the Adirondack high peaks than this. When I look back at the pictures of our hikes, and study the maps that trace our wanderings, I begin to see the mountains in a new, familiar light. They are becoming good friends, like some of the local Adirondackers we've come to know.

We're beginning to recognize the high peaks from a distance by their silhouettes. And later, back home, we fondly recall the quirky characteristics of each — their unique prominences and pitfalls, the heart-stopping overlooks, the boot-sucking wetlands, the unexpected waterfalls and silent pools.

A single trip to the high peaks is usually enough to lure anyone back from the busy world of business.

I'm beginning to believe that Jim and I will be successful in our quest of the 46. And after we've climbed them, I want to come back with him and take another, more relaxed look at each of them. A modified Fred Hunt circuit, you might say.

I am about to suggest this to Jim but think better of it. At 13 years of age, he is a creature of the moment — anything is possible today, but skip the long-range planning. Besides, we are both tired and with good reason. Our hike today is a half mile longer than the round trip to Marcy, and we have climbed 500 feet more of ascent. And, it is getting late.

At home, my wife informs me that I should have called to report that we were safely on our way home. It is past 10 p.m., she says worriedly; she was about to call the ranger.

She's right, of course. You tend to lose track of time when you're with friends. Next time, we'll make a point of meeting the ranger. He'll be a good man to have on our side.

Journal entry: Saturday, October 27, 1979. I've promised Ben that one of these days we'll retrace the route Jim and I took to Tabletop and Phelps.

Ben's thoughts seldom stray far from the Adirondacks. He has read and re-read my hiking journals. He has memorized most of the vital stats of the high peaks from the ADK guidebooks, and can tell you on demand the elevation, length and time of trail, degree of difficulty, and so on for all of them.

A budding Francis Parkman, perhaps. That eminent Adirondack historian decided during his sophomore year in college, in the early part of the last century, that he would write a story of "the whole course of the American conflict between France and England; or, in other words, the history of the American forest...My theme fascinated me, and I was haunted by wilderness images day and night."

I ask Ben if he had a theme like that in his dreams last night. "No," he responds solemnly. "I didn't get to sleep until two a.m. I kept dreaming there was an office building on my bed."

My fault, I'm afraid. Last week, I took Ben with me to the office to pick up some work to bring home, and showed him the view. My office building is in a suburban area of Albany called Colonie; it's too far away from the Adirondacks to get a view of the peaks. But my fifth-floor window provides a spectacular view of the triple peaks in the northern Catskills: *Black Dome, Thomas Cole and Blackhead.*

They're the next loftiest after Slide and Hunter, which we've already climbed. And they offer constantly changing vistas: sharp contours in the morning, fading to muted colors as evening inexorably creeps toward the horizon.

At this time of year, the big game season is booming in the Adirondacks so it makes sense to find an alternate target to Tabletop and Phelps. I suggest that we go down to the Catskills to climb the three mountains and see what the view from my office building is like in reverse.

Time out *for a hike in the northern Catskill Mountains. I follow Ben west from Black Dome toward Thomas Cole; we then return to climb Blackhead. Each is close to 4,000 ft.*

We have a glorious climb, as usual. But none of the wooded summits have an overlook to the north. Not that it would make much difference if there were: snow squalls combine with lowering clouds to blot out most of our views.

For the sake of Ben's sleep, I make a firm vow: stop bringing work home from the office.

***Journal entry: Saturday, June 14, 1980.** Ben and I decide that it's time to head for Tabletop and see if the trailless trek is any easier than it was 10 years ago.*

When we arrive at Indian Falls, Ben spots a well-worn, trampled path which leads toward Tabletop; he believes it is the route Jim and I took 10 years ago.

It speeds our way for a quarter of a mile to a well-used camp site and a major herd path marked with red ribbons, then peters out. A sweep of the mountain's flank fails to uncover any other path. We head back to Marcy Brook and start over.

This time we discover the problem. Blowdown has obliterated the normal herd path for a good 50 feet. Beyond it, the path is steeper than it appeared from Indian Falls because it was laid out by experts — climbers who wanted to get to the top as soon as possible.

At least, there is little chance of getting lost. We discover we will be on target if we head directly away from Colden, which sports the shape of a fat bottle when viewed from the northeast. It will be the beacon for our return.

There are no swarms of people as on the Marcy trail, but there are swarms of bugs. The temperature is in the '80s, and with no breeze it is stifling.

Fortunately, Ben and I have new mosquito shrouds which fit over our Adirondack crusher hats. I had to agree with Ben when he said earlier, "They'll look funny. Let's wait until we leave the trail to put them on."

But the pesky little devils changed our minds. In spite of Deet repellent, they peppered the cowlick on the top of my head with bumps, and bloodied both ears. To complicate matters, Ben got a bloody nose. When he removed the netting, the flies became very friendly and moved in.

Without warning, we top off on the ridge. After a short zigzag on the level, the herd path splits. Based on memory, I suggest that we go left to what I believe is the north.

Wrong, Ben says, as he spots a red marker tape on the right segment. And, mimicking what his brother Jim did 10 years ago, he plunges into the thicket and in a short time shouts: "I found the cannister!"

The brief, successful climax of both searches, it seems to me, is notable. The historian of the Forty Sixers reports that many people "assumed there was no cannister on this off-the-beaten-path mountain as they did not readily find it."

The previous entry in the summit register, nine days before, was made by park ranger Geoff May, here on patrol. Except for those who have to come here, such as the ranger, or aspiring Forty Sixers who feel they have to, it would appear this is not a favorite hangout.

Because of the heat and humidity and insects, we decide it is not for us either. It is a poor choice for lunch, even though the exposed summit rock is about the size of a picnic table. We jot our names in the register and begin our descent. The confusing blowdown makes the return trip as long as the ascent.

Marcy Dam pond is filled again, and lovely. Its serenity is broken only by yelps from two campers who dive in before toe-testing the mountain-fed waters.

Jungle conditions. *Blowdown wallowing in Christmas trees, black flies and oppressive heat often make Tabletop unbearable in midsummer. Two distant rises beckon; one is the true summit.*

Ten miles before reaching Schenectady, I begin to drive with caution. For one thing, it's hard to see at night on the newly-blacktopped surface of the Northway. But there's a more compelling reason: last night, a driver struck and killed a 400-lb. black bear lumbering across this portion of the Interstate. The car was badly damaged and the bear killed.

Journal entry: Sunday, April 19, 1981. *There is some question in my mind if this is too early in the year to again climb Phelps, this time with Ben. A week ago, when we came up for a warm-up stroll around Heart Lake at Adirondak Loj, there was considerable snow on the peaks. This morning, the man at the gas station was in no mood for hiking, early or late. "Cable TV's coming in," he beamed. "It's about time; there's not much else to do around here."*

Nor is a new young friend of Ben's in the mood — Greg Sanders, who spends most of his time at Elk Lake Lodge, where his father, Pete, is manager. Greg longs for the days when he can visit the big city down where Ben lives, while Ben longs for the days when he can return to Elk Lake. Or, for that matter, anywhere near the high peaks.

Ben and I are prepared for anything today — snow, rain, wind, mud or whatever. One never knows up here; most lakes are covered with a thin coating of ice this morning.

Blowdown on Phelps *complicates the ascent even though there is a trail. Climb from Van Hoevenberg trail is a little more than a mile, with only a few steep pitches along the way.*

We've traded in our old cotton wind-breakers for new Gore-Tex parkas, and both of us have new packs. At age 13, Ben is sprouting fast; his legs look twice as long as his body. And since as a consequence his feet have leaped two sizes since last fall, he has new boots. I've stopped growing, so I settle for new cleats in my old ones.

It seemed to me that when I was here with Jim, the trail from the junction shot straight up along the edge of the ridged shoulder to the summit. This trail, however, seems to wander all over, through new blowdown that I do not remember at all. Ben and I are

Avalanche Mountain *shimmers like a Chinese wall hanging in the late afternoon haze. Avalanche Pass is squeezed between it and Mt. Colden, left. Algonquin rises at right.*

out of condition since this is the first hike of the season, and it takes us two hours from junction to top, with frequent rests.

Nor is there fog this time — only high clouds which do not obscure the expansive views. Most of the Great Range is hidden by Tabletop, but a few of its peaks along with a good many other big ones parade in splendor — Marcy, Basin, Colden, Algonquin, etc. Nearby on the northeast, Big Slide grins with its clean-shaven face. The fair amount of snow on the higher peaks confirms that we made the right decision to take on this moderate mountain today.

Comparisons of Fred Hunt with Orson Phelps, the guide, are inevitable.

Both loved the Adirondacks and found solace in climbing the high peaks. But their different approaches to climbing confirm that Phelps Mtn. is the right namesake for Phelps the guide. Tabletop Mtn. is the locale where one is more likely to run into Hunt the bushwhacker, thrashing around in the blowdown.

It is true that Phelps pioneered many ascents in the high peaks. He cut two trails to Marcy, including the first from the east; he was a member of the first party to ascend Haystack, which is harder to climb than Marcy; and he made some of the earliest ascents of Giant, Nippletop, Gothics, Colvin and Skylight. But he is remembered more for his colorful companionship in guiding parties up established mountain trails in his later years. Phelps flowered in the company of friends.

Present-day hikers, on the other hand, know Fred Hunt not so much from personal encounters as from the repetition of his signature in trail-less summit cannisters: "The Lone Ranger." As he told the authors of *Forest and Crag*, "On well over half of all ascents, I was totally alone."

In that regard, Fred Hunt compares more favorably with the famed naturalist, John Muir, than with Orson Phelps. Muir jotted in his journal in the 1890s: "I am often asked if I am not lonesome on my solitary excursions. It seems so self-evident that one cannot be lonesome where everything is wild and beautiful and busy and steeped with God that the question is hard to answer — seems silly."

A few statistics highlight the similarities and differences between Orson Phelps and Fred Hunt.

It is said that Phelps climbed Marcy more than 100 times. It is a matter of record that Hunt climbed Marcy 110 times, in *consecutive* months, from September 1969 through October 1978. By December 1970, he had not only climbed the 46 Adirondack high peaks in each of the four consecutive seasons, but completed his grand scheme to climb each of the 46 in each month of the year. He wound up on Allen Mtn. in March 1973.

For an encore, Hunt then climbed all of the 46 peaks at night, prompting the Forty Sixers to add a new legend to his reputation: "Cat Eyes, the Moonlight Mountaineer."

Old Mountain Phelps lived his adult life in the Adirondacks and therefore could never fully appreciate the sanctuary the high peaks offered from the busy outside world. But Fred Hunt did. He had hiked since childhood in New England, and when he began to teach forestry at Paul Smiths, he turned to the Adirondacks to counterbalance the confinement of his classroom work.

In 1978, Fred Hunt moved to Vermont, where he promptly began setting records in climbing the 110 highest peaks in the northeast, during both day and night. But Adirondack climbers have not seen the last of The Lone Ranger. This time, according to the ADK's *Adirondac*, Fred

Hunt is the guide for his grandson, Danny Lombard, who urged that he introduce him to the never-ending pleasures of climbing the Adirondack high peaks.

They are near the top of the growing list of hikers who rejoice in the vision of people like David McClure, who argued for the preservation of the Adirondack wilderness at the New York state constitutional convention in 1894: "When tired of the trials, tribulations and annoyances of business and everyday life in the man-made towns, [the Adirondacks offer] a place of retirement...For man and woman thoroughly tired out, desiring peace and quiet, these woods are inestimable in value."

Amen.

Phelps' favorite. Some say Phelps Mtn. is an inadequate tribute to the famous Adirondack guide. But it has a magnificent platform for viewing Marcy, his favorite peak.

Nippletop and, on its right shoulder, Dial Mtn., from Elk Lake.

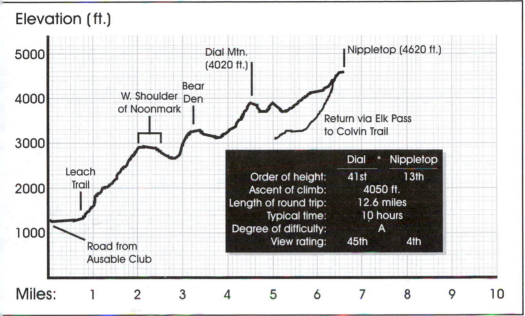

Elevation (ft.)

Dial Mtn. (4020 ft.)
Nippletop (4620 ft.)
Bear Den
W. Shoulder of Noonmark
Return via Elk Pass to Colvin Trail
Leach Trail
Road from Ausable Club

	Dial	°	Nippletop
Order of height:	41st		13th
Ascent of climb:		4050 ft.	
Length of round trip:		12.6 miles	
Typical time:		10 hours	
Degree of difficulty:		A	
View rating:	45th		4th

Miles: 1 2 3 4 5 6 7 8 9 10

or contour trails, see U.S. Geological Survey map, pgs. 120-121.

21, 22.
DIAL, NIPPLETOP

One can make a strong case that this is the most interesting climb in the Adirondacks.

The higher of the two peaks, Nippletop, thrusts its summit toward the sky with no dense woods on top to muddle your view. When standing on its tip, you'll know you have surmouted one of the highest mountains in the Adirondacks. Nippletop ranks 13th among the 46, sandwiched in between Giant Mtn., which is seven feet higher, and Santanoni Peak, which is 13 feet lower.

There are well-marked trails to the top. But the mountain is remote enough and the climb difficult enough that you have the feeling you are alone in wilderness, especially on the summit. From there, Nippletop's views rank among the best of the 46 high peaks.

There is also a storybook quality to scenes along the way — Gravestone Brook, for example, and Bear Den Mtn., Fairy Ladder Falls, Elk Pass, and so on. It's no wonder that romantic writers and artists were attracted to the peaks during the last century.

The climb also brings a bonus. In order to surmount the two high peaks, you must climb three more mountains along the way. In effect, you get five for the price of two.

These two high peaks are almost always climbed in combination; there's no rational reason for doing one without the other. There used to be a trail that followed the West Inlet of Elk Lake north to Elk Pass and then on up to Nippletop, but that has fallen into disuse. Hikers now follow a Great Circle route that begins and ends at the Ausable Club.

One segment of the route leaves the club road some three quarters of a mile beyond the Gate to head south over a shoulder of Noonmark, then on to Bear Den Mtn. and Dial to Nippletop. The return route descends to Elk Pass, then joins the trail from Mt. Colvin to the road from Lower Ausable Lake; this leads back to the clubhouse.

The best way to take the full measure of the two peaks is to follow the circle route both ways. It'll convince you that you've enjoyed two, distinctly different hikes.

And for a full appreciation of the challenge posed by the Nippletop range, scan it first from the four corners of the compass. Nippletop is a case study of a mountain with several personalities.

From Keene Valley on the north, you'll see a long ridge with a succession of ever higher bumps culminating in Nippletop at the southern end. A first-time visitor to the village could be convinced that a lower mountain on the left end of the ridge is Nippletop, because of its shape. But the mountain is Noonmark.

From the west, on Mt. Colvin, Nippletop is impressive but flattened on top. From the east, looking up from Hunters Pass which separates it from Dix Mtn., Nippletop's summit is nowhere in sight. The mountain, in fact, appears to be nothing more than a misshapen, amorphous mass.

At one time, Noonmark was called Dial. Then over the objection of the locals, the name Dial was transferred to Nippletop, to soothe the sensibilities and mores of outsiders who considered the view of the latter from the south as too descriptive.

The conflict was soon resolved. Noonmark again became Noonmark. The name Dial was bestowed on the peak in the middle of the range. And Nippletop regained its present name. Take a look at Nippletop from Elk Lake and you'll see why the locals prevailed.

The golf course and clubhouse which hikers pass today on their way to Dial and Nippletop from the Ausable Club look much the way they did in the early 1900s, with a few exceptions.

The original six-hole course was expanded to nine in 1928. The course (par 66 for twice around) is reserved for members and guests during July and August. But a sign notes a bargain out of season: "Keene Valley residents $10.00, Public $20.00, Mon. thru Thurs."

Golfers, like hikers, however, should be wary of June when the black flies begin to prey. As Alex Shoumatoff said in *Adirondack Life* recently of the "blood-thirsty little buggers" which frequent the course: "I saw a Canadian couple quit after three holes and demand their money back."

While the exterior of the clubhouse and outbuildings may look the same, some internal shifts reflect a change in lifestyles. A former small bar, for example, has been re-located in the more spacious Ladies Writing Room. As Edith Pilcher noted in *Up the Lake Road*, "Eventually it was realized that few ladies used the Writing Room, while the Bar was always overcrowded."

The club library has also been converted into a golf pro shop.

Journal entry: Saturday, September 19, 1970. The bustling action of preceding weeks has vanished. There are a couple of bitter-end golfers at the club, some frisky youths with packs on bicycles, and a caretaker in a pickup truck. A few leaves of modest color flutter across a putting green near the road; the good days are fast receding.

Son Jim has brought along his best friend, Bill Hume; we decide to take the trail that follows the ridge up to Nippletop. It's more than two miles longer to the summit than the route up Elk Pass, but the turn-off from the road to Ausable Lake comes a mile earlier, and the boys are anxious to start climbing.

The ADK guidebook says the first part of this climb is the hardest — a 1,600-foot shot up the west shoulder of Noonmark. It is correct, as usual. On one of my many pauses to puff and rest, two college-age boys, under full pack, charge up the trail. It makes me think of Fred Hunt. Or a passenger train whipping through my hometown in Iowa in the middle of the night. I always wonder if these vigorous young people, let alone passengers on the train, ever see anything.

Ah, youth. When Jim was nine, my wife and I used to worry that maybe one of his glands was out of control, because he'd pedal his bike furiously around the block, over and over. A check with the doctor was reassuring: "It's OK. He just needs to exercise his big muscles."

This trail makes it clear that Noonmark has a broad back. Time and again, one senses that the edge of the mountain's west shoulder is in sight, only to find that it's just another rib leading to the collarbone. Surmounting the shoulder, in fact, calls for about 400 feet less climbing than taking a separate trail which leads all the way to Noonmark's summit.

A pair of overlooks on the shoulder do not reveal Noonmark's summit on the east, but the first one offers a good view of peaks to the north. The second overlook unfolds the high peaks to the west, including Dix, as well as the Nippletop ridge, which ripples toward the sky. The latter is a substantial challenge.

The Adirondack Mountain Club rates the degree of difficulty for climbing Dial-Nippletop as anywhere from A to A+. The latter rating factors in the arduous roller coaster ride up the ridge. As the *Gazette's* Fred Fraser notes, it adds almost 1,300 feet of ascent to the round trip.

> *Journal entry: Saturday, September 19, 1970. The trail zigzags as it makes an easy descent into the col before Bear Den. There, we cross the headwaters of a north tributary of Gravestone Brook. There are traces of a wash, with damp areas supporting a patchwork of ferns, but no water. From the name, I would hesitate to fill my canteen from the "brook" anyway.*

> *The ascent to Bear Den is fairly easy. The crisp sunlight through the leaves enhances the promise of fall, so we stop and laze. How do you like it, Bill, I ask?*

> *"OK," he says. "It's better than the hike my sister Betsy and I made in June on the Long Trail in Vermont. We packed in overnight, and the flies were awful."*

> *I know what he means. A few years back I took our family there in the same month for a short walk on the Long Trail. We strolled from the car no more than 10 feet and came right back. The flies were unbearable. I wondered how Bill and his sister endured the night. Probably they were committed — too far in on the trail to turn back.*

Nippletop ridge ripples southwest from Noonmark Mtn., left rear, toward Nippletop. To right of Noonmark is Bear Den, then Dial. View is from Little Crow Mtn., near Keene.

Visual enjoyment builds on the way to Bear Den. At an overlook, Dix flaunts its scars — a posture that will remain in sight all the way to Nippletop's summit. On the right, to the west, the Great Range walls off many of the higher peaks. But they emerge one by one during the climb up the stair-steps formed by the peaks along the Nippletop ridge.

An outcropping which marks the summit of Bear Den offers a passable view. But it is marred by litter from past picnics and bonfires on the rocky table.

Aspiring Forty Sixers John Case and Mark Larsen are among those who can vouch that there are bears on Bear Den. While plowing through snow on their way to Dial in April 1994, Mark reported to *Adirondack Peeks* that he had stopped for a snack, while his partner moved ahead of him by five minutes or so. When Mark caught up with him, he informed John that fresh tracks showed a bear had been following him until Mark climbed close enough to spook the bear from its pursuit.

Journal entry: Saturday, September 19, 1970. As Jim and Bill and I move off Bear Den, a handmade sign confronts us with the warning: "Hornets, Sept. '70." We move around a fallen tree and, fortunately, encounter no problem. Jim and I saw the same warning about White Tailed Hornets on the bulletin board at the Ausable Club before our Gothics hike a month ago.

Beyond the col from Bear Den, the trail climbs some three quarters of a mile to the summit of Dial. Nearby on the right is a large boulder, which provides some views to the north and west. The boulder has no benchmark but does show the stub of a metal pipe imbedded in the top.

An easy dip and then a climb of a half mile bring the climber to what used to be called South Dial. It lost that distinction even though it's the same elevation as the real Dial — 4020 ft. — because it does not have a distinct peak; its summit is wooded, and it has no view. A peaked peak, no doubt, relegated to a bump on the way to Nippletop. The latter is not yet in view, but it is the powerful source that pulls the climber toward the end of the dark green arc soaring to the southwest.

A bare spot of land some five and one-half miles from the Ausable Club gives the climber a first good view of Nippletop. It sticks up like a gigantic cairn marking the way to the bulk of the 46 peaks beyond. To the southeast lurks monstrous Dix and its trailless neighbors, Hough, Macomb, and South Dix.

Journal entry: Saturday, September 19, 1970. We spot the trail coming up from Elk Pass and it tells us we have but a quarter of a mile to go. It also acts like a shot of adrenaline on Jim and Bill. They are off and gone. My fuel is stoicism; it is barely enough to propel me onward.

The unveiling of Nippletop's summit is so abrupt and breathtaking that one might think it was staged by a trail designer. The path becomes

*"**There is no sight** of man or his works in any direction," wrote Russell M. L. Carson in 1933 of the view from Nippletop's summit. So it is today. West Inlet, below right, leads to Elk Lake, beyond ridge at left.*

nearly level for the last hundred feet or so, coursing through a corridor of thickly-meshed conifers which block the views. Then, a last right turn leads to a huge, flat-topped boulder. It is perfectly canted for a sweeping view of the central high peaks, Elk Lake, Boreas Pond, Marcy Swamp, and a fair chunk of the rest of the world.

> *Journal entry: Saturday, September 19, 1970. As I turn to join Jim and Bill, Dix pulls like a magnet from behind — a horrendus hump. The two boys are transfixed by the Great Range. Jim has over-looked the two tough customers we conquered two weeks ago: Colvin and Blake, looking like two peanuts on the low ridge which squats unobtrusively before us.*
>
> *On our left, to the west, is a prime view of Upper Ausable Lake, with a glint of Marcy Swamp trailing off in the distance. Beyond? The mind reels with the sight of the big ones tracing the silhouette: Marcy, Haystack and the rest. And there, too, are some of the legendary trail-less peaks, such as Redfield and Allen.*

It's actually easier to calculate the peaks which can be seen from Nippletop by counting those which *cannot* be seen.

Marcy is a determining factor. It blocks out Gray, Colden, Iroquois, Marshall and the four Sewards to the west. Marcy's huge north shoulder also screens out Street and Nye.

Three lesser peaks are missing, too — Cliff, which is overwhelmed by Skylight; Couchsachraga, which at 17 miles away and 180 feet short of 4,000 feet, is lost from sight as usual; and East Dix, which though right next door is tucked behind big Dix, again as usual. Which leaves 33 of the 46 in sight.

While the panorama is impressive, a second view clamors for equal time: the endless wilderness. It makes the Adirondacks unique when compared with other famous vistas. A visiting exchange student from Switzerland, who leads climbing trips there, said "there is no real wilderness in the Alps." Reto Schultheas explained in *Adirondack Peeks*: "There's practically a village in every valley, and livestock roams the hills."

In the middle of the last century, the chances that present-day climbers would enjoy an Adirondack wilderness were slim. The earliest person to promote the concept, the writer S. H. Hammond, despaired that the beauties of the area were being ravaged. If left unchecked, he asked, "where shall we go to find the woods, the wild things, the old forests, and hear the sounds which belong to nature in its primeval state?"

Today, fortunately, Nippletop and the

Great Range stand-outs *line up to the northwest of Nippletop: Basin, left, Saddleback and Gothics. Sawteeth crouches before them like a wrinkled, Shar-pei guard dog.*

other high peaks are a part of the one per cent of the remaining land in the lower 48 states which is classified as wilderness. Even more meaningfully, the Adirondack peaks are among the one fourth of that land which is *protected* wilderness.

Russell M. L. Carson, author of *Peaks and People of the Adirondacks*, recorded the glory of that legacy in 1928, and it holds true today: "From Nippletop the silence of nature is unbroken and there is no sight of man or his works in any direction."

The alternate route to Nippletop via Elk Pass re-traces a little less than two miles of the initial part of the trail to Colvin, beginning where the Gill Brook trail branches off from the Ausable Club road. The climb toward Elk Pass moderates at first, then tilts upward through remains of virgin forest until the trail levels off as it passes an enormous, vertical rock face looming on the right.

Journal entry: Friday, July 10, 1981. Son Ben has scooted past the rock face to descend into the lower end of Elk Pass. His mother and I brought him with us to Elk Lake on Wednesday for some R & R. So far, it's been more Recreation than Rest for me, but I don't mind. Ben wants to see the sights on Nippletop that Jim and I have been telling him about. I suspect he's also responding to the same call that told Jim to exercise his big muscles.

Ben is like his brother's generation in another way: he hikes so fast that he misses things. He ignored the rock face against which I'm now resting. It's weathered and cracked in a way that makes it look like a frieze on the wall of a Mayan temple.

I take a breather and catch up with Ben a quarter of a mile down the trail. This time, he's standing still, as if in shock, staring at the setting.

Plunked on the edge of the narrow sliver formed by Elk Pass is a picture-perfect camp ground. It's sheltered by evergreens, enriched by blueberry bushes and is the setting for three, tiny, sparkling ponds which mirror the steep slopes surrounding it.

Two of the three ponds are gems, albeit rough cut by downed timber. They do not seem dead from acid rain, since bubbles puncture the surface around the lily pads. The third pond, the product of busy but unseen beavers, is secluded, still and questionable.

The shore trail leads us through whorls of sheep laurel; their rosy blooms magnetize clouds of butterflies. Ben says they are rare, and whips out his head net to try and snag one, but in vain. Before the trail heads upward toward Nippletop, it crosses the outlet of the ponds which sends their overflow toward Elk Lake via the West Inlet.

Adirondack literature tells us that other explorers have come this way, too.

When Verplanck Colvin and his surveying party came through Elk Pass in October 1875, the surveyor named one of the ponds Lycopodium, from the abundance of that plant near its shore. The plant could come in handy for weary hikers — the Indians valued it as a remedy for sore throats and runny noses.

On an early foray, Colvin and his crew erected "a shanty of boughs" for an overnight stay near the bottom of Elk Pass. It fronted, said Colvin, "an unknown waterfall, which from its silvery spray and step-like form I named the Fairy

"Stay awhile," one of the tiny ponds in Elk Pass seems to say to hikers. The passageway, well known to early explorers, sends its collected waters toward Elk Lake.

Ladder Falls." The falls are about a half mile south of the present-day Colvin-Nippletop trail juction on the upper part of the Gill Brook trail.

The next day, Colvin and his party, which included Old Mountain Phelps, made the first ascent of nearby Mt. Colvin. Later, Phelps served as guide for the writer Charles Dudley Warner and his companions for a climb up Nippletop. They also stayed at Fairy Ladder Falls in Elk Pass, but climbed some 300 feet to make camp at the top of the falls. It was, said Warner, "above the world and open to the sky...with a basin of illimitable forests below us and dim mountain-passes in the far horizon."

Warner was an incurable romantic. He had traveled widely in Europe, including Spain, and back home conjured up a cockamamie tale of a lost cave on the southeast side of Nippletop, which renegade

Spaniards had mined for — what else? — gold and silver. But as Warner and his party began the steep climb from Elk Pass, reality set in. Lamented the writer: "The pleasure of such an ascent...consists not so much in positive enjoyment as in the delight the mind experiences in tyrannizing over the body."

After climbing Nippletop, Phelps's charter was to guide Warner and his friends back to Elk Pass and then through the untracked wilderness to a log cabin on Elk Lake, then known as Mud Pond. But old Phelps became ill; he could not eat and had to make frequent stops to rest. Finally he could go no further and said, "I might as well die here as anywhere." As if to fulfill the premonition, he crouched into the hollow base of a towering pine tree, much as a bear might do, when an all-night rain began to fall.

But years in the wilds had conditioned him well. Phelps felt better in the morning and led his party to their destination at the southern end of Elk Lake. The legendary guide lived another 30 years before passing away at the age of 89 at his home in Keene Valley in 1905.

Warner referred to Elk Pass as Caribou Pass, but he was off by some 10,000 years. Caribou — which look like reindeer but are not domesticated — vanished from the Adirondacks along with the Ice Age.

The few elk that quartered in the high peaks later on were wiped out in the last century. An attempt to re-stock them was made in 1902 when a large group of the animals was set loose near Raquette Lake. Then, a smaller number was shipped in from Yellowstone National Park a few years later by, appropriately, the state's Benevolent and Protective Order of Elks. But, as Adirondack historian Donaldson noted, they were "stupidly and annoyingly tame."

As a logical outcome, a hunter shot the last elk in 1946. He must have thought "Wow!" when he mistook it for a whitetail deer. Both species *are* deer, but elk are a third taller and can weight three times as much as whitetails.

Journal entry: Friday, July 10, 1981. "Dad," says Ben. "I think we'd better get moving." He's studied the guidebooks and knows that we face a tough climb.

From Elk Pass, the trail seems to shoot straight up to the junction with the trail from Noonmark, then eases off for the short hike up the ridge to Nippletop's summit. That means we must climb almost 1,300 feet in a little more than a mile from Elk Pass. While the climb up the Dial-Nippletop ridge from Gravestone Brook started at some 500 feet lower, it stretched out over four times the distance.

When son Jim and his friend Bill and I came down by this route in 1970, we made it in less than an hour. In laboring upward today, Ben and I take a full two hours.

Once or twice as we struggle, I think son Jim, who now lives in Florida, has the right idea. When we visited him last year, we drove through the Everglades and passed a road sign posted by the National Park Service: "Red Rock Pass, Elevation: 3 ft." Refreshing — a bureaucrat with a sense of humor.

A short way up the steep trail, we stop on hearing a sharp retort. Probably a left-over firecracker, I suggest. Not so, says Ben. "There was a crashing noise along with it, like a tree falling." We conclude that the Nippletop slide, though not in sight, may be active again as it was on our trip to Colvin.

The nice thing about climbing a lot of mountains is that, ultimately, they do not all seem impossible. So it is with Nippletop today. Before we expect it, we reach the ridge junction and Ben races toward the summit.

The only ones on the exposed summit rock are two men who preceded us. I ask nervously if they have seen a young man. They smile and nod: "Over there."

Several feet below, on a similar rock ledge that has a better view of Elk Lake, Ben sprawls, shoes off, lunch under way. "The views are even better than you described," he says.

Before leaving our cabin at Elk Lake this morning, Ben told his mother to try and spot us with binoculars at 2:30 p.m. On the dot, 20 minutes after topping off, our binoculars can pick up no more than a fuzzy blur where the main lodge building should be on the south shore. That's good enough for us: it maintains the integrity of Carson's dictum: "There is no sight of man or his works in any direction."

Ben assumes his mother is waving, so he does the same.

Journal entry: Saturday, September 19, 1970. *It's hard to believe, but the boys have been so intrigued with the views from Nippletop that they have forgotton about lunch. It is 3 p.m.*

Bill nibbles gingerly around the blob that remains of his sandwich. Now, I find out, he dropped it on the patio before we left our house, and carefully put it back together, scraping off the dirt. A seasoned mountain man.

I offer him part of mine, but he declines. He digs out cookies from his pack, and they too are mashed. He eats them anyway. All of us are out of water.

A combination of exhilaration and exhaustion takes over on our way down to Elk Pass. For me anyway. The boys slither down the mixture of roots and wet mud that makes up the steep trail to look for water.

Trail from Nippletop descends northward over Dial and Bear Den toward Noonmark, right center, and Giant, right rear. Hikers will find no water on this trail.

At the first rivulet which offers its hesitant flow, they fill their canteens and plop in purification tablets.

At the pass, the languid waters from a marsh to our left laze across the swampy trail toward the quiet pond on the right. It has not been a half hour since they put the purifying tablets in their canteens, but Bill can't wait. The waters are dark and turgid, but I tell him to go ahead anyway — there should be no pollution from above. He flops on the mossy bank, dips his face into the black velvet mirror and slurps. "It's good," he says.

Journal entry: Friday, July 10, 1981. *The descent to the north via the ridge trail is easy to the point of being pleasant. But it seems endless on a sweltering day such as this. The first decent opening is a tidy little ledge on North Dial. The view, in my book, is as good in some ways as from Nippletop, and I am tempted to tarry. Ben, however, is hot and tired and thirsty, and states that he wants out.*

As we reach Bear Den, Ben moans for lack of water. Our last chance, Gravestone Brook in the col before Noonmark, is dry as usual. So we try to perk up by naming the drinks we will have at dinner and will bring home from the market: milk, lemonade, iced tea, fruit punch, pop of all kinds, orange juice, etc. Plus tall glasses of water, sweating with cold.

Ben slumps on the shoulder of Noonmark and drags out a left-over sandwich. "I never cared much about lettuce in these before," he says. "But I do now if there's moisture left." He wolfs it down and I give him my remaining water — not much more than a sip.

Ben and I elect to avoid the water in the stream near the road that leads to the Ausable Club. The Adirondack Mountain Club advised in the first edition of its guidebook back in 1934, that "All water from the streams from the mountain sides is pure and may be used for drinking."

That held true until some 10 years ago. Now, the risk of Giardiasis, or "Beaver Fever," caused by an intestinal parasite infecting mammals, calls for caution. We've been thirsty for four hours now, so we can surely go without for another half hour.

The day wanes as we hurry down the northwest shoulder of Noonmark. Annie Dillard, a self-styled "poet and walker," described the moment so well in Pilgrim at Tinker Creek: *"Shadows lope along the mountains rumpled flanks; they elongate like root tips, like lobes of spilling water, faster and faster."*

Tiny, carved signs mark side trails along the final stretch of the road to the Ausable Club. The last one announces the "Ladies Mile," a genteel reminder from pre-Women's Lib. A string of pipes along the road reveals that one water problem has been resolved: it brings a plentiful supply from Gill Brook to the Ausable Club.

Journal entry: Wednesday, June 11, 1986. *A surfeit of water does not guarantee a successful hike to Nippletop. My field notes for this day reveal what happened on an outing with son Ben and our friend Tom Stanwood: "Raining hard from club to Elk Pass. Low blowing clouds. Cold. Getting the chills. I tell Tom and Ben we* have *to go back. Nuts to Nippletop."*

Journal entry: Friday, August 22, 1986. *Ben and I decide to try again, and on this crisp, cool, and clear day we have no trouble. I am amazed to find on re-checking my field notes that the time for each of my three successful round-trips to Nippletop, on both good days and bad, was within 20 minutes of the others.*

On the summit, I recall that it has been 149 years since the first recorded climb of Nippletop, and 58 years since Carson remarked on its pristine loveliness. John Muir could have been thinking of this mountain view when he said, "In God's wildness lies the hope of the world — the great fresh unblighted, unredeemed wilderness."

It's also been 16 years since son Jim and I first climbed Nippletop. In all those years, thank goodness, nothing has changed. On the summit, at least.

As we pause on our descent at Dial, a pair of very large, black birds fly over us. They look like crows, but are bigger and soar instead of flapping their wings, as crows do. They confirm reports by the Adirondack Park Agency that ravens are returning to the high peaks after disappearing for half a century.

Ben has changed, too. I'm reminded of this by a left-over ticket for the Ausable Lake bus which I had tucked in my field notebook. It's marked "child"; Ben's now 18, and he couldn't qualify for that ticket if he knelt on his knees before the ticket counter inside the club.

Journal entry: Saturday, July 11, 1981. Back from my second trip to Nippletop, and finally relaxing at Elk Lake. For a while.

Ben asks me to go canoeing so he can try his luck fishing, which he's never done before. On his first cast, he hauls in a 15-inch, native, speckled trout. "Almost beats hiking," he grins.

Paddling back, we rout a kingfisher from the limb of a dead tree overhanging the lake. At first, it shakes its bushy crest and rails at us for spoiling the fishing. Then, still complaining as it takes off, it rattles away like a crotchety old man with a toothache.

Ben and his mother and I are the only ones staying at Elk Lake Lodge. In effect, we have our own 12,000-acre private preserve.

Journal entry: Sunday, July 12, 1981. Another party, a honeymooning couple, arrives. It is still like having our own 12,000-acre private preserve.

Journal entry: Monday, July 13, 1981. Ben hauls me out on the lake to try again. This time, no fish rise to the bait.

The Wood Duck houses are empty; they will be busy when we return in the fall. Nor do we see beavers at their lodges spotted about the islands. But otters frolic as usual near the dam at the lake's outlet.

On a cutoff trail leading to the main route to Marcy on the southwest shore of Elk lake, we are reminded of Verplanck Colvin when we find, as he reported, "in several places clear and unmistakable impressions, large, massive footprints." But ours were not made by panthers, as he asserted. Ours were made by bears.

Again tonight, as every night, we hear the eerie cries of loons on the lake. John McPhee came closest in describing them. They are, he said, "The laugh of the deeply insane."

Journal entry: Tuesday, July 14, 1981. *Rain again. An even cooler breeze prompts more blankets and a roaring fireplace. On a short hike, Ben and his mother and I come face to face with a mother black bear and her two cubs. We are all members of the Society of Mutual Mistrust — bears go one way, we the other. A visiting ranger says a bear seen here the day before would weigh in at close to 700 pounds.*

Our 12,000-acre private preserve, it would seem, is also a private zoo, sans bars.

Changing moods *enhance the beauty of Elk Lake. Rise of early morning mist adds a surrealistic touch to mountains reflected in the glassy surface.*

Macomb Mtn. from Elk Lake.

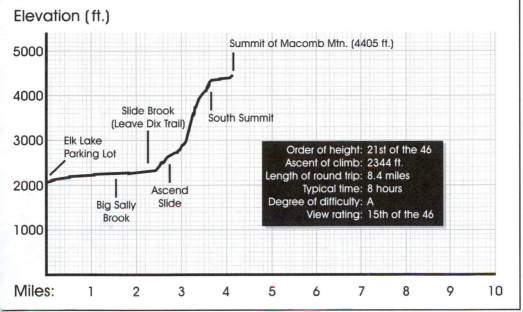

Elevation (ft.)

Summit of Macomb Mtn. (4405 ft.)

Slide Brook
(Leave Dix Trail)

South Summit

Elk Lake
Parking Lot

Ascend
Slide

Big Sally
Brook

Order of height: 21st of the 46
Ascent of climb: 2344 ft.
Length of round trip: 8.4 miles
Typical time: 8 hours
Degree of difficulty: A
View rating: 15th of the 46

Miles: 1 2 3 4 5 6 7 8 9 10

or contour trails, see U.S. Geological Survey map, pgs. 214-215.

23.
MACOMB

At the close of the American Revolution, New York state became owner of some seven million acres formerly owned by loyalists to the British cause or by the Crown itself. The bulk of those acres were wild lands in the northern part of the state, and included the four high peaks of the Seward Range in the Adirondacks.

The state was anxious to sell this territory for a couple of reasons. First, like the 12 other former colonies and the fledgling American government, New York's treasury was empty. And second, as Roderick Nash noted in *Wilderness and the American Mind*, "for most of their history, Americans regarded wilderness as a moral and physical wasteland fit only for conquest and fructification in the name of progress."

New York state decided that the most efficient way to fulfill this mission was to sell the land in big blocks to developers. They, in turn, would dispose of it to settlers.

One of the first bidders was Alexander Macomb, who no doubt shared the vision of noted American architect and city planner Daniel Hudson Burnham: "Make no little plans; they have no magic to stir men's blood."

Macomb and two associates responded in like mind. They petitioned the state to sell them more than half of the new "waste and unappro-

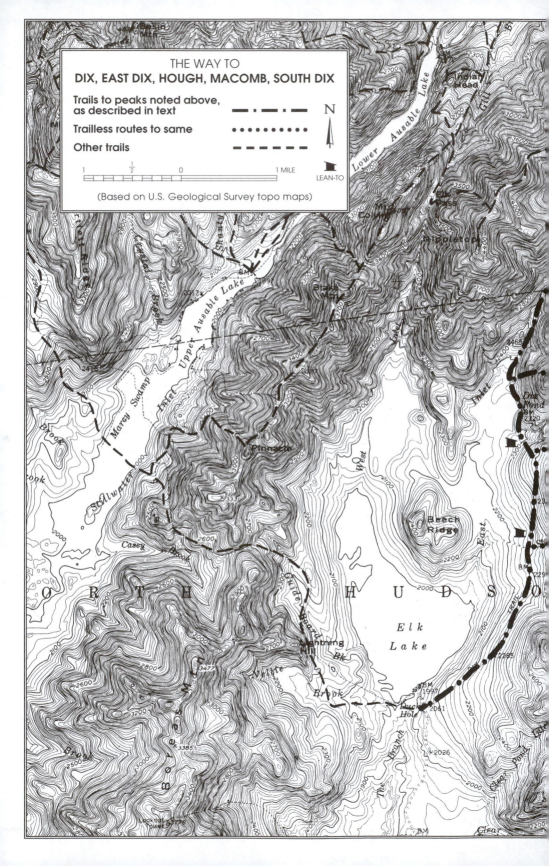

THE WAY TO
DIX, EAST DIX, HOUGH, MACOMB, SOUTH DIX

Trails to peaks noted above,
as described in text

Trailless routes to same

Other trails

N

1   ½   0   1 MILE

LEAN-TO

(Based on U.S. Geological Survey topo maps)

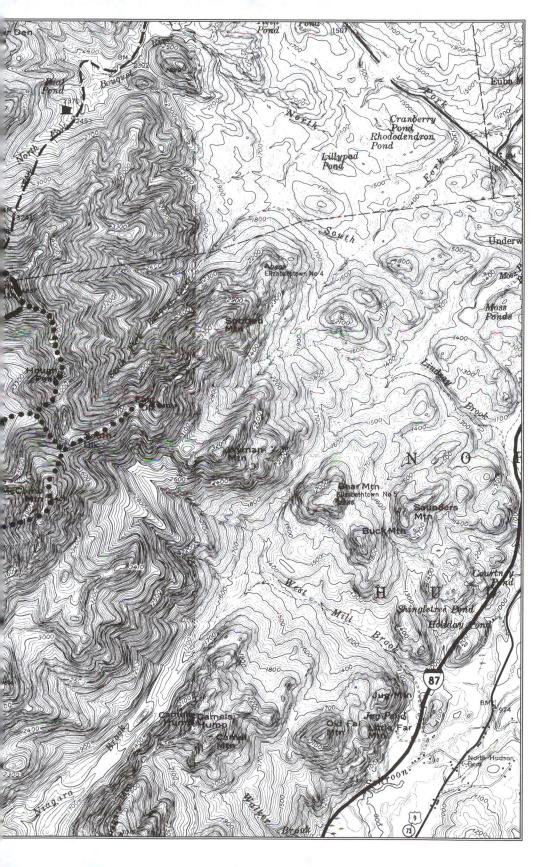

priated" public lands, which extended across Franklin, St. Lawrence, Herkimer, Hamilton, Lewis, Jefferson and Oswego counties.

They were either good salesmen or had connections, or both. In any event, they were astute businessmen. The state sold them 3,635,600 acres for eight pence an acre during a six-year period ending in 1798. It was like buying property today, but on a grand scale: they paid on an installment basis at six per cent interest.

There's no way to peg the sale in terms of present real estate values. But it was a bargain back then. In the middle of the transactions, the state fixed the minimum price for selling its remaining two million acres at six shillings per acre — nine times the price it had put on the Macomb Patent.

One would assume that the mountain which we know today as Macomb would be a part of that monumental purchase. But it is a good 10 miles away from the eastern boundary of the Patent. In fact, Macomb Mtn. is farther away from the Macomb Patent than any of the other 46 high peaks.

One might also assume, in spite of that anomaly, that Macomb Mtn. was named for the Alexander Macomb whose name will forever be associated with this landmark Adirondack purchase. Again, not so. The mountain was named in honor of his son, also named Alexander. He distinguished himself as the commanding general at the Battle of Plattsburg on nearby Lake Champlain, and later became commander-in-chief of the United States Army.

There is, however, a solid link between Macomb Mtn. and the wilderness which the two predecessors were associated with 200 years ago.

The side of Macomb facing Elk Lake still appears to be "waste" land, due to some of the most spectacular avalanches in the Adirondack high peaks. And the Dix Range of which Macomb is a part is labeled the Dix Mountain Wilderness.

There used to be a trail from Elk Lake to the summit of Macomb before the turn of the last century. Today, it is long gone and the mountain is trailless. The best way to explore the mountain is to climb the course of the slides, where one can examine the mayhem wrought by nature.

Climbing Macomb brings one face-to-face with conditions much like they were during the time of the two Macombs. As recently as 1934, the first edition of the Adirondack Mountain Club guidebook warned, "this territory is for the explorer, not the hiker."

Journal entry: Saturday, September 26, 1970. *Son Jim and I hope to climb not only Macomb today, but two other trailless peaks which adjoin it, South Dix and East Dix. The first two miles will be on the Dix trail, which starts near Elk Lake, which we will see up close for the first time.*

Elk Lake *from the lawn of the lodge; lone fisherman savors the loveliness. Pinnacle Ridge forms the horizon on the north, leading east to the Colvin, Nippletop and Dix ranges.*

We have caught glimpses of the lake from various high peaks. It surrounds a profusion of islands; sunlight on the glistening waters makes it look like a sackful of diamonds scattered on green velvet. We are also anxious to know more about Elk Lake Lodge — is it another Adirondak Loj, or what? We intend to find out.

As we leave the house, my wife gives me an extra cheerful goodbye kiss and says, "Have a happy September 26." That's nice of her, I think to myself. Son Jim and I are near our turn-off 90 miles to the north before it dawns on me — this is our wedding anniversary! Hmm. I may be a loser in the race for thoughtful husbands, but I picked a winner in a wife.

It also goes without saying that I've passed the test of a true mountaineer.

Half way up the five-mile, private entry road to Elk Lake which snakes northward from Blue Ridge Road, the ice-blue glint of Clear Pond sparkles through the trees on the right. The deep, glacial body of water is stocked with lake trout and landlocked salmon to entice the patrons of the lodge.

Beyond the pond's outlet, a caretaker's cabin appears on the left. It snuggles in a clearing where travelers heading west during the last century often stopped for the night at Israel Johnson's cabin. The site of his sawmill lies across the road near the Pond. Both have disappeared.

Where the road peaks another mile or so to the north, the bull-necked dome of Mt. Haystack rises to fill a break in the trees. Then, a trailhead marker at a small parking lot on the right indicates where the journey to Macomb begins. Elk Lake Lodge nestles a couple of hundred yards down the road, stolid and silent near the water's edge.

Just before reaching the lodge, the road dips to pass a dam and spillway. This reveals the means by which the place made a smooth name change from Mud Pond to Elk Lake.

Journal entry: Saturday, September 26, 1970. The lodge itself is a casual, two-story, log structure. No one stirs on the long front porch, nor inside, as near as we can see. The scene mirrored by the lake beyond explains why everyone is out and about. Paul Jamieson said of it in Adirondack Life, *"The High Peaks form a semicircle around the lake, composing the noblest of wild prospects."*

Elk Lake Lodge *is plopped in the middle of a 12,000-acre, privately-owned forest preserve. Guests enjoy the scenic panorama overlooking what* National Geographic *called the "jewel of the Adirondacks."*

Macomb looms the closest, to the northeast, sporting the biggest and ugliest landslide scars that Jim and I have seen. The peak in the center of the tableau, directly ahead to the north, is easy to identify by its profile — Nippletop. And the big one to its right has to be Dix — lofty, lordly, and wreathed in clouds. The Colvin Range trails off to the west toward Boreas Mtn.

Early morning steam rising from the lake does little to soften the challenge of the peaks. But it lends an ethereal quality to the lone fisherman in silhouette on the lake, and to the placid and peaceful setting of the main structure.

Elk Lake Lodge is not a clone of Adirondak Loj. The latter is owned by the non-profit Adirondack Mountain Club. The Loj is one of several facilities which the ADK makes available to thousands of visitors each year for lodging, meals, camping space and access to the high peaks. For hikers, the club offers accommodations which are among the best bargains in the Adirondacks.

Elk Lake Lodge, on the other hand, is privately owned. It limits visitors to seven cottages and one private camp, plus a few rooms in the central lodge which also houses a dining room and lounge.

Again, by contrast, the ADK owns a square mile of property surrounding the Loj, including all of Heart Lake and most of nearby Mt. Jo. Within the environs, one enjoys sweeping views of some of the high peaks — Street and Nye, the McIntyre Range and, dominating everything from the south, Marcy.

Elk Lake Lodge, on the other hand, encompasses 12,000 acres, almost 20 times more than the Loj. The splendor of the surrounding ranges is in sight from almost anywhere on Elk Lake. The lucky residents of Marcy cottage, fittingly, can sit on their side porch and study the tip of Mt. Marcy, which peeps over the Colvin range when its head is not shrouded in clouds.

It costs a bit more to stay at Elk Lake Lodge than at Adirondak Loj. But the people who come to Elk Lake must consider it a bargain. Many come back year after year to enjoy the same accomodations during the same seasons.

One should probably categorize Elk Lake Lodge as falling somewhere in between Adirondak Loj and the Ausable Club. Elk Lake Lodge has no courses for golf, tennis or lawn bowling, per the latter. But it has a bigger lake than the two Ausables put together and, like the latter, is off-limits to motor boats. Elk Lake is also right next to the lodge, not three and one half miles away, as Ausable Lake is to the club.

Elk Lake Lodge more closely resembles Adirondak Loj in one respect: it serves no liquor. Guests can bring their own bottles at Elk Lake, but there's no bar within 20 miles. Those who choose to belly up as their main exercise would be bored to death at Elk Lake.

Journal entry: Saturday, September 26, 1970. The first half mile of the Dix trail is brooding but beautiful. An occasional wispy shaft from the sun swings by like a ghostly pendulum as we amble beneath the dark forest canopy.

Jim momentarily comes to life to examine some strange markings on a huge boulder to the left of the trail. It is as if someone long ago had wrapped it like a ball of string, then cast it in stone for eternity.

The trail then spills out onto a wide lumber road, following it north for a mile or so. Someone has parked a pick-up truck to one side. There are no people in sight, but the keys are. Trustworthy country.

Before long, the trail again disappears into the forest, crossing a few small streams. Some are colored orange-red — no doubt from iron-tinged rocks which have been loosened by Macomb's slides.

Beyond, we cross two larger streams. Both are segments of Slide Brook, which was split by an avalance a quarter of a mile upstream to the east. The second is the home of Slide Brook lean-to. As we rest there, we note two packs inside, but no one is around. Nor do we yet see Macomb because of low clouds.

The ADK guidebook suggests two feasible ways to head for Macomb. One is the broad, stony brook bed of the first branch of Slide Brook. The other is an old tote road which leads east from the lean-to clearing. Jim and I agree that a trail beats a stony brook bed any time.

A trail of sorts leads to a leaning outhouse which offers precarious comfort. Beyond it, the trail splits. The right fork seems to be more well worn, but soon peters out; so does the left fork after a short distance. We take our chances with the right segment, since it leads in the direction of the brook, which comes from Macomb.

Right away we plunge into a maze of blowdown, and it is rough going. We decide to head for the brook, but find it just as bad, along with an added water hazard. As we clamber over and under and around the tangled, fallen trees, we do see footprints. It's comforting at least to know we are not the first to choose this route.

Nature has set its snares on this mountain. From the Slide Brook clearing, the hiker first must contend with blowdown from the 1950 hurricane. One emerges from that to face the sprawling remnants of the huge slides which rent the mountain from top to bottom in 1947.

As if that were not enough, fires ravaged the slopes so much in the early part of this century that Macomb has had to re-forest itself. First came grasses, and then pioneer trees such as poplar and birch. In places, they are so densely spaced that they hinder the hiker as much as help.

Journal entry: Saturday, September 26, 1970. For our ascent, Jim and I choose a slide which has formed a deep, rocky, V-notched gully. Through a break in the trees, we get a first glimpse of our target, far above.

A smaller branch of the stream cuts off to the left. Beyond, we note that the banks of the main gully are becoming very high and very steep with huge boulders jutting from loose soil on the sides. We decide the smaller gully we have just passed will be the easier and safer route. With difficulty, we surmount the bank on our left, leave a cairn to mark our return path, and continue up.

It is apparent from footprints that most climbers follow the portion of the slide that offers footholds in the rubble of reddish dirt and rock. The going is steep and somewhat precarious because of small rock slides we cause as we clamber ahead. We decide it is safer to climb side by side than one ahead of the other.

As Jim and I rest, we note three climbers gaining ground on us. Jim is annoyed; he does not want them to pass, because then we will be the target for their rockslides. With much huffing and puffing, we stay ahead.

This is one of our first forays where

Main slide ahead. *Multiple branches converge, all with loose rocks in crumbling soil. Overhanging ledges on cliff above guard the triple-crested summit.*

we can see the top of a high peak grow nearer as we climb. Of course, we know we cannot see the true summit of Macomb. According to the guidebook, that lies a half mile beyond the overhanging cliffs at the top of the slide.

The view from the top of the slide is breath-taking, and while we enjoy it we do a bit of breath-getting, too. Below us, to the southwest, Elk Lake shimmers through the soft, autumn air. To the west and north-west, we can faintly discern the outline of other, distant, high peaks.

The climbers below are no family out for a weekend picnic. They are pressing us, so we move up to skirt the rocky overhang of the steep cliffs. We follow a trail that moves to the left, then see many footprints in the damp ground moving steeply upward. We follow them, and reach a dead end at the vertical cliffs.

We make a short descent to the left, then move up at a sharp angle through cripplebush toward the summit. It is very wet and slippery, and for once we are grateful for handholds in the gnarled trees.

It is a relief to reach level ground and find a well-worn trail leading to an overlook on the right. Again we see the same sweeping views we saw from the top of the slide, only better. Jim flops down on the rocky outcropping to eat lunch, while I wander nearby to get my bearings.

There is no sign of a summit cannister. I spot two peaks to the north-east, one connected by a ridge from Macomb, and I assume these are South Dix and East Dix. On the Elk Lake side of the overlook, I see a big hulk looming ahead to the north. At first, I think it is Nippletop. A check of the map confirms that it is — big Dix, again. That means that the smaller pyramid this side of it is Hough.

It also means that the two peaks I saw from Jim's lunch table are not the little Dixes. I walk farther along the cliff edge to see if I can spot them. Instead, a long, rippled ridge leads to another summit, which is the real one, a hundred feet or so higher than our own. Obviously, we had been convinced like so many others that we had surmounted Macomb.

This momentary lapse reminds me again that in mountain climbing, you must never let hope take control of your senses. In my mind's desire, we had climbed Macomb and my search was for confirmation, not truth. I call to Jim to pack up the rest of his lunch, and we trudge upward along the ridge to the north.

Herd paths which fan out to false summits slow Jim and me on our way to Macomb's real summit. When we do reach it, I decide to recon-noiter to avoid any further blunders.

Just below the crest of the summit to the east we see the little Dixes — a long, flat twin-top peak that is the elusive South Dix and beyond it, separated by a deep pass, East Dix. Whoever dubbed them "little" had a great sense of humor. I am a bit skittish about heading over because both are trailless, and the weather is a dead ringer for the changeable conditions Jim and I encountered on Iroquois.

Jim wants to push on to the little Dixes, and really so do I. But reason tells me no. It is now two p.m. and other climbers have told me it will take us until six p.m. to return to Macomb's summit. Darkness comes at seven, so this means a major portion of our hike down the slide, plus the trail back to our car, would be in the black of the woods.

Sandwiches and a thermos of hot coffee assuage my disappointment. Jim is both malleable and resilient. He would love to knock off three peaks today, but he also loves to loaf. Which he now does.

As we sign the register, I discover why the pace of the three hikers on the slide below us was so brisk. They are the Chapmans from Newcomb, New York; Laura is a Forty Sixer, Ann has 41 and Walter 35. Obviously, the last two have caught the excitement of the chase and are forging to completion under Laura's leadership. It is clear, too, why they did not pass us. They must have made straight for the correct summit, heeding the guidebook's warning against climbing the cliffs, which are "too steep for safety."

The bold letters on the summit cannister read "Macomb." Yet I note that my topographic map and an Elk Lake map of the area label the peak "McComb." Early guidebooks, in fact, identified it both ways. And the first person to name the peak in print, New York state's pioneering geologist Ebenezer Emmons, labeled it " McCombe."

On a hunch, I search out the benchmark. It reads "McComb." The two Alexanders would be mortified.

For the first time on any mountaintop, it occurs to me that Jim and I are under no pressure to start back. The panorama toward Elk Lake is a pastel — mottled, pale green forests broken by the jagged mirror of the lake. The canvas spreads outward to an indistinct terminus, where misty peaks blend with misty sky. Low clouds sweep toward us from the flanks of the ridge which extends from the lesser summit of Macomb.

Idly, I glance at the tattered pages of the summit register. It reveals a vivid chronicle of those who have paused before us.

In June of this year, one Ian Heath of Sydney, Australia arrived, "Wet and haggard — 5:45 p.m." On July 12, that intrepid mountain climber, Trudy Healy, whom Jim and I have read so much about in Forty Sixer literature, urged those who follow to "send your news to Adirondack Peeks." She is its current editor.

View from Macomb *to the southwest emcompasses Elk Lake, shrouded in autumnal haze. In the distance, Boreas Mtn. range and Pinnacle Ridge struggle to proclaim their presence.*

July 16: Tim Smith of Keene Valley succinctly reports, "Boy, is this a crummy day!"

Aug. 1: Anthony Arcola scrawls, "At the top but don't know how I got here. Rock face pretty hairy."

Aug. 6: Linda Blum — "I'm pooped, but it's too great to miss."

Aug. 12: Tom McCormick, Yardley, Pa. — "No. 19 after three tries." An aspiring Forty Sixer, no doubt.

Aug. 15: Hall Stillman, Great Neck, Long Island — "No. 44, Couch and Marshall to come." And the same day, Kenneth Pur, Queens — "No. 42, very dangerous!"

Next, an undated cryptic note: "To the next person who arrives. Please take the glass with the 46 pennies in the cannister back with you to keep from Evan Kurtz, new ADK 46er, Bronx, N.Y., Camp Idylwold." (The second issue of Adirondack Peeks *the following year recorded this report from Peter Fish to the Forty Sixers' treasurer: "On August 22, a small party of us reached the summit of Macomb...there seemed to be little reason for leaving the pennies there, so here they are for entry in the organization 'cash receipts'").*

Aug. 28: Tric and Myrna Martin, East Rochester, N.Y., both now No. 43 — "We just have Dial, Nippletop and Sawteeth to go. We're clouded in, can see about 20 feet. We've heard thunder all morning, had a real downpour between East Dix and South Dix, noticed lots of hail all along the trail to the top of Macomb. Exhilarating!" It's revealing that so many notes are dotted with exclamation marks.

Sept. 1: Carolyn Reiners, Pittsford, N.Y. — "Cold and windy. It snowed (and hailed and rained)."

Sept. 20: John S. Signorelli, Newton, N.J., Syracuse U. '72 — "With this peak I complete the Dixes in one day, leaving it with fond and insistent injunctions to do itself well."

Jim yawns and points to the clouds racing in from the south. "Iroquois," he says. He's not worried about the descent; we can't miss the Dix trail if we keep going west. But it does seem like a good idea to make the bulk of our return trip below the clouds.

Journal entry: Wednesday, November 30, 1994. I have just uncovered a treatise which younger son Ben prepared some years back entitled, "The 25 Greatest Mountain Climbs in the Adirondacks."

It surprised me to see that he listed Macomb as ninth on the list, ahead of such stars as Colden, Algonquin and Santanoni. It surprised me also, but not as much, to see that he gave fifth rank to Sunrise Mtn., located a couple miles east of Elk Lake Lodge. While only 3,614 ft., Sunrise offers a marvelous, elevated panorama of the high peaks.

Marcy was number one, as expected. But the biggest surprise of all was to find that he gave second place to Snowy, a western peak near Indian Lake that one can barely discern from Sunrise. Snowy lacks a hundred feet of being among the exalted 46.

Ben and I climbed Snowy in May of 1980. It offers pretty much a reverse of the superb views one gets from Sunrise. But rankings are implanted in the hiker's psyche according to conditions at the time. All I remember of Snowy is debilitating humidity, hordes of black flies, and garbage spread around the abandoned observer's cabin near the summit.

Tonight, I called Ben, who's now living in Tucson, Arizona, to expand on my field notes about our hike up the Macomb slide in 1969 when he was 11 years old. He concluded with this observation: "Macomb was the scariest climb I ever made in the Adirondacks."

Journal entry: Saturday, September 26, 1970. The herd path leading back across Macomb is easy. However, Jim and I again can't find the path that's supposed to lead around the steep cliffs to the top of the slide. So we cut back through the cripplebush. The cliff is so near vertical it's frightening.

As we slither down from handhold to foothold, the register comments keep running through my mind. When I read them, I searched for the answer to the age-old question: "Why do we climb?" Jim slips, clutches a root, and momentarily half hangs, half leans against the black guck on the mountainside as he catches his breath. From that brief vignette flashes the real reason why so many people come to the mountains.

Climbing poses a real challenge; it's strenuous, adventuresome, and on occasion dangerous. Most of the notations reflect this, and it appears that with Macomb some of the climbers have had their fill.

Yet climbing is also exhilarating. When most people conquer a peak against a fair set of odds, they like to let off steam about it. Evan Kurtz did it with his cache of pennies. And I suppose my way is with this journal, which helps keep the memories alive for my sons and me.

As we rest at the top of the slide, Jim notes for his color-blind father that there are brilliant yellows and patches of red in the sea of green trees below. And the weather keeps changing the aspect. One moment there is a hint of Indian Summer; the next, scudding clouds predict the onrush of winter. In the distance, slanting sheets of rain fall on Elk Lake. The effect is a muted kaleidoscope.

Why do we climb? *Jim slips in the black guck and grabs for a handhold as I ponder the question. We descend a near-vertical path that's complicated by cripplebush.*

Jim glories in slithering down the loose slide on the seat of his pants, sending small rocks to tumble below him. His father descends more gingerly near the edge of the slide, taking advantage of overhanging scrub cherry trees. We note when glancing behind that one minute the top is in view, and the next it's obliterated by clouds.

Experience tells climbers to treat the Macomb slide with respect. Roger Harris of Troy, N.Y. reported to *Adirondack Peeks* in March 1975 that "four avalanches swept down the Macomb slide while we were climbing it. I was swept 500 feet downslope and par-tially buried in one of

Top of the slide: *only three and a half miles to go to the lodge. The haze of Indian summer competes with low, scudding clouds. Sheets of rain repeatedly sweep across Elk Lake.*

the minor ones." Climbers should be aware, said Harris, "that avalanches are quite possible in our mountains, and in this situation it could have led to serious injury or death."

Journal entry: Saturday, September 26, 1970. *Near the lower end of the slide, Jim and I hear the gurgle of water. A slight flow appears and disappears in the rocks, then emerges for good. It is the source of Slide Brook, or at least one of its tributaries. Scattered, square-faced chunks of orange-shaded rock confirm the source of the colored streams on the Dix trail.*

At our cairn we elect to follow the smaller gully to the right, avoiding a treacherous descent into the main streambed. Boulders provide the only handholds down the twisting course of the waterway. We keep our fingers crossed that the more exposed ones will not give way.

It's a welcome change to move back into the trees. There is a path of sorts along the stream, but not much. Jim and I stop for a breather at a small waterfall and fill our collapsible cups from the icy sheet of water. It rushes over the topmost boulder like a curved mirror of emerald.

The small trees thicken as we move downward, so we search for a path that will lead to the Slide Brook lean-to. Instead, we confront dense blowdown in every direction. And it is treacherous. Jim slips from a mossy log and sprains his wrist. I walk a tightrope of soil between two massive, fallen tree trunks and fall through to my waist.

We meet a welcome sight, although I never thought I'd call it such — the tilting John.

The owners of the backpacks we saw this morning loll in front of the lean-to, puffing on their evening pipes. The two men are from New Jersey, they say; they drove up in five hours last night. Yes, they have completed 25 of the 46 high peaks, and seem to want to talk about their favorite jaunts.

Hurricane Mountain, they allow, is excellent for families. But they admit their wives and daughters lost interest when they accompanied the men on some of their tougher climbs. From their relaxed sighs, I gather they will get along by themselves, somehow.

I ask them about the Pocono Mountains, just across the border from them in Pennsylvania. No good, they say: too many people. The Catskills are all right, but there is no water along the trails. "We love it here," one of them remarks. "The air is clear and there aren't many people. Last night, we were asleep at eight and up at seven to tackle Hough. It wasn't bad going up, but very difficult coming down."

I make a mental note for a future climb: Hough rhymes with tough. We trade wishes for luck, and Jim and I swing down the return trail.

Jim trips over a root on the trail ahead of me, and I am surprised to find it is almost pitch dark. The luminous pencil of our flashlight beam skips over an animal disappearing into the trees — probably a coon or a porcupine. As we drive past Clear Pond, we note another car parked at the trail sign leading to Boreas. For the sake of those laggards, I hope they have flashlights. The sky is like carbon black; the silence is total.

The quiet manner and inner peace of the two men from New Jersey makes me think of the beautiful little waterfall where Jim and I paused on the lower slopes of Macomb. Why was I tempted to stay longer, mesmerized by the soothing water? I suppose because there is nothing quite like it anywhere else.

Certainly not in my home state of Iowa. I relish the memory of corn and oat and soybean fields, which are rich and green. But the rivers are sluggish and muddy. I would guess there is nothing like this area in New Jersey either; almost eight million people in an area not much bigger than the Adirondacks dictates against it. And I saw nothing to match it in Colorado where we visited this summer — the waters of Big Thompson Canyon leading to Estes Park seemed cloudy.

To me, our little waterfall was a scene right out of Eliot Porter's magnificant photo book of the Adirondacks, Forever Wild.

Some critics suggest the colors of Porter's photographs are so glowing that they must have been doctored in the darkroom. Not so, from what I have seen today. Color blind or not, the green of our waterfall was the exact shade of the color of the waterfalls in his book.

Such watery gems are a major reason why so many people are lured to the Adirondacks. And the waterfalls are particularly welcome on this mountain, which is still very much like the wasteland identified long ago by Alexander Macomb.

Saddleback Mtn., foreground in shadow, from Gothics.

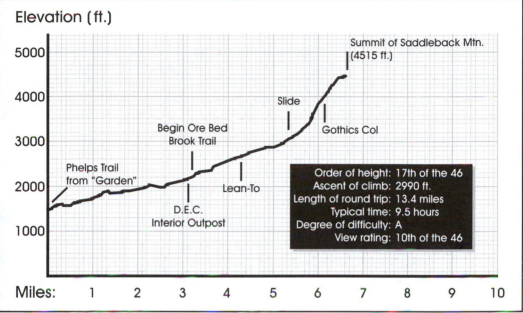

Elevation (ft.)

5000 — Summit of Saddleback Mtn.
(4515 ft.)

4000

Slide

3000 — Begin Ore Bed
Brook Trail — Gothics Col

Phelps Trail
from "Garden"

2000 — Lean-To

D.E.C.
Interior Outpost

Order of height: 17th of the 46
Ascent of climb: 2990 ft.
Length of round trip: 13.4 miles
Typical time: 9.5 hours
Degree of difficulty: A
View rating: 10th of the 46

1000

Miles: 1 2 3 4 5 6 7 8 9 10

or contour trails, see U.S. Geological Survey map, pgs. 120-121.

24.
SADDLEBACK

Journal entry: Saturday, October 10, 1970. *It's late in the hiking season and I am getting nervous about the weather. The forecast is no comfort: heavy fog through the morning.*

The prediction is half right. Jim and I grope our way toward the high peaks until we leave the Northway and head west on Route 73. There, the Ausable Valley greets us with a superb display of clear, crisp air.

It is fall at its loveliest in the Adirondacks. And, like an impertinent temptress, it flaunts an outrageous mixture of hues that overwhelms the hesitant, early morning light.

In Keene Valley a mature maple, sensing the change of season, paints up for a last fling. The sun, creeping above the mountain tops, reveals on the old matriarch a shameless display of gaudy golds and yellows and reds. They threaten at any minute to turn her finery into flame.

As we turn off the main road toward the Garden, Jim snickers at a couple of characters slouching by in nondescript clothes. We always wonder if they're for real, or visitors. My guess is that the man in the mashed felt hat, overall jacket and worn work shoes is one of the bankers. They know how to live.

Fallen leaves in Johns Brook Valley obliterate the trail and create the sensation of hiking through an impressionist painting.

Our targets today are Saddleback and Basin. The parking lot is jammed so we have to park our car down the road.* A Beetle pulls in behind us and an anxious young couple emerges to ask if we think there will be space in the lean-tos. From the looks of the lot, I say it is questionable; probably the annual Adirondack Mountain Club outing; or, fall foliage has hyped the hordes.

We go no more than a hundred yards into the forest when I get the distinct impression we are wallowing in the oils of a Van Gogh. Or is it Monet? Or Pissarro? Splotches of yellow and red predominate, slashed by random, vertical strokes of white and blue-gray.

Overhead, mottled green from lingering foliage blots out all but a few patches of blue. This can only have been done by my favorite, Seurat. He would cherish the millions of pinpoints that speckle our way.

For me, it is Saturday morning on the Island of La Grande Jatte, with saucy Johns Brook substituting for a placid river. And don't tell me it's Sunday Afternoon. The beauty of an impressionist landscape is timeless.

Others enjoy the freshening air. We meet a man and his wife and two children, all laboring under full packs; yet they whistle and smile as they pass. At Bear Brook, a teen-age girl waves as she descends from the lean-to with breakfast dishes to begin the morning chores.

---

* Parking on the road leading from the Garden is no longer permitted. When the lot is full, visitors must park in Keene Valley and hike the mile and a half back to the trailhead at the Garden.

Familiar landmarks fly by in the golden haze: the lean-to at Deer Brook; huge glacial boulders at trailside, with blackened sides showing where hikers have sought shelter; a small spring house where Jim fills his canteen; and a ranger's camp just beyond the three-mile mark.

We feel we know the ranger even though we have never met him. His name is Spencer Cram, according to the sign tacked to the eaves, but he's never around when we are. Other hikers tell us he's out working as usual — the reason why everything in the area looks shipshape.

A short distance beyond, a log footbridge crosses Johns Brook. It leads to outbuildings which are a part of Johns Brook Lodge — Winter Camp (now called Camp Peggy O'Brien) and Grace Camp. The lodge, a rough, rambling, comfortable structure, is deserted except for three hikers packing their bedrolls on the porch.

Jim and I cross the brook to the southeast and, a quarter mile beyond, turn south on Ore Bed Brook trail. The stream is named for traces of iron ore found in stones in the watercourse.

The patchwork of leaves makes it seem that we are walking on a soft comforter. We are tempted to lie down for a break, but the morning dew has not yet dissipated. As we climb, the pace of seasonal change quickens; erratic gusts of wind scatter the daubs of color in wild profusion.

Huge boulders *throughout the valley are testimony to the power of Ice Age glaciers. Blackened underside of this one reveals it has been the site of many campfires in the past.*

The going is easy along an old tote road. The babble of the brook to our right gradually fades as we climb. Then the road becomes a footpath again. It meanders up and down — mostly up — as we cross the tributaries of Ore Bed Brook while passing through virgin timber.

About half way up to the col between Gothics and Saddleback, we pass the Ore Bed lean-to. It's empty like the others except for packs left behind by campers. After a half mile of steady climbing, the trail slants steeply upward.

So much water action has been at work that it's hard to sort the trail from the eroded slopes. On the right, the former swift flow of Ore Bed Brook has softened to a silent sheet of water sweeping down a broad expanse of rock. The trail itself wends through and around a jumble of trees and soil and boulders from continuing landslides, both large and small. At the steepest spots where bedrock has been scoured clean,

the state has placed a series of long, log ladders to make the way safer and easier.

Just above the second ladder, we greet a pleasant, young couple who chart the way for us: "Yes, the Range trail junction is perhaps a mile ahead. There are three more ladders along the way. No, you won't find the Gothics lean-to in the col; it was destroyed by fire last year. Have a good journey."

At the junction, we rest in a clearing. It includes the remains of several campfires, a fair amount of garbage on the south edge, and two men lolling against their packs. So far today, they say, they have surmounted the two Wolfjaws plus Armstrong and Gothics.

They expect to go on over Saddleback and Basin before returning to their jumping-off point at the Garden. Jim and I smile at

Continuing landslides *call for caution on trail leading to col between Gothics and Saddleback. Ladders ease way over slick rock.*

their enthusiasm, especially when we find that compared to them we are veterans, of sorts. This is the first time out for one, and the other has climbed 12 of the 46 so far, including their four today. Jim and I will have twice that number, assuming we conquer Saddleback.

As we chat, a very young man — very short at least — vaults up the trail we have just climbed. He snaps a quick picture of the bald face of Gothics through the trees, then strides toward it at full speed. His long, disheveled hair flaps to keep up.

Why is everyone is such a hurry? Does the record book require such urgency? Our companions seem to think so, for they move on. It's not their pace but the inexorable push of time which dictates that Jim and I do the same.

The final half mile up the wooded trail on the east flank of Saddleback is moderately steep; we move slowly. I conclude it is not this 500 feet of ascent to the saddle, but the six and one half miles to the stirrup we have just left that did us in.

The geometrical cone of Gothics behind us grows bolder the higher we climb. Even the avalanches which have mutilated its north and south slopes do not detract from its noble posture. On the facing side, we see hikers clambering up and down, aided by cables implanted on the steeper slopes of Gothics. One climber in particular, a youngster with flowing hair, rockets upward. It has to be the young hiker who swept past us in the col below.

At Saddleback's lesser summit, I decide it is time for lunch and Jim agrees. As a matter of fact, I am ready to call it a day. The main west summit is a few feet higher, but who cares? If it is like most Adirondack mountaintops, fatigue will seem to make the ridge stretch for miles onward to a somewhat bigger lump which gets top honors.

Gothics' west flank *shows steep trail leading to the triple summit. In two places, cables offer handholds.*

As a consequence, we savor a long lunch. I enjoy the luxury of extra coffee in a large capacity Thermos bottle, a birthday gift from my children. It's gorgeous — sleek stainless steel, unbreakable, built to perform like an armored tank. And it weighs as much. Hereafter I think I will save it for family hikes at home where the wear and tear is greater and the distances shorter.

As Jim and I speculate about the names of peaks to the west, our two friends from the clearing appear from the main Saddleback summit, and stop to chat. It is an easy amble to the top, they say. However, there is nothing easy about the chasm between Saddleback and Basin. Enough is enough, they say; they are heading back.

I tell Jim I think we should do the same. It has taken us five and one half hours to climb here, and it is now three p.m. Judging from our pace, it will take some four hours to return to the Garden, and by then it will be dark. As a consolation for not climbing Basin, Jim and I decide to make a brief visit to the higher summit of Saddleback.

The climb to the summit, following a dip in the saddle, is less than a hundred feet. To me, that is enough like level ground to qualify for that most glorious of all hiking modes: strolling along at more than 4,000 feet in the air. Henry David Thoreau, I'm sure, would approve. Though he spent most of his life near sea level, he said of his daily walks, with obvious relish: "It is a great art to saunter." In my view, you can only saunter on the level.

Our hiking friends were right; it is a simple walk to the summit. And the stunning scene which unfolds affirms our decision to come.

Beyond the moderate rise, the trail drops to a broad, flat, rocky table that overlooks a deep valley. Through a haze burnished by the western sun, Basin and Marcy loom in soft green splendor. Oh, how the oriental merchants of jade and celadon who hawked their masterpieces during my tour of the Pacific would gnash their teeth if they were to compare their wares with these gems!

The magic of autumn is at work. The haze in the west undergoes a subtle change when we turn to see Upper Ausable Lake to the south along with Sawteeth, Colvin and Blake to the southeast, all bathed in azure blue. The transformation is even more dramatic behind us, to the east, where narrow wisps of white lace streak across what is otherwise a brilliant, cobalt sky.

I wonder how anyone can properly rate the views from Saddleback; so much depends upon the weather. When the Marshall brothers first climbed here in 1924, they judged it 25th. For me today, it is number one. But return tomorrow in a biting rainstorm or snow shower, and the rating will plummet on anyone's scale.

From Saddleback, *soft contours of Basin glow in the autumnal haze. Marcy, right center rear, marks the end of the Great Range trail, which begins some 14 miles away near Keene Valley.*

George William Curtis, who was editor of *Harper's Weekly* and *Harper's Magazine* during the middle of the last century, observed that "space and wildness are the proper praises of American scenery." Hikers who gaze out from the summit overlook on Saddleback might think he had this peak in mind when he penned the line. But he surely did not.

That patrician editor disdained the Adirondack wilderness. And since the Range trail, the first to traverse Saddleback, was not pioneered until 1911, it is a safe bet he never tried bushwhacking. Curtis was biased in favor of Europe and concluded, after extensive travels on the continent, that "we have none of the charms that follow long history. We have only vast and unimproved extent and the interest with which the possible grandeur of a mysterious future may invest it."

It's too bad he could not stand on Saddleback today. He would appreciate how prescient he was about the intense interest today's hikers have in the high peaks.

The Adirondack Forty Sixers affirm that Saddleback serves up some of the most spectacular views of our northern wilderness. They also say it contains the steepest section of trail in the high peaks: "Let no one belittle its strenuous offering to climbers on its western slopes."

The current ADK guidebook warns that when heading toward Basin, "The trail descends precipitously over ledges where extreme caution is needed." Because of this, most climbers feel it is easier to go from Basin to Saddleback, especially those who are carrying heavy packs.

In the summer of 1980, a Canadian named Keith Solomon set out to climb the steep trail from the col between Basin and Saddleback. The ascent of the latter was to be the culmination of his climbing the 46 high peaks over a period of two years. But he never made it up the last one on his own. One hundred and fifty feet from Saddleback's summit, he suffered a fatal heart attack.

The rangers who found him carried his body to the summit where it was removed by helicopter. The secretary of the Forty Sixers reported, "He had been writing to me all along and he had his papers with him when he died." He was awarded membership in the club posthumously for his perseverance and dedication.

Journal entry: Saturday, October 10, 1970. A growing coolness in the autumn haze tells me that Jim and I should begin our return from Saddleback. We retrieve our packs from the lesser summit and descend. Half way down the eastern slope, we meet a young couple on their tortured journey up. He is in the lead, impatient but solicitous, while she struggles to keep up. They are too intent on getting on with it to say hello.

The former, defiant slopes of Gothics are calm now as the softness of late afternoon closes in. But we still see the constant movement of hikers as they work the slopes.

The ladders on the trail are not much easier going down than up. As we descend in the deepening shadows, the lone, short tiger with the wind-blown hair who was on his way to Gothics skids to a stop before charging around us on the exposed rock face. Close up, it is apparent he is no adolescent.

He is a Forty Sixer, he avers, and suggests that for a real challenge, we try Cliff Mtn. for our next trailless climb. He struggled three times before he found the top. He is in a hurry to rejoin a group of 24 hikers who will stay tonight at Winter Camp near Johns Brook Lodge. Great, he says; only 50 cents a night.

The spirit of the Forty Sixers brings Jim's enthusiasm to a boil. "Dad," he says, "the second time around, I think I'll go alone if you don't mind." Since I answer with just a smile, he suggests a consolation: "You can bring Ben."

As a matter of fact, I plan to. The problem is that he's only two years old. I just hope Jim will put up with me until Ben is ready.

Twilight approaches as we cross Johns Brook prior to reaching the lodge. We startle a teen-age girl and two younger girls as they move across the path to a campsite. They do not answer our reassuring greeting.

The lean-tos and campgrounds near the ranger station have come to life. A few parents prepare evening meals while their children romp. But most of the campers are young people. The group of 24 at Winter Camp lounge on the river bank. Our pint-sized, energetic hiking friend waves from among a trio perched on a boulder in mid-stream.

It's almost dark as we move along the trail toward the Garden. We are somewhat surprised to see a party of four emerge from the dimness.

"Well, hello there," one of the young women says to me. She was a secretary in the building where my office is. She introduces her husband and the other couple and we shake hands. She casts a quizzical expression at me and says, "You're the last person I expected to meet here."

The surprise is mutual. In the office she was always dainty and in the height of style, with spotless coiffure. Here, her clothes are as casual as the next hiker's and, like the rest of her party, she shoulders a full pack. With kindness, I hope, I tell her, "I suppose I could say the same about you."

I'm glad to discover she's a believer.

It is now quite dark but Jim and I decide not to use a flashlight because a bulging harvest moon reflects a pallid glow. It turns Johns Brook Valley into a magical world — the kind Emerson said hides "every meanness in a silver-edged darkness."

Jim and I will have no problem even if we lose the trail. We can follow the squat telephone poles which lead from the lodge to the Garden.

Jim hears a noise behind us and suggests that we speed our pace. But the heavy footprints tell me it is a hiker who wants us to know he is coming. This proves to be right.

It is a man from Amsterdam, New York, not far from our home. The others in his party started out this morning for the Wolfjaws, Armstrong and Gothics. He set out on his own and expects to meet them at the Garden.

He loves hiking, he says. He has completed the Long Trail from northern to southern border in Vermont; the 120-mile Northville-Lake Placid Trail; and the entire Appalachian Trail from Maine to Georgia, which he tackled in four segments.

Through the windows of a camper truck at the Garden, we see two men drying dishes at the sink. They are the hikers we met in the col between Gothics and Saddleback, and again on the summit. It explains why they made such good time: they did not first have to drive 100 miles as we did before beginning our climb.

It is warm and quiet now, and the air is still. As I start the engine, a lone leaf flutters down to rest on the hood. With no wind, you wonder what critical chemistry in the woods told the leaf to let go.

It's nature's gentle warning, I suppose, that even though the weather is with us today, hikers must be on guard from now on.

Late autumn, said Adirondack veteran Gary Randorf in *Century Wild*, is "the start of the cozy season, for coming inside early to read and listen to music. The summer people have left. Many birds are following them south. Soon the hibernators will dig in, and soon the white stuff will come."

He could have added that the white stuff doesn't always wait for the proper season. An Explorer Post of Boy Scouts reported in *Adirondack Peeks* that they had "a new meteorological experience" while climbing Basin and Saddleback. They were completely enveloped by a snow storm, even though it was mid-August in 1982.

POSTLUDE: 1970

***Journal entry: Saturday, October 17, 1970.** Yesterday was a beautiful fall day. If the weather holds, it should be great hiking today. The forecast, however, is for temperatures in the 20s. Not good.*

On our way up the North-way, the radio informs us there is an inch of snow on Whiteface and some snow in the Helderbergs, an escarpment near Albany. Ten inches of snow fell in a southern suburb of Syracuse — no surprise

Wintry Elk Lake *does not encourage hiking. Clouds shroud surrounding high peaks, including Dix and Nippletop*

since as a rule residents there are buried from now until spring.

Jim and I agree we will try it anyway. Dix is our target.

Dense clouds of flurries slow our travel along the way. One trailing cloud, we discover, is condensation from a leak in the car's heater hose. The man at a filling station in Lake George Village grumbles: "I should have come to work in my snowmobile."

His wife mentions that two vacationing school teachers from Alabama are delighted; they were hoping to see snow before they leave. The station owner snorts: "Them we can do without."

A car leaving Elk Lake road is blanketed with snow; white chunks whip off like cotton batting. There is a good inch on the road itself.

Come again *next year, the weather seems to be saying. Spillway of Elk Lake dam is in center; cabin near lodge is on knoll at right.*

At the Elk Lake parking lot, a deeper fall covers the cars of a few hardy hikers. A cold, moist wind wrenches layers of snow from the evergreens. We hear a horrendous honking and there, etched against racing clouds in the metallic sky, is a V of Canada geese.

Could it be that nature is trying to tell us something, like "Get out of the woods"? Jim wears tennis shoes, and neither of us has cold weather gear. We decide to call it a day, and very likely a year.

A break in the clouds over Elk Lake releases a reluctant bit of sunlight. It's enough to generate a feeble rainbow over remaining fragments of color on the mountains.

For us, it suggests: "Better luck next spring."

Mt. Colden from Marcy Dam.

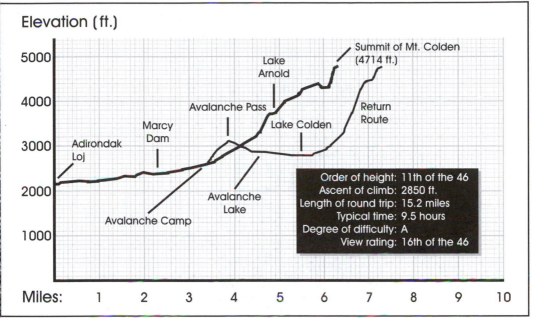

Elevation (ft.)

Order of height: 11th of the 46
Ascent of climb: 2850 ft.
Length of round trip: 15.2 miles
Typical time: 9.5 hours
Degree of difficulty: A
View rating: 16th of the 46

For contour trails, see U.S. Geological Survey map, pgs. 70-71.

25.
COLDEN

The genesis for the naming of three high peaks near Lake Colden stemmed from the early exploration of the area by a prominent American scientist named William C. Redfield.

Redfield visited the area early in the last century at the invitation of three men who a few years earlier had acquired a triangular tract surrounding the lake. The site was associated with an iron mine the trio hoped to develop some five miles to the southwest.

But Redfield was interested in more than mining. In his field notes of August 16, 1836, he wrote that he looked forward to "an expedition to the sources of the eastern or main branch of the Hudson [River] among the mountains."

Redfield's party followed the course of the Opalescent River northeast from the mine site to Lake Colden, which at the time had not been named. The area was, according to high peaks biographer Russell M. L. Carson, "then practically unknown." Hikers who enter the area today to climb trailless peaks will relate to Redfield's field notes: "The woods very difficult to penetrate."

Redfield also recorded, "the tracks of wild beasts abundant, wolf and deer tracks most frequent, and we saw the tracks of one moose." He also reported that when two members of the party circled Lake Colden, including the well-known guide John Cheney, the latter's dog roused a family of panthers.

From their base camp at Lake Colden, Redfield and two others in the party continued east up the Opalescent where they expected to find the highest source of the Hudson. They would have reached it if they had turned right to follow the course of a tributary, Feldspar Brook. Instead, they pushed north on the Opalescent a half mile or so.

Along the way, Redfield climbed a small peak on the south side of the river. From it, he saw a high mountain about a mile farther east. It was, he reported, "surmounted by a beautiful dome of rock the whole apparently of difficult ascent." What Redfield had discovered was the state's highest peak.

The following year, Redfield organized a party to climb the mountain, including the eminent New York geologist Ebenezer Emmons. This first expedition to the peak confirmed its commanding height. Emmons named the mountain in honor of New York's Governor William Learned Marcy.

When Redfield first sighted Marcy the previous year, he was near the back side of another, unnamed mountain to the east of Lake Colden. From Redfield's perspective, the mountain looked relatively bland. But he and his party soon learned that from the lake, it was anything but benign.

The whole western face of what would soon become known as Mt. Colden was ripped in several places from top to bottom, as if by some gigantic claw. This is likely why one of Redfield's contemporaries, the author and long-time director of the New York State Library, Alfred Billings Street, called Colden, "...the most savage mountain, by far, of the Adirondacks, — the very wild-cat of mountains."

Three of Redfield's colleagues had pushed a half mile beyond the northern end of Lake Colden to explore, as Redfield later noted, "a deep, narrow Lake bounded abruptly by the precipices of the two mountains [Colden and Avalanche] and discharging its waters into Lake Colden by a descent of 100 or more feet." The higher lake was aptly named Avalanche, because while it had once been connected with Lake Colden, a giant rockslide had separated the two.

Redfield also visited Lake Colden to see what his colleagues described as a trap dike. This was a natural fault where softer rock in the hard bedrock eroded to cleave the unnamed mountain from near-summit to Avalanche Lake. "The scene on entering the chasm," he wrote, "is one of sublime grandeur and its nearly vertical walls of rock, at some points actually overhang the intruder, and seem to threaten him with instant destruction."

Redfield, who was an adventurer by nature, climbed part of the way up. In fact, this trap dike was the route by which the first two people to climb Mt. Colden did so 14 years later. When one views it from the

MacIntyre Range across the lake, it is hard to believe that people can climb Colden via the seemingly vertical route. But hikers still do so today.

Verplanck Colvin explored the trap dike a week after a major slide scoured the fissure in 1869. It was, he said, "a wild, savage scene." Three years later, he and his surveying crew ascended all the way to the summit. Echoing the pattern of so many of his trips, he wrote, "of the dangers of the descent, finished at a quarter to eleven at night, I will not speak."

Redfield named Lake Colden for a member of his party when they first arrived at the site in 1836. David C. Colden was one of two people who had been invited to make the journey, as potential investors in the mine. Later, Redfield gave the same name to the unnamed mountain which adjoined the lake.

Others in the party who were connected with the mine wanted to name the mountain for Duncan McMartin*, one of the developers. But Redfield prevailed. One wonders if he made a rational choice.

Carson suggested that one of David Colden's main claims to fame came from his friendship with two prominent Englishmen, the author Charles Dickens and an actor, William Macready, who accompanied Colden on a separate trip to Indian Pass. David Colden was, it seemed, only a sometimes wilderness man. Redfield's notes show that on one occasion, Colden quit "an exploring expedition on Lake George because of rain."

This brings those who today explore the 46 highest Adirondack peaks face to face with a couple of good intentions gone awry. First, they encounter Mt. Colden, named for a man who didn't really live up to the hurly-burly image of his namesake. And second, they inevitably are drawn to Mt. Marcy, named for a man who never came close to the high peaks.

Two peaks down and one to go.

Thirty-six years after Redfield's exploration of the high country between Mt. Colden and Mt. Marcy, Verplanck Colvin discovered a watery gem nearby, which he recognized as the highest source of the Hudson River. With romantic ardor which matched the lofty setting, he named it Lake Tear-of-the-Clouds.

Three years later, in November 1875, Colvin and a guide descended south from Lake Tear to Uphill Brook. In heavy snow, they then climbed almost to the summit of another, unnamed peak. With typical Colvin luck, the explorers were forced to turn back because their boots were frozen to their feet.

Colvin named the peak Mt. Redfield, as a measure of respect for his predecessor. Anyone who thrashes through blowdown to climb it today

---

* One of Duncan McMartin's sons is the great-great-grandfather of Barbara McMartin, author of *Discover the Adirondack High Peaks*.

will agree it is an ideal appellation. Like the scientist himself, Mt. Redfield displays a mix of wilderness, pioneering and adventure.

Present-day hikers can feel affection for the scientist for another reason. When he was 17 years old and living in Connecticut, Redfield's mother remarried and moved to Ohio. Her dutiful son set out to visit her, walking 700 miles in 27 days. Five years later, the young Redfield hiked all the way back to Connecticut to begin a new life on his own.

Today, Mt. Colden is familiar to hundreds of hikers who come to the area from Adirondak Loj via Marcy Dam and Avalanche Camp, or from the western trailhead at the site of the old McIntyre mine. Their major goals are the camp sites at Lake Colden and a body of water to the south of it called the Flowed Land. This was formed when the developers of the mine dammed the Opalescent River to divert its flow to Calamity Brook for their use.

The Lake Colden/Flowed Land area accounts for some 80 per cent of camping in the eastern high peaks. With that kind of foot traffic, one may wonder if Mt. Colden retains any of the brute wilderness which confronted Redfield and his associates.

All you have to do to find out is to climb out of the valleys and take one of the two trails which lead to Colden's summit. The challenge of the Adirondack wilderness is still up there, ready and waiting for the adventuresome.

Journal entry: Saturday, May 29, 1971. This is an ideal day for Jim and me to start our hiking season. It is cool, sunny and cloudless. We expect company since it is the start of the Memorial Day weekend.

As we drive west through Cascade Pass on Route 73, we are startled to see that the monstrous snout of some high peak in the distance is covered with snow. "Well," says Jim, "that does it."

I am not so sure. The brown rock summit of Cascade Mtn. is bare. And at the Loj, many seem to share my optimism: cars are stacked along the road a half mile from the parking lot.

Just before reaching Marcy Dam, it is as if someone opened the floodgates holding back every hiker who planned an outing this year. The spring run-off of pounding boots almost engulfs us.

At the outer edge of the tide is a backwater of Boy Scouts, struggling to keep their heads above the wave of heavy packs. A chunky boy bringing up the rear, who has stopped to slow the panting, grins weakly at us and says, "Isn't this fun!"

It is apparent now why Marcy Dam was reconstructed last fall. It is not to contain surging waters from the hills so much as it is to brace the bridge against hikers. We note that Colden, some two miles due south, is flecked with white.

Jim and I are relieved to see that the majority of hikers head southwest for Marcy. We are mostly alone along the muddy trail that parallels Marcy Brook until we reach the Avalanche lean-tos, which are full.

As we head southeast up the trail to Lake Arnold, Jim is grumpy and slow. Suddenly, with only mild surprise, we pass patches of snow. And pesky insects. Jim points to the snow-capped top of Algonquin behind us. This has to be the mountain we saw when we rounded Cascade. Jim frets that the snow on the trail is getting deeper.

We meet a young man and his wife with two German shepherds. They are just out of college and had hoped to spend a few days at the Lake Arnold lean-to. But the snow was too much for them. We can see why: she wears tennis shoes.

A quarter mile farther we greet an energetic young man with flowing hair secured by a headband. "Good luck," he says. "I've been out for two days, and you can't move above here without sinking up to your hips in snow." He could not make it to the top of Colden.

Shucks. I have resolve and perseverance but Jim has the preponderance of good sense. He flops on a huge, flat boulder and suggests, "lunch?"

Why not? There may be snow above, and the glimmer of summer below. But our lunch table here is surrounded by the glory of bursting buds, and shining trees, and tiny rivulets which pulse away as the sun dissolves the snow crystals, one by one.

After lunch we loaf. For me, it stimulates warm thoughts of the poet and author, Samuel Taylor Coleridge, who may have been doing what we are

Great thoughts *come when you're flat on your back on a warm rock near a high peak in early spring. Deepening snow warns we should not proceed.*

when he wrote: "Winter slumbering in the open air/wears on his smiling face a dream of spring."

Journal entry: Saturday, July 24, 1971. *The weather has been incredibly pure the past three weeks. Jim and I have been slow to take advantage of it or even try and make up for our recent, abortive outing.*

This was partly due to my sustaining a minor back injury. But mostly it was lethargy, and intimidation for the challenge that lies before us. Of the 22 peaks we have yet to climb, only six have trails.

On the entrance road to Adirondak Loj, the peaks which stood out in stark brilliance two months ago are nowhere to be seen. The air is misty and foggy; the forecast is for rain.

Jim, the practical dreamer, sees none of the stuff that fun is made of; he suggests we try another time. His father, nurtured in business on a diet of long-range planning and lured by the computer to the achievement of impossible goals, decides otherwise. It is not exactly a consensus arrived at by committee.

To apply precision to the task, I bring along a pedometer to measure our progress.

The Loj area is bustling with campers, but we see no one on the trail until we reach Marcy Dam. There, brightly colored backpacker tents are splattered throughout the area, with a spate of young hikers milling about.

One of them, a boy about 16 with wildly unkempt hair, romps with a tiny, ball-of-fluff mongrel. He notices the map we are studying and gratefully thanks us when we confirm that this is Marcy Dam.

He is from Schenectady, he says, and journeyed up early this morning on his motorcycle with the pup in a cardboard box strapped to the rear fender. Today he will explore Marcy, he declares. Next weekend, he intends to come through here again on the Northville-Lake Placid trail.

Since that well-known walkway doesn't come within six miles of here, I urge him to buy a map before he finds himself in the predicament of young Douglas Legg. He is the eight-year-old who disappeared a couple of weeks ago while walking on a relative's huge, 12,500-acre tract near Newcomb, some 15 miles southwest of here. The papers report that hundreds of searchers have combed the woods for him with no success.

"The ranger says the Legg boy has been seen around the camps begging for food," our young friend tells us. "Bloodhounds picked up his scent on the Marcy trail and they're covering all routes."

Startling news, and hopeful if it is true. Jim and I will keep a sharp eye open for young Dougie on our hike today.

More colorful tents and shelter-halfs are sprinkled throughout the woods along the gradual ascent of the trail leading south from Marcy Dam. When we passed here last May, Marcy Brook roiled and roared. Today, the rill is gone; it flows in silence on our right. A feeble burst of sunlight pierces the overcast, encouraging us to move on.

Voluminous packs and gear are scattered in both of the Avalanche lean-tos, but we see only a lone, older man who greets us warmly. "Most everyone has gone to Colden," he says, leaning back against the damp warmth of the shelter nearest the trail crossing. It would appear he has made his peace between age and the urge to climb.

Jim and I almost reach the picnic-table rock where we stopped on our last hike here, when the old gentleman from Avalanche camp appears from below and chugs around us. He nods as we rest.

When we start up, Jim and I find that we can scarcely gain ground on him. It disturbs Jim, who says he will push ahead to catch him. By this time, I am puffing, so I wave him on.

I overtake them taking a break a mile above Avalanche Camp, where a crossover trail leads the three quarters of a mile east to Indian Falls. It is good to know that this hardy trooper rests like the rest of us mortals.

He tells us he is a Forty Sixer and that he finished on "Coochie" (Couchsachraga) last year. With a crony, he headed out and back over Panther Mtn. from an overnight stay at the Santanoni lean-to at Bradley Pond. It was "very tough," he says. "We just made it back to Bradley by sundown."

With an approving glance at Jim, he adds, "I was able to finish 24 of the 46 with my own son."

He says he will take the crossover trail to meet his daughter and boyfriend who should be heading back from a trip to Marcy. As he ambles onward, I think how happy I'll be if I can make that kind of time when I am his age.

Jim reads my mind. As we turn right to cross Arnold Brook and head up the moderate rise toward the lake, he comments from behind: "I always thought your hair was black. It looks bronze...with a few distinguished strands."

And I can read his mind. Last night, I flipped through his current issue of Mad *magazine. One page highlighted a truism: "You know you're getting old when you refer to gray hair as 'distinguished.'"*

Lake Arnold. *The tiny gem nestles at 3,772 feet on the northeast shoulder of Mt. Colden. Unseen bullfrogs croak a deep-throated welcome on this warm summer day.*

The Lake Arnold lean-to is dirty and in disarray; the names and boasts carved on the log walls are appropriate to the scene. A small sign on a tree points to the rear of the shelter, where a mound of litter overflows from a garbage pit.

Lake Arnold nestles nearby like a huge slab of jade. It does not glisten today, however. The surface is dulled by the lowering skies and mottled by lily pads. From the opposite shore, a bullfrog with an incredibly deep tone seems to say, "Go away." I note a huge paw print near the shore. A bear, no doubt, drawn by a free meal at the garbage pit.

At 3,722 ft., Lake Arnold is, as Old Mountain Phelps declared, "the highest natural lake known among the Adirondacks." Some people contest this, bestowing the honor instead on Lake Tear-of-the-Clouds which lies at 4,346 feet. But Phelps is right. Technically, Lake Tear is a pond like another body of water which nestles only 14 feet lower near the summit of Mt. Redfield — Moss Pond.

Either way, Lake Arnold is a gem. Contaminates from the site may have contributed blue-green algae to Lake Arnold during earlier times, but its color remains pretty much the same today. It would appear that Lake Arnold is not among the 25 per cent of Adirondack lakes and ponds which are "critically acidified" due to acid rain.

More than 200 of the lakes and ponds, according to the Adirondack Park Agency, are "totally devoid of fish life." Some, in fact, have the acidic level of vinegar, which is 400 times that of natural rainfall. The bullfrogs which tune up daily for their mid-day concert belie such a problem at Lake Arnold.

Journal entry: Saturday, September 20, 1980. Younger son Ben, who is now 12 years old, and I are heading for Colden for his first climb of it. His older brother Jim says he will join us since he is home from graduate studies in Florida. It will be his first hiking weekend in five years.

The hike is a long one and the days are getting shorter, so Ben and I get up at 3:30 a.m. I shake a sleepy Jim and ask if he's ready. "Go 'way, go 'way," he mumbles, and flops over.

Too late, I discover from his mother that he came in just an hour ago from his current, preferred mode of exploration.

"The rosy clouds mean rain," Ben predicts as we drive north. Since I'm red-green colorblind, that's no problem for me. But at Marcy Dam I am somewhat apprehensive about the high winds which are culling tree branches. Scudding clouds chilled by the water greet us at Lake Arnold. Even so, the place looks better than it did on my last visit here nine years ago.

In 1974, a joint effort by volunteers from the ADK and the Adirondack Forty Sixers removed the garbage pit at Lake Arnold. Two years later, the lean-to was removed due to new DEC regulations which prohibited such use above 3,500 ft. Camping activity at Lake Arnold, however, keeps much of the ground in flux between a texture of wet sponge and mud.

Today, there is an alternate, "spectacular" new route from Lake Arnold to Mt. Colden, according to those who have climbed it. The heavy rains which widened the slides on Gothics in June 1991 also loosened a new slide on the eastern backside of Colden. It is one of the longest slide paths in the high peak wilderness, extending downward to bisect the trail leading south from Lake Arnold to the Uphill lean-to.

Journal entry: Saturday, July 24, 1971. The conventional trail from Lake Arnold makes a series of lazy loops up the northeast ridge of Mt. Colden. Jim, scenting an imminent conquest, scoots ahead saying, "I'll wait for you."

The toll is telling on me. At one of my frequent rest stops in the blowdown, I note through the haze to the the southeast the huge flanks of what can only be Marcy. It recreates the kind of thrill Redfield must have felt when he first spotted the mountain from two miles closer than where we are now.

"Oh, no!" Jim shouts from a perch above. At first, I think he is in serious trouble. On scampering up, I discover it is all in his mind. Just above the edge of the ridge which we both thought was the summit of Colden, we see that we still have a stiff climb ahead.

Before us is a deep, wooded valley. Beyond is another rounded peak, a hundred feet or so higher than our elevation. Still farther on, separated by what appears to be another deep chasm, is the biggest bump on the block — it has to be Colden. The map confirms there are no nearby contenders.

Jim again leads, and as I join him at the summit of the next to the last knob overlooking Mt. Colden, I find him stroking a magnificent Irish setter. From a perch on the trail above us, two young people who belong to the dog wave a friendly "hello."

They sport the standard apparatus of their generation: blue jeans, leather jackets, a handlebar moustache on him and voluminous hair on both — his curly, hers straight and long. Both wear jaunty caps at a rakish angle.

"We talked to some rangers today who are looking for the Legg boy," says the young man. "They say he is big for his age, that he may have rifled some camps for supplies before he took off from Newcomb, and he could be living it up on the peaks nearby."

Living it up? I remind them that this is only an eight-year-old, two years younger than Jim was when he and I first started to explore the wild reaches of the Adirondacks. I cannot believe such a youngster would do that on a lark.

"Talk to the rangers," says the young man. "They told us, 'If you find him, tie him to a tree or rope him up and bring him down. You also have our permission to give him a swift kick in the pants.'"

This news is disconcerting. I hope they are right. A rebellious boy who wants to show the establishment he can outwit them is one thing. A very young, lost and frightened boy who is desperate to find his way out of the wilderness is quite another. I tend to believe the latter; however, I hope the former may be the case.

We descend into the col and begin the final push to Colden. The steep slopes, or maybe the cumulative frustrations, have gotten to Jim and he slumps at trailside. It suits my ego; the old legs are pumped full of hope and somehow I rocket to the top first. It is 1:30 p.m., four and a half hours after we left the Loj.

The weather may be a washout but the views are spectacular. The MacIntyre Range sprawls like a careless watercolor two miles to the northwest. It's fun to take a quick scan of the laborious route that took us so long on our previous hike — Wright, Algonquin, and over Boundary to Iroquois. I can barely make out the knob of Marshall beyond Iroquois to the south.

Behind me to the southeast is Marcy with the Great Range to its left, trailing off into the mist. Due south is a handsome trio: Skylight, Cliff and the elusive Redfield.

Jim straggles up to join me for lunch. We are delighted to find we are alone. We don't talk much as we eat; both of us, I guess, relish the pleasure of soaking up solitude.

Journal entry: Saturday, September 20, 1980. *It's been almost 10 years since Jim and I were here, and today son Ben and I find that again we are alone.*

The wind is blowing harder than usual on the summit. Ben and I maintain our hats by holding on tightly; at one point my glasses are blown askew. Since we have the summit to ourselves, Ben scouts the rock, sandwich in hand.

I crouch in a pocket, where tiny alpine flowers smile at me as they bravely bend in the wind. I can almost crawl into the mind of Old Mountain Phelps, who came upon some fragile flowers in the crevice of a rock, in a lonely spot like this. Phelps told his companion, the author Charles Dudley Warner, "it seems as if the Creator had kept something just to look at himself."

I wander over to the steep rock face that plummets downward. By leaning out with great care, I can look down the trap dike that leads from near the summit to Avalanche Lake. About a third of the way down, a couple climbs the slide after veering right from the dike. They do not hear my shouted greetings from where they huddle to avoid the screeching blasts.

The Gazette's Fred Fraser wrote that the trap dike "is not difficult to negotiate and resembles a series of steep flights of stairs separated by short landings." To me, that sounds more like a ladder than a flight of stairs. And from where I stand, there are no rungs, let alone risers. We'll stick to the trail.

The weather is deteriorating, so I suggest to Ben, who has just reappeared, that we leave. He is shaken. The wind was so rough, he reports, that he feared literally he would be blown off. Which stiffens my resolve to keep a better watch on my friend. Among the many reasons I like him, he is the only willing climber left in the family.

Trap dike — the crease on the left flank of Colden — offers a precarious route to the summit. Distant peaks, from left: Marcy, Gray and Skylight.

Journal entry: Saturday, July 24, 1971. Older son Jim joins me to spot a pale, bluish-green dot to the distant north. We conclude it is Marcy Dam. The map confirms we are four miles away as the hawk soars from where we started, at the Loj, or 6.52 miles via the Lake Arnold route.

Instead of returning the way we came, I suggest to Jim that we make the steep descent southwest by trail to Lake Colden — almost 2,000 feet down in a little more than a mile and a half — then head north past Avalanche Lake to Marcy Dam and the Loj. It's a mile or so longer, but it will cut out the rigorous ups and downs.

Jim and I move a bit below the summit to the south and pause on an exposed rock face, obviously a favorite lookout. We cannot see Avalanche Lake but there, to the southwest, is the faint outline of Lake Colden and beyond it, the waters of the Flowed Land. A peal of distant thunder rolls in from somewhere, so we decide it is time to get off the summit.

The trail winds around a bulbous summit dome on its way downward, then follows the ridge to a knob on the south before plunging to the west.

At timberline the trail disappears, descending into runt trees. We see no one. While slipping and sliding for more than an hour, we think several times we see a glint that should be Lake Colden, but it is only foliage rippling from below. We have been out of water since leaving the top, and are very thirsty in the warm, humid mist. Eventually, the shine shimmers and it can only be surface water.

Lake Colden is deserted. The narrow trail, which heads north near the edge of the lake, has been pummeled to roots and rubble by

Lake Colden lies below to the west from the summit; Flowed Land is at upper left. Approaching rain blots out peaks to the south and west.

hikers' boots. The gentle rain which has begun makes it slippery, but since it is level it is tolerable.

The rain reminds us that all sensible woodsmen have called it a day. We would like to do the same. But Jim and I have more than five miles to go on our return trip.

Journal entry: Saturday, September 27, 1980. *This is my third visit to Lake Colden. Today, younger son Ben and I have just arrived at Lake Colden with Tom Stanwood after an abortive try at Gray and Skylight. At Lake Arnold we headed southwest to pick up the Opalescent River, near where Redfield first spotted Marcy. We then continued to the Feldspar Brook junction to turn east. By that time, too many signs warned us to go back: snow cascaded down our collars from branches brushed in passing; twice we slipped part way into ice-coated streams as we crossed on logs; and Ben had tired noticeably due to an oncoming cold.*

Instead, we veered west to descend the Opalescent to Lake Colden. From here, we will loop around the northwest shore of the lake to reconnoiter. The trail is worth taking for a couple of reasons.

First, at the base of the lake, we pause to rest at Beaver Point lean-to, which offers a stunning view of Mt. Colden and Lake Colden. Many consider it the most beautiful campsite in the Adirondacks. And second, we pass the ranger's camp — a good man to know if you get in trouble.

Journal entry: Saturday, July 24, 1971. *On this first visit, Jim and I follow the trail which juts upward ominously beyond the northern end of Lake Colden. Erosion from hikers' boots make it rough going. Huge rock chunks, some as big as houses, litter the base of Mt. Colden. I assume these are the result of the big slide recorded by Colvin in 1869 and a more recent one in 1942, which destroyed the Caribou lean-to at the south end of Avalanche Lake.*

It is now raining steadily, but the setting for Avalanche Lake is still breathtaking. The lake itself, about a half mile long, is skinny; like the Cascade lakes, it exemplifies the U-shaped valleys scoured out by glaciers. On the right, Mt. Colden swoops upward at a near-vertical angle. Caribou, or Avalanche Mtn. on the western shore, rises even more precipitously. It is apparent that the western shore offers but a razor-thin tolerance for the trail shown on the map.

A short distance up the lake, the trail drops to the water and — thank goodness — where nature gave out, the Department of Environmental Conservation came to the rescue. The lake laps the

Avalanche Lake *is lovely, even in the rain. The half-mile-long lake squeezes its narrow width between Mt. Colden on the right and Avalanche Mtn. on the left, to the west.*

cliffs, but a crude, floating log bridge is chained to an underwater ledge; a wobbly rail adds to the fun.

Jim warns me to jump carefully where a four-foot gap in the bridge is missing. This calls for a springy take-off, which depresses the log path, already floating only an inch or so above water level. I make it, dragging a soaked shoe behind. With full pack, it would be ankle deep or, with a misstep, up to your armpits at least.

Across the lake, we spot the walled gorge that marks the start of the climb up the Colden trap dike. Mental note: any hiker — not a rock climber — who tries that is out of his mind.

Halfway up the lake, we cross another floating log bridge, this one longer but in better conditon. The stupendous rock face of Avalanche Mtn. not only rises above us but tilts menacingly outward. I assume that since it was 73 years between recorded major avalanches and 29 years since the last one, the odds favor our not having one today.

The rain is all that descends on us. In copious quantities.

We are no more wet than the party which forded this site more than a century ago, led by Adirondack guide William B. Nye of North Elba, for whom Nye Mtn. is named. He was much at home here, having cut

First of floating *log bridges proved the theorem that every action causes a reaction — in this case a wet one. Precarious bridge has been replaced by plank walkways bolted to rock.*

many trails in the Adirondak Loj area, including the Van Hoevenberg trail to Marcy.

Nye's job at this passage was to get the Fielding family past this spot, then unbridged. He decided to wade across on the underwater ledge and carry them one at a time, Mrs. Fielding first.

However, she was mindful of the civilities of the time, and attempted first to sit on one of his shoulders. Her husband gently reminded her this was not the time for "delicacy." So she looped her legs around his neck and off he strode into the lake.

The extra weight on Nye was bad enough as he tried to steady her legs with one hand while clutching the slippery cliff with the other. But she kept slithering down his back. Nye described his predicament, as related by Seneca Ray Stoddard in The Adirondacks: Illustrated:

"'Hitch up, Matilda! **hitch up** *Matilda! why* **don't** *you hitch up?' screamed Mr. Fielding, and I could hear him dancing around among the rocks and stones, while I thought Dolly (their niece) would have died laughing, and the more he yelled 'hitch* **up***' the more* **she** *hitched* **down***, and I began to think I would have to change ends or she would get wet; but by leaning over forward, I managed to get her across safe and dry."*

The current walkways are still called Hitch-up Matildas, but they are a far cry from the earlier, floating log bridges. ENCON rebuilt them in 1976 of sturdy planks bolted to the cliff walls.

While Avalanche Lake is beautiful, it is conducive to danger. The various slides from Colden dumped tons of debris and trees into the lake. Then, the hurricane of 1950 downed so many trees in the high peak area that the state closed the Lake Colden area to hikers for four years.

The trap dike has lured many over the years, sometimes with tragic consequences. The litany of accident reports illustrates why:

Peter Wollenberg, in *Adirondack Peeks*, 1977: "John, waiting on the lip of the lower waterfall, tried to grab me but my momentum carried both of us over the waterfall...found myself precariously balanced on a small icy shelf...thought my right arm was broken...later realized it was severe shock...(at the hospital) John had possible contusions of the kidneys."

David Lance, in *Adirondack Peeks* (of which he is the current co-editor), 1986: "I felt myself falling backward and quickly reached with both arms to grab anything to stop my fall...my left hand firmly latched on to an overhanging ledge...I felt my left shoulder go out — dislocated."

Rock climber Don Mellor, in the Annual Guide of *Adirondack Life*, 1992: "...the three accelerated toward frozen Avalanche Lake, only to be spared when their rope snagged on a scrawny tree growing from a crack in the slide...other climbers have not been so fortunate. A few winters earlier, a climber died after falling and crashing into a clump of trees."

Journal entry: Saturday, July 24, 1971. A stiff, half mile brings Jim and me to the saddle of Avalanche Pass. During wet seasons a small waterfall dashes from a Colden cliff to divide and form two streams, one gushing to the northwest on its way to the St. Lawrence River, the other flowing southwest to the Hudson. In fact, this along with Wallface Ponds, marks the northernmost source of the Hudson River.

Not today. It is hard to believe, with rain dripping from our noses, that this is not a wet season, and there is no waterfall.

Avalanche Pass *marks divide between waters flowing north to the St. Lawrence and south to the Hudson. Waterfall splits for the long trek.*

The gentleman we met on the trail to Lake Arnold greets us at the Avalanche lean-tos. His daughter and her boyfriend, back from Marcy, nod a hello as they bend to their cooking tasks.

As we pull out of the Loj in the murky drizzle, Jim analyzes the results of my corporate planning on this hike: "You included all of those interesting extra hills to climb, chose a perfect day to study the clouds close up, and got our feet wet a record number of times. How well did your pocket computer record the number of miles we hiked?"

I know from the maps that we have covered about 14 miles; the stiff climbing should add a couple more.

The pedometer reads: 26 miles.

Santanoni Peak from Panther Peak.

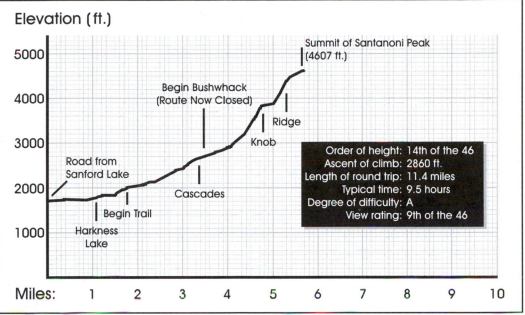

Elevation (ft.)

5000 — Summit of Santanoni Peak (4607 ft.)

Begin Bushwhack (Route Now Closed)

4000 —

Ridge

3000 — Knob

Road from Sanford Lake

Cascades

Order of height: 14th of the 46
Ascent of climb: 2860 ft.
Length of round trip: 11.4 miles
Typical time: 9.5 hours
Degree of difficulty: A
View rating: 9th of the 46

2000 —

Begin Trail

Harkness Lake

1000 —

Miles: 1   2   3   4   5   6   7   8   9   10

or contour trails, see U.S. Geological Survey map, pgs. 262-263.

26.
SANTANONI

Journal entry: Tuesday, August 31, 1971. What is the sign of a good hiking day?

For me, it is a sudden surge of energy, missing so often this season, coupled with the promise of a clearing sky. As son Jim and I head up the Northway, the distant peaks form an intricate pattern of gun-metal gray against a pale blue morning sky. It is as if some proud machinist has placed his handiwork on the horizon, knowing that warming streaks of yellow and red will soon burnish and enhance its beauty.

Other signs are not favorable. Jim's mood is bearish; it appears his winter hiking hibernation has already begun. As we turn at Frontier Town to head west, he poses a grumpy challenge: "Where did you put my shoes?" He is right — they are missing — but he is also wrong — I did not bring them. Now this is an interesting prospect: how do you tackle a trailless mountain like Santanoni without shoes?

The road is desolate and deserted except for an early-hour highway crew, fighting a losing battle against frost heaves. They say our best bet for a spare pair of shoes is Newcomb, some 10 miles farther on.

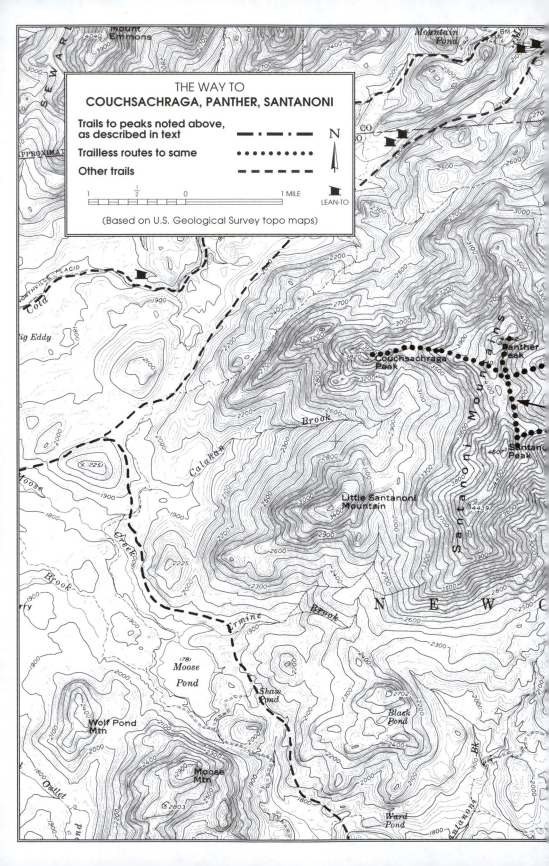

THE WAY TO
COUCHSACHRAGA, PANTHER, SANTANONI

Trails to peaks noted above,
as described in text

Trailless routes to same

Other trails

N

1   ½   0   1 MILE

LEAN-TO

(Based on U.S. Geological Survey topo maps)

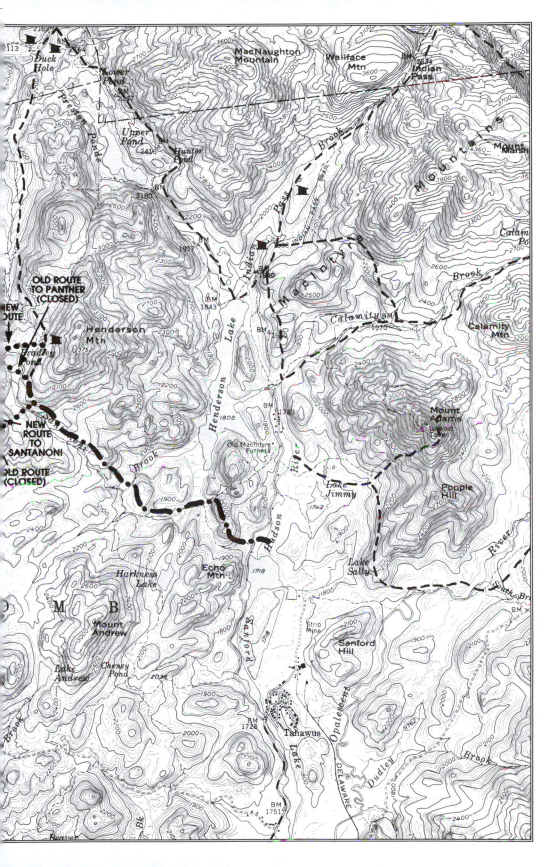

Another sign, and how do you read it: a couple of miles this side of Newcomb, Jim sits bolt upright and shouts, "a wolf!" A gray, bushy animal the size of a large dog bounds across the road. Some insist that wolves have returned to the Adirondacks after being wiped out during the last century. Others say they are wild dogs or coy-dogs, a mixed breed of coyote and dog. For Jim and me, though, this one is a wolf.

It's hard to find your way around Newcomb; it's laid out more like a wilderness settlement than a conventional community. Homes are scattered for a good five miles along both sides of Route 28N; the highway meanders another 15 miles west to Long Lake.

Interspersed among the houses at Newcomb are a town office, a pocket-sized bank branch, a tavern, and two general stores. The latter establishments, fortunately, stock sneakers along with food and sundries.

Newcomb's population in 1995 hovered around 550, a precipitous drop from the 1,500 it registered in the '50s. Logging and mining fueled its growth, but it perks along now on half empty because the mine at Sanford Lake, some 12 miles northeast of here, shut down in 1989.

The school at Newcomb has shrunk along with its people. The cacophony of 400 students which at one time rocked the hallways has modulated to a pleasant roar of 60. Newcomb's school district is now the smallest in New York state.

Newcomb tries to pique the interest of students by focusing on themes relating to the Adirondacks. For example, students do field work with experts at the Newcomb campus of the state university's College of Environmental Science and Forestry. One focus: coyote populations.

Students learn that the dog-like animals they see now and then are not wolves. The last bounty for killing an Adirondack wolf was paid almost 100 years ago.

What they see are coyotes: not hybrids of the wolf, nor the Western Coyote, but a true species of the Eastern Coyote. ENCON's Gordon Batcheller said recently in the Albany *Times-Union* that the breed has been in the northeast for most of this century, but has now become firmly established in New York state.

The color of coyotes varies widely, from brown to gray. Males can weigh up to 50 pounds, about half as much as wolves. But coyotes look bigger than they really are because of fluffy fur and long legs.

One thing coyotes are not, said Batcheller, is coy-dogs. Coyotes, he averred, "are more likely to eat domestic dogs than breed with them."

Journal entry: Tuesday, August 31, 1971. *For some time now, Jim and I have noted on maps that there is an active mine at Sanford Lake, on the road that leads north from Rt. 28N to the trailhead for Santanoni. I've always assumed, or maybe hoped since it's in the high peaks, that it involved no more than an innocuous hole in the ground.*

But when we mount a crest in the highway near the lake, we are stunned to confront gigantic piles of slag. They squat like interlopers in front of a picture postcard of lovely mountain peaks. A jumble of industrial buildings, railroad tracks and smokestacks rounds out the mining complex of NL Industries, formerly known as National Lead Co.

All of those mountains of slag had to come out of something, and the void falls away beyond a screened visitors' platform on the left side of the road. Mining is open pit; tiny diggers and trucks far below are actually monstrous vehicles doing their best to enlarge the hole. The man-made chasm is enormous.

I glance at the Santanoni Range rearing beyond the pit to the west, and suggest to Jim that we move out. At the rate these rocks are being hauled away, the mine may soon put our target on the list of endangered species.

The original developers of the mine at Sanford Lake would be shocked and chagrined at the changes which have taken place at the site. During the early part of the last century, they first started and then abandoned a modest iron work at North Elba. At their Sanford Lake site, they envisioned that "works of great magnitude will be erected and carried on at our place." But in those days before mechanized equipment, their plans for the new venture fell far short of the gaping hole in the ground we see today.

The developers had been tipped off in 1826 about a large area of iron ore some 12 miles south of their original works at North Elba. They were guided to the site by a St. Francis Indian whose father, appropriately, had come up the Indian River to settle near Indian Lake. The youth led them, again appropriately, through Indian Pass. Near Henderson Lake and Sanford Lake, he showed them, according to Adirondack historian Donaldson, not only "vast deposits of ore all around," but "boundless forests for the fires, and endless waters for the power."

The developers quickly bought surrounding tracts of land to protect their interests. They then hacked out a road through some 30 miles of wilderness from Lake Champlain, and built a small settlement near Henderson Lake. At first, it was called McIntyre, and later, Adirondac. Some of the buildings in the village, now deserted, still stand. The site was referred to as the Upper Works, since it was farther up the Hudson River than a second location three miles to the south on Sanford Lake. The latter was officially named Tahawus when a post office was established there; it was referred to as the Lower Works.

The developers soon confronted two serious obstacles to success. The first was an impurity in the iron ore, identified as titanium, which caused problems in smelting. The second was transportation. It became

a continuing nightmare due to primitive roads, severe weather and the remote location.

At the peak of operations near the middle of the last century, a force of 400 people was in place to sustain the iron works. By that time, it included a large stone blast furnace.

Outlet to Harkness Lake offers a pleasant interlude a mile from the Santanoni trailhead. Sheer cliffs of Wallface Mtn. gleam in the morning sun five miles to the north.

Hikers can still see the weed-covered remains of it on the right side of the road just before reaching the head of the Opalescent River trail. That was the route which Redfield and the developers took on their way to explore Lake Colden and Marcy.

Eventually, the obstacles made the venture unprofitable, and operations were shut down in 1857. Today, the three developers are known more as Adirondack explorers than titans of industry.

The name of the lead developer, Archibald McIntyre, is perpetuated in the Adirondack's MacIntyre Range, even though Archibald never spelled his name with an "a." He was a member of the party which Redfield led on the first ascent of Marcy, and was with the same party which made the first recorded ascent of Algonquin three days later.

Henderson Lake is named for a second developer and resident overseer at the mine, David Henderson. He accompanied McIntyre on the ascents of Marcy and Algonquin.

The third partner, Judge Duncan McMartin Jr., came up short. His associates thought the mountain to the east of Lake Colden should be named in his honor. But Redfield's choice — Mt. Colden — won out.

It's ironic that the problem which gave the developers so much trouble early on became the impetus for reopening the mine in 1941. The "impurity," titanium, was recognized as a strategic resource during World War II, and played a key role in the production of paint, tires, paper and other products. A railroad was extended from North Creek to the mine in 1943 to enhance wartime productivity; the iron ore was considered merely a by-product.

The new owner, NL Industries, expanded the mine until its closure in 1989. Unfortunately, as Sharp Swan noted in the Adirondack Forty

Sixers' *Of the Summits, of the Forests*, "the mine dumped tailings into Lake Sanford until practically nothing remained of that precious little jewel."

Journal entry: Tuesday, August 31, 1971. The trailhead for Santanoni is on the opposite side of the road from where the Hudson River flows into the north end of Sanford Lake.

The initial portion of the trail follows an old lumber road covered with jagged ore tailings from mining. These would be brutal on tires, and are also hard on footwear — including tennis shoes, so Jim informs me. Bright patches of foliage on either side mark the change of seasons.

After about a mile, the sharp rocks disappear and the dirt road dips to cross over the outlet to Harkness Lake. This is a potentially beautiful meadow, but is marred by swamps and rotted stumps. They are counter-balanced somewhat by the rosy glow of Wallface Mtn., whose precipitous cliffs shine against the blue sky five miles to the north.

The road then meanders upward to peter out at the junction where the trail to Santanoni, Duck Hole and Bradley Pond disappears into the woods. It soon dips to cross Santanoni Brook, slithers back and forth over a tributary, then returns to head up the right bank of the main brook in earnest.

Series of cascades *tempt the hiker to tarry on the upper reaches of Santanoni Brook. North River Mountains crease the horizon some six miles to the southeast.*

We meet two young couples descending. They stayed at the Santanoni lean-to at Bradley Pond for two days and say it is in poor shape and extremely wet.

"The view from Santanoni is fantastic," one of them says. But they warn that the jumping-off point from the trail is unmarked and hard to spot. "It's to the left just beyond a waterfall up ahead. Watch out after you cross a brook; there are a million trail branches."

The waterfall is a series of cascades including a sizeable pool above a fine overlook. Jim checks for fish, but finds none.

A short distance beyond, we see the beginning of the Santanoni herd path. It leads over a narrow log bridge with a taut-wire handhold, meanders through a small clearing — legacy of a bygone beaver pond — then splinters into a maze of herd paths.

With the help of blazes and occasional, antique trail markers that are made from square pieces of tin painted red, Jim and I creep up the steep slope. Often, we shoot off on a side branch, but have little trouble in returning to the main path.

Our seventh edition ADK guidebook says: "This peak is approached by a trail originally cut from the Tahawus Club many years ago, but is no longer maintained. Its condition depends upon the amount of usage and whether some ambitious fellow climber recently cut the way."

Judging from the roots and rocks exposed by hikers' boots, there have been many ambitious climbers through here; none, however, were intent on trail clearing. It would be welcome in the fierce blowdown.

We resolve to keep our eyes peeled for Douglas Legg, the eight-year-old boy who was lost a few miles south of here on July 10. If he strayed into this area, I fear for him.

As of 1979, hikers were no longer allowed to turn west from the Duck Hole trail just above the cascades and bushwhack west toward Santanoni Peak. The owner, Finch, Pruyn & Co., had decided to lease the land to a hunting club.

However, the company did cooperate with the Adirondack Forty Sixers in blazing a new herd path toward Panther Peak along the dividing line between state land and its own property, which reaches just to the north of Bradley Pond. As a result, once hikers mount the connecting ridge between Panther and Santanoni, they can follow it south to the summit of the latter. Both the old and new routes to Santanoni are shown on the U.S. Geological Survey map on pgs. 262-263.

The one-mile herd path along the ridge to Santanoni is still difficult because of the hurricane of 1950, which hit Santanoni harder than most other Adirondack high peaks. Laura and Guy Waterman proclaimed in *Forest and Crag* that the area is, "the most genuinely wild and difficult in the Northeast."

The rough conditions are likely the reason why no trace of Douglas Legg was ever found. There was a glimmer

"Ghastly," *"appalling" and "terrible" were typical reactions to the Santanoni climb following the hurricane of 1950. It's still bad.*

of hope that his remains had been located in 1993 on an island near Newcomb. But a contingent of some 40 searchers, including state police, an agent from the FBI crime lab, state forest rangers, and a rescue squad from Plattsburgh Air Force base, concluded that skeletal remains were from an animal.

The eight-year-old youngster was not the only one to disappear into the wild maw of Santanoni. The Forty Sixers reported that in 1958 a lone climber signed his name as "Howard Gilroy" in the summit register of the peak. "He then entered a notation that visibility was poor but apparently proceeded and then disappeared." An extensive search turned up nothing but his bicycle hidden in the woods near the mining complex.

The two disappearances underscore why the Adirondack high peaks can be so dangerous. As naturalist John Burroughs said, "Nature is not benevolent. [It] never tempers her decrees with mercy, or winks at any infringement of her laws...It is a hard gospel; but rocks are hard too, yet they form the foundation of the hills."

Journal entry: Tuesday, August 31, 1971. The varied herd paths begin a steep climb toward Santanoni. As we stop to rest, we think we see Panther to the north and Henderson Mtn. behind us to the east, with Algonquin and Colden beyond. It's difficult to tell because the latter peaks are some eight miles away. Also, we're used to seeing these peaks from the east. From here, it's like trying to identify long-time friends when all you can see are their backsides.

All of the peaks, including Henderson at 3,752 ft., are higher than our present elevation. I don't give Jim the bad news that we still have a long way to go. It is two p.m.

No need. As I catch up with him at a level spot beyond a slight rise, he slumps to the ground with head in hands, literally. He thought we had topped off. But beyond a slight depression is a heavily wooded, abrupt shoulder leading up to Santanoni.

I try to console Jim with an anecdote, courtesy of the ADK guidebook. The name Santanoni derives from Saint Anthony, filtering down through the French Canadians to the Abenaki Indians, who pronounced it in their own way. Jim reacts in his own way: "This is Colden all over again."

The strain is relieved by inspired views of Algonquin and a big bump we thought was Colden, but which now clearly has to be Marcy. When viewed from the east, Marcy's broad base is its trademark. From here, it looks pointed and almost skinny.

With relief we pull up a final, 10-foot cliff and clear daylight on the 4,000-foot spur which adjoins the summit ridge. We see no sign of a herd path to a summit or a cannister, as promised by the two couples we met below. But the guidebook does identify a "fine open space" some 75 yards before arriving at the summit, so we head toward it.

A twisting path dips down past a small, exposed rock face to the open area. There, Jim suggests that instead of stopping, we reverse our way and lunch on top of a 15-foot high chunk of rock back up the herd path. We surmount it by climbing a tree near its side, and break out lunch.

Robert and George Marshall and their guide, Herb Clark, who were the first to climb all of the the 46 high peaks, rated Santanoni's view as second only to Haystack. On a glorious, clear day like this, Jim and I are tempted to rate it number one.

Due north beyond a deep col, one can see Panther, its summit only 150 feet lower than Santanoni. Jim points to a smaller

Couchsachraga! *Jim points with excitement when he spots the reclusive and elusive peak. At 3,820 feet, it is the shortest of the 46 -- 800 feet lower than Santanoni and 600 feet lower than Panther.*

mountain that juts from the end of a shoulder reaching west from Panther, and shouts, "Couchsachraga!" Sure enough. It is our first view of this little peak, at 3,820 the lowest of the 46 and so remote it is often the last to be climbed by aspiring Forty Sixers.

Its size and apparent ready access from Panther makes Couchsachraga appear to be an easy conquest. It is only 2:30 p.m. and the prospect is tempting. But we heed the stern admonition in the ADK guidebook: "Do not try to include the other two Santanoni peaks (Panther and Couchsachraga) with this peak in a one-day trip. This was quite an ordeal in 1950, but since the hurricane it would be sheer folly to try it."

Other views make up for the disappointment. This is our first close-up of the Sewards. We conclude that if we try to climb all four of those trailless bruisers in one day, we will sleep soundly that night.

Long Lake and a myriad of other mirrors shine amid the Lake Country to the west and north. MacNaughton, Street and Nye rumple the carpet of forest that stretches northward, splotched by the puddles of Henderson Lake and Bradley Pond.

Through the gash in the greenery at Indian Pass we see the notch made by Cascade Mtn. Together, they appear, as Robert Marshall noted, "like looking through the sights of a gun." Farther east, Jim and I identify the MacIntyre Range, Colden, and most of the other high peaks which shape the crumpled folds.

We can't pick out Marshall; it nestles too demurely near the south flank of its taller neighbor, Iroquois.

Twenty miles or so to the east, there appear to be two Giants, both streaked with slides. But a check of the map shows that Giant, along with most of the peaks in the Great Range, is hidden by the towering trio of Marcy, Haystack and Skylight. The slides mark Dix and Macomb, their now-familiar profiles sharpened against the soft tones of the Green Mountains in Vermont.

For the first time, because of the clear air, Jim and I can identify Redfield and Allen with confidence. We're not sure about Cliff; it is indistinct, like Marshall. We don't spend much time looking toward the southeast. The ugly wound of NL Industries' open pit offends the sensibilities.

Santanoni has long been a prime spot for scanning the Adirondack wilderness. But it has not always been the best place to go for peace and quiet.

Before the mine shut down in 1989, climbers often were startled by blasting, which as a rule took place around noon. On the summit, one could hear not only the faint din of big machines but the toot of a loco-motive at the industrial complex.

The activity fulfilled the worst fears of the Northwoods Walton Club, which in the last century called for laws to protect the northern wilds. As Roderick Nash noted in *Wilderness and the American Mind*, the club argued that the result of preservation would be a "vast and noble preserve" where fish and game could flourish and where "no screeching locomotive [would] ever startle...Fauns and Water Sprites."

It's hard to stop the onrush of "civilization," of course. Thoreau found one way to cope by retreating to Walden Pond near Concord, Massachusetts. Those who visit there today may be horrifed to hear the sound of a nearby train. But in the fourth chapter of *Walden*, titled "Sounds," Thoreau observed pleasantly that, "the whistle of the loco-motive penetrates my woods summer and winter, sounding like the scream of a hawk sailing over some farmer's yard."

Journal entry: Tuesday, August 31, 1971. Jim and I start back up the trail and it seems extra long. Something's wrong; we don't recognize this segment of the herd path. Then we understand. A slightly higher bump rears a short way ahead; it is the true top.

Jim suggests that since the guidebook says there is no view, we skip it. I agree. Why jot our names in the summit cannister when we have the whole marvelous record on film? If the Forty Sixers want to drum us out of the club for a measly 50 feet, so be it. We are tired.

It takes awhile, but we locate the spot where the steep path moves off the summit ridge. No wonder we missed the way to the summit at this point on the way up: clustered branches hide both the path and the peak.

It soon becomes obvious we are following a maverick branch of the herd path, not the main one. While leading, I start to step forward, pull away the branches before me, and peer down a 10-foot vertical drop. We move more gingerly.

On occasion, through the trees, we see the nub that was base camp for our final assault on the way up. Our "trail" leads to the right of it, so we bushwhack to the left and recognize the ascent route by bits of yarn and cloth attached to twigs by previous climbers. We follow them to the nub, then start the long five miles to our car.

Santanoni has been an exhilarating experience, giving us a taste of the rigors we will face in the Cold River region. My head swims with the complexity of the challenge: what's the best strategy to conquer the four Sewards? And is it easier to do Panther and Couchsachraga together from Bradley Pond, or should we tackle "Coochie" alone from the west?

Per the latter, most likely not: Bob Marshall wrote that he and his two partners who first explored the 46, climbed Santanoni from the Cold River region on the west and "found it to be the hardest mountain we ever attempted."

I conclude that whatever we decide, it should be based upon enjoying the Cold River region for what it is: a lovely place which acts like a magnet on those who wish to be alone.

Journal entry: Saturday, September 6, 1980. *The two angular men who approached me yesterday in front of the Department of Environmental Conservation building on Wolf Road in Albany were familiar. But the clucking sound they made was not.*

Old friends Bob Rehbaum and John Goerg, photographers for the state's Conservationist *magazine, gave me their standard greeting, prompted by the favorable weekend forecast: "Heading for the Adirondacks?"*

Yes, I said. But it was not for them. "We'll be out tracking turkeys in the Catskills." And off they went practicing their calls, oblivious to the noon-time hordes.

Son Ben and I are the first to sign in at the trailhead register for Santanoni. On the way here, in fact, we saw more deer than people; we passed but one workman in a town truck. The lonely cry of a loon suggests we may have the mountain to ourselves.

But a message on a paper plate tacked to the register suggests otherwise: "Bob: you are so overdue I've gone out for help. If you go out please leave this at the sign-in register so we'll know you are OK. Jon. 8:30 a.m." Jon and friend(s) apparently left just before us.

Ben hopes for a day that's perfect for pictures, like the one Jim and I enjoyed. The forecast, at least for Schenectady, promises to deliver: mostly sunny, temperatures in the '80s, with only a 10 per cent chance of rain.

A little more than a mile in, we pause near Harkness Lake to capture on film the sheer side of Wallface, ablaze in the morning sun. To ensure good results, I use a normal lens, add a polarizing filter, then do the same with a new telephoto lens.

Problem: the film is not advancing. Too late, I remember I did not reload after completing my last roll, and have brought no spare. Harkness has become my Calamity Pond! Fortunately, Ben has his camera.

As we rest at the boundary post marking the private land of Finch, Pruyn & Co., Ben unlimbers his encyclopedic memory of high peak facts: "We have an ascent of 800 feet to the junction where the herd path begins. At that time, we will have climbed 1,000 feet from the road. We will then have 1,900 feet of climbing to the summit." Above the cascades, the clouds threaten and coalesce, in spite of the forecast. The mine's open pit in the valley far below prompts another unnecessary observation from Ben: we have gone two thirds of the way in to Santanoni but only one third of the way up.

The sprinkles, urged on by the clouds, turn to rain. It makes the maze of paths in the beaver dam area, the blowdown and steep rock faces slicker and more difficult. We push through a thicket of low trees; they are soaked with water, so we are soon drenched.

We top off on the ridge at one p.m. to find there is little view, no cannister, and the rain is now pelting. We slosh on through the wet trees toward a dark, indistinct mass on the south. A sharp dip and climb bring us to the same ledge which opens to both west and east, where Jim and I stopped. It exposes Ben and me to fierce, new blasts of rain; we put on our plastic jackets, but all they do is intensify the cold.

Another dark shape, slightly higher and farther away, offers promise of the true summit. After another brief descent and slightly longer ascent, Ben spots the cannister. One thing has not changed since Jim and I visited Santanoni's summit ridge: the last 50 feet are the hardest.

The actual summit is clogged with scrub trees, even though Verplanck Colvin and his crew cleared the top when they came here

On a clear day, *you can see most of the Adirondack high peaks from Santanoni. In 1926, the Marshalls ranked its view second among the 46. Then there are days like this one.*

on their Adirondack survey. Ben and I spot the three eyebolts and holes they drilled in the rock to secure their surveying equipment.

I would guess that Colvin came here on a miserable day like this, and for the moment lost his cool. In his Seventh Report to the state legislature, he said: "Elsewhere in those rich borders where nature has lavishly given iron sinews, veins and arteries to each mountain crag...new mines, new tunnels, new roads and iron tramways, new mills and forges, will minister to the needs of the modern nation.

"But the great forests on the mountain slopes will remain...these forests will yield New York more than the untold millions of dollars, which the European State forests annually give their governments; will show a State taxless and debtless."

New York state? Taxless and debtless? Colvin lost it for sure.

Back on the open ledge, a brief break in the clouds relieves our frustration. Tiny patches of sun help, racing over Panther and Couchsachraga before disappearing.

As we begin our descent at 1:20 p.m., the rain lessens but both wind and clouds rush to follow. We return to the knob to huddle under its larger trees for a standing, dripping lunch.

While it is now muddier, we make good time descending. Ben monitors our progress by the increasing height of our two mountain benchmarks, Panther and Henderson. I'm more interested in monitoring my rain-soaked pants, which threaten to fall down.

A short distance beyond the junction, we are both startled by a furry, brown animal which looks like a small fox. It darts across the trail, then climbs a low tree and stares at us. Since it is as curious of us as we are of it, and is in no hurry to move, I sketch it and make notes about its rounded ears and bushy tail so I can confirm its identity later on.

At first, I think it is a mink or fisher. But the distinctive shape tells me it must be a pine marten. They were hunted so much in the past that it was believed they had been wiped out in the Adirondacks. It is obvious they are making a comeback.

What a time to forget film!

The eighth edition of the ADK's guidebook, which I haul out as we cross over the outlet from Harkness Lake, tells us we have beaten the odds: "One's chances of standing practically alone on the summit of a trailless peak are considerably less likely than they were in Porter's day" — referring to L. Morgan Porter, the editor of the previous edition. Ben and I have been lucky: we have been alone on almost every trailless peak we have climbed this year.

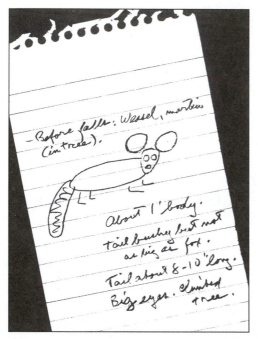

My field notes describe a furry, brown animal which climbs a small tree and stares at us. Later we confirm that it is a pine marten.

Just then, I note a movement in the backed-up, black waters of Harkness, and shout to Ben: "Beaver!" Sure enough, one paddles by. This is unusual because beavers usually sleep during the day, coming out in early evening to begin their work. This one displays the grave countenance of a slow swimmer who is determined to stay the course, diving occasionally to avoid floating logs.

Experts tell us beavers are back in full force in the Adirondacks. It's hard to believe that by the turn of the century, trapping had reduced their numbers in New York state to less than 10 animals.

For the five minutes this beaver stays in view, Ben snaps away. I watch in utter frustration, empty camera in hand.

I feel better when I see the response to the urgent query we saw on the paper plate at the trailhead this morning: "Jon. We are OK. A cold wet night on Panther Brook. Thanks for your concern. Bob."

At home, Ben discovers in our new 10th edition of the ADK guidebook something we should have known: the herd paths to Santanoni, on private land, are now "abandoned" and "closed to the public." So, I am sorry to admit, we climbed Santanoni illegally, albeit unintentionally.

I also note that a good many ADK guidebooks, beginning with the first one, report that "this peak is in wild country." Indeed it is. Counting today, I can confirm that we have seen deer, bears, grouse, loons, foxes, a coyote (which still looks to me like a wolf), and now both a beaver and a pine marten.

The luxuriant fur of the pine marten is known as sable, which made it a major target of trappers and Indians. The latter prized it for their robes.

Verplanck Colvin reported seeing one in August 1878: "...we came suddenly upon a beautiful sable in a tree beside the trail, peering down upon us with great curiosity, his bright brown eyes, soft, rounded ears, and dark brown fur, giving him altogether the appearance of a *Lemur*."

A Cornell researcher noted in the *Conservationist* in 1980 that, "the marten is so solitary and cautious in its ways, seeing one in the wild is an uncommon event." No more. In 1992 the magazine updated the report: "Pine martens have become so numerous in the High Peaks region that...they raid hikers' packs to steal a meal of raisin and nut gorp or freeze-dried food."

The upper reaches of the Cold River region, including Santanoni, were the ancestral haunts of the pine marten. The old herd paths to Santanoni were an ideal habitat because, as an old-time Adirondack trapper was quoted in the *Conservationist*, they made their home "in the wildest, and most mountainous sections of the United States and Canada."

The old route to Santanoni, of course, is now closed. But another, even more remote route to the summit has been discovered that would make an excellent habitat for pine martens. It is on the opposite side of the peak, on state land.

The route follows a sinewy, shiny new landslide triggered by torrential rains deposited on Santanoni in September 1985. The cause was another errant hurricane which skirted the peaks after ravaging the U.S. east coast. Barbara McMartin, author of the *Discover the Adirondacks* guidebook series, calls it in *Adirondack Life*, "the best hiking trail that has ever been created in the High Peaks."

Journal entry: Wednesday, May 3, 1995. The desolation of the now-closed buildings of the titanium mine at the Lower Works, coupled with the deserted village at the Upper Works, solidify the area's reputation as the loneliest spot in the Adirondacks.

The creatures of the wilderness sense it, too. A pair of Wood Ducks, so shy that one rarely sees their finery, paddles at leisure across the remnants of Sanford Lake.

As Ben and I turn left on the road to drive back toward Blue Ridge, a coyote — bushy tail bobbing, a limp cottontail hanging from its mouth — saunters across the blacktop into the brush. A few miles beyond, three deer munch on their own kind of dinner as we pass a pickup truck. Its occupants are the first humans Ben and I have seen since leaving the Northway two hours ago.

Hikers no longer have to journey to the high peaks to see coyotes. Almost a month ago to the day, I nearly ran over a coyote as it crossed the highway next to the GE Corporate Research & Development Center in Niskayuna, New York, a suburb of Schenectady. And earlier this year, the local paper reported that a coyote had been struck and killed by a car on one of the busiest highways in the nation, the Major Deegan Expressway in New York City.

Dix Mtn., left center, from Elk Lake. Hough Peak is at right.

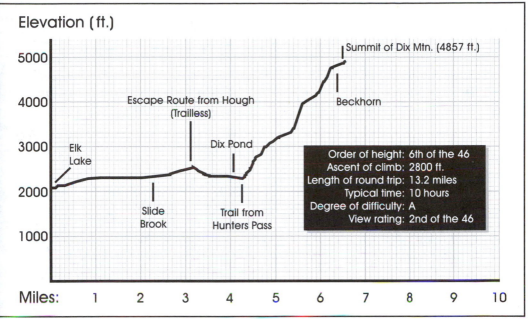

Elevation (ft.)

5000 — Summit of Dix Mtn. (4857 ft.)

4000 — Escape Route from Hough (Trailless) — Beckhorn

3000 — Elk Lake — Dix Pond

Order of height: 6th of the 46
Ascent of climb: 2800 ft.
Length of round trip: 13.2 miles
Typical time: 10 hours
Degree of difficulty: A
View rating: 2nd of the 46

2000 — Slide Brook — Trail from Hunters Pass

1000

Miles: 1 2 3 4 5 6 7 8 9 10

For contour trails, see U.S. Geological Survey map, pgs. 214-215.

27.
DIX

If you want to know what's on the minds of young teenagers, take a couple of 14-year olds along on your next hike. All you have to do is keep up, and listen:

Journal entry, Saturday, September 25, 1971. This has not exactly been our finest year for the hiking record. Son Jim and I have been out six times, and topped only two peaks. It surpasses our conquest of one in 1967, but is far behind our eight in 1969, and 15 last year. There are various reasons: a slow start due to the late snow melt, a back problem in mid-season, and inertia. The latter is spelled "l-a-z-i-n-e-s-s."

It is time for us to get cracking and get down to business. Besides, there are only two weekends of safe hiking left if my calcuations are correct. After that, snow could thwart us.

Jim's buddy, Bill Hume, has agreed to come along. I ask Jim to make sure Bill brings the proper gear. "Don't worry," says Jim. "He's hiked a lot and knows what to bring." When Bill gets in the car he has a paper bag containing two small plastic bags of compressed chicken — no canteen, no flashlight, no poncho, and no jacket.

He must subscribe to Thoreau's philosophy: "Our life is frittered away by detail...Simplify, simplify." Oh, well. If Bill has survived a five a.m. paper route the year round, he can survive some discomfort in the mountains.

It is cold — 40 degrees as we leave the house and, according to the radio, in the 20s at our destination. But it is a beautifully clear, crisp morning.

A few early risers at Elk Lake Lodge stare at us as we get our first unobstructed view of Dix beyond the mist rising from the water. Dix does not appear to be much higher than its neighboring peaks, Nippletop and Hough. Unfortunately, the point where the bulk of Dix thrusts upward is at least four miles away, and that base point is about the same elevation as here. No wonder Adirondack Mountain Club veterans say, "Dix is rough from any direction."

The first few miles roll by quickly. Jim snickers as he shows Bill the sign marked "Cadillac Lane," an old logging road that cuts across our trail a little less than a mile from our start. The two ham it up through the windows of an old, ramshackle logging shanty on skids. Then they begin an interminable discussion about food: have they brought enough, is it the right kind, can they hold off eating until we reach the top, etc., etc.

As we rest in the cool quiet of the morning at the 1.94-mile benchmark, Bill says to Jim: "Are you going to smoke when you grow up?" "No," says Jim, "I think I'll stick to ginger ale."

"Me, too," says Bill. After a few steps in solemn contemplation, he adds, "and an occasional root beer."

Along the muddy trail leading to Slide Brook, we strain for a view of Macomb's slides to the east, as described in the ADK guidebook. It was published in 1962, however, and it is obvious that new growth nearby prevents us from seeing the great scar that slashed from summit to base in 1947. We settle for the orange-colored brooks complete with peculiar odor, as promised in the guidebook, and hurry on.

In spite of the numerous packs in Slide Brook lean-to and the many colorful backpacker tents spotted around it, we see few people on the trail. As we pause at the clearing, a man and two boys about seven and eight years old hurry by. "Which way to Dix?" the man asks. I motion to the trail heading north and they charge onward.

Along the trail we note the swift onrush of fall — bright splotches of color that appear as haphazard drippings from the autumnal paint bucket. Just to the north of the lean-to, a young-adult maple seems to have been totally dunked. Even though it is in the shadows, its crimson swatches ripple gloriously in the soft morning breeze.

It would appear from a cursory glance at the topographic map that the way from here to the base of Dix is on the level. However, it is anything but. From the Slide Brook lean-to the trail descends gradually, climbs to a painted-rock benchmark at 2.84 miles, continues a moderate ascent, and then dips again.

As we loll at a rest stop, Jim leaps to his feet and points back up the trail: "There are two of the biggest dogs I've ever seen!" When Bill and I

Autumnal magic. *Why would anyone want to be anyplace but hiking in the Adirondack high peaks in the fall?*

turn, we see nothing. "I hope they're not wolves," says Jim, recalling the huge animal we saw loping across the road to Newcomb on our last hike.

We are relieved to see three couples under full pack emerge from behind a large boulder, accompanied by the dogs: one obviously a St. Bernard, the other what appears to be a sheepdog, only oxford gray in color.

"It's a Bouvier," says one of the hikers. "You've probably never seen one because there are only 100 registered in this country. They're trained as guard dogs." He adds, parenthetically, "I'm in the dog business."

They tell us they will make camp at Dix Pond, leaving their packs behind for the assault on Dix. Our packs go with us: for lunch on top and for supplies we will need if we decide to come back over trailless Hough.

Somewhere near here there is supposed to be a cairn marking an old tote road that's the favorite route to and from Hough, which is to the east of us. Apparently we missed it. Any help in climbing that peak would be valuable. Huge, jumbled masses of blowdown surround and, in some cases, arch our trail. Even a path would be rough going up those tangled slopes.

The trail to Dix drops steeply, levels off somewhat and, just beyond the three and one-half mile mark, comes to a lean-to at Lillian Brook. It is the main waterway flowing from the col between Macomb and Hough, and has scoured a fine swimming hole just below the boulder which serves as a trail crossing.

There are no swimmers today; it is too cool. The packs at the deserted lean-to and surrounding tents tell us their owners are off for the peaks.

The boys' conversation has ranged from food to vacation to food to fishing to food, etc., and has never stopped. Now they switch to ways to earn money to get some of the real pleasures of life like — well, you know, food and other things.

Says Bill, "I've caddied for my Dad, but with my paper route it shoots the whole day. Maybe you could do it for him sometime."

"I asked him once," says Jim. "He said I talk too much." They solemnly follow me as the trail dips to Dix Pond, and switch to another subject: what they will order for dinner tonight at the restaurant on the way home.

The pond languishes gloomily and still to the west, just beyond an overgrown lumber clearing. The trail courses over the log corduroy slopes that ridge down from the east to the shoreline, then abruptly descends to a second, larger clearing. This should be the junction of the red trail which continues north through Hunters Pass, then loops east and back up the north flank of Dix. Our route will follow the yellow trail. At two and a quarter miles, it is three quarters of a mile shorter than the red trail but much steeper. We will see if it is faster; that is why we chose it.

From the clearing a very high peak thrusts upward dead ahead. We debate whether it is Dix. I conclude that it can't be: our trail branches right from here and heads toward our target. A deep valley separates the other mountain from the one we are climbing, which is Dix. The silhouette of the peak in sight is confusing because it is somewhat flat on top from this vantage point. But it has to be Nippletop. That means Hunters Pass is the deep notch between Nippletop and our target for today. Dix is still not in sight.

A lone hiker passes us at the clearing and glances at the yellow trail signpost. We pass him and then at our first rest stop he scoots around and disappears. I don't tell the boys why I doubt we will pass him again. There are no up-and-down swings on this trip: it's straight up all the way, some 2,600 feet in a little more than two miles. It will be tough, but I'm sure we can make it with our packs if the boys will just keep their minds on the reward for reaching the top: lunch.

After a moderate, half-mile upgrade through a fine stretch of hardwoods, the trail merges with a rocky brook bed. We rest and again are surprised by the charging dogs, closely followed by the three young couples, bounding up easily without their packs.

They stop for a breather. Have you been up Dix before, I ask the bespectacled one studying the map? "Six times," he says offhandedly. "This time we'll traverse Hough on our way back," and he reels off the intricacies of the route. Thanks, I say weakly; we may see you.

The three couples move up a short distance, find water for their dogs at a sparkling spring, and forge out of sight. Good idea — I check our water supply, for this may be the last chance for a refill. We have plenty; a month ago in hot weather we would likely be dry by now.

Crest of Macomb, *two miles south of Dix, pierces sky on left; Sunrise Mtn. huddles behind it, overlooking Clear Pond, at right. Hoffman Mtn. looms large on the horizon.*

A brief leveling of the trail leads to a steeper pitch through birch and balsam; then the profile is repeated at an even steeper angle. We see no sign of the summit of either Dix or Hough.

We have climbed about a mile now and as we slump by a large rock, we can see through an opening to the south the hazy shimmer of Elk Lake with Clear Pond a mile and a half beyond. To the east of them is a three-crested peak. It should be Macomb but I see no slides. Then it occurs to me why — the slides are on the southwest slopes, out of view.

For the first time, Hough comes in view. It is a good deal higher than our position and since at 4,400 ft. it is 450 ft. lower than Dix, we can see we have much climbing yet to do.

A few hundred yards on the trail above we meet an older man, alone, descending leisurely. "You're about a mile away and an hour to go," he says. "It's easier without a pack," he observes ruefully looking at ours and his own. "I would have left mine below to do Dix alone, but originally I intended to swing over Hough to the other Dixes and back. I would have needed it if I didn't make it back.

"No problem, though," he adds with a chuckle. "I got lazy." As he moves downward, an ADK patch on his pack prompts me to ask him to stay and tell me what he knows of the adventures that lie ahead for Jim and me, here and elsewhere in the high peaks. Since it is nearly one p.m., however, I decide we had better push along. Our pace is slow enough without further dawdling.

Before we go, Bill and Jim point to what they say is a flaming red tree on a hill far below. At 20 yards, I might see it. At a mile away, however, to me it is like staring at an Ishihara color-blind chart with one tiny pinpoint of red among a thousand green and yellow dots. The boys snort in disbelief; gamely, I tell them to move on.

On occasion through the trees, we get a glimpse of peaks beyond Hough which should be South Dix and East Dix. It brings to mind the fine newspaper articles in the Schenectady Gazette *by Fred Fraser, describing these remote, trailless peaks. I haven't seen any stories in the series this year, and since I know Fraser works for Bill's father, who's publisher of the paper, I ask him if there will be more.*

"Beats me," says Bill. "I'll ask the O.M."

Mentally, I run down the list of names that might match these initials, when it strikes me: this must be the term our offspring use in regard to their fathers — the "Old Man." While it is difficult to gauge the degree of affection, it is comforting to note that it smacks of respect for authority.

Shortly we slump into a grassy sag and see our target dead ahead, at a sharp angle upward and perhaps a mile away. The top appears to be a thin, barren ridge that slices the clouds. Just below it, jutting to the right, is a protruding, rocky bulb that has to be the "Beckhorn." This is the name applied by Old Mountain Phelps, who thought it resembled the "beck-iron" or pointed end of a blacksmith's anvil.

Halfway up the rocky climb to the Beckhorn, we note a profusion of tiny, blue berries. They appear to be too small for blueberry fruit but Bill, sniffing, says they must be. Good old master-taster Jim, with a big smile on his face, says from below, "they taste like it, too." He's been stuffing.

Rocky bulb of the Beckhorn, a tag applied by Old Mountain Phelps, comes into view at the 3,100-ft. level, a mile below the summit.

A lone youth perches on the westerly promontory of the Beckhorn as we approach, crouching to shield himself from the stiff wind. We decide to stop at the exposed prominence where the view is magnificent. The heat of the climb wears off quickly, however, so we move our gear to a sheltered area above.

The great moment has arrived! One can almost hear the saliva pumping as Bill fumbles in a frenzy to pull out two bags of pressed chicken — and nothing else. Jim matches him in a dead heat to hold aloft — a small cardboard tin of tuna spread — and nothing else. No bread. No celery or carrots to moisten the mouth. No orange or apple to sweeten the feast.

Judging by their actions, they hold trophies fit for winners. Bill fingers each morsel with a loving glance before devouring it. Jim stirs his

Almost there. *Son Jim and Bill Hume survey the short, remaining climb from below the Beckhorn. Elk Lake shines to the southwest. Trail came up over a shoulder of Dix, below the boys.*

diminishing, gooey mess from one side of the tin to the other, then gobbles a bit more. They trade bites, comment on the other's exquisite taste in cuisine and make a vow: next time they will switch roles and relish the full impact of the other's judgment.

The sight of this moveable feast, added to the rigors of the climb, makes my peanut butter sandwich taste like sirloin. I save the hot coffee till last as a special treat to ward off the chill and — it is stone-cold. Too late, I recall that my three-year-old, Ben, was playing with my Thermos a few days ago.

Bill and Jim, expansive after a hearty meal, debate whether the knife-edge ridge to the north is really higher than our perch on the Beckhorn. It appears to be almost level with us. They wander over beyond a slight sag to see for themselves.

My inclination after eating is to loaf. And the surrounding sights suggest the same. Scudding clouds are moving in rapidly, and the variegated patterns of sun and shadows on the peaks and valleys keep the views interesting and ever-changing.

To the east, Giant and Rocky Peak — the "Giant's Wife" — nuzzle together like a pair of oversized whales. Giant is belly up, its white slides simulating the pattern on the underside of an ocean mammal.

Almost two years ago to the day, Jim and I peered from Giant at the same peaks surrounding us today, and wondered which was which. Today, after our 27th conquest, many of them are as familiar as old friends.

The lesser peaks of the Dix range cluster benignly to the south. Nippletop, which still looks like a plateau from this viewpoint, crowns the southern tip of the long ridge that stretches to the northeast. It descends to the Dials, partly obscured from where we are on the Beckhorn by the main summit of Dix, and on over Bear Den and Noonmark to Round Mountain. Beyond Nippletop is Pinnacle Ridge, with Blake and Colvin the major humps to the north.

How much higher? Narrow ridge of the Dix summit on the north seems almost level with our perch on the Beckhorn. Map shows it is 100 feet higher.

Beyond them, the Great Range — except Lower Wolfjaw, which also is hidden by Dix — is etched in sharp relief on the northwest, culminating in Marcy to the west. Whiteface, remote but dignified, stands stiffly some 22 miles to the north.

The autumnal haze is still thin enough to spot the MacIntyre Range over the right shoulder of Marcy and the faint outlines of the Santanonis far to the west. There's one ringer with a double bump on top looming in solitary contempt this side of Henderson Lake, beyond Marcy Swamp. I haul out the map and confirm my guess. It's Allen, a loner that's trailless and second only to Couchsachraga as the peak most often climbed last by aspiring Forty Sixers.

My casual observations are interrupted by — people. Hordes of them. The leader of a young people's group clusters his charges around me, then coaxes them on to some urgent objective. Two men with *unsmiling wives (I thought the plural of spouse was spice?) wend around me.*

The two dogs, closely followed by the three young couples, almost trample me as they pass. None of the girls smile; one frowns. It suddenly dawns on me that the yellow paint marker partially hidden by my pack on the rock face that has served as a lunch table is the center of the trail. As a matter of fact, the only suitable spot for lunch anywhere on the ridge is near or on the center of the trail.

Descriptions of the Dix summit vary but all describe it as "very narrow." Elijah Simonds, who was a guide for Alfred Street, a writer of Adirondack ramblings in the 1860s, insisted that, "the top of the ridge at the south rises as sharp almost as a knife. It isn't more than a foot wide." From where I sit near the Beckhorn, the main summit to the north appears wider but is still a hogback, maybe five to six feet of rounded ridge which falls off sharply on either side.

I decide it is time to head for the main summit and check up on the boys. They wave from the highest boulder as I approach and point to the Colvin bolt. It's a silver dollar-sized peanut compared to most of the four-inch, copper benchmarks in the Adirondacks. The stamped words are obscure, worn smooth by countless shuffling feet. But it still evokes memories of the Colvin crew, urged on by their single-minded leader, who was determined to complete their surveying in the foul weather that seemed to dog his Adirondack explorations.

Dix is a prime example of the deterioration of summit peaks from the incessant pounding of hikers' boots. The narrow summit ridge is covered with a soft, spongy layer of organic material like peat moss that in places is a foot or more deep. The trail cuts into this springy mass to bedrock, and the surrounding ground cover and alpine growth are badly decimated from hiker forays.

We return to the Beckhorn and wave to the last of the hordes who seem determined to return via Hough. It is now three p.m. and, based on a sound hiking pace, it will take a good four or five hours to return to Elk Lake by our ascent trail, let alone a circuit over a trail-less peak. It will be dark by seven p.m.

I can only conclude that most of those hikers will return to their packs at Lillian Brook and Slide Brook and, therefore, have the luxury of several hours less hiking than us. We decide to retrace our steps. Anyway, what's the hurry? Hough will make an interesting hike another day.

We have gone no more than 50 feet down when Bill and Jim begin a discussion of — food! As a matter of fact, it appears that their time on the summit was devoted to planning a survival plan for the return ride home: dinner at nearby Frontier Town, a stop at Dairy Queen near the Chestertown exit a few miles beyond for a cold drink, then a visit to a hometown grocery store for a snack before set- tling down to late night television. I can't believe it, but I close my mouth. It's the only way I can think of to bridge the generation gap.

Shortly below the Beckhorn, the sun breaks clear to highlight Hunters Pass on the northwest. It is tempting to a hiker and, I presume, irresistible to a hunter, in season.

We are surprised to meet a young man and his wife, about a mile below the summit. They are resting quietly on the trailside. He asks how

Trail to Beckhorn from Dix reveals the knife-like edge of the summit ridge. Return trail drops off to the right, toward the southwest.

far it is to the junction with the red trail at the base of Dix.

My guess is about a mile, according to the topographic map. "I hope so," he says. "We both have new hiking boots, and she has blisters an inch long on both feet."

No wonder. Both wear the kind of hiking shoes that look like ski boots, beautifully sculptured and probably indestructible, but monstrous. They've broken a basic rule of climbing: never climb an Adirondack peak in new boots or shoes. Clomp around the block a couple of weeks in advance, and you may be ready.

Dix Pond, so placid this morning, has now come alive. The fish are feasting. Their incessant lunges for insects are marked by widening circles that overlap to form ever-changing, geometric patterns. At the north end of the lake, a V-shaped ripple moves toward land — proba- bly a muskrat or beaver. A strange, shrill bird call floats toward us from the dusky, distant shore.

A lone figure with a fishing pole startles us. He, or she, wears jeans, a baggy sweater and sports a wad of brown hair culminating in a pigtail. He is heading upstream, to the north, in search of trout. "For dinner?" I ask. "We don't really need it," he answers. And, with an enigmatic smile, he disappears into the deepening shadows.

"If he has to count on that for dinner," says Bill, "he's in trouble. His rod and reel are mismatched; you couldn't catch a fish in a bucket with that setup."

We are even less sure now if it is a he or a she.

The thought of fishing perks up the boys and they relate to me their career objectives after they finish high school, which they have just begun as freshmen. Bill will settle in Florida on a resort acreage, stocking its lakes with all sorts of staple and exotic fish. Of course, it will border the ocean so he can alternate the stream and lake fishing with deep-sea adventures.

Not so Jim. He will live on a ranch in Arizona. Half of it will be desert that has artificial lakes teeming with golden trout, bass and sunfish. The other half will be high plateau country so he can enjoy snowmobiling in the winter. To accomplish this, according to my calculations, the ranch will have to be split with an escarpment at least a mile high. It'll be a nuisance to climb, but the view of the back yard from the front should be magnificent.

Lillian Brook camp, deserted this morning, is now a bustling outdoor city. Most campers are eating, and Bill and Jim slow their pace to cast longing looks. We pass two young men about to dig into a huge, steaming bowl of stew, and it is too much. The boys turn their heads and scurry around.

I note that none of the hikers who headed for Hough from Dix have yet returned to this base camp.

As we move steeply up and down the trail toward Slide Brook, Jim and Bill again bring up the matter of eating, but their tone is desultory; it smacks more of petulance than promise. It's been a long day. And we still have three and one half miles to go to our car.

In the gathering dusk we do spot this time the cairn that marks the recommended trailless route to Hough. It's supposed to follow an old tote road, but no such path is in sight. The tangled blowdown sprawling upward to the east is forbidding.

It's almost dark in the leafy shadows of Slide Brook, and our approach startles a lone girl washing dishes in the stream. She quickly gathers her utensils and scurries off to join her hidden companions. She does not acknowledge our greeting.

It occurs to me on the long, rolling, return path that Dix is just like most of the remaining 19 high peaks that Jim and I have yet to conquer: remote and tough. Maybe the approach we've taken on all of our preceding hikes — in and out in one day — is wrong. Most of the people we see are prepared for the long pull with enough gear for at least one overnight. Once they unload their packs at a "home" shelter, they can jaunt from peak to peak unencumbered, and enjoy a relaxed dinner and rest on their return.

Tonight, however, it makes no difference to me. Jim and I struck out twice before in tackling Dix, but this time we made it.

The climbs ahead may be rough, but Jim and I will figure out some way to surmount them, in one day or whatever it takes. And Bill can come along any time he likes. He's a good hiker.

Perk up, boys. There's lots more food ahead!

Street Mtn., left, and Nye Mtn. from Algonquin Peak.

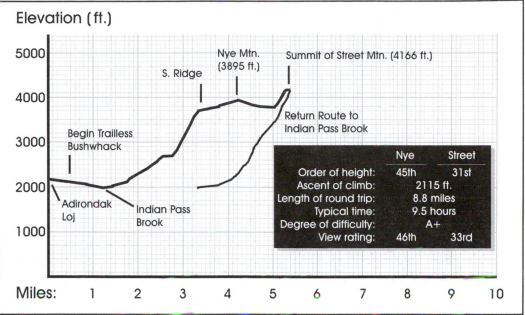

Elevation (ft.)

Begin Trailless Bushwhack

S. Ridge

Nye Mtn. (3895 ft.)

Summit of Street Mtn. (4166 ft.)

Return Route to Indian Pass Brook

Adirondak Loj

Indian Pass Brook

	Nye	Street
Order of height:	45th	31st
Ascent of climb:		2115 ft.
Length of round trip:		8.8 miles
Typical time:		9.5 hours
Degree of difficulty:		A+
View rating:	46th	33rd

Miles: 1 2 3 4 5 6 7 8 9 10

For contour trails, see U.S. Geological Survey map, pgs. 70-71.

28, 29.
NYE, STREET

"Nature," wrote Ralph Waldo Emerson, "never wears a mean appearance."

The poet and philosopher visited the Adirondacks in 1858 as one of several eminent vacationers at Philosophers' Camp on Follensby Pond. But modern-day climbers are convinced, in the light of his remark, that Emerson never came within a country mile of Nye and Street.

The two mountains are among several dozen high peaks which spark a gleam in the eye as you turn south from Rt. 73 on the road to Adirondak Loj. Most of the other mountains stand erect to display inviting profiles. Nye and Street, on the other hand, crouch nearby, to the west, like shapeless lumps. In the context of the 46 high peaks, they seem almost like an afterthought.

Aspiring Forty Sixers consider Nye and Street, on a comparative basis, as necessary evils, to be tolerated and then done with. Louis P. Fortin spoke for many of his peers when he wrote in the *Conservationist* that they are "two of the dullest mountains in the Adirondacks."

This is ironic in a way, because Nye and Street have not always been condemned to this kind of Adirondack purgatory. Before mid-century, the Forty Sixers reported that "climbing the mountains was easy and pleasant in the spruce and balsam forest." Bob Marshall agreed that Nye, at least, was "quite an easy climb."

The hurricane of 1950 changed all that. Since then, climbers have described the mountains as "a booby trap of hidden blowdown," "a nightmare obstacle course of deadfall and debris," and "a truly horrible place." Veteran Fred Fraser said getting to the summit of Nye took "hours of inching upward through an almost impenetrable barrier of blow-down timber hidden beneath jungle-thick strands of Christmas trees."

As a consequence, most climbers today rate Nye and Street as the most difficult of the 46 high peaks to conquer. One will not find much compensation when reaching their summits, either. The original view ratings applied by the Marshalls ranked them, respectively, last and second to last.

Street fares better today because climbers have discovered some new vistas overlooking the MacIntyres, Santanonis and Sewards. The view rating for Nye, however, remains rock solid: it is firmly imbedded at the bottom of the scale.

Both mountains were named for men whose works are linked with Adirondack lore.

Alfred Billings Street, historian, state librarian and poet, was the more widely known of the two. He authored a couple of Adirondack travel books, including *The Indian Pass*, which told of a trip through "the Notch" to the abandoned mine at Tahawus.

William B. Nye was celebrated in his own way as an Adirondack guide. It was he who hoisted a lady on his back to keep her dry as he waded across the underwater ledge at Avalanche Lake. As recounted by Seneca Ray Stoddard, it fostered the name which has since been associated with the place: "Hitch-up, Matilda." Nye was also with Verplanck Colvin when they discovered that Lake Tear-of-the-Clouds did not flow to the Ausable River but was the highest source of the Hudson.

There is no record that either Street or Nye climbed their namesake mountains. It's quite possible that they did, however, since both frequented the area. The Marshall brothers and Herb Clark made the first known ascent of the peaks in 1921.

Nye the guide came within a whisker of being a celebrity of another sort. He was a friend of the fiery abolitionist, John Brown, whose farm nestles a few miles north of Nye Mtn. At one time, the popular guide considered joining Brown on the latter's fateful trip to Harper's Ferry in Virginia. Nye thought Brown was recruiting for the Underground Railroad, which helped southern slaves flee to freedom in the north. Instead, of course, Brown had decided to attack a federal arsenal, which led to his death by hanging. Brown is buried near his farmhouse.

No fugitive slaves made it to Brown's farm. But Mary MacKenzie, historian for Lake Placid and the Town of North Elba, says that some 15 black families from other parts of the state did come there to farm in the mid-19th century after receiving land grants from a wealthy abolitionist, Garrett Smith. By the 1970s, she says, all of the families had moved elsewhere.

There's no point in exploring these mountains separately. If you do one, you might as well see if you can crawl and slog your way over to the other.

It's instructive that most climbers refer to the pair as Street and Nye. Yet invariably they tackle Nye first and then head for Street. One suspects the order of mention was initiated by the revulsion generated when climbers came face-to-face with the blowdown on Nye.

Not much has changed since the 1950s. In 1994, Mike Hendricks of the Associated Press said in the *Albany Times-Union* that, "Street and Nye are so challenging that even the most experienced hikers can wind up traveling in circles in the confusing maze of herd paths, mistakenly climbing the same summit twice, and frequently returning without finding the top."

It's no wonder, then, why Adirondack Forty Sixers warn that Street and Nye earn the record "for creating the largest number of lost hiking parties and unintentional bivouacs."

Journal entry: Sunday, May 25, 1975. Son Jim and I are getting cold feet about conquering the remaining 19 Adirondack high peaks we have not yet climbed.

Correction: I am.

Our last conquest was almost four years ago when we scaled Dix. A month later, Jim and I failed in an attempt at Haystack from Keene Valley. So we assuaged our disappointment with a hike up Hunter Mtn. in the Catskills four weeks later. Interesting; but the Catskills are not the Adirondacks.

Next, we attacked our old nemesis, Marshall, which eluded us twice before in August of 1971. We tried again in August 1972 and in June of 1973, but failed both times.

Last week, I noted in The Lookout, *monthly newsletter of the Schenectady Chapter of the Adirondack Mountain Club, that members are welcome to join a trip planned for today up the trailless twins, Street and Nye. The answer to our dilemma of climbing all of the 46 high peaks, or at least inching up on them, becomes clear: we must cast off this spirit of individual adventure and, as members, join the club. The ADK, that is.*

The prospect of gearing up again for the remaining peaks arouses mixed feelings in us.

Jim is ambivalent. As a soon-to-be high school graduate who will enter the University of Miami this fall, his current aspirations do not include any more climbing; Florida is flat. But because of our long and close association, he's willing to humor his fearless father and give it one more shot.

The only problem is that I am not fearless. In fact, I am getting downright cautious.

I keep thinking of the unfortunate incident three years ago, in the late spring of 1972, when two men attempted to set a record by climbing the 46 Adirondack high peaks in five days. As related in The New York Times, *they never made it.*

On the fourth day, 26-year-old Chris Beattie of Lake Placid, N.Y., developed "shin splits," a pain in the lower leg which often affects runners. He realized he could not go on, but shook hands with his partner, 31-year-old Patrick Griffin, as the latter moved out to climb the remaining targets for the day, including Marcy. The weather was deteriorating due to a mixture of torrential rains and gale winds unleashed by Hurricane Agnes. Temperatures plummeted to near freezing, even though it was late June.

One hundred and fifty yards below the summit of Marcy, after he had completed close to three-fourths of the peaks they had set out to climb, Griffin slumped dead of a massive heart attack.

Other signs tell me to take it easy. The Times *also related the admonition of professional mountaineer Mitch Michaud, who recently became the first man to scale the highest peak in each of the 50 states in one calendar year.*

"Football, hockey and baseball are sissy sports compared to mountain climbing," reported Michaud. "The Journal of the American Diabetes Association states that in one hour, climbers can burn up twice the calories used by tennis players and three times the energy of golfers or bowlers."

The logical question asked of Michaud by the Times: *Why do you head up the slopes? "It's fun," he said, "and it's a challenge."*

I agree. But I intend to keep one eye cocked on the weather. It has become a controlling factor since Jim and I were stumped by snow when we tried to climb Colden four years ago on Memorial Day weekend. Jim wore sneakers, I moccasins. And we both wore all cotton clothes.

This time, I tell Jim, we will take no chances. I insist that we wear down jackets, wool pants and boots. Mine are a new, nine-inch pair of insulated Chippewas with Vibram cleats. We will be ready for whatever Street and Nye offer in the way of drifts or deadfall.

We rendezvous with the ADK group at the new Hikers Building at Adirondak Loj and wait for late comers. When our hiking group gets ready to move out, Jim sheds to his T-shirt, noting, "It's spring. I'm hot."

He's right, even though it doesn't calm my nerves. I shuck my down jacket in the car with his, but convince him to bring his sweater for protection when we plunge into the jungle.

The initial stroll of a little more than a mile west from the Loj to Indian Pass Brook borders on the bucolic. It skirts Heart Lake, then follows a portion of the old cross-country ski trail built for the 1932 Olympics.

At Indian Pass Brook, the two mountains lie due west. Yet our ADK leader, Eugene Brousseau, leads us downstream a quarter of a mile to a small clearing. We prepare to cross where the brook makes a right angle, turning from a westerly flow to the north.

Indian Pass Brook is like Marcy Brook when Jim and I first tried Colden: clear as rippled glass, yet so frigid one expects it to shatter at the touch. Others in our party search up and down for an easy crossing; Jim and I join those who leap from rock to rock.

We follow a herd path which leads west toward Nye. The first part is gently rolling, with little gain in elevation. The weather is balmy. My insulated boots are bad enough; a down jacket would have been stifling. Then we turn to start up a tributary of the brook which descends to the southeast from a source only a half mile below the summit of Nye.

At first, we follow what appears to be an old, reasonably well-defined hunters' path. But in a short time, the hunters either gave up on game, or on the blowdown. As we crisscross the stream and the slope becomes steeper, a scattering of trees and brush gives way to an incredible jumble. It slows us to a creep.

This is a carbon copy of the herd paths Jim and I faced on the high plateau of Tabletop, except that these are canted at an impossibly steep angle.

It makes me think of Charles Dudley Warner describing how his "motley party of the temporarily decivilized files into the woods." It was exhilarating, he said, but it also brought "the weariness, from the interminable toil of bad walking...and the grim monotony of trees and bushes, that shut out all prospect, except an occasional glimpse of the sky."

He could have been writing about us.

I also remember our leader's warning about this climb in the club newsletter: "All in the party must have compass and map as you will be leaving the herd paths, especially near the top."

Ascent of Nye is, according to one veteran climber, "a nightmare obstacle course of deadfall and debris from the 1950 hurricane." We know.

It is 12 noon, two and a half hours from Adirondak Loj, when someone ahead shouts, "we've made it to the ridge!" Our challenge now is to trudge a half mile over the two intermediate knolls which lead to the summit. True to form, Nye teases us when we get there; it takes a spreading search of five minutes to locate the cannister holding the register.

There is no danger of getting even a mild chill as we lunch. Nye's welcome is warm, and windless. It adheres to its reputation: there is no view.

A few hardy souls have climbed Nye from the west, going up a major tributary which joins the Chubb River at Wanika Falls, on the Northville-Lake Placid trail. Stuart McCarty told *Adirondack Peeks* in 1985 it "must be the most beautiful approach in that region and very lightly traveled."

He also reported that on the way up, his party found on a side feeder of the main stream the decaying remnants of "a pair of gaiters, khaki pants and red flannel shirt with matches, tissue and snacks in the pockets...It was kind of scary." According to McCarty, there was no trace of an owner.

Even by the conventional route from the east, there seems to be an almost infinite number of ways to climb Street and Nye, limited only by the number of herd paths.

One complicating factor is the number of "bumps" on the Nye ridge. Topographic maps indicate there are three. Yet trail veterans vow that from Adirondak Loj at Heart Lake, you can see five. Also, some climbers have had so much trouble following the advice of those who went before them that they have vowed that the summit cannister must have been moved from one bump to another.

Climbers reach Nye by circuitous routes. Some, to convince themselves they made it, climb all of the bumps. One party's report:

"Attempting to climb Street first, we suddenly found ourselves atop Nye." And for an unfathomable reason, one newcomer chose Nye as his first Adirondack climbing challenge. There is no report that he ever tried another.

Journal entry: Sunday, May 25, 1975. Henry David Thoreau may have been right when he said, "the mass of men lead lives of quiet desperation."

But he did not speak for those of us on this hike. Our lot can best be described as active frustration. Jim and I decide to just plod along and let our leader deal with the obstacles.

I note that we surmount only three bumps as we retrace our way along the Nye ridge on our way to Street. Then we descend into a col, which is our first easy stretch since leaving Indian Pass Brook.

Even here, we step with care through the downed trees. A couple of years ago, a man was forced to go for help when his wife fell, tearing the ligaments in her knee and fracturing an elbow. He left her in the col with four boys, the oldest only 13, while he struggled back to the Loj alone. He reached there at nine p.m., and returned with a dozen people in a rescue party, including three rangers. From the col, it took them five and a quarter hours to make their way out.

The 400 feet of ascent to Street from the col leads through continuous blowdown. It is, I tell Jim, the closest thing to the jungles of New Guinea and the Philippines I've seen since my tour of the South Pacific.

In exactly one hour from the time we left Nye, we reach the summit cannister on Street. The weather, usually as unpredictable as the mountains, this time is in our favor: it is superb. A comforting mantle of fluff-ball clouds crown the surrounding peaks.

Our group could not have planned better for a special occasion. One of the climbers, 17-year-old Mark Baldwin, announces that he is now a Forty Sixer.

Son Jim is only a year older, so I compared notes during the climb with Mark's father, Robert. But he gave me no inkling that the two of them were so close to their goal. Now, he tells me, they were in such a rush to complete the 46 that they climbed Cliff last week, Esther yesterday, and these two peaks today.

When Robert Marshall climbed Street, he noted that "the top is flat" and "heavily wooded." And, he said, "we saw nothing." That was before the hurricane, of course. So it must be that the wind knocked down enough trees to boost the low view rating Marshall gave it.

Just prior to reaching the summit, a herd path on the right leads to a close-up view of the MacIntyres that's much like the one from Indian

Falls, only from the opposite side of the range. The Santanonis also beckon from the southwest and the Sewards from the west.

Nye sprawls lazily to the north with Whiteface looming beyond. On a clear day, the climber can spot Giant and a chunk of the Great Range to the east.

Alfred Street, the mountain's namesake, oozed sentimentality when writing about the Adirondacks. Of the wilderness, he once said, "I was more and more impressed with the utter savageness of the scene, and my entire helplessness should I be left alone."

Modern climbers are anything but sentimental about Street and Nye. Kirk Luchtenberg recently reported to the Adirondack Forty Sixers' historian that the two peaks, his 41st and 42nd, were "the longest day of climbing — fourteen hours! Got back to the lean-to just as the last rays of light vanished. A day to remember, or forget."

> *Journal entry: Sunday, May 25, 1975. Since it is going on three p.m., Jim and I again plunge into blowdown with our group on the eastern slopes of Street and head downward. Brousseau says a trail marked by red blazes is our best escape route.*
>
> *But Street, like Nye, does not loosen its grip gracefully. Deep, lingering patches of snow in the tangles make the going slippery and treacherous. We find no markers.*
>
> *One could become very nervous pondering the recent advice of ENCON's ranger Gary Hodgson: "The Street and Nye mountain area is one where we carry out many search and rescue missions because people get turned around by the many stream tributaries and get caught up in the swamps."*

Finally, one of our group discovers a red blaze, and we perk up our pace. Brousseau sighs and smiles at the sharp-eyed climber: "You get a quarter for spotting the trail. That's cheap, for I told myself many times I'd give

From Street, *Nye sprawls lazily to the north. Whiteface preens on the horizon; Giant and the Great Range are out of sight, at right.*

a million dollars to the first one who found it."

Indian Pass Brook brings a lift both in spirits and in temperature. The return- ing warmth of the low- lands also attracts other, unwanted celebrants: hordes of

Indian Pass Brook's *icy waters are no deterrent to outing leader Eugene Brousseau. Others rock-hop to begin our last mile to the Loj.*

black flies. In our haste to outdistance them, some of our group ignore the icy brook waters and splash across barefoot. Jim and I revert to rock hopping, on the assumption that motion works better than moisture in repelling the flies.

By the time we reach Adirondak Loj under forced march, Jim and I are soaked in sweat. No matter. We made it. With a couple of tough ones like Street and Nye, it is better to be safe, and warm, than sorry.

Journal entry: Saturday, May 23, 1981. *My recounting of the dangers of hiking in the high peaks has son Ben on edge. I tell him to relax.*

First, this is our eighth straight day of flawless hiking weather; we couldn't get hypothermia if we tried. Second, he and I are going up Street and Nye on another Adirondack Mountain Club jaunt. This one will be led by John E. Winkler, whom club members call "Bushwhack." They say John could find that dauntless British explorer, David Livingstone, if he were lost in the Adirondacks, whereas his compatriot, Dr. Henry M. Stanley, might fail.

This is another Memorial Day weekend, so Winkler hustles our group of 10 away from the tumult of the Loj area. We cross Indian Pass Brook and head up a herd path he determines to be the proper route west. We halt for rest a half hour up the slopes at an old lum- ber clearing.

Winkler tells me, "I'm at the Loj for the weekend." I suggest that after today's hike, he'll probably rest up. "Oh, no," he says. "Tomorrow I'm leading a group up Wright over the Whale's Tail."

When I point out there is no trail there, his eyes begin to dance: "Yeah, I know." But there are limits even for a bushwhacker like John Winkler in this area of the Adirondacks. "One thing we're not going to do today is come down off Street," he says. He reminds me that he was one of those with Jim and me when our ADK group thrashed our way down from there six years ago.

"This time," he vows, "we'll return to Nye and come down the way we came up."

There is something about these two mountains that mesmerizes me. I see and hear things along the way, but don't retain anything. Mostly, I suspect it's caused by the follow-the-leader rhythm set up by a group hike. Also, the compelling need to keep up dictates against looking around.

An hour after leaving the lumber camp, we top off the ridge and face a latticework of herd paths. It is like a maze with multiple entrances.

John frowns for a few minutes, then heads along a path that looks much like the others. It wanders up and down through a dreary wasteland, then an hour later moves past a small depression to a modest blister that is Nye's summit.

Again, I don't recall anything about it from the last time. This is not surprising, because visually Nye is a zero; it's easy to forget. The tiny clearing near the cannister is surrounded by woods.

There isn't room for all 10 of us to have lunch there, so Ben and I shuffle back to the slump. Ben corrects me: "It's the pits."

When we leave, vague glimpses of Street through the trees tell us we are descending in the right direction. But in 20 minutes our herd path vanishes at a jumbled mass of windfall and underbrush. "No prob-

John Winkler is known as "Bushwhack" to fellow ADKers. He views the tangled, fallen trees as challenges, not obstacles.

lem," says John. "I'll just take a compass reading on Street, and we'll head straight for it."

Nine voices plead for reason: let us retrace our steps, find the proper path, then arrive on Street together. Most important, we suggest, let us arrive.

Fortunately, John Winkler is good-natured. We backtrack and choose a well-trod course which brings us to the col between the two peaks. It harbors a grass-lined pond, the source of the Chubb River, which here begins its long journey to the St. Lawrence.

MacIntyre Range *comes into sharp focus from Street. Tip of Marcy peeks above saddle between Wright, left, and Algonquin. Iroquois is at right, the slope to Marshall beyond.*

Our second target mountain is often in sight, so we arrive at the summit in less than a half hour. A journeyman jaunt this time, it seems to me. Not to Ben, though. When he returns from confirming the overlook to the MacIntyres, he says, "It's spectacular." He also reports he's found out what we have to do to climb Marshall.

That makes me nervous again. My next try of Marshall will be number six; Jim and I lucked out again in 1975.

The journey back to the Nye ridge is uneventful, except when we hear shouts from climbers thrashing around in the jumble. Soon, a party of four emerges under full pack. We ask where they are headed, and they say, "out there," pointing west.

They are either woefully ignorant of what they are getting into, or are out of their minds.

At the junction where the ridge juts downward from Nye, Winkler determines that another, wider herd path to our right would have been a better course for us in ascending Nye. It is too late for that now, of course. But a member of our party who is scheduled to lead a group here soon, lags behind to prop up logs as markers. He wants no mistakes when he returns with his group.

Strangely, the descent from the ridge takes as long as the initial climb of it — two and a half hours. And I revise my opinion about this being a journeyman climb. Even with a wilderness expert like John Winkler leading, the circuit takes an hour and 55 minutes longer than it did the last time.

John "Bushwhack" Winkler exemplifies the legendary Adirondack explorer as well as any current climber.

He finished climbing all of the 46 high peaks in 1975, the year Jim and I made our first ascent of Street and Nye with him. After three more years of climbing, Winkler came to the conclusion that existing trails and herd paths were "conventional." So he determined to go back

We hate to leave. *View is to the south on the exit road from Adirondak Loj, a mile and a half from Rt. 73. Indian Pass, center, is flanked by MacIntyre Range, left, Nye and Street on right.*

and climb each of the 46 again, this time by a brand new, trailless route, from base to summit.

Consciously or not, Winkler had adopted the philosophy of that fabled Adirondack guide, Old Mountain Phelps. Each climb would be "a random scoot" — a bushwhack into the trackless forest.

John completed his mission in 1985. The Forty Sixers, recognizing that his accomplishment was anything but conventional, appended B#1 to his club membership number. The "B", as you might expect, stands for Bushwhack.

But Winkler was not finished; not when there were more mountains in the Adirondacks to climb and explore. He studied all Adirondack Mountain Club maps of the high peaks and, excluding the 46 highest, pinpointed the 100 highest with names. Many had no record of being climbed, so he determined to set the record straight.

One of the 100 he targeted was a mile south of Street Mtn. Winkler had already climbed part way toward it via the Roaring Brook which flows to the southeast from Street. In 1990, he vowed: "Sometime when I have the time and energy, I would like to explore the fork that leads to Lost Pond."

The 3,900-ft. peak had no official name, but it was referred to as Lost Pond Peak. Eventually, Winkler climbed it and found out why it was given that name. Two hundred feet below the summit is a sizeable body of water. John notes this is not visible from the surrounding high peaks. Lost Pond can only be seen from Lost Pond Peak, because the multiple summits of the latter surround it.

The names among the other mountains which John climbed were intriguing: Old Far, Jug, Peacock, Claybed, Wolf Pond, and so on. Many called for fierce bushwhacking worthy of Street and Nye. Rist Mountain, a part of the North River Ridge, topped even that level of frustration.

The ascent to the summit from the base camp, where Winkler and a partner bivouaced, was only a mile long. Yet, according to John, the round trip took 12 and a half hours. "That's one sixth of a mile an hour! Horrendous! Unbelievable!"

But in true bushwhack spirit, Winkler added: "Had a good time though!"

John's exploits are documented in *A Bushwhacker's View of the Adirondacks*, published in 1995 by North Country Books of Utica, New York. The volume, illustrated with four-color photographs and sketches, was edited by Neil Burdick, editor of ADK's *Adirondac* magazine.

Among the others on the 1981 climb of Nye and Street noted above were John Wiley, who drew the sketches for Winkler's book, and Neil Woodworth, who today is the Adirondack Mountain Club's deputy executive director for public and legal affairs.

Hough Peak, center right, from Nippletop. Dix Mtn. is at left.

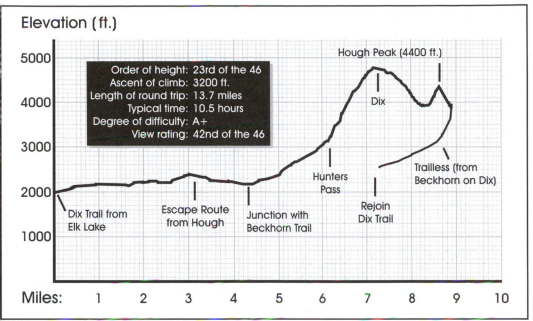

Elevation (ft.)

Hough Peak (4400 ft.)

Order of height: 23rd of the 46
Ascent of climb: 3200 ft.
Length of round trip: 13.7 miles
Typical time: 10.5 hours
Degree of difficulty: A+
View rating: 42nd of the 46

Dix

Hunters
Pass

Trailless (from
Beckhorn on Dix)

Dix Trail from
Elk Lake

Escape Route
from Hough

Junction with
Beckhorn Trail

Rejoin
Dix Trail

Miles: 1 2 3 4 5 6 7 8 9 10

For contour trails, see U.S. Geological Survey map, pgs. 214-215.

30.
HOUGH

Journal entry: Tuesday, October 3, 1995. Until recently, the last chance to stock up on trail snacks before climbing Hough came at the general store in Blue Ridge, New York. The store, some two miles west of Frontier Town, is the first one on the right on the road to Newcomb. In fact, it is the only store along the 20 lonesome miles leading to that hamlet.

At one time, the century-old business was called Bruce's, and the store pictured its quaint exterior on post cards taken in both summer and winter. The cards look the same except for the one with a loaded logging truck parked next to snow drifts four feet deep.

Hough is not my climbing target today. My two hiking sons are off on their own, so my wife and I are taking a pleasant, exploratory drive in the Adirondacks. I stop at the general store anyway, out of habit; our family always liked to chat with the woman who most recently ran the place.

Everything looks in order inside, but the door is locked as it has been for some time. Nobody's at the house behind it either, so I knock at a home across the street to see if I can find out if and when the store will reopen.

We are greeted with a warm smile by Mildred Dobie, who makes us feel right at home. She tells us the store was operated by Katherine Atkins, an older woman who has not been well. "We all call her Nannie," says Mrs. Dobie. "She likes to run the store because it gives her a chance to meet people. I don't know if she'll reopen it or not."

I devoutly hope so.

Going inside the old store was like stepping back in time. This was no ersatz emporium stuffed with fake old fittings and fake new souvenirs. The store's wooden counters and cases were darkened and polished from use — more inviting, one would guess, than when they were new.

Mrs. Atkins displayed a modest amount of necessities, geared to the frequency and wants of patrons: staples like bread, milk and beverages; gloves and hats; fishing gear; film; and, of course, snacks. All were enhanced by the glow of daylight coming in through the old-fashioned store windows in front. Signs outside advertised trapping equipment and "Ice Fishing Supplies."

The kindly, white-haired proprietress greeted customers in front of a row of shiny, penny candy jars lined up against the back wall. She dispensed wisdom for the children about what was in the jars, a pat on the back for her cat and the black Lab which followed her everywhere, and patience for those who couldn't make up their minds about what candy to buy.

Mrs. Dobie, we learn, is supervisor of the Town of North Hudson. In 1980, she tells us, "the town had 179 people. Since North Hudson covered 190 square miles, that gave each of us a little over a square mile."

But, she says ruefully, "The town grew to 266 people in 1990. I wish we could go back to the old days. We don't want to get too big."

Later, I checked to see how much the world was pressing in on them, on a comparative basis. They can relax.

The United States as a whole has 71 people per square mile. New York state doesn't fare so well: 381 people per square mile. Things get dicey in Rhode Island; it squeezes in 962 citizens per mile. And Mrs. Dobie and her constituents can feel blessed compared to the people of Hong Kong. They must be layered in vertically; every mile includes 14,547 of them.

Journal entry: Friday, July 27, 1979. *Hough is trailless, so I think it may be wise if Ben and I schedule our exploration with a group outing sponsored by the Adirondack Mountain Club. On the spur of the* *moment, I call Elk Lake Lodge to see if they can accommodate my wife and me and Ben tonight, and again tomorrow tonight after our hike. No problem, the innkeeper reports.*

At dinner, through the ground-glass haze settling over Elk Lake, we think we spot a mother loon and her brood along the shore. "No," says a knowledgeable lodger at the next table. "They're mergansers.

"Even at this distance," he says, "you can tell by the number of chicks. A female loon will lay only one or two eggs. But a merganser will lay from eight to 12 eggs, sometimes even more.

"Once in a while," he continues, "you'll see a mother merganser with up to 20 or so chicks. That happens when another merganser lays her eggs in the mother's nest because she can't find a site of her own. Rangers call it 'egg dumping.'"

As the mother merganser draws near, with the chicks paddling behind her, she dives beneath the surface. The chicks panic until she resurfaces. The chicks then skitter over and, as many as can fit, climb onto her back for reassurance.

Today's hike *will take us six miles from Elk Lake to Hunters Pass, left, then over Dix, center, to Hough, right center. Trek to the latter and return behind spur of Macomb, right, are trailless.*

Journal entry: Saturday, July 28, 1979. Ben and I rendezvous at eight sharp with the Schenectady Chapter ADK crew, whose car-pool has just arrived. "I'm already dragging," reports one. "We had company, so I didn't get to bed till midnight. And since I live 15 miles west of Schenectady, I had to get up at 3:45 a.m."

Even so, he looks to be in vigorous condition, as do the six other men in the party. They wear shorts; bulging calves above sturdy boots tell us they're not strangers to hiking.

This is reinforced by their hiking club patches and comments. Several are Forty Sixers. One has completed the 130-mile Northville-Lake Placid trail. Another has hiked a great deal in the White Mountains of New Hampshire. The face of one is familiar: it identifies Mindaugus Jatulis, a neighbor whom I've seen jogging but didn't realize was a hiker. He tells me he's completed 21 of the 46.

A woman with a smile as wide as our surroundings rounds out the roster. She has hiked with her husband and three sons, now grown, but is apprehensive about this outing. Her last time out, she says, was on Gothics last December.

Gothics in December? Anyone who can do Gothics in mid-winter should have no problem.

Our leader is Tom Stanwood, whom I met while working on United Way projects. He was with Jim and me on Street and Nye, and again on an abortive ADK attempt to climb Marshall four years ago in June.

"Do I remember Marshall?" laughs Tom. "When we came down, I was so cold I couldn't unbutton my jacket. I went back and made the attempt twice again before finally reaching the summit."

Our failure on Marshall in 1975 prompted me to quit climbing. I started again only last year, with Ben. It's obvious that Marshall fueled Tom's desire. He was just beginning to explore the high peaks then. But when and if we reach Hough today, it will mark his second time around the 46.

"Our route today," says Tom, "will be through Hunters Pass. Then we'll go up the red trail to Dix, and on over to Hough. We should top out on Dix at 12:30 p.m., and get back here by five p.m."

It is 8:10 a.m., and the sturdy calves go churning up the trail. One of our hikers, named Allan, surges ahead and disappears. Since I expect to have trouble keeping up once the trail starts to rise sharply after about four miles, I position Ben and me just behind the two front runners.

Dix Pond, at 10 in the morning, is at a lower level than I remember when I was here eight years ago. It also looks lifeless, as if victimized by acid rain.

The Adirondack Park Agency advises that "the normal appearance of a lake or pond turned sterile by acid precipitation is that of extreme clarity tinged with blue." In my red-green color blind judgment, the pond is dead.

But the Department of Environmental Conservation suggests otherwise. Most damage from acid rain has occurred on the slopes and higher elevations of Adirondack peaks farther west. At Dix Pond, reports the DEC, brook trout and other fish thrive.

Rampant clusters of tiny, wild, red raspberries in the old lumber clearing just beyond Dix Pond perk us up. When we leave the junction, the red trail begins a steep assault of the slopes leading to Hunters Pass. Ben surges ahead with the leaders, while I fall back, puffing.

I'm pleased to see that one hiker is slower than I am. He is the sturdy, lively chap with 46er/Northville-Lake Placid patches on his pack. "I'm the sweep," he says. "On club hikes, someone lags behind to watch out for stragglers."

"Wrong," some smart alec yells from up ahead. "That position is known as the drag." My companion says nothing, but smiles at me.

We soon catch up with the main members of the group, who promptly cut short their rest period and charge off. This happens twice more before they take a major break at the notch in Hunters Pass. Finally, a moment to relax. We have made a little over six miles in two and three quarter hours.

It seems a shame that everybody is in such a hurry. I had hoped we might pause a half mile back to look for a lost cave where, according to a yarn dreamed up by Adirondack writer Charles Dudley Warner, outlaws stashed away a booty of gold and silver. A stream which crossed our trail flows down from Nippletop and, per the legend, goes by the hideout-sized cave.

Until the middle of the last century, Hunters Pass was known as the "Gorge of the Dial." That reflected the name given at the time to Nippletop, which rises on the western side of the corridor.

In 1878, Hunters Pass was, according to Warner in his book *In the Wilderness*, "one of the wildest of the mountain passes...There is no trail...it is rare to find a guide who has been that way." That was fine with Warner: "The tin-can and paper-collar tourists have not yet made it a runway."

Some 50 years later, writing about a trip through Hunters Pass in *The Adirondacks*, T. Morris Longstreth said it was in "gloomy and savage country." Of the high peak passes, he said, it is "the highest of all in the Adirondacks." That will prompt an argument today: Elk Pass looks to be the same elevation on U.S.G.S. maps.

From the crown of Hunters Pass, Longstreth observed that "another pair of these contrasted stream issues, the Schroon finding its way to the Hudson, the Bouquet to Champlain." Warner discovered the phenomenon the hard way: "The pass is narrow, walled in on each side by precipices of granite, and blocked up with the bowlders (sic) and fallen trees, and beset with pitfalls in the roads ingeniously covered with fair-seeming moss."

Said Warner, "When the climber occasionally loses sight of a leg in one of those treacherous holes, and feels a cold sensation in his foot, he learns that he has dipped into the sources of the Boquet."

Hikers who don't watch their step have the same problem today.

Journal entry: Saturday, July 28, 1979. I hardly catch my breath when Tom Stanwood routs the group to start climbing. We take the trail which skirts the north edge of the cliff notched in Dix's shoulder. To me, it seems to go straight up.

The main party, including Ben, moves out of sight. Soon, one after another of the adults lags back to see if I'm still coming.

Finally, Tom comes back to ask: "You OK?" Yeah, I tell him through the heavy breathing. I'm just slower than you young Turks. Go ahead. I'll catch up on top.

Solace to slow climbers comes from thinking about Verplanck Colvin and his survey crew, who climbed from the same location in 1871: "Paths stamped by the footprints of deer, panther and bear," wrote Colvin, "showed us where these creatures had found spots amid the cliffs which they could climb. Availing ourselves of these runways, we slowly toiled upward."

Dix summit looks more like a neighborhood park than a windswept wilderness. The only hiker I seek is a small figure on topmost knob: Ben.

The distance from the pass to the summit is just a mile. But it calls for 1,800 feet of steep climbing, relieved only by spectacular outlooks.

Journal entry: Saturday, July 28, 1979. *A beeping walkie-talkie breaks the silence. It announces the arrival of a modern-day Colvin — a park ranger — who nods as he scoots by under full pack. I follow until he pulls out of sight.*

At one p.m., I top off; Tom Stanwood predicted we would arrive at 12:30. Close.

Dix's summit, like an inverted chopping knife, appears today to be a lofty state park; climbers perch all along the top.

Ben waves to me from the topmost summit knob, where Colvin implanted a silver-dollar sized benchmark. I slump for lunch below him to avoid the frigid effect of the stiff breeze on my sweat-marked clothes.

The views, as on my first trip here, are inspiring. They're matched by an exhilarating confidence that Ben and I will now complete this twin conquest.

I finish no more than half a sandwich when Tom notes a touch of gray in the scudding clouds. He stands up and says, "Let's go."

As usual, the hiker named Allan, who lingered briefly while we were on Dix, is long gone toward Hough. Hikers are supposed to stay with their groups on ADK outings, but Allan is irrepressible. Tom would call him back, I'm sure, if he did not feel he was an experienced hiker.

It's comforting to see that Ben stays close to two

Nearing the Beckhorn, *what we thought were scraggly trees on its top are hikers — lots of them. Route to Hough lies beyond to the southeast.*

others who lead us down the well-worn herd path, which is a contin-uation of the knife ridge that characterizes Dix's summit.

It is also nice to know that I have moved from last to fourth place in our party. I begin to think my worries are over. Except for Ben, who is nowhere in sight through the tangle ahead. I call for him twice, with no answer.

"Don't worry," says Tom, who is right behind me. "He can't get lost." However, there is a serious reason why the ADK designates a "sweep." A club spokesman noted in Adirondac *that, "the conse-quences of missing the trail are far greater on the way down since one could end up almost anywhere while, going up, all routes at least tend to converge at the summit."*

As Ben observed earlier, this herd path is more distinct than some marked trails. Still, it's a mighty big wilderness out there and, by comparison, Ben is mighty small. And he's my son.

Herd path to Hough, *center, follows ridge, left, descending from Dix. Steep escape route plunges to the west this side of Macomb, at right.*

As soon as we begin the steep, 400-ft. ascent to Hough from the col, the others scoot out of sight. I'm dragging again.

I haul onto the crowded summit at 2:30 p.m. It's a flat rock slab about the size of a large dining room table, with conifers forming three walls. The fourth con-stitutes an open picture win-dow fronting Elk Lake to the southwest. Beyond the window sill, for a long way down, there is nothing.

They're all there, including Ben — plus the elusive Allan. Without a word, however, he packs up and heads out again.

"Congratulations on your 30th," says Tom. The same to you, I say, on your second circuit of the 46. With a wink, Tom smiles to Ben: "And to

you for climbing the same number as your age."

Hough ranks in the middle of the high peaks, 23rd in height, seventh among those which are trailless. Hough shares characteristics of many of the others, as cannister comments revealed in a 1979 issue of *Adirondack Peeks*.

In July, for example, Richard Mecklenborg asked: "Why, whenever I come to the Dixes, is it threatening or making good on those threats?" Red Bromfield of Dallas, Texas, wrote in the same month that Hough is not unique: "Have climbed many of your 46, perhaps half of them. Nearly all made in pouring rain. It's still worth it." Neil Longer was of like mind in July: "Dark, wet, cold, but very happy."

Hough summit is about the size of a big dining room table. Vista to the southwest encompasses Elk Lake with Boreas Mtn. beyond.

Journal entry: Saturday, July 28, 1979. The lure of the Adirondack high peaks seems to be universal: the last three people to sign in before us are a man from Olney, New York, another from Brooklyn, and a woman from Oakland, California.

We take a swig of water — better than champagne for our kind of celebration — and begin the five-mile descent to Elk Lake.

A sharp branch bloodies my upper arm, so I ask Tom to bandage it. He does in great haste. "It still looks like rain," he says, "and I don't want to lose sight of our party ahead."

Fine with me. Ben's down there out of sight, again.

We catch up at a low saddle between Hough and a hogback ridge to the south, which climbers call Pough. Makes sense: Huff and Puff. The marshy clearing spawns a profusion of herd paths; none in our party is sure which is the right route down. Campers in tents confirm they all are. "Your choice," one says.

Hough's western slope, littered with debris and scoured by slides, matches the drop of Macomb, which at its best is scary. A spider web of paths plunges erratically along the courses of various streams, all tributaries of Lillian Brook. The paths are so steep they are looked on more as escape routes in bad weather than conventional paths from Hough, or for those descending from the lesser Dixes to the south.

As we fill our canteens at a cool glade, I discover that my wristwatch is gone. Small wonder: my glasses have already been flipped off twice by snagging branches. The watch could have come off anywhere during our last mile and a half and 1,500 hundred feet of descent. Searching for it would be like hunting for a needle in a very large haystack.

A main herd path finally levels off and threads back and forth across the stream. It then merges with a meandering old hunters' trail which angles away to the left from Lillian Brook. "It's a piece of cake now," says one of our group.

He's right. In no time, we reach the cairn on the Dix trail, and by 4:30 p.m. flop down at the Slide Brook lean-to. The sleeping bags we saw this morning have been joined by their owners, two hikers from Schenectady who greet their fellow ADK members.

One man announces that he has completed 41 of the 46, and he is on the prowl to complete the circuit next week. "Very shortly," he says, "we're moving out to camp at the base of Allen. We'll do that tomorrow, then camp out on the uplands to do Redfield and the others."

The only one of the "others" I can make out is Marshall.

Tom, who is conversing with the man some distance away, jerks his thumb in my direction and chortles: "You two have something in common. You still have Marshall to do, and you both lost your wristwatches."

"I was coming off a mountain in early spring," the man relates, "when I slipped and plunged forward into deep snow. When I pulled out my arm, the watch was gone. Of course, I didn't know that until later."

Our hiker from Amsterdam allows that he is really tired now. But Tom urges us on. "Don't say I didn't warn you. I said at the start I push harder than I should."

Tom and his assistant outing leader, Bruce Wadsworth, stride out in front. Ben and I struggle to keep up with them so we can soak up trail wisdom.

Wadsworth, we find, has written a book entitled An Adirondack Sampler, *which the Adirondack Mountain Club will release this year.* It describes modest mountain hikes which are good for families and for those who may not be ready to tackle the high peaks.*

Not Tom. "My next hike," he vows, "will be in the Sawtooth Range in the Cold River region. It's really wild, I understand."

"Tomorrow?" asks Ben.

"No, next weekend," Tom responds. "Tomorrow I sleep." Good news: this high-speed dragster is human like the rest of us.

We reach the parking lot at 5:40 p.m., a half hour behind schedule, per Tom, but still respectable. I had predicted, based on my cadence, that we would arrive around eight.

As we check out at the trailhead, I leave a note about my watch, along with my name and address. It's a bigger long shot than winning the lottery, I suppose. But, hey, you never know.

From the lodge during dinner, we again see water birds on the lake. Their forlorn calls tell us that this time they are not mergansers.

As the waterfowl approach, we are amazed to see six full-grown loons cavorting near the shore of the lake. Yet another comes lumbering in for a landing, doing a long-distance belly flop before settling next to the others. They all dive for food, surfacing helter-skelter in front of us. This morning's wildlife expert, again next to our table, tells us, "That's a sight you may never see again. There are perhaps only 200 pairs left in the U.S."

The lodge's manager, Pete Sanders, confirms that this gathering is unusual because loons, which mate for life, are highly territorial. "Normally," he says, "only one pair will reside at either Elk Lake or Clear Pond. They even drive off their young when they reach adulthood. But last year was like this — there were eight loons here at one time."

Our stay at the lodge seems like a continuation of today's hike. Wife Betty was startled by a deer while taking a stroll this morning, and fresh tracks dotted the path in front of the lodge. Our friend nearby also reported on canoeing past a beaver dam at the north inlet of Elk Lake this morning: "We could hear the murmur of little ones inside."

---

* Wadsworth also wrote a second Sampler *book on backpacking, plus three* ADK Guides to Adirondack Trails: *Northville-Lake Placid trail, Central Region, and* The Catskills. *He also has authored a* History of the Adirondack Mountain Club, *scheduled for publication late in 1996. Wadsworth and his wife have been active in the club for more than 20 years, and are co-chairs of the ADK's 75th Anniversary Committee.*

The walls of the sitting room in the lodge, too, remind us not only of the animals here today but of those which roamed the area in the past, including moose, wolverine and elk.

In the morning, Ben and I are stiff, so my wife joins us for a six-mile circuit of Clear Pond, a part of the lodge complex. The trail along the north edge of the pond, which is two miles south of the lodge, traces the route of the long-gone Cedar Point Road. It was built to haul iron ore from the old McIntyre mine at Tahawus to what is now Port Henry on Lake Champlain.

From Elk Lake, Hough looks like a geometric cone tapped onto the right shoulder of Dix. During earlier times, in fact, Hough *was* called Cone Mountain.

Over time, Hough Peak was known by other names: Marshall, after the brothers who first climbed it in 1921; Middle Dix; and then Little Dix. In 1937, the state's Committee on Geographic Names settled on the present one. It honors Dr. Franklin B. Hough, known as "The Father of American Forestry," who first headed what is now the U.S. Forest Service.

At sunset from Elk Lake, Hough Peak often matches the image of a lovely scene decribed by Francis Parkman: "The glow of the vanished sun behind the...mountains, darkly piled in mist and shadow along the sky."

Journal entry: Thursday, September 20, 1979. I have just received an acknowledgment for the "thank you" letter I sent to Mark E. Blazka of Lake Placid, New York. He found my watch the day after I lost it when he came down the same, steep, trailless slopes of Hough.

"I couldn't believe it," he said. "It was one foot from that little stream you followed." Mark has just entered Tufts as a freshman. The hike was a nice break, he wrote. "I spend an average of 12 hours out of 19 of my waking hours studying."

A great break for me, too.

Journal entry: Tuesday, August 19, 1986. Up again for five days at Elk Lake Lodge, so Ben and I decide to try Hough on our own, this time via the Yellow trail to Dix which Jim and Bill and I took.

Today, Ben is six foot four, with a stride that even Tom would find hard to match. So our stay on Dix is no sit-and-go affair this time. We spend an hour and a half enjoying lunch and the view. We compare it with the one from Black Mountain, overlooking Lake George, which Ben and I climbed three months ago. We gave that a

Lake George from Black Mtn. Ben and I climb this 2,646-ft. peak in the southern Adirondacks, but conclude it has too many people to match Elk Lake's tranquility.

top rating. But the view of Elk Lake from Dix is better; there are no power boats here, only canoes and rowboats.

The col between Dix and Hough is, if anything, worse than ever. It's littered with blowdown; we have to search for accessible holes to slither through.

In the cannister notebook on Hough, Ben chuckles at an illegible signature following a note from a hapless hiker: "Took the wrong turn at Dix and wound up here."

My wavering field notes illustrate the problem: "Down — lost — multiple paths, cuts, bugs. Terrible."

All hikers agree: Hough is tough.

Journal entry: Saturday, August 23, 1986. *The general store at Blue Ridge has upgraded its wares. It now offers a T-shirt emblazoned with the name of the store and a promotional slogan.*

Its marketing niche, however, is pretty narrow. The last line of copy after Blue Ridge, New York reads: "Pop. 36."

Basin Mtn. from Mt. Haystack.

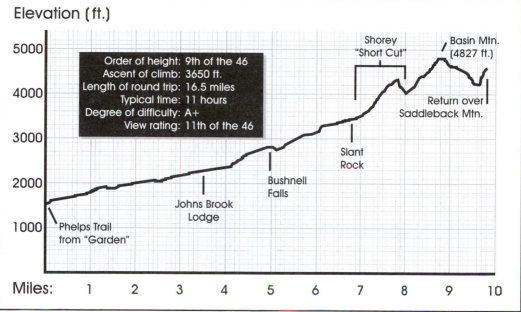

Elevation (ft.)

Order of height: 9th of the 46
Ascent of climb: 3650 ft.
Length of round trip: 16.5 miles
Typical time: 11 hours
Degree of difficulty: A+
View rating: 11th of the 46

Shorey "Short Cut"
Basin Mtn. (4827 ft.)
Return over Saddleback Mtn.
Slant Rock
Bushnell Falls
Johns Brook Lodge
Phelps Trail from "Garden"

Miles: 1 2 3 4 5 6 7 8 9 10

or contour trails, see U.S. Geological Survey map, pgs. 120-121.

31.
BASIN

The challenges in climbing the remote mountains of the northeast —
steepness, distance and that old bugaboo, time — force climbers to
choose one of three strategies.

First, slim down and travel light, so you can get up and down a
mountain before running out of daylight.

Second, lug along the considerable baggage of food, shelter and
bedroll you need to camp out overnight.

Or third, choose a mountain with an on-site facility which provides
food, shelter and bedding.

The last option can make your hiking life easier, even though it puts
constraints upon what you do and when. How much it will ease your
task depends upon the philosophy of the mountain climbing club whose
facility you use.

In the northeast, the two major clubs — the Appalachian Mountain
Club and the Adirondack Mountain Club — have followed divergent
paths in serving climbers.

The Appalachian Mountain Club, older and larger of the two, focuses
on the White Mountains of New Hampshire. Scarcely more than 10

years after its founding in 1876, the club began to build a series of "huts" at high elevations to accomodate climbers.

Its first stone structure, according to the Watermans in *Forest and Crag*, was little more than a "simple, one-room stone dungeon, dank and dark, equipped with stove, bunks, and cook-gear." Over time, the club constructed eight, more elaborate ones, some with as many as seven rooms. Each hut had a resident crew to provide food and do the cooking.

Obviously the sturdy huts promoted safety when severe weather plagued climbers. But that was not the initial motivation, according to the Watermans. It was "the convenience of a high base for tramping excursions."

The lofty huts have received mixed reviews. While most Appalachian Mountain Club members like them, some arch eyebrows at what they see as "hotels" intruding on the wilderness. Suzanne Lance, a visiting Adirondack Forty Sixer, underscores why. As she reported in *Adirondack Peeks* (of which she is co-editor), "we checked into the hut which was crowded with hikers...[ours] accommodates 90 guests and this time our bunk rooms held 18 people."

She also learned, in climbing Mt. Washington, why the Whites are termed rocky. "We weren't climbing a mountain, we were climbing a slag heap. What looked from a distance like a mighty and majestic monolith, was really just a giant rock pile up close."

The Adirondack Mountain Club was formed in 1922, almost a quarter of a century after the Appalachian Mountain Club erected its first hut. Not long thereafter, the ADK thought it might be a good idea to mimic its sister club in the White Mountains and build a similar system of shelters.

But New York state's Conservation Department, the forerunner of today's Department of Environmental Conservation, put an end to the proposal; the huts would be incompatible with the "Forever Wild" provision of the constitution. Besides, at the time there was no real system of trails in the Adirondack high peaks.

Today, the only shelters allowed for hikers on public lands in the high peaks are Adirondack lean-tos. These are unique, log structures enclosed on three sides, with an overhanging roof shielding an opening designed to face a stone fireplace. Most of the lean-tos are in mountain valleys; at one time, some were built above 4,000 feet, but these have been removed.

Two exceptions, both private facilities of the Adirondack Mountain Club, offer hikers an upgrade from the primitive lean-tos, an outgrowth of the shanties originally built by old-time Adirondack guides. One is Adirondak Loj, which can be reached by car. It provides access to many of the central high peaks, including Mt. Marcy.

The other is Johns Brook Lodge, a rambling, informal, wooden structure which provides basic amenities similar to those of Appalachian Mountain Club huts. At both the lodge and the huts, climbers need reservations and must hike to the remote areas where they are located. Johns Brooks Lodge is three and one half miles south-west of the trailhead at the Garden, near Keene Valley.

But the Johns Brook Lodge is not a "hotel in the clouds" like White Mountain huts. It can be reached after a climb of less than 800 feet from the parking lot at the Garden. Its central location in Johns Brook Valley serves as the hub for trails which emanate like spokes to the surrounding high peaks. When climbers head skyward from the lodge, they leave civilization behind.

Johns Brooks Lodge fulfills a basic need for hikers. It is a halfway house, a jumping-off place for those who want to climb and explore the high peaks.

Like Basin, for example. Many Adirondack climbers consider this mountain the crown jewel among the peaks which make up the majestic Great Range.

Journal entry: Monday, August 6, 1979. Ben and I have a reservation tonight at Johns Brook Lodge. Early tomorrow morning we will try to conquer the peak which Jim and I failed to complete after climbing Saddleback nine years ago.

As we register the date and our destination at the Garden, we note we are the 68th and 69th to log in today. We will not be alone tomorrow.

We also see for the first time warning signs posted at the parking lot: "Do not leave valuables in your car. There have been many deliberate break-ins. Report thefts to the State Police," and so on. Before, we have parked here only for day trips, so there has been little cause for concern.

The need for caution is reinforced by a lone man in his late 40s at the Bear Brook lean-to, a little less than a mile from the Garden. He shouts, "Hey! How would you like to buy $450 of camping equipment for $100? Someone stole all my money."

I decline, but he persists. "Then how about a camera for $20?" His aggressive, belligerent attitude grates on us; it is like stumbling on a garage sale in the wilderness.

Farther on, a young woman sits at trailside, babbling into a walkie-talkie; it does nothing to induce solitude in the woods. There is no one in sight at the ranger station.

Not far beyond, the trail passes a bridge on the left which leads to the two small, satellite camps of Johns Brook Lodge: Camp Peggy O'Brien, formerly known as Winter Camp, and Grace Camp. A short distance farther on, the forest opens on the lodge itself.

Johns Brook Lodge was opened by the Adirondack Mountain Club in 1925, three years after the club was organized. Its facilities, including

Johns Brook Lodge *is the Adirondack hiker's home-away-from-home in the central high peaks wilderness. It's reachable only by trail from the Garden near Keene Valley.*

resident staff, are available by reservation to all hikers from mid-June until Labor Day, and on a caretaker basis on weekends for about a month before and after those dates.

Camp Peggy O'Brien and Grace Camp offer hikers bare necessities: no food, but pots and pans and cooking facilities plus mattresses and bunk beds. Propane heat and light are provided along with outdoor toilets, but there are no showers and hikers must arrange for their own water.

The two satellites are open year round, accommodating the spillover from the lodge when it is open, and for an increasing number of people who climb in wintertime. In that regard, they serve as critical base camps. As ranger Peter Fish noted in *Adirondac*, "Winter comes to the mountains long before it comes to towns, cities and villages in lower-lying country. Winter also stays in the peaks long after the leaves are out in the lower elevations, where most people live."

Journal entry: Monday, August 6, 1979. Ben and I receive a cool reception at Johns Brook Lodge. The two young, college-age men in charge — Brent and Stephen — fret as they bustle about the kitchen. "No one phoned in your reservation; we'll have to make-do for dinner," they say.

They report no problem with a room, however. They have a reservation for only one other person, a woman. Since dinner will take a while, Ben and I wander the half mile back down the trail to see if the elusive ranger, Spencer Cram, is there yet. He is not, but we are hailed by two young women who ask if the lodge is much farther.

"I thought it was only a mile in," sighs the leader, obviously the one with the reservation. She wears a day pack but her guest appears to be a first timer in the woods. She lugs a large, heavy suitcase and searches for a comfortable way to hold it, with no luck.

When we return to the lodge, Brent and Stephen have spread out dinner on an enormous harvest table in the lodge's central room. The menu is hearty and healthy: boiled fish, green beans, cinnamon applesauce, and some dark, crumbly bread. There is coffee with powdered milk, honey instead of sugar and, for dessert, walnut pie. Plain, but delicious.

The dining room is the center of lodge activities, taking up a third of the front of the structure. The addition of another long table with benches near a book-lined side wall provides a kind of lounge for reading, writing, playing games and so on, under suspended gas lamps.

Two small private rooms lead off from the rear of the lounge, one on each side. The remaining space to the rear includes a commodious kitchen in the center, with a double-bed bunkroom on each side. One is for men and the other for women, each with its own toilet and tiny shower.

Brent and Stephen have their quarters in a small structure detached from the lodge itself.

The private room for Ben and me is furnished, like all the other facilities, for crude Adirondack comfort. The room, perhaps nine feet square, includes a double bunk bed constructed of logs, pushed against the outside wall, and a low bed jammed tightly from bunk to front wall beneath a large window. This leaves perhaps three by six feet of open floor space in the middle.

We rent sheets for the bunk beds, as required by state law, and discover it is almost impossible to make them up due to the cramped quarters. This explains why most hikers bring sleeping bags.

In spite of this, it's a bargain. Bed and board — three hearty meals, or two with a trail lunch if you prefer (two sizeable sandwiches, chocolate bar, orange and raisins) — is $16.20 per day for ADK members, $18 for non-members, plus tax. Sheets rent for a dollar.

We laze in the lounge; the traditional deer head gazes blankly from a high perch. Along the wall opposite from the books are essential items for sale — trail guides, maps and, locked up in a chicken wire enclosure, candy, gum and raisins.

The walls are splattered with pinned-up miscellany: watercolors and old prints of mountain scenes, clipped cartoons, a large portrait of an old-time Adirondack guide and, not surprisingly, a small poster Ben and I have seen at almost all Adirondack trailheads.

Robert L. Thomas of Remsen, New York seeks word on the fate of his brother, Steven Paul, who was lost on Mt. Marcy on April 12, 1976: "Steven was last seen at the Lower Lean-to by the five members of his climbing party. He left alone in the direction of the Upper Plateau lean-to. He gave no definite location as to where he was going. The night of April 12 was a full moon. The snow was hard packed and offered ideal walking conditions. It was cold @ 10 degrees F. and windy. The sky was clear."

We feel for them both.

On the walls also are the inevitable snapshots. A yearly progression of previous "Hut Boys," like Brent and Stephen. Ruddy, happy faces of hikers ready for or returning from jaunts. A collage of those who gathered here four years ago to celebrate the 50th anniversary of the lodge.

It's only eight p.m., so I flick to the crossword puzzle in a tattered Sunday New York Times Magazine. *Unfortunately, either Brent or Stephen has half finished it. So, not wanting to be inhospitable, I practice a nonsensical diversion — trying to complete it mentally. It is hard enough at home; the flickering light here makes it impossible.*

My eyes wander to an old book on the table: Mushrooms and Toadstools. *It's not very interesting, but a handwritten sheet which falls out, is. A neat, feminine script records: "Found at and about JBL 1938." The writer then lists certain specimens outlined in the book. The list ends abruptly, unsigned, with this find: "Boletus Indecisis."*

(My high school Latin is rusty, so I looked it up later. The Roman scholar, Pliny the Elder, called it "the best kind of mushroom." But I see that he also remarked, "the emperor Claudius is said to have been poisoned by them." Hmm.)

From the front porch, we see the glowing disc of a full moon just beginning to bulge over Big Slide. Ben checks the thermometer. It was 57 degrees at eight p.m.; now, a half hour later, it is 54.

Ben, who is now swaddled in three blankets in the upper bunk, does not answer my call five minutes after we turn in at nine p.m. A good omen: excitement has kept him up half the night prior to many previous hikes.

Journal entry: Tuesday, August 7, 1979. *Steaming bowls of oatmeal with brown sugar plus stacks of blueberry pancakes moderate the 43-degree breakfast chill. Brent is apologetic about the pancakes. "There's only about three berries per cake; they're hard to find around here."*

"Sorry about the coffee," Stephen adds. "I ordered 30 one-pound cans of drip grind and after I packed them in, I found they were regular. We're trying different ways to see how to use them."

"This is obviously not the way," he frowns as he sips. "Anyway, it's hot. And one thing's for sure. I'm not going to lug them back for exchange."

The 10-mile trek to town and back is the reason Brent and Stephen cultivate a postage stamp-size garden near the edge of the lodge's clearing. One suspects that few of the brave little plants will beat the odds they face.

For a brief time in the 1940s, food supply problems at Johns Brook Lodge were eased when the Adirondack Mountain Club enlisted a burro named Nubbins to help the Hut Boys haul in rations from the Outside. The beast's career was short-lived because, as Gary W. Koch noted in *Adirondac*, it was "the most notorious employee ADK ever had...A penchant for blondes, cigarettes and neck-biting cemented his infamous reputation."

Today's meals at JBL are perked up by the little garden, but it's not exactly bountiful. The growing season at Keene Valley barely surpasses 100 days; at the timberline on Basin, it's two months. Prime time here at the lodge is somewhere in between.

The short summers are one reason there is only one operating farm left in Keene Valley; it's devoted to truck gardening, raising produce for the market. Potatoes are one part of a dual crop grown along the entrance road leading to Adirondak Loj. In early spring, you'll see the other part of the crop heaped in piles by the roadside. That part is made up of rocks, almost identical in size to the potatoes. They'll be hauled away to spare the plows and cultivators.

Early observers were convinced the Adirondack wilderness could be tamed for farming. Even that sage New York state geologist, Ebenezer Emmons, affirmed in the middle of the last century, "the axe has been laid at the foot of the tree, and ere long where naught now greets the eye, but a dense, and to appearance impassable forest, will be seen the golden grain waving with the gentle breeze..."

The Reverend John Todd, who pioneered a church at Long Lake at about the same time, preached a similar theme: Cut down the trees and let the sun in; then you can plant and harvest the crops. He predicted that the land could "easily support a million people."

The Adirondack climate, however, had proved earlier that the answer wasn't quite that simple.

The writer Joel T. Headley noted in a letter to *The New York Times* in 1844 that "There is a good deal of tolerable land in this region." But, he added wryly, there is "a good deal more that is intolerable." Todd observed the following year that a British soldier had written home during the American Revolution of his duties in the Adirondacks: "They have six months of hard winter and six months of awfully cold weather."

An early history of Essex County reported the summer of 1917 was so cold that farmers had to dig up seed potatoes in order to keep food on their tables. When Redfield stopped overnight at Israel Johnson's sawmill near Elk Lake in 1836 on his way to explore the high peaks, he wrote: "Cold heavy frost and grass frozen stiff — potatoes killed — oats and rye not yet ripe." That was in August.

Adirondack entrepreneurs soon discovered that economy of scale was no answer either.

The grandaddy of all the enterprises — the more than three and a half million acres assembled under the aegis of Alexander Macomb — was never a howling success. Macomb soon became insolvent.

Another John Brown — the one for whom Brown University was named — also carved out 210,000 acres from the Macomb purchase about the turn of the century near what is now Old Forge. After his death, his son-in-law took it over, declaring, "I will settle this tract or settle myself." After going broke, he chose the latter course, and shot himself.

A Frenchman, Pierre Chassanis, bought another 210,000 acres from the Macomb holdings to the west of Brown's Tract. He lured emigrants from the French Revolution to what he promoted as "unusually fertile and well watered" lands. The venture collapsed.

In the 1880s, a state commission evaluating the prospects of Adirondack forests concluded that soil and climate mitigated against successful farming. In the end, said Adirondack historian Donaldson, each failed venture "left another name in the history of these untractable tracts."

In minuscule form, the Hut Boys' garden at Johns Brook Lodge qualifies for the list.

Journal entry: Tuesday, August 7, 1979. I mention to Brent and Stephen that we are headed for Basin via the Phelps trail to Slant Rock and then by the Shorey cutoff trail to the Range trail. For our return, the map indicates it should be shorter with less climbing if we come back by the Range trail over Saddleback. I solicit their advice.

"You're probably right," says Stephen. "And I can guarantee the sheer rock on the top of Saddleback facing Basin is a lot easier going up than down.

"Also," he gestures toward a cartoon on the wall, "once over the Shorey cutoff is enough."

The New Yorker *cartoon shows two men in a canoe confounded on their way upstream by an enormous waterfall. The one in the rear asks, "Know any more short cuts?" Someone has scribbled on the margin, "Dedicated to A. T. Shorey." Ben and I are anxious to check out the trail, a long-time butt of ADK jokes, though the man who cut it was the respected former chairman of the ADK guidebook committee. We move quickly up the moderate grade to Bushnell Falls.*

The falls were named by Keene Valley guides in honor of Dr. Horace Bushnell of Hartford, Connecticut, one of the most popular 19th century residents of that hamlet. Of all those who guided him, however, the one who prized most his association with Bushnell was Old Mountain Phelps.

In his essay, A Character Study, *Charles Dudley Warner asked the old guide if money would be a factor if he had his life to live over again. Said Phelps, "To have had hours such as I have had in these mountains, and with such men as Dr. Bushnell...is worth all the money the world could give."*

Most campers today in the lean-tos at Bushnell Falls are still asleep. They have suspended their food supplies from long poles high off the ground. Stephen told us last night that bears roam the area nightly, foraging from camp to camp.

The beasts also have visited Slant Rock, according to a pencilled note at the empty lean-to: "8/5 — Bear seen to reach 14 ft. at least. Hang all food off of rock. Not afraid of people!!!" Then, a welcome add-on below: "8/6 — No bears tonight."

We reach the junction for the Shorey trail a short distance beyond, and find another scribble on the sign: "Bad trail." The way leads sharply upward and is erratically wet and uneven and heavily wooded; we cannot tell for sure if the peak which thrusts ahead is Basin. My guess is that it is not, because a shoulder slants higher toward the east. But there is no mistaking Big Slide, shining like a beacon through the green five miles to the north.

In less than an hour from the junction, Ben and I top off on the Shorey trail, then begin the steep dip downward. One can see why climbers joked about the trailblazer. "When we hiked with him we were the last group to return because of his notorious short cuts." This "short cut" leaves the Phelps trail at about 3,450 ft., climbs to 4,300 ft. and then descends to join the Range trail at 4,000 ft.

While the stats for the climb to Basin are about the same as for Dix and Hough, the going seems easier. It has to be a combination of cooler weather, low humidity, and no bugs. Plus, a good sleep last night helped along with no long drive this morning.

At the junction with the Range trail, Ben and I get our closest-yet view of Haystack. If my calculations are correct, it cannot involve more climbing than what we will do today. We resolve to tackle it next.

The ascent of Basin by the Range trail — due to better conditions or whatever — is not difficult. The ever-lowering profiles of Haystack, a little more than 100 feet higher than Basin, and Marcy, not much more than 500 feet higher, produce a powerful incentive.

We also confirm my hunch about the bulbous knob we saw coming up the Shorey trail. It is not Basin's summit but a prominence on its northwest shoulder.

I know we are topping off when Ben, just out of sight ahead, shouts: "Elk Lake!" Then, "Skylight!"

Climbers who make it to Basin's summit can still share in the thrill of those who pioneered the ascent. Verplanck Colvin and his guide, Orson Phelps, were likely not the first to make the climb, but were the first to record it while exploring the area between Basin and Marcy in 1875. Of course, they had to bushwhack because the Range trail was not cut through until a quarter century later.

The mountain was named because it overlooks, on the east, as described by Colvin, a "great circular gorge — a mountain walled amphitheatre." The summit view, Robert Marshall wrote almost 50 years later, was such that "no words can describe a person's feeling as he looks over this enormous hollow and gets perhaps the finest view now possible of the type of forest which once covered all of the North Woods region."

It's there for the viewing today.

Journal entry: Tuesday, August 7, 1979. *Lunchtime for Ben and me on Basin is 12 noon, only five hours from Johns Brook Lodge. Pretty good; I had predicted we would reach the summit at 1:30 p.m.*

We welcome an arriving couple accompanied by a boy about 14, all under heavy packs. They stayed at Slant Rock last night and will head over Saddleback and Gothics, and then out.

Shortly after they leave, we are joined by a vigorous young man under even heavier pack, who is hump-hopping in

Summit of Basin *offers a front-row seat for viewing the king of them all, Marcy, two miles to the west. Mt. Skylight rises on the left, a mile beyond.*

reverse. He slept over at the col between the Wolfjaws and has already surmounted *Upper Wolfjaw, Armstrong, Gothics, Saddleback* and, of course, *Basin.* His target for camping overnight is Panther Gorge, between *Marcy* and *Haystack.* He may go by way of Haystack,"if I feel like it," he says.

That kind of hedge-hopping is intimidating to me. But on checking the topographic map, I find that if we were to throw in the Shorey short cut, Ben and I have climbed 300 feet more than he has. And we still have almost 400 feet more to climb on our way out, while he can scoot more or less straight down to the Gorge.

"It's lovely out here," he says as he relates other

Mt. Haystack *looms a mile and a half southwest of Basin. Little Haystack is on its shoulder, right; if on its own, latter would be among 10 highest peaks.*

exploits. Ben is elated to find we have climbed one peak he has not: Sawteeth. Because of that, I tell him I gather he's not an Aspiring Forty Sixer. "No," he replies, "I just like to be out here anywhere. I spent a summer here and got spoiled."

During an hour on the breezy summit, Ben and I agree that this hike has been one of our best. We also note that Ben did not see Elk Lake; it is blotted out by Pinnacle Ridge. What he saw was Upper Ausable Lake.

As we make the easy half-hour descent to the col before Saddleback, clouds tinged with gray race overhead. At this point, even rain could not spoil our picnic. But if the weather worsens, it would be great to have an escape route from the col between Basin and Saddleback. The Forty Sixers' Jim Goodwin notes that Chicken Coop Brook, which leads north from the col to the Phelps trail near Bushnell Falls, offers a "pleasant" way out. But hikers who try this route can expect to find rough country. I decide not to chance it.

Saddleback thrusts a mile away; trail from Basin climbs the sheer cliffs at left, steepest in the high peaks. Trail leads over Gothics, right, and lower end of the Great Range, to left.

The sheer, near-vertical rock face looming up toward Saddleback for more than 100 feet poses a difficult challenge: no ladders, no tree roots or branches, and only vague, widely-dispersed handholds. Ben is nervous, and so am I; we climb in close combination.

Five men who have just scaled the wall shout encouragement from above. To be frank, I'm more encouraged by the fact we do not have to lug up the heavy packs they carry.

"The weight of the packs is bad enough," one relates as we pull up to them. "But the wind acts on them like a sail pulling you outward. I was about to take mine off and rope it up." He sighs with relief: "But I made it."

They have come from Marcy by way of Haystack and Basin, and plan to go out tomorrow via the rest of the Great Range. Their biggest concern is that they are out of water. This means that one of them will have to descend at one of the cols to fill their canteens at the nearest stream, and then return. Volunteering to be waterboy in these hills is tough duty.

Johns Brook Lodge is a welcome sight after descending two hours from Saddleback's summit. At the ranger station, it appears we may finally meet Spencer Cram. My guess is that he is the one with the World War I-type hat among a group of five people on the porch.

I wave, but there is no response.

As we rest at trailside just before reaching Deer Brook lean-to, the same group passes us: a young couple holding hands, two other men including the pseudo ranger

On Saddleback, *stiff breeze from bowl-shaped valley southeast of Basin Mtn. affects hikers like a wind tunnel. Marcy's huge dome, right center background, is pervasive in this highest of high peak areas.*

and, bringing up the rear, a barrel-chested, middle-aged man with a glorious handlebar moustache. He wears outrageous, checked green pants tucked into pack boots, carries an army canteen on his belt, and sports a T-shirt emblazened with "Philadelphia Orchestra."

The younger crew again does not answer my greeting. But the musician does, in a booming, well-modulated "Hello!" Summering in Saratoga, no doubt. I would lay odds he plays a wind instrument.

The peddler has vacated the lean-to nearest the Garden. In his place is a covey of collegiates, smiling happy thoughts of peaks to be conquered. Or something.

The checkout register confirms they will have plenty of company tomorrow. Nineteen more signed in after Ben and I did last night, and today's listing covers two full pages.

Friends greet the Saratoga ensemble at the Garden parking lot, and they all pile into two cars. The pseudo ranger, behind the wheel of one, promptly backs into a Volkswagen parked in the middle of the lot. One of his passengers, much concerned, steps out to investigate damage, not to the VW but to their rear bumper.

As Ben and I walk by the battered bug, I see that they may have a point. It is impossible to discern new dents from the old.

Our car is safe and secure, with no break-in. Or dents. We no more slam the door than rain spits on the windshield, and then lets loose in earnest. It is as if someone is telling us what we already know: we have some control on when we go and where we stay, but not when it comes to weather.

Haystack from the Great Range trail, at col west of Basin Mtn.

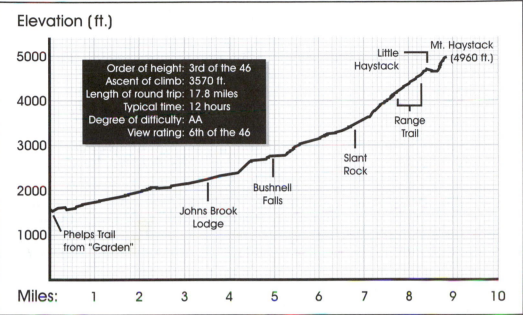

Elevation (ft.)

Order of height: 3rd of the 46
Ascent of climb: 3570 ft.
Length of round trip: 17.8 miles
Typical time: 12 hours
Degree of difficulty: AA
View rating: 6th of the 46

Mt. Haystack (4960 ft.)
Little Haystack
Range Trail
Slant Rock
Bushnell Falls
Johns Brook Lodge
Phelps Trail from "Garden"

Miles: 1 2 3 4 5 6 7 8 9 10

For contour trails, see U.S. Geological Survey map, pgs. 120-121.

32.
HAYSTACK

Journal entry: Sunday, October 3, 1971. "Do you want to go hiking with us tomorrow?" son Jim asked his three-year-old brother last night.

"No," said Ben solemnly. "There are too many Indians." With that, he toddled off to the family room for more TV.

Jim and I expect to confront no more than our old hiking adversary, time, on our jaunt to Haystack today. From the Garden, it will take us almost nine miles southwest to the farthest reaches of the Great Range.

As the clouds gather before we reach Keene Valley, two large V's of Canada geese wobble south. Their time mechanism is sharper than ours: while the air is cool, it has none of the crispness and bite that is overdue.

Johns Brook Lodge is closed and deserted. Jim decides to travel with only a snack and canteen, so he leaves his backpack on the porch. A mile and a half up the Phelps trail, the lean-to at Bushnell Falls perches securely on a high knoll above the brook in front of a glowing backdrop of fall foliage. The lean-to is deserted as were the others along Johns Brook.

A sharp dip in the trail brings us to the falls. The meager flow of the brook encourages hikers to rock-hop to the other side to continue the trail. While the route from the lodge has been gradual, it now rises more steeply for a mile or so through a magnificent stand of evergreens, then moderates and becomes wet and muddy.

We greet a weary young couple, both toting monstrous packs. They tell us we have a bit more than a mile to the base of Haystack. Then, they say, "the trail goes straight up."

The map indicates we are heading in general between Haystack and Marcy. The peak we spot through the trees ahead, however, does not resemble either. We conclude it must be Little Haystack or Little Marcy, with the big ones hidden beyond. To me, this is disheartening.

The dilemma is resolved at Slant Rock lean-to. As we rest in the muted solitude of fall, the soft babble of Johns Brooks seems to affirm my hiking philosophy: what's the hurry? There's always another day. Jim is never obstreperous about putting a hike on hold, so we lunch and loaf.

It's obvious that Slant Rock, looming before the lean-to opening, is a popular spot for hikers. Its plank shelves are loaded with left-overs, and busy-beaver campers have cleared the surrounding area of fallen

Slant Rock *camping area is a long-time favorite of climbers on the way to Marcy and nearby high peaks. The glacier-deposited boulder lies between the lean-to and Johns Brook.*

branches; small trees have been felled for firewood. An indiscriminate few have settled for lumber in the outhouse — its top half and door are missing.

Jim devours his snack, then eyes my remaining lunch. I remind him that he should watch his intake to keep in shape for his judo lessons, not to mention mountain climbing. My own concern, I tell him, is not weight but keeping up with him on our hikes.

"I wish I had your problem," he snorts with a glance at my skinny frame. "I'd eat a lot."

Just before returning to Johns Brook Lodge, we glimpse a huge bird gliding through the shadows by the brook. My guess is it's a great horned owl, primed for a nightly foray.

As we mount the porch, we notice a swarthy, bushy-haired man admiring a gleaming Buck hunting knife which he holds in his hand; it's like the one Jim left in his pack. As Jim rifles through his opened pack, the man sheaths the knife and says, "You shouldn't leave a valuable knife like this in your pack. There are people around who will steal it in a minute."

I retrieve it for Jim and the man, grinning nervously, shuffles off the porch with two embarrassed companions. "Better be careful," he finishes. "You can't trust anyone."

This is distressing. You'd think The New York Times had gotten its wish when it ran an editorial more than 100 years ago. It proposed running a railroad from the city into the Adirondacks. It never came about, fortunately, but this incident suggests we may be edging close to the Times' objective: to make the area a "Central Park for the World."

At the grassy opening near the ranger station, we identify the large bird we saw earlier: a Canada goose, standing stiffly, eyeing us imperiously.

The ranger, Spencer Cram, joins us to explain: "Several flights were confused last night trying to find their way out of the valley. I hardly got any sleep because of the honking. This one injured itself in a tree, but it'll be on its way soon. It happens often here."

The trail to the Garden is deserted. We meet only one party: three matrons who plod slowly toward the lodge in the deepening dusk. They nod and give Jim an especially warm greeting.

A few yards beyond, Jim winks and nudges me: "It sort of arouses the tiger in you, doesn't it, Dad?" He's an impertinent cub, but I like his spirit. I just hope he saves a little for our future hikes before he takes out after girls in earnest.

Marcy has all the attributes of the novice hiker's dream: pyramidal shape, relatively easy access, and premier height. Haystack, while no great beauty, is loaded with character. It reminds one of a gnarled, weatherbeaten old timer who's wary about letting you get too friendly too fast.

Well, not entirely. From Basin, Haystack appears to have a thin ridge leading from little to big Haystack that is but a gentle stroll. The map also indicates that while the total climb to Haystack is slightly longer than Basin and Saddleback combined, it entails 80 less feet of climbing.

But there is a touch of the hermit in Haystack. Whereas from Basin one can know that Marcy's summit will almost always be alive with hikers, it is rare to spot more than one or two on Haystack. For explorers, these are compelling reasons to head for the latter. Also, Haystack's view is rated number one by the first three Forty Sixers, the Marshall brothers and their guide, Herb Clark.

Journal entry: Sunday, August 26, 1979. Son Ben, who is now 11 years old, has read all about Haystack's attributes. But he also hopes for good weather that will make this the "perfect hike." My regret is that son Jim can't join us. He was graduated from the University of Miami in May and is about to begin a program leading to a Master's degree.

Ben and I had planned to tackle Haystack yesterday, but rain was forecast. At the Garden, a couple with teen-age son confirms that our decision was correct. They were no more than a half mile out from Adirondak Loj when the skies opened up. Today, they will try again here to fulfill their high intentions. But they are not home free yet; the same storm swept through yesterday. One of the Johns Brook tributaries named Dry Brook is wet. And a fallen tree at the first lean-to has pulled telephone lines to the ground.

Ben and I had intended to say hello to our new lodgekeeper friends whom we met three weeks ago at Johns Brook Lodge on our way to Basin. However, only Brent is there, oblivious to us. He and another lodgekeeper, a young girl, chatter away with a ranger. They are on a different channel, so we do not try to tune in.

The spongy trail to Bushnell Falls is not encouraging; it's lined with tree roots shaped like mangroves from the incessant pounding of hiking boots. The racing clouds scatter only thin slices of sunshine around us.

At the first lean-to, an owner holding snapping dogs in check prompts Ben and me to descend and cross Johns Brook. We will do no boulder-hopping today, however. The river, roaring from the rains, is impassable. We follow an alternate trail a couple of hundred yards upstream to a rickety, iron-grated suspension bridge, a high water route; a single-wire handhold sways dizzily at the touch.

The trail to Slant Rock is not hard. But Ben acts as if it were the most important challenge in the world which must be overcome, right now. Each time I catch up with him to rest, he says not a word but races on like one possessed. And I know why: his thoughts are on the promise of Haystack.

Slant Rock is deserted. Even the bears have gone, if you can rely on the absence of notes from the lean-to walls. The skies now reveal a cheery note: the mottled clouds expose wider patches of blue.

At the trail junction a few hundred yards beyond, we note a prominence on the right called Point Balk. It's aptly named, because the trail gives pause to climbers: it swings around the prominence to climb sharply up a ravine to the mountainous lip perched above Panther Gorge, connecting Haystack and Marcy. It's a letdown to learn that the point was named not for trepidation but for Dr. Robert Balk, a geologist who studied the area.

The trail, which still traces the course of Johns Brook, looks steeper than it in fact is. While it is riddled with corduroy log patches over swampy stretches, the climbing is moderate.

Ben, who has just dunked his foot to the ankle on a wobbly log floater, disagrees. We go no more than 50 feet beyond when he mistakes black guck for firm footing and again sees his foot disappear.

No problem. Once his outrage passes, he can wear the caked mud on his pants as a hiker's badge of honor. "Ice cream pants," Jim used to call an old tan pair of mine, blanched by years of washing. The trousers had a flair for displaying mud.

The steep, three-quarter mile climb to the junction seems interminable. On arriving, we discover that instead of the expected spectacular view of Panther Gorge, we face a flat expanse of trees. It doesn't really matter: climbers from Elk Lake, Johns Brook, Adirondak Loj and the Great Range all converge on this short, dull trail segment, scooting through to enjoy the great sights just ahead.

The half-mile scramble toward Little Haystack is also steep, but we are heartened by emerging visual benchmarks: first, Big Slide to the north, then the gradual uncovering of the upper contours of Little Marcy and, finally, the sharp tip of Marcy itself. What looks like sticks on its summit are not trees, but are moving: busy climbers, vibrating like slivers of metal from the magnetism of Marcy.

Mt. Haystack and its not-so "Little" companion, left, come into view after turning south from the Range trail. The last haul calls for 350 feet of stiff climbing to the summit from the col between the two.

Mesmerized by Marcy. Haystack dominates every peak in sight except Number One, rising 384 feet higher. Marcy blocks out the second highest, Algonquin, four miles away.

Scrub trees, receding toward a bald rock face, suggest we are nearing Little Haystack. The map indicates we will have only a brief, almost level walk from a bulbous knob preceding the Little summit.

Ben, as usual, is first to reach the knob and shouts his excitement. When I drag up, my hopes sag on seeing the deep col into which we must first descend.

But that's my concern, not Ben's. He points beyond to the long-time dream he now sees up close: the two bare bulbs of Haystack — the first like half a fractured egg shell, and the main summit beyond, staggering upward in a semblance of sharpness.

"It looks different than I expected," says Ben. Certainly it's a far cry from what we saw on Basin. From there, the jaunt to the top of Haystack looked like a breeze. Yet from here, cols lie like moats on both sides of Little Haystack.

Cairns to guide climbers over the open rock have been moved from the logical route to keep climbers from stepping on fragile alpine vegetation. The climb itself, while steep, is manageable. The only problem is the journey Ben and I have already made from the Garden. As we rest, I calculate that in six hours we have hiked almost nine miles and climbed close to 3,600 feet. That's farther and higher than a trip up Marcy.

A four-foot, rounded boulder near the minor summit catches my eye. It's studded with what appear to be ancient fossils and marine shells. Geologists say such fragments in the high peaks were destroyed long ago by erosion. This suggests otherwise.

"Little Haystack is nice," says Ben. "But let's go on to the big one."

Little? If it were rated among the 46 high peaks, it would outrank all but nine.

As on Dix, Ben hones in on the bolted summit and waves from there as I puff up. But this mountain is no crowded Dix. As of now, the mountain is ours; we are alone. We are also exhausted, so we break out lunch. As if by invitation, a burst of bugs joins in to lunch on us.

The clouds are losing their battle with the sun; ever-widening windows of blue let golden splotches race across the peaks. This may not meet Ben's specs for a perfect day, but it has to be a close second.

While there are no people on Haystack, we are not without friends. We are plopped in the center of a glorious cluster of 27 of the 46 highest peaks. It's easy for Ben and me to spot all of the 14 we have climbed except one. The jumbled mass of the Great Range, rippling toward us from the northeast, obscures Lower Wolfjaw.

Northeast from Haystack, the Great Range trail surmounts Basin, left, and Saddleback, center. Then from Gothics, right, it follows the descending peaks to the northeast toward Keene Valley.

This also is our nearest approach to others we have yet to climb. Elusive Allen, now asserting itself. Redfield. Bashful Gray, huddled behind Marcy's western flank. And there's no mistaking that monstrous hump a bit south of due west. "Let's do Skylight next," suggests Ben.

Binoculars reveal twitching sticks on that fourth highest peak, as well as on Basin and Saddleback; I count at least 20 hikers on Marcy.

High peak explorers are ambivalent about Haystack. Members of the Forty Sixers Club almost never rush in to climb it first. Nor do they savor its pleasures for the last climb; that's usually reserved for Whiteface, which is easy to get to, or Allen, which is hard to do because it's out in the middle of nowhere.

It seems to have been ever thus with Haystack. As high peaks biographer Russ Carson noted, the two pioneering Adirondack explorers, Emmons and Redfield, ignored Haystack as well as Skylight and "made no mention, directly or indirectly, of either peak." The soaring prose of nineteenth century writers such as Joel Tyler Headley and Benson John Lossing sang the praises of lesser peaks but took no note of the big pair. Even Verplanck Colvin, ever voluble about his summit surveys, dubbed Haystack "the Matterhorn of the Adirondacks" but said nothing of its views.

A major reason for Haystack's obtuse image is remoteness; it's difficult to climb from any direction. A few years back, Don Greene outlined the challenge of the trail from Elk Lake, in *Adirondack Life*: "We have only to put one foot in front of the other some sixty thousand times, and ascend the equivalent of a dozen Washington monuments while crossing two ridges and a swamp, to reach the Garden, in Keene Valley."

The first party to climb the peak in 1849 affirmed what hikers know today: the climb is more rugged than Marcy. One of those three early climbers was Old Mountain Phelps, who gave Haystack its name. Anyone who has ever been on a farm will recognize that this is some load of hay.

Phelps named Haystack for its shape, not its texture. The huge, lumpy summit is mostly bare rock. Even so, more than six acres of its 18 and a half acres of open alpine summit are vegetated.

The Marshall brothers recognized Haystack for more than its views. Wrote Robert, "It is the sense of being in the center of a great wilderness which gives the greatest charm." From Haystack, he said, "You can look over thousands and thousands of acres, unblemished by the works of man, perfect as made by nature."

His comments reinforce the profile of a rugged but wary individual who's lived most of his life alone, enduring the rigors of the winds and the seasons. And peaks such as Haystack have had a very long life

Little Haystack *looks like an enormous cracked egg perched on the north shoulder of Mt. Haystack. Descent calls for caution to avoid trampling fragile alpine plants.*

indeed, according to Edwin H. Ketchledge, distinguished forester and retired professor of botany. As he observed in 1993, "The concept of time disappears when thoughtful people on a high summit free their minds momentarily from the dramatic impact of the summit scenery and realize that in truth the surrounding alpine meadow is a continuation of ancient times into this very day."

Journal entry: Sunday, August 26, 1979. Ben has long talked of enjoying an hour and a half on this summit. I remind him that the sun will set at 7:30 p.m. and it is now 2:40 p.m. We have nearly nine miles to hike to our car, so we limit our stay to 40 minutes.

"Look, Dad," says Ben. "Here's a lady bug." He carefully lets it crawl on his finger, then deposits it out of the stiff wind behind a rock.

Lucky lady, lucky for us; the weather keeps improving.

We gain one more impetus for leaving the summit: people. A man and his son, decked out as if detoured from the Tyrolean Alps, pose and snap their way up Little Haystack. Atop the knoll we must climb beyond that peak, we see a half dozen other hikers, some heading our way.

After we move out on the Range trail for a short distance, Ben cries out, "Oh, no!" I look up and in an instant know what he means. In

our haste, we have descended by mistake on the Range trail toward Basin instead of Slant Rock. "We're headed for the Shorey cut-off," says Ben, in horror. We scamper back up, make the right turn at the junction, and head home.

Despite the slippery wet gravel and mini-swamps, we make good time by moving with care. The landmarks which grudgingly gave way on our ascent now gracefully rise again. I calculate that from the summit to the Marcy trail junction, we have halved the time of our ascent.

Slant Rock is now a bustling community of 10 young men and women, cooking, eating, washing dishes and, per the bathing suit of one, back from a dip. All I can think of as I fill my canteen is, True Grit: the water is frigid.

Precipitous slopes *of Panther Gorge are exaggerated by three surrounding peaks: Skylight, ahead, Haystack at left, and Marcy, right.*

Down the trail we meet two, big-boned girls lugging bulging packs. They pose the standard query: how far, and how many?

You're about a quarter of a mile away from Slant Rock, I tell them. Adds Ben: "There are only 10 people in the lean-to."

"Ten?" one responds querulously. She is not a happy camper.

For some time, Ben has rhapsodized about the snacks he will buy at Johns Brook Lodge. But a "Closed" sign on the door tells us there will be no candy and lemonade tonight. For customers, anyway.

On the porch, the young girl caretaker sets a rude table with cloth, goblets and utensils. Like a master chef, Brent comes forth with a battered tin of...pizza. As they dig into it, Stephen ambles out with a ranger: Spencer Cram.

Their dining is as gracious as at any club in the city, but with a difference. Here, there is no need for canapes, cocktails and witty conversation. The ingredients at hand blend well: good friends, a camaraderie forged from a common interest, and a relaxed rapport with nature.

Ben asks me to break the rules and see if he can buy candy. But their warm greetings and well-wishes suggest otherwise. I give him the remains of my rations, and we move on to rest on the bench at the ranger's cabin.

At Deer Brook, a camper separates from his lean-to companions to greet us in the dusk. He asks where we climbed today; he surmounted Haystack yesterday. "It was blah," he says. "No view at all."

In the dim light at Bear Brook, both Ben and I stumble face-on against the downed phone lines. My retort startles two occupants of the lean-to. One gives us a wary hello; the other, a silent rebuff.

I suggest that we pull out our flashlights, but Ben says no. "It'll be good practice if we have to do it for real." Where there is space between trees, we have little trouble with our footing. But where overhead branches converge, they curtain the twilight and the dark, damp trail disappears. We are in a losing race with nightfall.

Ben jerks back to me and points at an obscure, upraised object ahead. "It looks like a giant beaver!" he says.

To me, it looks like a huge woodchuck, or ground hog, pausing from a snack of tender plants to rear up, stare and sniff. "Whistle hogs," they used to call them in Iowa. At your whistle, they'd stand up and offer a ready target.

But this object is immobile. It is a misshapen stump which broods benignly as we pass. At the Garden, we need a flashlight to sign out because total darkness is minutes away.

What do you think, I ask Ben: Was Haystack easier than Basin and Saddleback? And are you tired? "Harder," Ben replies softly. "And yes, I'm tired."

I muse out loud: Maybe we're trying too much. Maybe we ought to cut down.

"Oh, no," says Ben. "This was the best of all." He flops in the back seat of the car and is gone with the droop of an eyelid.

East Dix, left, and South Dix, center with softly-rounded summit, from Giant Mtn. Macomb Mtn. is at right.

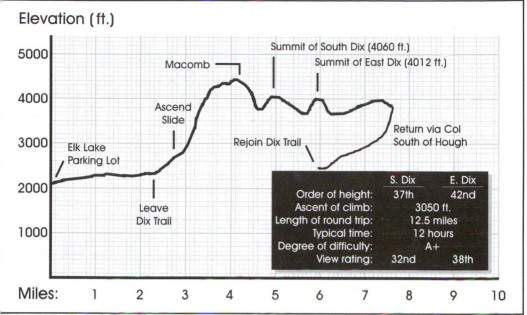

Elevation (ft.)

Elk Lake Parking Lot

Leave Dix Trail

Ascend Slide

Macomb

Summit of South Dix (4060 ft.)

Summit of East Dix (4012 ft.)

Rejoin Dix Trail

Return via Col South of Hough

	S. Dix	E. Dix
Order of height:	37th	42nd
Ascent of climb:	3050 ft.	
Length of round trip:	12.5 miles	
Typical time:	12 hours	
Degree of difficulty:	A+	
View rating:	32nd	38th

Miles: 1 2 3 4 5 6 7 8 9 10

or contour trails, see U.S. Geological Survey map, pgs. 214-215.

33, 34.
SOUTH DIX, EAST DIX

Climbers who rhapsodize about Haystack or Marcy or Colden almost never do so when asked about the trailless little Dixes. One reason is that climbers rarely see them. In fact, climbers are less likely to see South Dix and East Dix from Adirondack summits than any of the other high peaks.

The lonesome twosome comes into sharpest focus, as you might expect, from their closest neighbor, Macomb. They're also in view from the other high peaks in the Dix Range: from Dix, particularly on the long slope leading to the southeast toward Hough; and from Hough itself, if you can find an open view to the east on its tangled summit.

Two other mountains, Giant and Rocky Peak Ridge, offer decent views of South Dix and East Dix. But even the highest of the high peaks gives up on East Dix: from Marcy, South Dix and Couchsachraga are the only two of the 46 not visible.

Close up, the little Dixes don't look like much. South Dix's summit is a flat ridge, and East Dix appears to sport no more than a miniature pyramid on top.

Robert Marshall, the pioneering Adirondack Forty Sixer, did nothing to bolster their images when he wrote in 1922 after making one of the first climbs of South Dix the previous year: "This is one of the most desolate views I know of — nothing but burned wasted land on all sides. A few fine mountains in the distance could not seem beautiful when seen over the dreary foreground."

As a result of such bad press, many climbers think of the two little Dixes as being in a kind of Never-Never Land, a Valley of the Lost. Yet Adirondack explorers do not look on the little Dixes with trepidation. There's always the chance, they say, that the forlorn may turn out to be fun.

There are a couple of unconventional ways to seek out the little Dixes from Exit 30 on the Northway. One is to head northwest from Route 9 via West Mill Brook, just above North Hudson, or via Lindsay Brook, a couple of miles farther north. Another way is to hopscotch to the southwest from Rt. 73, first going up the North Fork of the Boquet River and then switching to the South Fork.

The conventional approach to the Little Dixes is to climb Macomb from Elk Lake, then head east over a ridge line which leads up and over the reclusive twins. This route is the preferred path for climbers for an obvious reason: if you lose the herd path, you can regain it by climbing to the top of the ridge. So they say.

But even this conventional, trailless trek to the little Dixes is by no means a sinecure. A glance at the degree of difficulty noted on the mountain profile at the chapter heading will tell you why.

__Journal entry: Saturday, September 1, 1979.__ Two things make me skittish about this hike.

First, it's long and difficult; when son Jim and I set our sights on the two little Dixes nine years ago after first climbing Macomb, we ran out of daylight.

And even if Ben and I do climb them today, the return poses a dilemma. There are two options: one is to go back over Macomb, adding some 650 feet to the total climb; the other is to try and find the right herd

Sun's rays *reveal multiple spiderwebs on early stage of trail to Dix. Bushwhack to Macomb begins at Slide Brook, 2.3 miles from trailhead.*

path down the escape route to the west of South Dix, as our group did two months ago when coming off Hough.

It seems to me we have one crucial factor in our favor: this is Labor Day weekend. There should be plenty of hikers to keep us from getting lonely, or lost. Or both.

Beyond Warrensburg, we plunge into the deep fog that's common there on the Northway this time of year; it obliterates the cheery "Hello" sign on a knoll to the south of Chestertown. But Ben notes a pleasant substitute: a spotted fawn nibbling at the roadside, its nervous mother peering at us from bordering trees.

At the trailhead, we are surprised to find that only three other groups have signed in this morning. And just one is headed for our first target, Macomb.

This time, I decide we will head toward Macomb via Slide Brook instead of the herd path near the lean-to just beyond, which caused Jim and me so much trouble. The brook bed is dry as we leave the Dix trail, but it soon brings us to flowing branches that crisscross a network of herd paths. At the first major fork, a sizeable cairn marks the route suggested in the current ADK guidebook.

As Ben and I approach a minor slide, an expanse of loose, crumbly debris, we hear what appear to be shrill cries for help. We race ahead to discover it is only the exuberance of three children clambering up the treacherous slide with their parents. We wave and continue up the stream bed until it joins the main slide, sweeping toward the summit. At the base, we circle a waterfall and begin the long haul up.

The climb, which alternates over flat, exposed bedrock and residue from the slide, is steep and slippery. Almost at once, Ben and I find ourselves boxed in a gully whose slopes of rubble appear to be too dangerous to surmount.

We retrace our steps to try the edges of the slide, where we are passed by the family of climbers. They greet us, and warn whenever they dislodge modest boulders from above.

Ben soon clambers ahead to mingle with the boys. One is in the seventh grade, a year ahead of Ben; the other two are younger. By the time I reach the top of the slide, Ben is having an animated conversation with the younger two and disappears with them along a path at the base of a rock ledge to the left. The father, who points the way for them, follows.

The older boy climbs as if he were returning to school after summer vacation. His mother stands solicitously at the top of the slide, so I join her to wait for the laggard. It's a good feeling to wait for someone else; climbers usually have to wait for me.

Steep slide calls for both hands and feet to maintain balance. The route gains 1,800 feet in a mile. Surface of Elk Lake shimmers below.

The three of us follow the trail, which twists through stunted conifers to the top of the ridge, then loops gently to the summit. When we arrive, Ben and the two younger boys are enjoying the shade of the small tree which holds the trailless register. It is 12:10 p.m.

Macomb's summit is the perfect place to admire Elk Lake. The faultless day makes the facets of the lake sparkle in its high peak setting. Ben and I laze on the lower summit ledge while the family sprawls on a huge boulder above us, near the cannister.

Henry James captured my unspoken feeling, which I'm sure is shared by the others: "Summer afternoon...To me, those have always been the most beautiful words in the English language."

Our new friends carry a couple of light packs and canteens. These contain only a sparse lunch, so I suggest that Ben share his large bag of M&Ms. The boys politely take a few.

On signing the register, I find that our new-found friends are Pete and Dorothy Seagle of Delmar, New York, a suburb of Albany. The boys are James, Tommy and Charlie.

In spite of their scanty gear, this is no first-time outing for them. Mr. Seagle tells me he has completed 42 of the 46 high peaks, lacking only Allen, Redfield, Whiteface and Esther. He will save Esther for his last conquest.

The boys also have climbed varying high peaks but, Ben tells me with great satisfaction, none as many as he. Mrs. Seagle volunteers no statistics, but by the way she scampered up the slide, she appears to have energy and good humor aplenty.

The Seagles also intend to explore the two trailless Dixes; the father preps by giving his sons a cram course in map and compass. Since they face the challenge of a return route, too, I suggest we join forces. They agree.

An ADK trail veteran warned in our local paper: "Time marches on for the hiker atop East Dix, who should start the return trip back to civilization by 2 p.m. in a race to beat the setting sun."

Let's see, it is now almost one o'clock and, according to the vet, it will be 3 p.m. before we reach East Dix. That could pose a problem. But the weather is supposed to stay calm and pure, so we should face none of the fall haze and changeable conditions that Jim and I did nine years ago.

An open ledge below the northeastern crest of Macomb offers a preview of the two little Dixes. The skinny pyramid of East Dix juts up by itself two miles away, forlorn and lonely. Hans Steiniger of Buffalo, New York, who was one of the first to climb it in 1917, suggested to *Adirondack Peeks* an apt name for it: "Dragon Tooth." The long, scrubby ridge which shapes its neighbor, South Dix, shows no more than a couple of knobs to indicate a summit.

As a high peak, South Dix seems inconsequential. Yet the mountain is actually higher than such better-known peaks as Colvin and Porter.

The well-worn herd path to the col between Macomb and South Dix is three quarters of a mile long, but the downward slope is gentle. At the col, a side path of sorts leads to the left, or north.

A short distance beyond the col, climbers confront a huge rock face. It is not quite as steep as the bald face on the southwest slope of Saddleback, but it slows the going, with the way marked by cairns.

Climbers may not bring back many raves about the little Dixes, but they are unanimous in praising the outlooks along this segment of the path. One of them, Forty Sixer Tim Tefft, reported, "The boulder slope along the flank of that little peak seems as wild and wonderful a spot as any place I've ever been."

Journal entry: Saturday, September 1, 1979. *Mrs. Seagle suggested when we reached the col that we mark the escape route with a stick poked into the ground. To me, it seemed superfluous, but we did it anyway.*

As we climb, she tells me she is originally from California and has climbed Mt. Whitney. At 14,494 ft., it is of course the highest mountain in the contiguous United States. She reports that she and her husband climbed Dix, crossed over to trailless Hough and returned to Dix. To me, that rigorous trek enhances their climbing stature.

The thought stimulates me to surge ahead to the top of South Dix to keep up with the three boys. Mr. Seagle is close behind me, while his wife again waits for James. I'm convinced now that the boy at the very least has an aversion to mountaineering school.

On South Dix, at first we think 3,300-ft. Wyman Mtn. on the east is our next target. But the tip of another mountain which descends gradually to the northeast over the shoulder of South Dix proves us wrong: the tip is East Dix.

Behind us, to the southwest, Macomb now looms more sharply upward than our casual descent suggested. It adds a strong argument against descending by the Macomb slide, which is more treacherous going down than up.

The boys head off like young colts, with Ben in the lead. Since we are still in unknown territory and have met no one, I push hard to keep them in sight. Two pair of ruffed grouse, one on either side of the trail, take off in noisy flight, instilling enough caution in the boys for Mr. Seagle and me to catch up.

He stoops to pick a bunch of what appears to be clover, and chews it with a smile. "Wood sorrel," he says. "Helps slake your thirst." Then he adds, "We only have two canteens and they're empty."

As he reaches for another handful, he tosses off an appropriate quote from Rudyard Kipling, but I miss it. Since I'm now a bit weary but still unbowed, I can recall only one of Kipling's Departmental Ditties:

> "The blush that flies at seventeen
> is fixed at forty-nine."

Growing up in the circumscribed, rolling prairies of Iowa, I never saw a real mountain before age 17. Yet there must have been some hidden urge in me to search for more lofty goals, and I found them in the Adirondacks. All 46 of them.

To satisfy Kipling, I could bump that total to 49 with ease. Add McNaughton Mtn., which is 4,000 ft.; Green Mtn., a companion to Giant which is higher than three of the 46; and either Moose or Snowy mountains, both of which outrank Nye and Couchsachraga.

The urge to explore them all is, as Kipling said, "As immutable as the hills."

The Seagles stop to fill their canteens at a dark, shallow pool near a house-sized boulder in the col between the two little Dixes. I move beyond a couple of hundred yards to corral Ben and Tommy who are racing to surmount East Dix on their own. Ben frowns but the youngest Seagle, a bright-eyed towhead, relaxes with a big smile.

Such good nature!

The herd path up East Dix is relatively easy, but side branches bear witness to previous herds which have been restless or lost. I help the boys sort out the right path, and then hear Ben shout from a rocky bulb that appears to be the summit: "Where is it?"

He means the trailless cannister, of course. A low thicket on a rise to the west looks just as high, so Ben scurries over to search further. Just then, Mr. Seagle arrives and discovers the cannister, bolted to the hidden side of the bulb. We record our deeds, then savor the views to the east.

Spotted Mountain, true to its name, squats a mile to the northeast like a fun-loving pup, held in check by the leash of the Northway. Beyond it stretches the north-south corridor, including Lake George and Lake Champlain, which pioneers and Indians used for their warring encounters between central New York and Canada.

James Fenimore Cooper related in *The Last of the Mohicans* how the Mohican warrior Chingachgook and his son Uncas, with the scout Hawkeye, pursued the Huron warriors who had captured the daughters of the defeated British commander of Fort William Henry at the head of Lake George.

"The party had landed on the border of a region," he wrote, "that is, even to this day [1825], less known to the inhabitants of the States than the deserts of Arabia or the steppes of Tartary." In Cooper's day, he wrote that the area was surrounded by rich and thriving settlements, "though none but the hunter or the savage is ever known, even now, to penetrate its wild recesses."

The little Dixes have embellished that reputation. The first two people to climb South Dix in 1913 did so by mistake. They set out to climb Dix and became confused along the way. And so it goes. Stan Lucas of Malta, New York, reported recently in *Adirondack Peeks* that in searching for East Dix, which was to be his last of the 46, he stumbled on Hough by mistake, then South Dix before finally reaching his objective.

The summits of both peaks, like those on Cascade and Porter as well as Giant and Rocky Peak Ridge, have been laid bare by forest fires. This has improved the views, but there wasn't much to be seen anyway. The other peaks in the Dix Range to the west tower over the lesser ones. They also block the view of the high peaks farther west. Old Mountain Phelps noted the predicament in Bill Healy's *The High Peaks of Essex*: "It's more like the man in the city that could not see the city because the houses were in the way."

From East Dix, climbers with binoculars can study Marcy, with Haystack in front of it, by focusing in the notch formed between Hough and Dix.

Journal entry: Saturday, September 1, 1979. A subtle softening in the hues of the mountains tells us we should head back. The English art critic John Ruskin described the late afternoon color change in Modern Painters as, "The grave tenderness of

From whence we came. *Herd path traces down from Macomb, left center rear, then over South Dix, right, to this site on East Dix.*

the far-away hill-purples."

But I think pioneering conservationist Aldo Leopold came closer to the essence of it when he wrote in A Sand County Almanac: *"Our ability to perceive quality in nature begins, as in art, with the pretty. It expands through successive stages of the beautiful to values as yet uncaptured by language."*

Before going, we all heed Ben's suggestion: the summit thickets are loaded with blueberries and, while tiny, they are delicious. Word from a previous climber in the summit cannister noted the outcome: *"Too many blueberries to make better time."*

I wander back to the summit a final time to linger with the loneliness of the moment, and find a kindred spirit in the Seagles' eldest son James. He is placidly picking blueberries in his own private patch. I think I understand. In a few days he will be entering Junior High School where a broader world will start churning his sensibilities along with those of his classmates. East Dix proffers a beguiling calm before the action begins.

It is now 3:30 p.m., well after the deadline the trail veteran warned me about, so we head back. Mr. Seagle guesses we will reach Elk Lake at 7 p.m.; I think we need to tack on another hour.

This time, all of us fill our canteens at the murky pool in the col. The Seagles add iodine to purify their water. Ben is repelled by the color, so he and I stick to water purification tablets.

It's a struggle to keep Ben and Charlie in sight because of the tricky, multiple herd paths on the slopes of South Dix. They have moved far *ahead and, from somewhere behind me, Mrs. Seagle's calls to them show her concern. I round up the boys so we can all regroup at the top. From here on out, Mr. Seagle and I agree, we will keep a tight rein on the herd.*

We exchange addresses while relaxing on South Dix's summit. Mr. Seagle's business card identifies him as John P. Seagle, Associate Professor of the School of Business at the State University at Albany.

It was probably inevitable that John Peters Seagle and his wife Dorothy would one day be seized with the urge to climb the Adirondack high peaks.

In 1989, Pete and Dodie, as they are called, assumed ownership of the Seagle Colony for singers, located on Charley Hill Road to the south of the village of Schroon Lake. Adirondack mountains surround the 500-acre site and the high peaks, which begin thrusting some 25 miles to the north, offer tantalizing views for lake residents.

The Seagle Colony, which has been in the family since 1915, was the first of the summer music colonies which now dot the area. When Tanglewood initiated its summer programs in Lenox, Massachusetts with the Boston Symphony Orchestra, the Seagle Colony had already been presenting programs for singers of musical theatre, operas and concerts for 25 years.

It would be another quarter century before the Saratoga Performing Art Center (SPAC) would open for works by the Philadelphia Orchestra, and by the New York City Opera and New York City Ballet.

The Seagle Colony has been a magnet for aspiring singers for summer study and for renowned artists from all over the country. Metropolitan Opera star Patrice Munsel and composer Randall Thompson are among those who have visited the colony.

It's no wonder that for Pete and Dodie Seagle, the nearby Adirondack high peaks are a magnet which brings them again and again to climb and enjoy tranquil moments in a magical place.

Journal entry: Saturday, September 1, 1979. *Before we leave South Dix, a huge bird soars nearby, much like one Ben spotted while we were on Macomb. It seems to be an eagle since it is much too big for a hawk. Suddenly, the bird plunges downward, not so much in pursuit of prey, so it would seem, but to head homeward. Which reminds us, since it is 4:50 p.m., we should also move downward.*

Four young men with bulging packs greet us as we descend over the bald prominence below South Dix's southwestern shoulder. "We're doing it the hard way," one says, eyeing our day packs. He confirms that our planned return route around the north base of Macomb is best.

Escape route *leads from South Dix toward Dix, center rear, and Hough, right. It skirts left side of hogback, foreground. Latter is dubbed Pough (as in Huff and Puff).*

As the younger boys slither down the rockside, Tommy announces, "This is like the western mountains." I ask his mother at what elevation the climb up Whitney began.

"About 10,000 feet," she replies. "Actually, that trail is not as steep as what we've done today because of the many switchbacks. It's also a lot drier and hotter on Whitney. We'd need more than two canteens." As an afterthought, she adds, "Of course, there was a house on the summit of Whitney."

At the trail junction in the col before Macomb, Mrs. Seagle's stick points in the direction we are to take. A good thing: the four, spreading trail segments have disoriented me. If Ben and I were alone, I would have led him in the wrong direction with complete assurance.

The steep, descending trail soon splits into erratic herd paths which cross and recross a stream. The younger boys lead, then draw back in confusion. Mr. Seagle and I finally decide to bracket the stream, and lead everyone downward over deadfall, slippery moss and jumbled rocks.

Eventually, the overgrown paths converge into a distinct one on the east side of the stream. Faint blazes identify it as the promised escape route, an old hunter's path which should lead to the marked trail from Elk Lake to Dix.

Lengthening shadows prompt hikers to head for Dix trail in a hurry. High peaks beyond Pinnacle Ridge, center, are from left, Allen, Redfield, Skylight, and Marcy.

While James and his mother catch up — I'm beginning to wonder if that boy will ever make it to school — the younger ones and Ben frolick forward. Ol' good nature himself, Tommy, is exuberant. He steps on a bent sapling, discovers it is springy, and pumps up and down. One has to marvel at his store of energy: we've already gone eight miles and climbed 3,500 ft. during the past nine and a half hours.

But we still need caution. On crossing the stream, a branch snags Ben's glasses and flips them into the water. Charlie, anxious to please, hops to a rock in mid-stream and retrieves them. In the process, he traps himself; it is too awkward for him to jump backward, and the gap forward is too far for his short legs. I stretch for his hand and yank him across.

The course of the path brings us to a much larger stream. This is Lillian Brook, which swings to the north, flowing far below and away from us. The hunters' path angles south, bringing us to the giant cairn marking the junction with the Dix trail. It is 6:45 p.m.; we have only a bit more than three miles to go on a clearly marked trail.

As we rest, Ben offers the boys the last of his M&Ms. This time, hunger overcomes politeness; they dig in with enthusiasm.

As we move out, the boys again flush a ruffed grouse, which whistles away in the dusk.

"Why do you carry such a heavy pack?" Mrs. Seagle asks Ben. He has read my tales of trouble on Algonquin and Tabletop, so he rattles off our supply of emergency items. I explain that on a good day they may be superfluous, but on a bad day they make eminent sense.

It is now almost 10 hours since we began hiking with the Seagles, and all seem to relish the camaraderie that comes from hiking together. Our pace slows, and the lead changes often.

"Have you stayed at Johns Brook Lodge?" asks Mr. Seagle. Just last month, I tell him, when Ben and I climbed Basin and Saddleback.

"I took my father there once," he replies. "I couldn't get a call through for a reservation, so we took a chance and went anyway." I nod sympathetically, remembering the problem I had with our reservation.

"The lodge was filled, so they put us in Winter Camp nearby." He shrugs: "It was in sad shape and we had no food. There was a Grab Box there, but all that was left was oatmeal. The outing was supposed to be a special occasion for my dad, but we ate the oatmeal anyway. Now I always carry spare rations," he says, patting his pack. "Freeze dried chow mein and my Army canteen, so we can prepare it with hot water."

Pete's father, John Seagle, had a distinguished career as a voice teacher at Trinity University in San Antonio, Texas, as well as a singing career on radio, television and the concert stage. He directed the Seagle Colony during summers for 40 years, retiring in 1987. He had taken over from his father, Oscar, Pete's grandfather, who founded the Colony in 1915. Oscar, a concert baritone and voice teacher of international acclaim, died in 1945.

Journal entry: Saturday, September 1, 1979. *The faint cry of a loon is a sure sign we are nearing Elk Lake.*

The pace of the two younger Seagles is more languid now, and they lag behind with me. Tommy the towhead is solemn and determined; Charlie still sports the bright eyes and ready smile that predict a burst of activity.

But the main source of energy on this leg of the hike comes from the seventh-grader, James. He acts like he really does care if school will keep, and forges to the lead with Ben, bubbling with enthusiasm and babbling with banter. "Look at him go," says his mother. "He has his second wind."

I'm relieved because until now, I wasn't sure he'd even gotten his first.

I tell her he is a carbon copy of my own son James. On many hikes, I had to mentally drag him up the slopes, then find on descending that he perked up to race me to the bottom.

It is 7:45 p.m. as we leave Cadillac Lane and plunge into the quiet woods on the last half mile of our adventure. Neither the afterglow from the just-set sun nor the dim shine from the rising half moon are enough to pierce the dark, deep shadows. But we decide to forgo flashlights and enjoy the stillness.

"What does your son like to do?" asks Mrs. Seagle. Probably the same as yours, I reply: airplane models, baseball, sports of all kinds, and a hundred other things. Her reply is interrupted in the enfolding darkness by two young voices seeking reassurance: "Mom?"

But, I add, Ben likes hiking best of all. And, I tell her, it's my favorite, too. It's the only sport I know where I can be with my sons, uninterrupted, for so long.

The young voices beckon to her again, and I note a contented smile as she moves ahead to be with them.

Journal entry: Friday, March 1, 1996. *I called the Seagles today to catch up on their family doings. Mrs. Seagle told me they're looking foward to the 81st summer season of the Seagle Colony.*

It's easy to keep up with the Seagle Colony on a regular basis because it gets good press each year with articles which detail their new season and update the family.

The July 8, 1990 issue of the Albany Times Union, *for example, described Pete as "an engineer by profession and by his own admission 'not very musical.'"*

It also noted that the Colony closed down during the summers of 1986 through 1988 after Pete's father, John, retired. It was saved and reopened after Pete and Dodie and their children joined with his father in rescuing it, largely "with the sweat of their brows."

Perseverance, I'm sure was at the core of it.

For I also discovered in the spring 1986 issue of Adirondack Peeks *that both John P. Seagle and Dorothy "Dodie" Seagle of Delmar, New York persevered to become Forty Sixers the previous year. The historian of the Adirondack Forty Sixers, Grace Hudowalski, noted wryly in her report for 1985 that "Number 2126 John Peters Seagle took 40 years" to accomplish the feat.*

Allen Mtn. from the west, near south branch of Opalescent River.

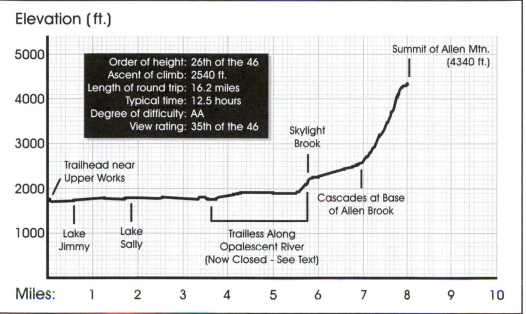

Elevation (ft.)

Order of height: 26th of the 46
Ascent of climb: 2540 ft.
Length of round trip: 16.2 miles
Typical time: 12.5 hours
Degree of difficulty: AA
View rating: 35th of the 46

Summit of Allen Mtn.
(4340 ft.)

Skylight
Brook

Trailhead near
Upper Works

Cascades at Base
of Allen Brook

Lake
Jimmy

Lake
Sally

Trailless Along
Opalescent River
(Now Closed - See Text)

Miles: 1   2   3   4   5   6   7   8   9   10

For contour trails, see U.S. Geological Survey map, pgs. 362-363.

35.
ALLEN

The first edition of the Adirondack Mountain Club guidebook, published in 1934, made no mention of this mountain.

The second edition, seven years later, gave it one paragraph, including this succinct summary: Allen "Stands apart on the S. side of the 'big mountains' and all approaches are long." By the seventh edition, in 1962, directions had ballooned to three pages because, as it explained, Allen "has always been one of the hardest trailless peaks to attain, mainly because of its remoteness."

Advice in the next edition was trimmed by half; in the edition of 1977, it was further shortened to just two paragraphs. These indicated that the conventional route, "via Marcy trail from Sanford Lake by the way of the Opalescent River is now closed to the public by the owners of the property in this area."

The conventional route had followed gravel lumber roads owned by Finch, Pruyn & Co., which logged the area for papermaking and leased lands to hunting clubs. But club members began to complain about increased rental costs while hikers passed through for nothing.

The closure left hikers with several options. First, they could go a couple of miles farther north on the Opalescent River trail, then loop around to the east and south and follow the border of state land to the

THE WAY TO
ALLEN, CLIFF

Trails to peaks noted above,
as described in text

Trailless routes to same

Other trails

N

1   ½   0   1 MILE

LEAN-TO

(Based on U.S. Geological Survey topo maps)

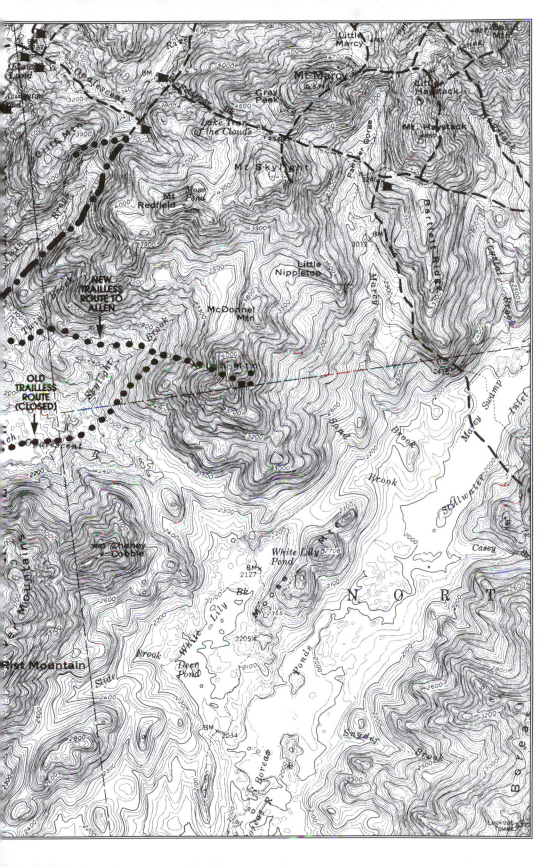

base of Allen. Eventually, this was the general course of a new herd path agreed upon by Finch, Pruyn & Co. and the state Department of Environmental Conservation, with the way to be flagged by the Adirondack Forty Sixers.

Or, hikers could bushwhack to Allen from neighboring Redfield, on the north, or do the same from Elk Lake, which was even farther away, on the south. Neither of these routes were enticing because they meant penetrating blowdown without benefit of herd paths.

In fact, *Adirondack Peeks* reported that *any* of the climbs meant a long, hard struggle. One of the first groups to climb by the new route bordering Finch, Pruyn & Co. lands in 1981 said it took them 18 hours. The same year, another group fared even worse, telling of their 32-hour approach from Elk Lake. The comment of another frustrated hiker was typical: "Took four attempts to climb it."

Others pioneered their own routes. The Forty Sixers' first book quoted a good woodsman who knew the locality well: "Started for Allen in heavy weather and ended up on Mt. Redfield." Another party from Elk Lake: "Contended with high winds, thunder, lightning, dense clouds and driving rain. Following a brook not shown on the map, we ended up on McDonnel Mtn.," a mile northeast of Allen. And yet another group targeting Allen: "Confusion. Much to our chagrin, we arrived at the cannister on Cliff Mtn."

It was clear that climbers who wanted to explore all of the Adirondack high peaks faced a serious obstacle: Allen was becoming harder than ever to find and climb. The solution seemed obvious: get an experienced guide to show the way.

Such a guide should be able to lead the way to Allen, starting from the nearest trailhead at Tahawus. That would probably rule out a clone of the most colorful guide of them all, Orson "Old Mountain" Phelps. Phelps worked at the mine during his early years, but moved to Keene Valley when he was 29, spending most of his career thereafter climbing the high peaks on the east.

The best example for a modern-day guide would be someone like John Cheney, the first of the legendary Adirondack mountain men, who was at Tahawus when the author Richard Henry Dana visited the mine site in 1849. His guides, said Dana, were "as good a set of honest, decent, kind-hearted, sensible men as one could expect to meet with."

However, there is a problem with using any of the old-time Adirondack guides for a modern role model: none of them, including Phelps and Cheney, ever climbed Allen. The Golden Age of Adirondack guides was over by the end of the last century, and there is no record that Allen was climbed until 1921.

Journal entry: Saturday, June 28, 1980. After agonizing over the problem of Allen for 13 years, I decided this year to look for a guide.

I asked Adrian Edmonds in Keene Valley and Pete Sanders at Elk Lake if they knew of any latter-day Cheneys. They didn't, but Pete suggested I ask around Newcomb, since Cheney had lived in the area. No luck.

Then an unexpected solution came from a logical source: the Adirondack Mountain Club. Tom Stanwood, a club member with whom son Jim and I climbed on two ADK club outings, told me he was scheduled to guide two people to Allen and would be glad to have Ben and me come along.

Tom said he does not believe the route from Tahawus has been posted off limits, but that we will make sure before passing through paper company land. He has climbed Allen twice before by this route.

When we rendezvous for the hike, Tom informs us the two others have cancelled out. Great. Ben and I will get to know Tom better, and see how he matches up with early-day guides.

During the drive up, Ben and I pump Tom for trail tips about climbs he has made which we have not. He responds from a wealth of experience; he's a Forty Sixer twice over and is now working to become a member of the 111 Club, open to those who have climbed all peaks over 4,000 feet in New England and New York state. To date, he has completed 70.

Most classic Adirondack guides were said to be tactiturn on the trail. But Tom is not. As we begin our trek, he stops me to hear a bird call, and identifies the species. On a recent climb of Hurricane Mtn. we made with him, Tom pointed out three falcons cavorting near the summit.

He also pulls Ben off the trail to provide an answer which has always escaped me: how to tell the difference between evergreen leaves. And, since I don't know as much about wild flowers as I'd like to, I ask him about a specimen at trailside. Without hesitation, he replies: "Bunchberry."

You know a lot about nature, I tell him.

"Not at all," says Tom. "I'm just getting into woodcraft, and then I want to go on to birds and geology. I'm learning."

Maybe so. But he seems to have earned the quality which Charles Dudley Warner credited Old Mountain Phelps with in an essay in Atlantic magazine in 1878: "A special communion with nature." Tom is completely at home in the mountains.

Warner described Phelps as "a sturdy figure, with long body and short legs." The analogy limps a bit here. Tom has a long body, but also long legs. One can tell from his strong, determined gait that he is well-suited for climbing mountains.

Ben and I race to keep up. The three of us slice through the early morning mist on the infant Hudson River, clatter across Lake Jimmy on a long log bridge, then catch fleeting glimpses of Lake Sally as we pass to the east of it.

Most old-time guides were hunters. For example, David Colden referred to John Cheney as "the Mighty Hunter of the Adirondacks." The record shows that he was indeed...but never on Sunday. In Masten's The Story of Adirondac, *the guide related, "I have always been able to kill enough on week days to give me a comfortable living. Since I came to live in the Adirondacks I have killed 600 deer, 400 sable, 19 moose, 28 bears, 6 wolves, 7 wild cats, 30 otter, 1 panther and 1 beaver."*

I pose the question of hunting to Tom. "Only with a camera," he replies. "I've never hunted with a gun and never will."

Ben mentions two incidents we heard of last fall while at Elk Lake. In one, a guide led a hunter to a bear in hibernation. Another guide condoned the shooting of a fawn. "That's terrible," says Tom. "But that's not much different than some hikers. A few can spoil it for the many." He stoops to put a discarded beer can on the trail for pick-up when we return.

All three of us have been busy swatting mosquitoes and black flies. As I pull out my Cutter's repellant, Tom advises, "Try this." He pokes a stick into a small bottle whose contents have congealed, and daubs it on Ben's arm.

"Save-the-Baby," he says matter-of-factly. The label reveals it is a remedy used for more than a century to treat spasmodic croup in children. It's easy to tell why it's effective: the insects dislike the smell as much as we do.

Where the trail meets a ford along the Opalescent River, a state Conservation Department sign proclaims rules to protect private hunting camps on the south shore: "The owner has permitted the marking of this trail for the benefit of the traveling public. But hunting, fishing and camping are not permitted."

"Just as I thought," proclaims Tom. "We're only hiking, so there's no problem." He leads the way a short distance up the trail, and we swing and sway on a suspension bridge to the other side.

Earlier guidebooks charted a clear course for us: from the bridge, a herd path leads to the right past hunters' camps, over a wooden bridge crossing Dudley Brook, the south branch of the Opalescent, then down a road heading southeast toward Allen.

We rest at a T in the road where we will turn left. The right fork, Tom says, leads to Tahawus. I ask the logical question: Why didn't we drive in and start from here?

"It's only open to lumber company vehicles," Tom replies. "Besides, that would be cheating." He recounts how one aspiring Forty Sixer surmounted trailless Esther. "He hitchhiked by road to the top of Whiteface, then traversed the shoulder between the two mountains. I don't believe in that," he adds.

"Here's little Miss Opalescent," said Old Mountain Phelps of the upper reaches of the river. When asked "Why don't you say Mr.?", he replied: "Oh, she's too pretty!"

Another prized attribute of a guide from any era: honesty.

At a fork in the road near another hunter's cabin, Tom hesitates, then heads left to cross a plank bridge spanning a major stream. The road coils through the woods along the stream, then veers away from it.

Tom falls silent and, straining to see beyond each bend in the road, strides so fast that Ben and I fall behind. As we catch up near another cabin, we find him staring at...the end of the road. "I blew it," he says. "We went the wrong way."

Ben and I are puzzled along the road by several trees with crude steps leading to platforms high in their branches. "It's for deer

Platforms for hunters *dot many trees around private camps on way to Allen. Boards nailed to this tree provide a makeshift ladder.*

hunters," says Tom. "It's legal because this is a private preserve.* But I think it's pathetic."

Up to this point, we have had but fleeting glimpses of our target. Each time, Allen has adhered to the phenomenon noted by Warner when he tracked Giant while heading east in the Ausable Valley: "It kept its distance, as only a mountain can." But now at another cabin clearing, Allen comes into unobstructed view for the first time.

We have already hiked five and a half miles and must go more than two miles to the base of Allen before we begin our climb of 1,740 feet. But the mountain now looks doable. Less than a mile beyond the clearing, Tom identifies Cheney Cobble, nearby on the southeast. It is, at 3,683 feet, an imposing monument to the legendary guide.

Out of view, six miles to the west, is Cheney Pond, where the guide accidentally shot himself in the ankle while on a deer hunt. As historian Donaldson noted, Cheney "reasoned that a mangled foot was less likely to prove fatal to a man alone in the woods than an empty stomach." So Cheney overtook the deer he was pursuing in the lake and towed it to shore. After dressing out a portion of it, he packed up the meat, fashioned crude crutches and hobbled 14 miles through dense forest before reaching help.

The trail to Allen now becomes a herd path clogged with blowdown. Tom flops his gear near a fallen log and hauls out map and compass. "It's not for now," he explains. "I need a reading for when I climb

*Permanent platforms are not allowed on state land.

here next winter." One more of Tom's goals: climb the 46 in winter. He has already completed 20.

Tom sorts out one of the multiple herd paths and follows it to the rush of Skylight Brook. "Something's wrong," he says. "This is not it." So we return to our log break where he sights a shoulder of Allen that bristles with blowdown. He plows into it, shouting, "Follow me."

After thrashing around for 15 minutes or so, Ben and I are getting edgy. Then, out of sight ahead, Tom shouts, "I've got it." He has crossed the main herd path. "I goofed again," Tom adds. "But don't worry. We'll make it." After such astute needle-threading, I'll follow this guide anywhere.

A short stroll brings us to a sparkling waterfall at the base of Allen Brook. Tom points out a level spot nearby, protected by a rock overhang: "Great spot for an overnight." Then he adds, glancing at the herd path which disappears among high cascades of the brook, "Now we go to work."

The final ascent, as always, generates a mixture of fatigue and blurred impressions: constant blowdown that one must go round or over; the dwindling brook, which must be crossed and re-crossed by jumping or slithering over moss-slicked slabs; and the slow encouragement that comes as we gain on Mt. Redfield, at our backs to the north. The latter, however, is discounted by Allen's summit ridge, which seems to be locked in place each time it appears.

Tom had promised Ben he would see a mini-slide much like the one on Macomb. In fact, Allen's is miniscule by compari-

***Cheney Cobble**, named for the legendary guide, rises 3,683 feet to the southwest of Allen. Cheney Pond, six miles west, also honors him.*

Waterfall at base of Allen Brook marks the beginning of the one-mile, 1,740-ft. climb to summit. Rock overhang reveals a tempting campsite.

son but just as treacherous, so we skirt it.

Tom is far above us now, and shouts encouragement from the top of a sizeable rockslide. "Keep to the right," he suggests. But we have already started up what appears to be a major herd path on the left. We rejoin his path at the top, then follow his fading shouts until he is out of range. Ben and I are too tired to protest. We struggle upward in short bursts, punctuated by rests.

Then Tom reappears. He had said we would top off the ridge without warning; my guess is that he has already been there because he insists we go ahead. Ben leads, and we gain a few glimpses of Dix, Giant and other familiar shapes to the east and northeast. Tom suggests we not tarry because, as if on schedule, the clouds are beginning to roll in.

As Tom predicted, the ground succumbs to the contest, falling flat before us; it is the summit saddle. Tom points to the highest knob peering through the trees a few hundred yards beyond. Minutes later, we reach the cannister, record our triumph, and lift our head nets to share lunch with the bugs.

It is 2:50 p.m., almost eight hours from the time we left Tahawus, ten and a half hours after leaving Schenectady.

A hiker on Allen Mtn., says Associated Press writer Mike Hendricks, "may arguably be the most isolated New Yorker at that moment, miles from the nearest person and a day away from the nearest road."

The mountain was completely alien to hikers when named in 1869, three quarters of a century before it was first climbed. A small group caught in a cloudburst on Upper Ausable Lake decided to commemorate the incident by calling a nameless peak after a member of their party, the Rev. Frederick Baylies Allen.

Years later, high peaks biographer Russell M. L. Carson asked him what he thought of the honor. Allen confessed that he had

Dense wooded summit *provides minimal view of Marcy with Skylight at center foreground. Other restricted views target Redfield, the MacIntyres, Haystack and Gothics.*

forgotten all about it. He said he was grateful, however, but felt "somewhat as did the inhabitants of the West Indian Island where Columbus first touched: 'Thank heaven we are discovered at last!'"

Allen's twin summits are wooded, but exploration brings rewards. Among the good views: Redfield and the MacIntyres to the north, and Marcy, Haystack, Skylight and Gothics to the northeast.

Allen's isolation makes it attractive to other species. Ken Bruno told *Adirondack Peeks* that when he and his son were on Allen's summit in 1981, "There in a tree, not 10 feet from us, sat an eagle. He stared at us as if we were invading his land."

The dense woods on Allen's summit also act like a magnet on insects during midsummer. Most of them are bloodthirsty, as Jeffrey Duflo of Wilmington, NY related recently in *The Wall Street Journal:* "A mosquito injects a small tube, like putting a straw into a box of Kool-Aid. But black flies rip the top off the box with a knife," with "razor-sharp mouth-parts."

Even politicians have enlisted the pests to serve their legislative purposes. In her book, *The Forest Preserve of New York State*, Schenectady conservationist Eleanor Brown noted that in 1949 an assemblyman called for "reconsideration of the constitutional provision that keeps the Preserve serving 'no one but the bugs.'"

Farley Mowat, the naturalist and anthropologist, proposed a rational answer relating to the Canadian arctic in *People of the Deer:* "The flies are not the least of the Barrens' defenses and they have greatly assisted in protecting the land so long from white men's violation."

But the poet Ogden Nash best expressed the feeling of most hikers:

"God in his wisdom made the fly
and then forgot to tell us why."

Journal entry: Saturday, June 28, 1980. The wooded summit of Allen has a tiny clearing. But to me, at this point, it is a triumphal auditorium suited for the feasts of victory: sheer joy, first, from having made it here and, second, a Spam and cheese sandwich.

Tom cocks a quizzical glance at my fare. He's like so many others who don't appreciate how popular and versatile Spam is. It tastes so good, according to The New York Times Sunday Magazine, *that South Koreans rank it as a gift item right up there with jewelry and premium whiskey. The* Times *reports that it can also be used to keep condensation off the bathroom mirror. And I can vouch that it repels black flies.*

Ben wanders off to take pictures, so I thumb through the register. A previous climber, Robert E. Mound of Hudson Falls, lamented:

> *Let me climb Mt. Marshall with my hands tied behind my back,*
> *Let me climb Street with no arms,*
> *Let me climb Nye with no eyes,*
> *But don't let me climb this AGAIN.*

Tom sits across from me on our log lunch table, munching on an egg salad sandwich and morsels of health food. I try to visualize him as one of the old-time Adirondack guides.

He's not like Old Mountain Phelps, whose stubby pipe protruded from a cherubic face; Tom doesn't smoke. And he's not like the Keene Valley guide Harvey Holt; as George Marshall wrote in the Forty Sixers' book The Adirondack High Peaks, *"Holt had a great weakness for moose hunting and at times apparently killed more than was reasonable." Tom doesn't like hunting.*

And Tom is not another Verplanck Colvin. That renowned Adirondack surveyor was so oblivious to time and weather that he often delayed leaving a mountain top until darkness forced an overnight. Tom, eyeing the threat of rain, looks at me and suggests, "Let's get going. We'll be lucky to reach the car by 8:30 p.m." It is 3:15 p.m.; we have been on the summit 25 minutes.

Tom adds, "Pick up," as he stows litter in his pack. "I'm surprised there are no corks. So many Forty Sixers save Allen until last, my friend John Winkler calls this the Champagne Trail."

The descent to the base of Allen is as steep and slippery going down as coming up. Ben follows in lockstep with Tom; first one falls flat on the tilted rock stream bed, then the other. Neither are hurt.

"Reminds me of Snow Mountain, a mile and a half south of Keene Valley," says Tom. "I was descending with a friend and walked right off a ledge. Broke my shoulder in three places and banged up my head."

Good thing you weren't alone, I sympathize.

"Maybe," says Tom. "But if so, I would have paid attention and not talked so much." It's hard to tell what might have happened if Richard Henry Dana were hiking with us today. The best part of his stay at Tahawus, he said, was the "hard walks and good talks."

We rest briefly at the waterfall and refresh with a refill. At the first hunter's camp, we are brought up short by a notice tacked on the main porch wall, out of our sight when we passed this morning. The message: no hiking permitted.

Tom Stanwood *typifies modern-day Adirondack explorers who head for the hills in every free moment. They emulate the best qualities of 19th century wilderness guides.*

"Oops," says Tom, stooping to pick up litter. "Well, the least we can do is respect their property."

Ben is limping by now, so Tom unstraps his pack. "Blister," he says automatically, hauling out moleskin, scissors and tape from a bulging first-aid kit. But his best medicine is a small tin of fruit, which Ben gobbles gratefully.

The array of articles in Tom's pack guarantees both succor and survival. All of them are protected from the rain now falling by garbage can liners. The lengthy list of items fulfills another requirement of a competent guide: preparedness.

It's a good feeling to know that he's here. I am covered with cuts, scratches and insect bites; in fact, both ears are bleeding from the black flies and deer flies. At one nasty stretch of blowdown, if it were not for my glasses and felt hat, a branch would have poked my eye. My calf muscles are sore and my shoulders ache from the pack straps. But I'm sure if I asked, Tom would have a remedy for all.

Probably Save-the-Baby.

The bridge crossing the Opalescent leads us to a welcome transition from gravel to humus. Yet the thought of nearly four miles yet to go on the trail makes our feet feel leaden; the legs swing automatically, like pendulums with only a tenuous relationship to our bodily clocks.

Tom does his best to keep us moving, suggesting that first Ben, then I take the lead. But Ben is very tired and the ruse is transparent. We lag behind. The darkness in the woods, even though it is only a little after seven p.m., is discouraging.

As we drag into the parking lot at 8:10 p.m., a ruffed grouse bullets off at Ben's approach. On the lonely exit road we startle four deer and a raccoon. And while Ben and Tom chat about future hikes, I drive clear of a furry creature with long legs and short tail bounding across the road: the elusive bobcat.

Even the familiar mountains, now seen in unfamiliar silhouette, reflect a warm glow from the sinking sun. The two-pronged summit of Allen is a southern mime of Saddleback; Marcy, with only a nub visible from here, strains to add its goodbye.

Heading east on the road toward Blue Ridge, Ben asks about a rounded mountain whose furrowed silhouette evokes the head of a sleeping gorilla. Tom identifies it: "Owl Pate. It's sort of interesting up there, but there's no view to the south."

And on he goes on the return trip with an enthusiastic outpouring of trail tales, camping cautions and his joyous view of the views from on top. Ben alternately slumps with exhaustion, then shudders bolt upright so that no revelation escapes him on the way home.

"Hiking," Tom wrote to us shortly thereafter, "or climbing as I often call it, is like peanuts. I get out every chance I get. Guess I'm happiest when I'm on the trail. There are so many feelings I have toward it that just cannot be expressed in words."

The one who came closest to expressing them perhaps was John Cheney the guide, who described the moment when he stood with the first group to climb Mt. Marcy: "It makes a man feel what it is to have all creation placed beneath his feet." But Tom Stanwood is no reincarnation of John Cheney. Tom will guide friends to hard-to-find and hard-to-climb peaks. Yet he does not do so for money. And he wants no part of the hunting and fishing that so many seek.

Tom Stanwood is one of a new breed of Adirondack mountain climbers who are becoming legends in their own time. John Winkler is another. And I suspect the veteran mountain men who climbed the Wright slide with Tom and Ben and me in May 1982 — Phil Corell, Wally Herrod and Tom Ellis — would also qualify.

Climbing, they claim, is their avocation. But to the observer, it appears to be their primary goal in life; all else is secondary and subservient. They revel in the joy of climbing; the more the better.

These dedicated climbers seem to know most everone on the peaks. When Ben and I were descending from Algonquin in August of 1981, I chatted with a woman heading up the trail, who was acting as sweep for a party from Glens Falls. It was Pat Collier, a Forty Sixer and member of the ADK's Conservation Committee, who knows a good many of our hiking friends.

"Of course I know Tom Stanwood," she avowed. "He's a wild man."

Since Tom is one of the gentlest of the good-natured people we know, she obviously referred to his hiking prowess.

And members of the new breed celebrate with gusto. When Stanwood climbed Mt. Colden to complete his first circuit of the 46, friends brought along not only a sumptuous trail lunch but table linen, silverware, and a candelabra (which wouldn't stay lit in the summit winds). They dined while a melody from *The Sound of Music* floated over the summit from a portable tape player: "Climb Every Mountain."

To this day, Stanwood signs off all of his correspondence by adding after his name the initials, C.E.M., for that evocative melody.

The October 1980 issue of *Adirondac* carried the following notice: "The Adirondack Mountain Club has been notified by Finch, Pruyn & Co., Glens Falls, New York, that persons who travel on their property to climb Allen Mountain will be subject to arrest. Finch, Pruyn & Co. has agreed to take no action until after ADK members have had the opportunity to read this notice in the October 1980 issue of *Adirondac*."

The company offered help in cutting a new route that avoided the hunting clubs which leased land in the area. The new route to Allen was marked by the Forty Sixers in 1983 and is now the accepted herd path giving access to Allen. Both the new route and the old one are shown on the U.S. Geological Survey map on pgs. 362-363.

Cliff Mtn. from Twin Brook trail, now abandoned.

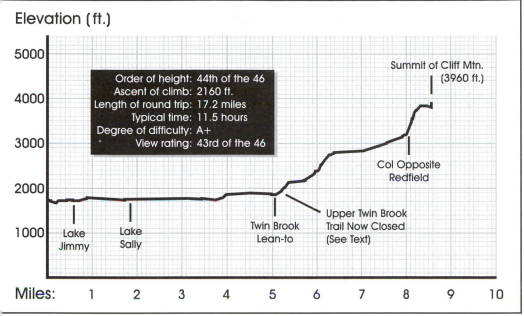

Elevation (ft.)

Order of height: 44th of the 46
Ascent of climb: 2160 ft.
Length of round trip: 17.2 miles
Typical time: 11.5 hours
Degree of difficulty: A+
View rating: 43rd of the 46

Summit of Cliff Mtn.
(3960 ft.)

Col Opposite
Redfield

Upper Twin Brook
Trail Now Closed
(See Text)

Twin Brook
Lean-to

Lake
Jimmy

Lake
Sally

Miles: 1 2 3 4 5 6 7 8 9 10

or contour trails, see U.S. Geological Survey map, pgs. 362-363.

36.
CLIFF

Adirondack surveys conducted during the last half of this century show that Cliff Mtn. is a fraud. It does not qualify as one of the 46 high peaks reaching 4,000 ft. or more.

The U.S. Geological Survey of 1953 pegged it at 40 feet below that level. The metric survey of 1979 indicated that Cliff was another 18 feet lower. In fact, three other high peaks among the 46 — Blake, Nye and Couchsachraga — have been proven to rise less than 4,000 ft.

For the purpose of the Adirondack Forty Sixers club, however, the shortfalls are academic. Members adhere to the original listing because those were the 46 high peaks first climbed by the Marshall brothers and their guide, Herb Clark. At the time, according to George Marshall, both Cliff and Blake were thought to be "exactly 4,000 feet."

When viewed from its big neighbors to the north, such as Colden or any of the MacIntyres, Cliff does not live up to its name. It is just one more sizeable bump on the folds of green carpet which ripple toward the south. There isn't a cliff in sight.

But the mountain does have redeeming features. Those who approach Cliff from the south and east see in an instant the rugged rock face for which it was named. The venturesome can also climb to the summit via a slide up the soaring mountainside beginning about a quarter of a mile south of the col between Cliff and Redfield.

As a rule, those who conquer this trailless peak will find themselves alone on the summit. One reason is that it's a long hike: more than 17 miles round trip via the Opalescent River-Twin Brook trail (the latter segment is now abandoned), and only a few miles less via the Calamity Brook trail from the Upper Works near Tahawus.

And, Cliff is inching its way up there to rank in a class with its bigger siblings. Geologists estimate that the high peaks are growing at a rate of three millimeters or more a year — close to a foot every 100 years. At that rate, Cliff will become an official member of the Forty Sixer club in less than 6,000 years.

Journal entry: Friday, July 4, 1980. Two weeks ago, Ben and I chose the longest day of the year — the first of summer, June 21 — for a very long hike: Cliff Mtn. from Sanford Lake near Tahawus.

The forecast in Schenectady was for a 10% chance of rain. But Adirondack reality set in on the Opalescent River trail. After slogging for an hour and a half over three miles in the face of an approaching storm, rain gave way to reason. We turned back.

Today we intend to try again.

Without exception, experienced hikers describe Cliff as "hard." Even Tom Stanwood urged caution last week: "It's tricky." Ben and I wish he were here to guide us today.

Then it occurs to me: four years ago today, Ben and his mother and I celebrated the nation's bicentennial at the Saratoga National Historical Park where one of the crucial battles of the American Revolution was fought. At the time, Ben was a wispy, eight-year-old boy engrossed in chasing butterflies instead of mountains.

Since then he has fostered an admirable combination of strong limbs and strong will. In 1978, he pulled me up five of the 46 Adirondack high peaks, and 13 the following year. This year, discounting a repeat of Cascade, we have completed three tough ones, culminating in Allen. Only three of those in previous years were trailless; all have been so this year.

Therefore, I tell Ben, we hereby declare our independence in the Adirondacks. We will journey to Cliff, sans guide, and climb the mountain, sans trail. Ben cheers like a patriot.

Ben commandeers a stout hiking staff leaning against the trailhead register, which is three miles north of the mine at Tahawus. It is 8 a.m. As we move out on the trail, Ben sketches a battle plan for our revolution. We will conquer 10 more trailless peaks this year, he says, plus Skylight. Then we will launch an unexpected raid. The target: a nameless, near-4,000 foot mountain bordering Lost Pond on the south side of Street.

"We'll name it Mt. Benjamin," he smiles.

Why not, I tell him. A man whom I worked with in the General Electric News Bureau, Clyde Wagoner, early in his career set up short-wave broadcasts for Admiral Richard E. Byrd and his lonesome crew members when they explored Antarctica from Little America. The grateful Admiral conferred the name Mt. Clyde Wagoner on a peak near the tip of the continent.*

Ben warms to the challenge: "I told Mom we heard a geologist at the State Museum say that the Adirondack high peaks are rising a little bit each year." He snickers: "She says at your speed we may wind up climbing the highest mountains in the world."

Very funny.

The bugs bore in so we don our head nets. I'm convinced that if our climb were higher than the Himalayas, we'd still expend more energy scratching than hiking.

A quarter of a mile after crossing Lake Jimmy, we rest at the junction of the side trail to Mt. Adams. I suggest to Ben that we add this peak to our list, because it played a role in molding the career of the pioneering high peak explorer, Bob Marshall.

Paul Schaefer tells in ADK's Adirondac *magazine of meeting Marshall on Marcy in 1932 and pointing to lumbering operations on Adams. Marshall was devastated: "We simply must band together — all of us who love the wilderness." Said Schaefer: "The people Marshall banded together were the founders of the Wilderness Society."*

At a bit less than four miles, we cross the Opalescent suspension bridge and for the first time explore the graceful rise of the trail that leads a mile and a quarter to the Twin Brook lean-to.

A flutter of voices tells us various hikers are camping in the area; only one young man is in sight. He's been to Cliff and, "the trail is not hard up to the col, but it's in bad shape." He starts to proffer advice on the actual climb, but a nervous call from his partner sends him packing.

Another young man, breathless with anticipation, asks if we have climbed Allen; he plans to try it tomorrow. Ben and I assume the mien of trail veterans and warn him of nature's ambushes he can expect.

---

*In 1937, Wagoner also arranged the program on the summit of Mt. Marcy celebrating the 100th anniversary of the peak's first ascent by William Redfield and Ebenezer Emmons.

Suspension bridge crossed Opalescent River a little less than four miles from trailhead near Tahawus. It has since been replaced.

The former yellow-marked trail from the site of the Twin Brook lean-to to the col between Cliff and Redfield was officially closed in 1981 and is no longer maintained. With care, however, it can still be used as a route to the two mountains. It offers an alternative to the red-marked trail which tracks the Opalescent River to Uphill lean-to on the north side of the two peaks. The latter was the route pioneered by Redfield and Emmons on their Marcy expedition.

The Twin Brook lean-to was removed by state rangers in 1992. Since the site was private property, hikers now must continue on to state land for camping.

Journal entry: Friday, July 4, 1980. *I hate to veer away from the Opalescent, which historian Donaldson referred to as "the embryo Hudson." He noted that state geologists found the bed of the stream glittering with labradorite, or opalescent feldspar.*

Normally, the rocks are supposed to be a rich blue, although they sometimes show as green, gold or even bronze, and can be iridescent. To me, they all look the same, from pebbles to boulders, because of my red-green color-blindness. But the river is entrancing anyway.

After a short dogleg on a lumber road beyond the lean-to, the trail again resumes a comfortable rise up the south bank of Upper Twin Brook. It's hard to believe that this trail was an active road when lumbering was conducted in the area. The ancient, slippery, corduroy log surface may have once been usable, but it now tilts sharply like a worn-out washboard. It reminds me of Indian Pass near Wallface, since the sheer face of Cliff Mtn. soars majestically on our left.

A party of six from New Jersey lunches where the trail crosses a second waterfall. They have no gear and all wear tennis shoes. "We're off to Marcy," says their jovial leader. "Are we close?"

I tell them they have nearly five tough miles to Marcy's summit, and warn that they may not make it back before dark. If they're staying at Twin Brook lean-to, their total round trip will be more than 12 miles; if they came from the parking lot near Tahawus, their day's trip will be almost 23 miles.

Younger members in the party look askance at their leader, but he is unconcerned. Seeds of disaster.

Four hours from the parking lot, the trail curves to round a knoll in the middle of the pass between Cliff and Redfield. The other side of the knoll, we discover, is the saddle of the col. An ancient blaze on a tree at trailside marks a well-worn herd path which snakes northwest toward the slab slopes of Cliff. It is one p.m.; the first skirmish is about to begin.

A short distance upward, the path splits in a T. The left branch leads toward the exposed walls; the right branch is blocked by a log which appears to be placed as a barrier.

Old logging road *offers precarious footing on Upper Twin Brook trail, now abandoned. It takes hikers heading for Cliff three miles from Opalescent River to col between Cliff and Redfield.*

The guidebook admonishes climbers: "Head W keeping well to R of the cliffs." This suggests a right turn, but in light of the barrier we decide to go left. We suspect a previous hiking party was trying to tell us something.

Apparently. Because at the base of the vertical cliffs, the path enters a narrow opening cleft by a stream, and follows it steeply upward. Over and over, the path dead-ends at rock outcroppings. Sliding footprints mingled with stripped-branch handholds show how forerunners circumvented the challenges.

At one nasty stretch, Ben slips and his new walking staff goes clattering to the base of a rock face some 30 feet below. He grabs a tree, panting: "It's dangerous. Steep. Tough. Wet. Slippery. Hard. Horrible."

Then he adds, in frustration: "I wish I knew more adjectives." We decide to leave his staff and retrieve it on our return.

From false summit, *top of Cliff rises a couple of hundred feet and a half mile away. Same thick growth carpets the true summit.*

The path keeps branching. Yet almost without exception brush placed on one fork suggests we take the other. Where there is no clear choice, either Ben or I form a reconnaissance party of one and investigate the most likely branch, marking a blaze to guide our return.

As on Allen, the mountain abruptly surrenders and the first summit, entrapped with blowdown, sprawls before us. It has taken an hour and a quarter from the col.

Tom Stanwood warned us that a huge jumble of logs at the southwestern end of this false summit would seem like an impenetrable barrier. "Just walk over it," he advised. "On the other side, you'll see the true summit dead ahead."

At this point, one deadfall looks like all the others to me. But in 15 minutes we

*clamber over the logs, then skitter down to the narrow col separating
the two summits. In 10 minutes more, we can climb no higher. We
have bested Cliff.*

Tim Tefft, a former director of the Adirondack Forty Sixers, said of
Cliff Mtn. in *Of The Summits, of the Forests*: "I know of no other place
that seems so private and removed from the rest of the world."
One would think it had ever been thus. Cliff was one of the last of
the 46 high peaks to be climbed, in 1921. It had been named almost 50
years before by Verplanck Colvin, who viewed it when he and a guide
were on the side of Mt. Redfield. "Opposite us," he said, "arose the
black and singularly rounded and embossed front of Cliff Mountain."
When the Marshall brothers climbed it in 1924, they claimed they
"saw some 29 of the high peaks from its upper slopes and ledges by dili-
gently looking for views here and there." The scribbling in the summit
register, per *Adirondack Peeks*, suggests that later climbers had other
priorities in mind.
1967, Karen Schoebel and Clyde Babb: "We defy anybody to descend
by exactly the same route they ascended." 1968, Stan Ashley: "Hard to
pick the easiest route with so many 'trails' on this 'trailless peak!'"
1970, Peter Mark: "We had a time finding the summit, but the bugs
knew right where to come."

*Journal entry: Friday, July 4, 1980. Ben and I record our victory
in the register for the historians. Lunch is brief, for the bugs are more
adept at biting than we are.*

*Ben wanders off but returns to report he can only spot two peaks from
a ledge on the east: Marcy nuzzling Gray. While he wanders back for
a photo, I pull down my head net and resume my favorite sport:
doing nothing.*

*It is deathly quiet on Cliff. There is no wind. In fact, it is downright
spooky.*

*No wonder. Except for a small spot worn bare on this table-sized sum-
mit, it's probably just like it was two centuries ago during the
American Revolution. I doubt if the Indians even came here before
that, since hunting would have been better and easier on the lowlands.*

*What a rush of history since the United States was founded! Thirty
nine presidents, from George to Jimmy. And now we are in the midst
of our quadrennial convulsion to see who will be our next commander in chief.*

*The political conventions are a game of chance, and the implications
are sobering. Twenty five years ago I was asked to be the personal
public relations representative for Ronald Reagan as he fulfilled one*

Mt. Marcy dominates the limited viewing scene from Cliff some three miles to the east. Gray Peak nestles below on its left.

aspect of his role as television host of the GE Theatre. I declined and went on to other things in General Electric. If I had accepted the job, it's hard to know if I'd be on this peak today.

Not everyone wants to influence the course of history. A GE associate, Guy Waterman, did want to but in a different way: he decided to reverse it. During our one brief encounter, we met during rehearsals in New York City for GE executives for whom we were writing speeches.

The next I heard of Guy, years later, was through an article he had authored in Backpacker *magazine. He and his wife* had chucked it all and settled in a primitive cabin in the backwoods of Vermont. No running water. No electricity. No normal comforts. According to Guy, just happiness.*

Ben interrupts my musings: "We'd better be going." He sees my placid expression, and wonders if I'm all right.

I'm with you all the way, good buddy. I appreciate the rigors of the revolutionists and admire the spirit of the Watermans. But good days give me enough of the wilderness. Good nights dictate soft beds.

Before we leave, I note a June 14 scrawl in the summit register by Gerald "Tody" Edwards: "God give me 'Couchie' [Couchsachraga]. I'll do anything. Bugs - scratches - sun is close to setting. Heavy loss of blood to the Black Fly Foundation."

*In 1989, the Watermans authored Forest and Crag, *a superb "History of hiking, trail blazing, and adventure in the Northeast Mountains," published by the Appalachian Mountain Club, Boston.*

His companion, Claire Herred, added a shaky PS: "Get me back to the lean-to." Not exactly my sentiments, but close.

While our battle is won, the war is not over. Slapping bugs will have to do for firecrackers on this independence mountain. Ben and I begin our 10-mile return hike, plus a 100-mile drive home.

The views we missed on ascending now unfold before us: Marcy, Gray, Skylight, Redfield, Colden. Marcy is a good four miles away, and 1,500 feet higher. If the Jersey group went for it, they will sleep well tonight. Possibly in the woods.

A couple climbing from below shouts for guidance. Ben worries they will find and take his staff. No problem, I tell him; they are a hundred yards off the main path, thrashing around in a thicket.

We set them straight and answer their inquiry: you're an hour from the top. The woman slumps in discouragement. She looks too tired to even register a complaint in the register.

Ben perks up on retrieving his staff. At the trail junction in the col, he props up a stick in the cairn and affixes an arrow locating the herd path. Moral reinforcement for future assault troops.

Litter at the first waterfall is the calling card left by the group from New Jersey, but it gives no clue as to their intentions. We heed Stanwood's example last week, and clean up after them.

An enormous, snarling dog greets our approach on the rear side of the Twin Brook lean-to. At his master's call, the dog returns to a group of young people seated in a circle at the front. We nod and marvel: they are all in shorts, oblivious to the bugs.

When we reach the suspension bridge crossing the Opalescent at 6:30 p.m., Ben slumps to the ground with a bad case of battle fatigue. He's too heavy to carry, so I exhort him to honor God, home, and country. He responds mostly to home, in particular my graphic reminder of his soft bed.

Under his revived leadership, we finish the three and a half miles to the parking lot by forced march. It takes only an hour and 20 minutes, which is 10 minutes less than we took with Tom Stanwood on our way from Allen. Inspiration from independence.

The listing of heights for the 46 Adirondack high peaks in the ninth edition of the ADK guidebook ranks Cliff number 44. Yet the trailless description in the same volume refers to the peak as number 43. I can understand the confusion. I wouldn't rank it number one on a scale of difficulty. Yet at this point, I can't think of too many others which are longer and therefore more difficult.

Ben is asleep as soon as he plops in the back seat of our car. I am tempted to arouse him at the sight of Fourth of July fireworks along our way home. I can't resist at the obvious climax of a spectacular display at Glens Falls.

Only half awake, he stares and asks, "Is that for us?" Then he flops down again.

A good conclusion to a successful campaign.

Journal entry: Friday, July 4, 1986. *It's been six years to the day since Ben and I conquered Cliff, and 10 years since the bicentennial.*

It's like another birthday in a way, so we decide to celebrate by climbing Mt. Adams. The trail branches off on the way to Cliff, a little less than a mile from the parking lot near Tahawus.

"Trail" is a euphemism for the route up Adams. The eleventh edition of the ADK guidebook refers to it as "a less than attractive climb." One reason is that the trail has not been maintained for years. As a result, the brush is encroaching and when it's wet, hikers get soaked. With the usual winds on top, they can expect to get chilled. Also, the fire tower has been abandoned so there's no view from the heavily wooded summit.

Hikers cross *Lake Jimmy, then skirt Lake Sally on way to Mt. Adams. Origin of names is unknown. Story of their romance, we learn, "is shrouded in antiquity."*

The forecast calls for cloudy and cool

weather. We dress accordingly.

My climbing companion is now an 18-year-old collegian who takes huge strides up the faint trail. By degree, the slopes become steep and then very steep. We finish the two and a half miles and 1,800 feet of ascent in a little over two hours.

It makes for a happy birthday. Old lumbered areas have been perked up by newly grown, glistening birch trees. Just before reaching the summit, we are welcomed by a cacophony of chickadees. And while the fire tower is called "unsafe to climb," we find that a half-way climb brings rewarding views.

From Mt. Adams, *Mt. Colden presents an unfamiliar profile four miles to the northeast. It's like the view from Phelps on the opposite side.*

The forecast is wrong; it has been a perfect day. Well, almost. Ben shucks off his trail pants to show me the cool summer shorts he wears underneath. Unfortunately, I took the weatherman seriously: my long johns are totally out of place.

But again, we are alone. Thoreau was right when he said, "I never found the companion that was so companionable as solitude."

Couchsachraga Peak, lower right, and Panther Peak, left, from Seymour Mtn. Santanoni Peak is at center rear.

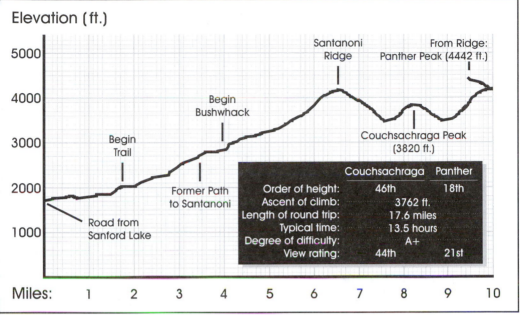

Elevation (ft.)

	Couchsachraga	Panther
Order of height:	46th	18th
Ascent of climb:	3762 ft.	
Length of round trip:	17.6 miles	
Typical time:	13.5 hours	
Degree of difficulty:	A+	
View rating:	44th	21st

Santanoni Ridge

From Ridge: Panther Peak (4442 ft.)

Begin Bushwhack

Begin Trail

Couchsachraga Peak (3820 ft.)

Former Path to Santanoni

Road from Sanford Lake

Miles: 1 2 3 4 5 6 7 8 9 10

or contour trails, see U.S. Geological Survey map, pgs. 262-263.

37, 38.
COUCHSACHRAGA, PANTHER

Journal entry: Saturday, July 26, 1980. All of the 10 mountains left on my list are difficult. But the one that tops them all is Couchsachraga Peak. It prompts horror stories from climbers who have tried it and failed; it prompts horror stories from those who have succeeded. Couchsachraga is in a class with Allen, Tom Stanwood told us. "They're the toughest two of the 46."

The renowned woodcut artist Rockwell Kent, who lived and worked in the Adirondacks for many years, seemed to anticipate the logical question one might conclude about climbing Couchsachraga: Why bother? In his book, N by E, which Kent wrote while living at Ausable Forks, he postulated the answer: "Who can deny the human soul its everlasting need to make the unknown known."

Fine, but I had a more practical motivation: I wanted Ben and me to get home safely. So I called Tom and we scheduled the trip for today.

"While we're at it," said Tom, "we might as well climb one of the two peaks we pass along the way. You've already done Santanoni, so we'll go for Panther."

People have long had trouble coming to grips with Couchsachraga. In the context of the high peaks, it's like an orphan at a family reunion.

There have been questions about its lineage. In 1784, Thomas Pownall wrote in his *Topographical Description of North America*, "the Country...called by the Indians Couxsachrage...[is] very little known to the Europeans; and although a hunting Ground of the Indians, yet either not much known to them, or, if known, very wisely by them kept from the knowledge of the Europeans...I own I could never learn any Thing about it."

Nobody heard much about Couchsachraga until it was first climbed in 1924. But even after that, the Marshalls and their guide were ambivalent about that first ascent. They called their conquest the Cold River Mountain, after the region in which it was located. They applied the name Couchsachraga to the mountain now known as Mt. Emmons, then later switched the name to its present owner.

Chronicles of the high peaks gave Couchsachraga short shrift in the family album. The first ADK guidebook, issued in 1934, said the peak was 4,000 feet, but gave no directions on how to climb it. It wasn't even listed in the index.

One reason is that Couchsachraga is the runt of the litter. It's almost 200 feet shorter than the original 4,000-ft. benchmark for the 46 high peaks, and 75 feet below its nearest sibling, Nye Mtn.

Even spelling its name has posed a conundrum. At various times in its brief history, the peak's namesake region has been known as Cooughsaghrage, Couxsaxrage, Cou-a-cra-ga, and Kohsaraga.

The base word comes from the Iroquois, and means "beaver hunting ground" or "habitation of winter." Most hikers, however, equate it with an ancient Algonquin word for the Adirondacks: "Dismal wilderness."

It may be that explorers search out Coughsachraga simply because it is little known, isolated and lonely. Samuel H. Hammond, an Albany preservationist who made annual trips to the Adirondacks beginning in the 1840s, expressed the feeling when he said he "loved the old woods, the wilderness, and all the wild things pertaining to them." They fulfill, he said, the "streak of the savage" in all of us.

Journal entry: Saturday, July 26, 1980. When I first talked with Tom Stanwood about this hike, he offered an option: "It'll be long, so we can either camp out at the trailhead to get an early start, or shove off from home at 4 a.m." Ben and I opted for the latter, not exactly by choice: we have no equipment for camping out.

Fortunately, we do have the perfect hiking wife and mother. She's up and getting things under way for us at 3 a.m.

The sights along the entry road bring back memories of the hike son Jim and I made to Santanoni nine years ago: Wallface peeping through the morning mist on the north; a field covered with raspberry bushes — sure sign of an old lumber camp; the two brook crossings; and the boundary post marking Finch Pruyn & Co.'s property at two and a half miles.

And then, the long sweep upward along the course of Santanoni Brook, past the sparkling cascades at three and a quarter miles, and, just beyond, the junction with the old herd paths to Santanoni Peak.

We climb briefly to a high point in the trail, then descend to where a large, blazed tree indicates a trailless cutoff toward Panther Brook. The trail beyond leads a short distance to Bradley Pond and, on the right, the Santanoni lean-to. The trail then continues for three and a half miles to Duck Hole, near the northern entry to the Cold River region.

Adirondack Peeks magazine noted in mid-1981 that, "Most 46ers by now have learned that the popular approaches to Allen as well as those to Santanoni and Panther have been closed by Finch Pryun Corporation." The dilemma for hikers wanting to climb Panther, and in turn Santanoni and Couchsachraga, was resolved by the company, which offered to cut a new path to Panther Brook near where their property borders state land.

The new path veers west from the trail at a beaver dam some 200 yards south of the Santanoni lean-to. The path skirts the north edge of Bradley Pond near the boundary of state land to the northwest corner of the company's property. It then assumes a new route marked by Forty Sixers to Panther Brook, where it follows the old herd path up to the ridge connecting Santanoni and Panther.

Volunteer trailwork *by Adirondack Forty Sixers eases the way for hikers at swampy areas.*

Panther Brook *has been called the most beautiful in the Adirondacks. But it ensnares hikers tracing its course to trailless peaks.*

Journal entry: Saturday, July 26, 1980. At the blazed tree, Ben and I follow Tom, who plunges into a maze of herd paths criss-crossing Santanoni Brook. Soon, however, he sorts out a side branch heading up Panther Brook and we begin a steady climb.

Tom notes that I have blood on both of my sleeves. "Must be scratches from tree branches," he says. "There are two generations of black flies each year, but these are from the second one, and aren't supposed to bite."

Someone forgot to tell them.

It has grown muggy, and our pace slows. But a slight breeze freshens our prospects as we leave the diminishing brook; it has disappeared underground. We plunge into blowdown for our final assault toward the ridge. "We have five or six hundred feet to climb," says Tom. He predicts we'll top off in 45 minutes, by noon.

Scrub trees, sure summit signposts, foretell our arrival at the Santanoni-Panther ridge line. We slump, catch our breath and reinvigorate with half a sandwich.

Ben suggests we go to Panther, which squats only a couple of hundred feet higher and less than a half mile to the north. "Coochie first," advises Tom. "We'll do the hard one, then enjoy the view when we come back here."

The focal point for hikers on the Santanoni-Panther ridge is a cross-roads known as Times Square. It connects the herd paths coming from Bradley Pond and the Duck Hole trail on the east, from Panther on the north, Santanoni on the south, and Couchsachraga on the west.

Panther is a relatively easy jaunt from Times Square. Santanoni is another matter. It looms more than a mile away at the end of the

Santanoni Ridge. That height of land ascends more than 400 feet and is guarded every step of the way by tough, scruffy trees which have learned how to put up with incessant, year-round winds.

From Times Square, Couchsachraga projects the unknown. One cannot see the peak from the crossroads. Contour maps suggest that it is inconsequential; to the climber it is anything but. To reach it, one must descend some 800 feet into a col, then climb 300 feet to the summit over a series of frustrating knobs.

Much of the route to Couchsachraga leads through tangled blowdown, a product of the 1950 hurricane. The resulting debris was so bad, according to the Forty Sixers' first book, that it "meant a man could lose himself within feet of a highway and not be rescued." Hikers heading for Couchsachraga are miles away from a highway, not feet; an escape route through the Cold River region takes even longer than returning by the trail near Bradley Pond.

Such speculation lies in the future: the initial problem for hikers is to find the correct path leading west from Times Square.

Journal entry: Saturday, July 26, 1980. At first, Tom is confused as to direction since the ridge is thickly forested. Ben and I follow him as he scouts a short distance each way along the top, then points to a faint herd path descending west into the tangles. "That'll get us there," he states with conviction. The three of us plunge down the slope.

He has allowed us 10 minutes for half a lunch.

No more than a hundred yards downward, Couchsachraga comes into view for the first time. It appears to be an easy conquest, squatting like an old-fashioned, jumbo ice cream cone just beyond a sizeable, rounded bump dead ahead.

Couchsachraga *raises its diminutive snout a mile to the west from below the ridge connecting Panther with Santanoni.*

Easy? Perhaps. But Ben and I are tired. In effect, we have bested Panther and are headed into a forbidding wilderness. We have been on the road and the trail nine hours since leaving home. Before returning to our car, we'll hike another eight and a half miles for a total of more than 17 miles, climb an additional thousand feet including Panther, then repeat the 130-mile drive home.

And it looks like rain.

"This part is easy," Tom states as if reading our minds. In the sense that we are going downward, he is right. Ben and I decide to follow, for a while anyway, through thicket and thin.

Only 20 minutes after leaving the ridge, we near the top of the bump. If we can believe what I saw when we started off the ridge, this should be an easy conquest, with "Coochie" but a brief jaunt beyond.

Wrong, as usual. From the hump of the bump, we see that there are other ones between us and our target, which is as distant as ever.

The gurgle of a turgid stream offers refreshment. It's surprising how good dirt can taste when you're out of water.

The path dips precipitously into another col, then wanders aimlessly up and around a succession of prominences. The topographic map promises a flat, final approach to Couchsachraga; the actual climb is more like a roller coaster.

"Hey, cheer up, gang," says Tom. "We're almost there." The only other cheerful note comes from the birds. It's beyond me why they would choose to visit this desolate location.

We drag up to the summit cannister at 1:50 p.m. and share the other half of our sandwiches with the flies. I'm too tired to take more than a cursory glance around. No great loss: the mist is rolling in with a greater hint of rain.

Voices announce the arrival of two sturdy, confident hikers who are camped at Bradley Pond. They say they are Forty Sixers and have lost count of the peaks they have climbed. They plan to head west for Cold River, follow it northeast to Duck Hole, and then loop back south to Bradley.

Revolting. I have completed 37 peaks but am not even at first base in their league. Or Tom's either, for that matter. Tom senses our deflation. "Come on, Ben. You're half way through your 46. Let's go get the others!"

Twenty-three skidoo. And Panther looks like it is a million miles away.

Hikers do not come to Couchsachraga for the views. To be charitable, it is the most diminutive of the 46 Adirondack high peaks. In fact, more than a dozen peaks outside of that charmed circle are as high or higher. Also, Couchsachraga's summit is densely wooded; one can eke out tolerable views only to the south and toward the Santanoni-Panther ridge on the east.

For many years, climbers mostly approached from the Cold River region on the west. Among nature's mischievous pranks awaiting them were a tortuous swamp and a confusing patchwork of abandoned lumber roads leading to a blind search for the mountain. Frustrated hikers often found themselves by mistake on Little Couchsachraga or one of the other lesser peaks near the main summit.

Summit cannister on Couchsachraga is about to be engulfed by encroaching conifers. Black flies elevate head nets to high fashion.

Few climbers come from the west today. Those who do find it more confusing than ever because the old herd paths are overgrown. There are other changes, too. A park ranger has confirmed that plentiful moose droppings have been found on the slopes of Little Couchsachraga.

Hikers found an added reason for approaching Couchsachraga from the west in 1934 when they discovered an authentic hermit, Noah John Rondeau. He not only helped them find their way to climb the peak but welcomed them in his capacity as "Mayor of Cold River, pop. 1."

Beginning in 1915, Rondeau had served as an Adirondack guide in summers, then made his home in the woods during winters. But in 1928 he had a spat with the state Conservation Department. As a result, he took off for good to a wilderness area which was about as remote as one could find in the park.

Rondeau located his Hermitage at a high bluff on the Cold River some five miles southwest of Duck Hole. He used materials scrounged from old lumber camps to build crude huts, along with wigwams made of logs notched to fireplace length. His "city" included a Town Hall and a Hall of Records — containing the most crucial papers, toilet tissue — flower and vegetable gardens and, nearby, good views of not only Panther and Couchsachraga but the Sewards to the west.

Photos of the hermit show him dressed for the part: tattered clothes, floppy felt hat and a full beard. Yet he did not go completely native: visiting hikers recorded that he wore boots from L. L. Bean.

Rondeau had no use for calendars, radios and clocks. But near the end of each year, he strapped on snowshoes and headed west toward Corey's to stock up on supplies and visit with friends.

When Noah John set off for his annual visit to civilization in late November 1950, he noticed an ominous, rising wind whipping through Ouluska Pass, the col between Seward and Seymour mountains. Fortunately he was able to get through before the arrival of the hurricane which devastated so much of the high peaks. It also forced the closing of the Cold River region and ended Rondeau's life as a hermit. He died in Lake Placid in 1967 at the age of 84.

Noah John Rondeau, like Couchsachraga, was diminutive compared to his peers; he was barely five feet tall. Yet his memory looms large in the minds of those he welcomed while Mayor of Cold River. One can still spot remnants of his stay at the Hermitage: fragments of the Town Hall, a scattering of wild flowers, even a few peas in the garden.

His legend lives on, too, in a reconstruction of his Town Hall at the Adirondack Museum, Blue Mountain Lake.

Journal entry: Saturday, July 26, 1980. Our slow return over the roller coaster to the Santanoni-Panther ridge is not exhilarating. But, as at a carnival, a cold drink at a spring near the end of the ride lifts our spirits. We reach the ridge at four p.m.

In the sag before the final, brief push to Panther, we note a red rag marking what appears to be the main herd path leading down to Panther Brook. "We missed it coming up," says Tom. "But it'll be our quickest way down."

We sign in at the summit cannister, then flop on an open rock ledge 50 feet or so below. Santanoni soars at an intimidating angle on the south, while the chasm between us and Couchsachraga makes even that modest peak look fearsome. We note that more clouds are moving in from the west to blot out the Cold River region beyond it.

Henderson Mtn., a couple of miles east of Panther Mtn., was called Panther until the turn of the century, and MacNaughton Mtn., some three miles to the north, was called Henderson. The U.S. Geological Survey straightened things out in 1904, and Panther Mtn. gained its present name.

Regional preferences would have suggested the peak be called Mountain Lion if it were located in the Rockies, Puma in the southwest, Cougar in the northwest, and either Catamount or Painter in New England.

Summit of Panther *makes great viewing platform for Couchsachraga, center rear, Cold River region and the Sewards.*

All names refer to the same animal.

Any of the names would be justified in the high peaks, because in the last century the area was infested with panthers. "Amid these mountain solitudes," wrote Verplanck Colvin, "the panther has his den among the rocks, and rears his savage kittens undisturbed." During his work as state surveyor, Colvin told of being attacked by one of the beasts.

Officially, the last panther in the Adirondacks was killed by a bounty hunter in 1894. In the contiguous United States, there is a shrinking colony of panthers in southern Florida and a growing population in California. In the latter state, in fact, they have become a problem.

A hiker near San Diego and a jogger near Sacramento were killed by mountain lions in 1994. The following year, the *Los Angeles Times* said the state's fish and game department reported more than 350 serious mountain lion incidents — including attacks and threats to humans — since 1993.

Experts fear the animals may be losing their reputed shyness of humans. One reason, environmental writer Edward Hoagland asserted in *Walking the Dead Diamond River*, is that "They are susceptible to an odd kind of fascination with human beings." Often, he said, mountain lions will seek them out, "hanging about a campground or following a hiker out of curiosity, perhaps, circling around and bounding up on a ledge above to watch him pass."

Philip G. Terrie, Jr., who edited an update of Carson's *Peaks and People of the Adirondacks* in 1973, avowed that, "Practically no scientist will say with certainty that panthers are extinct in the Adirondacks." The Catamount Investigation Network, which conducts studies on the matter, recently said in *Adirondack Life* that, "Sightings of the large cat have been reported almost every year in locales across the park."

Tony Goodwin, editor of the ADK's current High Peaks Region guidebook, wrote in *Of the Summits, of the Forests*, that he "is quite certain that he saw a panther in 1983." And ADK's *Adirondac* editor, Neal Burdick, wrote in 1994 that a "12-week-old lion cub was shot on the southern edge of the Adirondacks in mid-January — the fourth such shooting since 1968."

The official line, he said, is that "these are escapees from or intentional releases by private owners." But, noted Burdick, conservation officials say privately they have seen a half dozen panthers in recent years.

There have also been increasing sightings of panthers in Maine. And in 1994, *Business Week* reported that the National Fish & Wildlife Forensics Laboratory "has just verified the good news" that "three catamount-like creatures were spotted bounding through the snow" in neighboring Vermont.

Good news for some, but perhaps a time for nail-biting by Adirondack high peak hikers. At the least, they ought to weigh the advice of that joyful American versifier, Ogden Nash:

"If called by a panther,
don't anther."

Journal entry: Saturday, July 26, 1980. *"I suggest we move out,"* Tom says, scanning the puff-balls building overhead. *"I want to be sure we hit the trail from Duck Hole by seven p.m." It is now 4:45 p.m.*

The new return path seems to plunge much more steeply through the dense woods, and in no time we reach the first faint seepage of Panther Brook. Herd paths trace either side, but for speed and ease of travel we mostly rock-hop down the middle.

Weariness forces some rest stops. At first, an occasional pinch of blue sky accents the loveliness of the brook. Then as we descend, the air takes on a growing milkiness. A rumble of thunder induces an increasing tempo of sprinkles, and gusts confirm what Emerson observed: "All the trees are wind-harps."

The now pelting rain lends an urgency to our descent. Ben and I put on the only protection we have — windbreakers — which are ineffectual, while Tom dons a new, full set of raingear. We slosh in a hurry down the trail, slowing only for log walkways, which have become slippery.

Almost as if programmed, the rain halts as we reach the car at 8:35 p.m. It is accompanied by a feeling of joy and relief. Tom, who now has climbed Couchsachraga and Panther three times, is sure to come back again. Ben and I may, but there is no problem if we do not: we have comquered these two peaks for the first time, the one time that counts.

Journal entry: Saturday, July 29, 1995. The hermit of our back-home neighborhood is gone.

Realistically, I suppose he was not a hermit. But he looked like one and he acted like one for the 10 years that I knew of him.

I used to look for the old gent every morning and evening on my way to and from work. He lived in what appeared to be a one-room shack in the town of Colonie, a bedroom community squeezed between Schenectady and Albany. His "home" was tucked into a grove of trees a few doors away from an old farm; both sites were across the street from a settled area.

The man was short like Noah John Rondeau, but portly and more neatly dressed, in work-clothes with suspenders. In summer, he sat near his house on an old, tubular-framed, springy metal chair, stubby pipe in mouth, companionable dog by his side.

The only time I saw him in winter was when he came out to shovel a path through the snowdrifts, or to go into a small outbuilding to the rear, possibly his version of Rondeau's House of Records. An oil drum on the outside of his house supplied fuel for heating; smoke from a tin stovepipe indicated the inside was cozy.

I never saw him with other people. And gradually, the burgeoning waves of houses began to flow into the farm fields behind his place. Then one day he was gone and, shortly thereafter, so was his house. I never learned if he left because a new housing development swallowed him up, or if he simply gave up when the developer's gilt-lettered sign went up nearby. Only a small patch of green — remnant of a garden in the midst of a grove of small trees — shows that he was ever there.

I never met Noah John Rondeau, who was gone before I explored the Cold River area. And I never met my "friend" on Vly Road in Colonie, who has been gone now for four years.

But I miss them both.

From Stony Creek Ponds: Seward Mtn., left, Mt. Donaldson and Mt. Emmons in center. Lesser peak at right is to the west of the range.

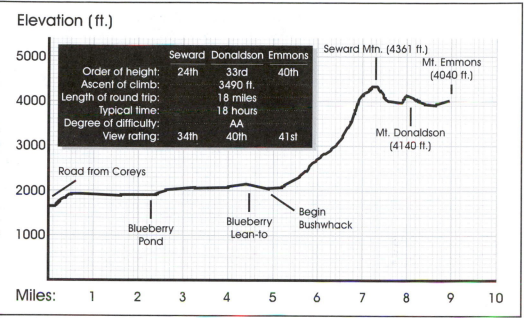

Elevation (ft.)

	Seward	Donaldson	Emmons
Order of height:	24th	33rd	40th
Ascent of climb:		3490 ft.	
Length of round trip:		18 miles	
Typical time:		18 hours	
Degree of difficulty:		AA	
View rating:	34th	40th	41st

Road from Coreys

Seward Mtn. (4361 ft.)

Mt. Emmons (4040 ft.)

Mt. Donaldson (4140 ft.)

Blueberry Pond

Blueberry Lean-to

Begin Bushwhack

Miles: 1 2 3 4 5 6 7 8 9 10

For contour trails, see U.S. Geological Survey map, pgs. 402-403.

39, 40, 41.
SEWARD, DONALDSON, EMMONS

Journal entry: Tuesday, July 29, 1980: A month ago, during a casual conversation with a neighbor who was a member of our ADK group that climbed Hough last year, I made a pact to join him for a try at the Sewards. His son, who is 11, and Ben, a year older, were to come along. We would pack in the first night, climb the group of three the next day, then sleep over again and finish Seymour, the last of the four Seward Mountains, the following day.

Doing four peaks in a three-day sweep seemed like a marvelous way to get the final act of my high peaks performance under way. Then I promptly forgot about it as Ben and I went about the tough business of climbing Cliff, Allen, Couchsachraga and Panther.

Today, three days before our agreed-upon date, the neighbor — Mindaugus Jatulis — calls and announces: "Tommy and I are all set. How about you and Ben?"

Sure. At least, Ben is: he just returned fully-equipped from a week at Boy Scout camp.

As for me, I have no sleeping bag, no pack or frame, no portable stove or utensils. Literally, I have nothing but the desire to act. As a

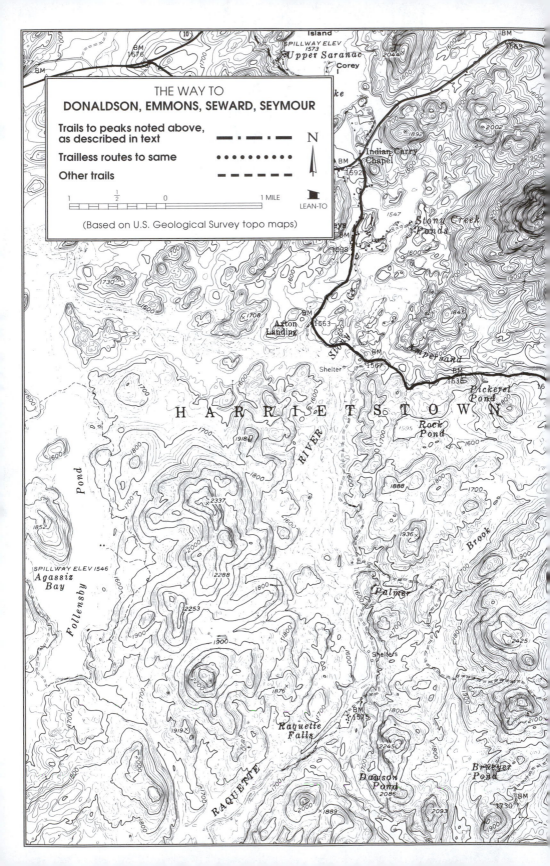

THE WAY TO
DONALDSON, EMMONS, SEWARD, SEYMOUR

Trails to peaks noted above,
as described in text   — · — · — · —

Trailless routes to same   · · · · · · · · · ·

Other trails   — — — — —

N

1   ½   0   1 MILE

LEAN-TO

(Based on U.S. Geological Survey topo maps)

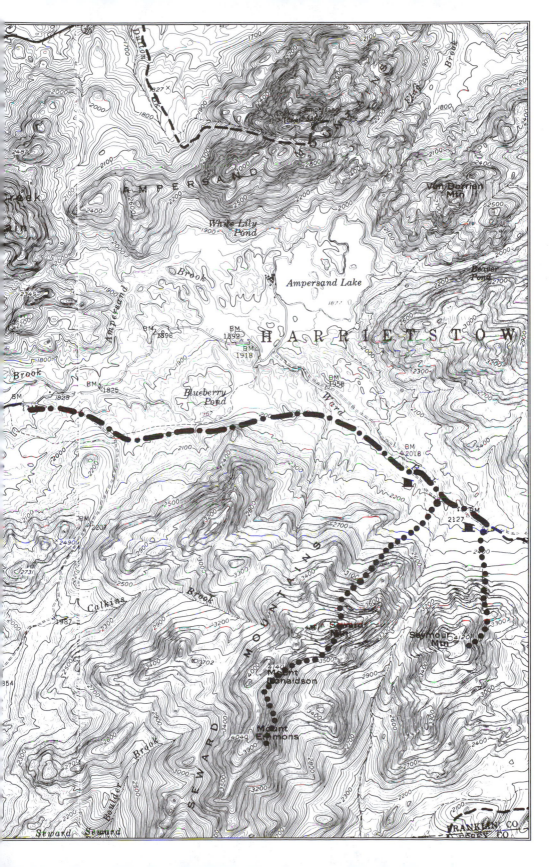

matter of fact, I have not camped out since my Army days with the infantry.

"No problem," says Mindy. "You can borrow my wife's pack frame and pad, share our stove, and use an old tent of mine that doesn't weigh much because it has no floor or side zippers. I'm sure you can scrounge the rest."

The rest was easy to assemble: my daughter Gretchen's Girl Scout sleeping bag, four plastic bags of camp food, a loaf of bread, and a jumbo sack of M&Ms.

Journal entry: Friday, August 1, 1980. *The prospect for this adventure is not promising. As we drive north to flank the Sewards from the west, we are overtaken by a violent thunderstorm.*

At Axton Landing, two miles south of our turnoff from Highway 3 and a mile south of the little settlement of Coreys, the curtain of storm clouds raises as if on cue. It is, however, still misty, hot, humid and threatening.

There is only one other car at the parking lot where the road ends and the trail begins, some six miles from the highway. Weekend or not, there are a lot of no-shows.

I don't dare mention it, but there are also no bugs.

Early exploration of the western Adirondack high peaks came in fits and starts. Pioneers found it hard enough to penetrate the foothills, let alone the interior.

One of the earliest settlers on Upper Saranac Lake, Jesse Corey, in the middle of the last century built a popular lodge on the site that bears his name, near the ancient, mile-long Indian Carry between Stony Creek Ponds and Upper Saranac Lake. It's one of many portages in the network of waterways throughout the so-called Lake Country, so popular with canoeists today.

As the name of the canoe "carry" indicates, the Indians were there first. In fact, the western region was almost unknown to the civilized world before the 1830s.

In 1836, New York state appointed Professor Ebenezer Emmons of Williams College to conduct a geological survey of northern New York state, including the Adirondacks. Emmons never got around to climbing Seward, but his survey provided the first description of the peak, as seen from Long Lake.

Seward appeared to be a cluster of mountains, and in one of the peaks, there was "a remarkable white spot, which is always distinctly seen when the mountains are not enveloped in fog." "Great eye," the Indians called it.

Emmons estimated the height of Seward to be 5,100 feet. That erroneously put it in the lofty company of Algonquin and Marcy.

The following year, Emmons was among a group of scientists who made the first recorded ascent of Marcy. Another member of that party was William C. Redfield, who had first sighted the "High Peak of the Essex" in 1836. On his way back to Tahawus after climbing Marcy, Redfield found traces of "an Indian trail going from Lakes Sanford and Henderson and the Preston Ponds to the headwaters of the Raquette River."

The trail passed to the northeast of the Seward Mountain Range. There is no record of Indians climbing any of the mountains in that range. In fact, no one knows of any permanent Indian settlements in the Adirondacks.

The first recorded climb of Seward Mtn. was made in 1870 by Verplanck Colvin and his guide, an ex-hermit named Alvah Dunning. They paddled down Long Lake and up the Cold River, then took two days to climb several prominences before reaching the summit of Seward. Records are fuzzy but it's likely that, in the process, they made the first ascent of Mt. Emmons and Mt. Donaldson.

The day before topping off, Colvin voiced the refrain of many climbers on today's trailless peaks: "The balsam trees continued to dwindle in height until we stood upon an open crest. The world seemed all below us; but northward, half a mile away, a lofty summit reared itself, grizzly with dead and withered balsams, struggling to keep their hold on the rock that here and there looked out gloomily; it was Mt. Seward. Between us and it was an abyss through which clouds floated."

In later years, others have suggested that Colvin may not have been first. A good case has been made that in 1863 a geologist doing field work for the Smithsonian Institution, Arnold Henry Guyot, or at least his nephew and climbing companion, Ernest Sandoz, surmounted Seward from a base at the McIntyre Iron Works. And, in 1872, the hunter and guide John Cheney wrote to E. R. Wallace, author of *Guide to the Adirondacks*: "I know of no one, except myself, and four others with me, that ever ascended Mt. Seward, and this was about 25 years ago."

In any event, during the eight decades following Colvin's ascent, an average of only one person per year climbed the Sewards along with all of the other 42 Adirondack high peaks. That slow pace stopped dead when the great hurricane of 1950 hit the Adirondacks. The Sewards and the Cold River region were devastated more than any other area in the state, and as a result were closed to hikers for five years.

An Albany newspaperman named Samuel H. Hammond was one of the first to urge that the Adirondacks be protected from exploitation. In 1854, he wrote in *Hills, Lakes and Forest Streams*, "There should be left some broad sweep of wild woods, where a man can get free of the sights and sounds of the clearin's, and look upon nater, as it came from the hands of the great Creator, with all the wild animals, and nateral things that belonged to it in the times of old."

It was clear to Hammond that explorers were not the only ones to set their sights on the western Adirondack high peaks.

Loggers began operating near the mouth of the lower Raquette River around 1810 and gradually worked their way up the waterways, their highway system for transporting timber. By 1846 the state designated the Raquette River as a "public highway" throughout its entire length. This included the segment of the river formed by Long Lake, which at one time was called Wide River.

At about the same time, logging began on a large scale in the interior of the mountains. By the turn of the century, lumber roads reached up beyond the 3,000-ft. level in the Sewards. By 1920, fortunately, the state purchased the area containing the four high peaks, and lumbering halted.

Each year, there is less evidence of that logging. The forest is reclaiming a big lumber camp clearing in Ouluska Pass, along with outlying tote roads. The clearest evidence remains in fire truck roads and horse trails which follow old logging routes.

The horse trails parallel and criss-cross many hiking trails. The state maintains two horseback loops from the trailhead near Coreys: one is 13 miles long and the other is a 32-mile segment through the Cold River region. A peripheral trail from the latter extends to Newcomb.

Today, thanks to new growth and the remains of the hurricane of 1950, high peaks explorers will find the Sewards as challenging as Colvin did a century and a quarter ago. And those who climb the four mountains in the range will confirm the judgment of the first ADK guidebook: this is "wild forest country."

Journal entry: Friday, August 1, 1980. Mindy says I'll get used to my pack frame in a short while. But my first short while, about 15 minutes on the Blueberry foot trail, ushers in slippery log walkways followed by a very steep rise.

According to our bathroom scale, Ben's pack weighs 23 pounds and mine 28, plus the weight of various items thrown in at the last minute. Mindy carries the bulk of their gear, so Tommy needs only a day pack. Ben's pack is grossly out of proportion to his frame; I just hope his skinny little body can take it.

It's a good thing his mother is not along. I can hear her now: "What are you doing to my little boy?" I could use a little sympathy myself; I'm not sure my 125-pound frame can take it either.

In a little more than a mile, though, we rest at the Calkins Brook horse trail crossing and feel better after taking salt pills. And, our foot trail begins to level off with occasional, pleasant glimpses of Blueberry

Pond to the north, on our left. It cranks me up for one more dress rehearsal before tomorrow's performance.

Ben senses my apprehension. In the gathering murk at six p.m., he conjures up the night: Will there be animals? Snakes? Or what?

"Don't worry, Ben," says Mindy. "This is gentle wilderness."

It is my pack, however, and not apparitions which causes me to fall behind. Then, from beyond a rise ahead that's out of sight, comes for me the sweetest soliloquy of the forest: Ben anxiously asking, "Where's my father?"

I catch up and haul my heavy thoughts to the Blueberry lean-to. It's empty, so Ben and I don't

Blueberry lean-to is a welcome sight after four-plus-mile trek from Axton Landing. Brooding weather indicates the shelter will be needed.

have to struggle with the pup tent. All of us unload, exhausted, have a quick, cold trail dinner and fall into our sleeping bags. It is 10 p.m.

We're all restless and have trouble getting to sleep, with me the last to go. In the old days, we would have had our guide cut fragrant balsam boughs as underpads for our sleeping bags. But, of course, in these days that is an environmental no-no.

To keep my mind off the hard floor of the lean-to, I stare through the protective opening to the stage of the forest beyond. Then the show begins and I have a front row seat.

Act I: Heat lightning, largo tempo, builds a soundless overture. As it draws nearer, the alternating blackness and glowing silhouettes heighten the sights and dialogue of the wilderness. It makes clear what Adirondack writer Charles Dudley Warner had in mind when he said on a similar excursion: "We are prisoners of the night." And, relating to his shelter: "The world is only ten feet square."

At first I think I hear a bear climbing the foremost tree to snatch our food bag suspended from above. But it is only Mindy, grunting as he turns and gets tangled in his sleeping bag. Then the take-off of a ruffed grouse breaks the silence from the opposite end of the lean-to; it was startled when a freshening breeze blew one of our packs against the side wall.

And what I think is thunder is only Tommy, reacting to his hay fever.

Act II: A kettledrum of real thunder now begins, followed by the staccato of rain. I am tempted to awaken Ben, because at home he and I like to watch approaching storms from our upstairs window. I don't, however, because even the flash of a brilliant bolt does not disturb his deep sleep. He will need the rest for our start up Seward.

Act III: The play is totally absorbing, and suddenly the hard bed is soft. In my mind, I shift from one to another of the truly great beds in which I have slept — my grandparents' feather bed, back in a little town of 600 in Iowa, made inviting in winter by a hot brick wrapped in flannel; the luxurious comforters on the straw mats of an R&R resort hotel in Atami, Japan; and my first, real, state-side bed in San Francisco after returning from nearly two years in the Pacific with the Army.

There is only one sour note from the orchestra: the whir of a lone mosquito.

The curtain of sleep falls.

Journal entry: Saturday, August 2, 1980. Mindy Jatulis awakens us at 7 a.m. with the bustle of breakfast; he has prepared hot items for himself and Tommy. I discover, too late, that the food packets I brought must first be boiled in water, then fried for 20 minutes; Ben and I have neither a frying pan nor the time. We each wolf down half a deviled ham sandwich, and pack the rest for trail lunches.

The rain has stopped, but there are still grumbles of thunder.

The start of the herd path to Seward is easy to find. From the Blueberry lean-to, a short hike brings us to a clearing where our trail joins the Ward Brook truck road; the latter comes in from private lands on the north near Ampersand Lake and continues nearly six miles to Duck Hole on the southeast. Seward's well-worn herd path begins a tenth of a mile on the right beyond the trail junction with the road.

At first, the path lazes up the left side of the stream coming off of Seward. The flow, alternately placid and rushing, reminds me of Panther Brook — gorgeous, and refreshing. The weather is very hot and humid, but so far there are no bugs.

Ben, in the lead, spots where the path crosses the brook and leads us on a moderate ascent through second growth. Before long, the path tilts upward at a sharp angle through the dense blowdown.

Summit cannister *on Seward Mtn. holds notebook for climbers to register names for the Forty Sixer Club. Son Ben checks gear with Tommy Jatulis; his father signs in.*

Little by little, we gain on the ridge looming on each side. A glimpse of the valley far below is promising, as are fleeting patches of sun and blue. We can see Whiteface on the northeast and Ampersand Mountain to the north, with the Saranac lakes beyond.

As if on cue, Ben and Tommy exit upward. Soon, their shouts tell us Seward's cannister is in sight. Mindy and I drag up to the summit, which like most trailless peaks is covered with scrub trees. It is 11:25 a.m., three and a half hours from the time we left the road.

One of three previous climbers has left a vivid scrawl in the summit cannister: Eddie Stone. It looks like the autograph of a harried stage star, dashed off on the eve of a premiere. His signature is followed by a cryptic "#42" — his current total of high peaks climbed.

Seward Mtn. was named for William H. Seward, Secretary of State in President Lincoln's cabinet during the Civil War. In the same post in 1867, he negotiated the purchase of Alaska from Russia. It's hard to believe that at the time it was called "Seward's Folly." A half century earlier, Alexander Macomb had paid eight pence an acre for his huge land holdings in the Adirondacks; Seward paid just two cents an acre.

Naming of the mountain, however, came for Seward's earlier service as governor of New York state and U.S. senator in Washington.

Verplanck Colvin climbed Seward a second time in 1872, two years after his first ascent. By mistake, he climbed Seymour Mtn. first, then was forced to descend into Ouluska Pass, an Indian word for "a place of shadows." He then made the rugged climb up Seward. The view from the summit, he reported, "was magnificent, yet differing from other of the loftier Adirondacks in that no clearings were discernible; wilderness everywhere; lake on lake, river on river, mountain on mountain, numberless..."

Seward offers great views of the Lake Country: Long Lake beyond Emmons with Lake Lila farther west; Tupper Lake due west from Seward; the Saranacs on the north; and this side of them, both the lake and the mountain named Ampersand. From a sizeable boulder a hundred yards south of the summit, one also gains a new insight into the bulk of the 46 high peaks when viewed from the west: they look like strangers, with different slides and different profiles.

Journal entry: Saturday, August 2, 1980. While Mindy and the boys crane for a better view of the other two leads in this mountainous play, I assume the role which suits me best: sitting and munching on trail snacks. I can't help but think about Colvin's trips here.

His reports to the legislature were replete with problems: "clambering upon hands and knees," "wetted to the skin, waist high," "chilled us through our wet clothing," "out of provisions," and so on. He would have made a great dramatic actor.

Yet I have a growing fondness and admiration for that dedicated explorer. In his report on Seward, he laid down arguments for the eventual creation of the Forest Preserve, and was the first proponent to record the term "Adirondack Park."

Adirondack author and editor Philip G. Terrie calls Seward Mtn. "one of the most remote spots in the park, maybe in the eastern United States."

The only sign of life is a White-throated Sparrow which cocks its perky, yellow and black-striped crown and talks to me with its plaintive whistle, "Poor Sam Peabody, Peabody." Whoever has heard a Whitethroat in this kind of setting, said T. Morris Longstreth when he explored the Adirondacks in the last century, "has been bound with invisible strings to the wilderness."

I join the others on an open ledge to the south of Seward's summit to assess our best route to Donaldson and Emmons. When Ben and I stood on Couchsachraga, we concluded that the trip would be an easy romp of a couple of miles along the level ridge of the Seward Range. But that's not what it looks like from here.

There are several sizeable, mountainous bumps between Seward and Donaldson, with a cavernous valley between them. Veterans advise climbers not to head for a high ridge, called West Seward, though it's supposed to boast spectacular views. Instead, we follow the herd path a short distance to where it plunges steeply to the south.

At first, it appears we are taking an escape route off the ridge into Ouluska Pass. But after a quarter of a mile or so, the herd path levels off and heads west toward Donaldson. We see the reason for the detour as we pass below the sheer cliffs of West Seward.

From Donaldson, *climbers can see where the herd path from Seward, right, dips south below cliffs of West Seward, left. Donaldson is named for famed Adirondack historian.*

A steep haul of a half mile brings us to the summit of Donaldson and its trailless cannister. Eddie Stone's signature has degenerated into a broad squiggle.

It seems a shame to me that the man who wrote A History *of the* Adirondacks, *the first and only one of its kind, could not savor the view from his namesake mountain. But historian Alfred L. Donaldson, who left New York City to come to the mountains for his health, was not well enough to climb the peaks. I find it incredible that an invalid could complete such a monumental, two-volume project.*

Mt. Donaldson's summit is tiny, but its views seem as good as Seward's. The sight of Marcy and its friends basking in the afternoon sun to the east is breathtaking. So is the dazzling array of lakes spread out below us from an open ledge on the west side of the summit.

Try as I may, I cannot spot any of the Great Camps built near the lakes on the west not long after the Civil War by transplanted city folks: the Durants, and the Lehmans, Morgans, Rockefellers, Vanderbilts, Whitneys, and so on. Nor can I track below us on the east the 132-mile Northville-Lake Placid trail, completed by the ADK in 1924, which winds through the Cold River Valley.

I ask my favorite fisherman, Ben, to come look for a "Lost Pond" among the lakes. Another New York City resident named Henry Abbott, who fled to the Adirondacks every summer for more than 50 years, told his friends about it in a series of tiny volumes called The Birch Bark Books.

Summit of Emmons offers limited views, including this look-back to Seward, some two miles away. Hurricane blowdown makes it slow going.

In his 1915 edition, he told of finding a legendary pond somewhere below where we are now standing. In its clear, cold water, he wrote, "The trout climbed out, stood on their tails, and reached for the fly long before it hit the water." All the other lakes shine up to us. But Abbott's Lost Pond is still lost.

Half-sunny skies lend encouragement for our final assault on Emmons. This time, the path dips deeply to the west into a col. Breaks in the blowdown give occasional glimpses of our target. Strange — the mountain rises to a sharp point, unlike any view it has shown from afar. Typically Adirondack: each side shows a different character.

Emmons' summit could be a theatre in the round if there weren't so many trees sitting in front of us. But Ben and I do manage to spot our recent conquests, Couchsachraga and Panther, which lie submissive on the southeast. The next peak we will try, Seymour, broods alone a couple of miles to the northeast. Looking back, we see Seward, now blotched with shadows; it's beautiful in a way, like the streaked face of a child devouring a treat.

We register our names in the summit cannister. Eddie Stone's signature covers half a page.

It's appropriate that the mountain named for the renowned geologist should be placed next to Mt. Donaldson. In his two-volume history, Donaldson noted that Emmons not only gave the Adirondacks its name, but "was the first to herald authoritatively the scientific wonders, the scenic beauties, and the natural resources of the region."

Emmons displayed a quirky side in one of his reports to the state. The Adirondack hills, he averred, "will afford good pasturage, and herds of cattle and flocks of sheep may one day give life and animation where the silence of the day is broken only by the rustling of the wind through an unbroken forest." It is clear that Ebenezer Emmons never climbed Mt. Emmons.

Journal entry: Saturday, August 2, 1980. When the Marshall brothers and their guide climbed Mt. Emmons in June 1925, they became the first to climb all 46 high peaks of the Adirondacks.

Mt. Emmons is the end of our journey, too. Sort of. First, however, the four of us have to re-climb two tough peaks on on our way back. Then, Ben and I must climb five more peaks to complete the 46.

After a few minutes, Mindy says, "It's 2:20 p.m. We'd better go. Tommy and I have no flashlights." Good point: we'll be lucky to reach the road by 8:30 p.m. Ben and I have flashlights, but it will be less risky if all of us get to our seats while the house lights are still up.

Mindy also announces, "This will be enough for me without doing Seymour tomorrow. I have to get up early the day after and go to work."

At the bottom of the col before Donaldson, Mindy notices that his Melton shirt jacket has disappeared from his pack. "I'm going back for it," he announces.

Tommy remains with us and, to cheer him up, Ben plays a fractured tune on his harmonica. He then gestures grandly at the peaks through the trees: "Aren't the Adirondacks beautiful?" But Tommy's mind is not on the peaks. He echoes Ben's earlier refrain: "Where's my father?" Mindy has been gone a half hour.

Then, Mindy appears with a sheepish grin. "It was on the summit. But twice while returning I started down the escape route to Ouluska Pass which is very steep. The last time, I went down far

Who can resist *throwing a stick from a perch 4,100 feet in the air? Ben watches his hiking companion toss one west from Donaldson.*

enough to see Duck Hole before I realized my mistake.

The open summit on the west overlook of Donaldson's false summit gives us a welcome rest and a sweeping panorama through the soft haze. The threat of rain has vanished.

Not so the bugs, which come front and center to put on a show of their own — you might say, a revival. Ben and I don our head nets. Tommy and Mindy have none so they make do with frantic stage gestures, swatting and slapping. Then we begin the long loop down and up to Seward.

On its summit, the views, even with head nets, are lovely, as through a scrim. Mindy is unimpressed; insect bites have swollen his ears to half again their normal size. So we limit our encore to five minutes' rest. My reluctant thespian, the sparrow, has left the theatre.

Dusk descends along with us. Finally, our flashlights penetrate the growing darkness to identify the end of the herd path.

At the lean-to, which is empty, we heat up beef stew. I doubt that any playgoer at Sardi's, before or after the show, has savored a better meal.

Ben and Tommy zip into their bags even before Mindy and I begin to clean up. Ben had promised to play his harmonica tonight, but cancelled the act on short notice. It's just as well; an incessant drumbeat of rain begins. It brings, as Thomas Merton said, the talk that rain makes: that "wonderful, unintelligible, perfectly innocent speech, the most comforting speech in the world."

Journal entry: Sunday, August 3, 1980. *Instant macaroni is not bad for breakfast, if you're hungry. Ben agrees that the rain is reason enough to save Seymour for another day.*

As we shoulder our packs to leave the lean-to in mid-morning, prospects brighten. The rain diminishes and the others urge me to assume

Hiking builds hunger. *Even the most plebeian dishes seem fit for the gods when you "come home." Ben, left, digs in at the lean-to with Tommy Jatulis and his father.*

the lead role on our way out. It's a nice psychological lift: I'm no longer the drag.

One of the reasons I started hiking was to strengthen my back following an injury. Hiking hasn't changed my weight much — for decades, it's hovered around 125. But it's helped me become strong and confident in the high peaks. I could never have handled a horrendous pack like this on earlier hikes.

We sign out at the trailhead at 12:50 p.m. The solitary Sewards have lived up to their reputation: in two full days we have not seen a soul.

What's changed in the high peaks from the first pioneers to the present? Not much, in spite of all the incursions.

Alfred Billings Street, who wrote two books on his Adirondack travels in the 1850s and '60s, expressed his impressions in poetry:

> "The wilderness has vanished like a curl
> From nature's brow, save where the grand peaks
> Of the stern Adirondach (sic) challenge heaven."

Longstreth, that latter-day Baedeker, reinforced the impression in 1917 when he wrote in his book on the Adirondacks that it is "so extensive that no one can know it thoroughly, so forbidding that only the accomplished can know parts of it intimately [and] only the most foolhardy will seek to know it all."

One might suspect that Jay Summerson led his group of Adirondack Mountain Club hikers to the Sewards during Longstreth's days, when he reported: "I'm soaking my weary feet in Epsom salts and reflecting on this particular long Saturday jaunt...one of the most difficult days I've encountered."

Yet his report appeared in the August/September 1994 issue of the Schenectady ADK's *Lookout*. In the spring of the same year, George Hrubenak reported to the ADK's *Adirondac* magazine that it took his party 22 hours to complete the Sewards: "A blinding snow storm in August slowed us down to a snail's pace as we walked through the night with flashlights to get out."

One of the original Forty Sixers, Bob Marshall, felt that wild scenery in the Adirondacks compared to great works of art. Roderick Nash, in his book, *Wilderness and the American Mind*, recalled that someone once asked Marshall how many wilderness areas America needed.

His reply: "How many Brahms' symphonies do we need?"

Seymour Mtn. from Mt. Emmons. Shoulder of the Sawtooth Range is at left.

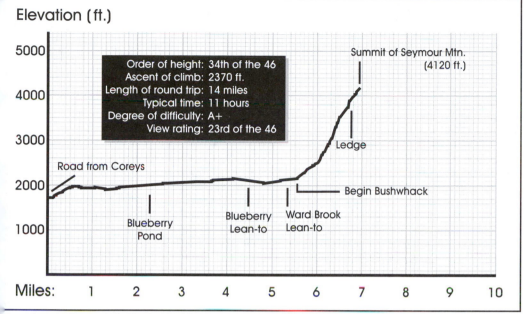

Elevation (ft.)

Order of height: 34th of the 46
Ascent of climb: 2370 ft.
Length of round trip: 14 miles
Typical time: 11 hours
Degree of difficulty: A+
View rating: 23rd of the 46

Summit of Seymour Mtn.
(4120 ft.)

Road from Coreys

Ledge

Begin Bushwhack

Blueberry
Pond

Blueberry
Lean-to

Ward Brook
Lean-to

Miles: 1 2 3 4 5 6 7 8 9 10

r contour trails, see U.S. Geological Survey map, pgs. 402-403.

42.
SEYMOUR

Journal entry: Saturday, August 9, 1980. From all reports, this mountain appears to be a duty climb that's of interest only to those who want to become Adirondack Forty Sixers.

Club members mention it as an afterthought to the other three Sewards. Even Tom Stanwood said, "There's nothing to it." But he neglected to tell us if that was good, bad or what.

Ben and I decide to tackle Seymour in one day rather than packing in for an overnight. That will make it a long hike: five and half miles to the base of the mountain before the climb begins. To get an early start, I make a reservation at Marion Biesemeyer's Mountain House on East Hill Road, some three miles up from Keene.

Mrs. Biesemeyer, chatting with two other couples in the parlor of the main house, approves of our target. "That's nice," she says. But she does not tie the sentiment to Seymour.

One of the husbands joins me on the porch of the house to share night air and mountain thoughts. He and his wife have brought their children here from Pennsylvania for many years. But this year the siblings balked, so he and his wife will hike the hills alone.

"You're lucky," he says, "living so close to the Adirondacks." He talks knowingly of the peaks, but has never heard of Seymour.

At least we know that the mountain is in rarified company. Seymour stands next to peaks named for the two best known Adirondack explorers and the park's first and only complete historian. Fortunately, Ben is a know-it-all when it counts. He parrots the current ADK guidebook: Horatio Seymour was "several times governor of New York." But that's all it says, he reports.

Before turning in at our cabin, we savor the fading yet stirring silhouettes of the Great Range, the Crows, and Cascade and Porter.

Journal entry: Sunday, August 10, 1980. *It's cloudy and cool at five a.m. when we turn at the Elm Tree Inn in Keene to head west on Rt. 73. Pity the proprietor: only a stump remains of the monster tree which gave its name to the inn wrapped around it. It was 80 feet tall and five feet in diameter at the base when it succumbed to Dutch Elm Disease in September 1974.*

The weather brightens and a gorgeous sunrise greets us in Lake Placid. But no one else is up to enjoy it. The only signs of life are two hawks circling above the turn-off at Coreys. There are just two cars at the trailhead: another measure of the lure of Seymour?

I tell Ben: let's go meet our mysterious partner for today and get it over with. It's like going on a blind date. And I'm not well dressed for the occasion — my boots are moldy from our trip here last weekend.

No more than a mile up the trail, we meet two young men and a young woman on their way out. "We've been four weeks at Duck Hole as instructors in wilderness training," says one of the men. The girl smiles: "I've forgotten what a shower feels like. But I'm going to find out real soon."

They have hiked by Seymour twice; it is the dominant peak to the west of Duck Hole. But none of them knows anything about the mountain.

Blueberry lean-to, our home away from home a week ago, is deserted. So is Ward Brook lean-to, about a mile beyond on the road to Duck Hole. And there is no sign of anyone as we leave the road on the far side of the first stream beyond the lean-to, and head south up the herd path toward Seymour.

It is like being invited to a party where nobody else comes.

Ben leads, as on our climb of Seward. The path has been well-travelled, but the way is still tricky because of misleading side branches. The initial grade is easy.

The ascent of Seymour marks an astounding turn of events for me. Adirondack literature I've read over the past 14 years has portrayed this area as a forbidding unknown, as if it were the end of the earth. Up until last weekend, I hesitated to tackle it alone.

Yet here we are, six miles from the nearest public road, and heading up in the midst of the trailless wilderness. Worst of all, from what I can gather, the peak promises little or nothing to the conqueror.

Not quite. After a leisurely climb of little more than a half mile, we reach a steep slide that the guidebook tells us is the best route to the summit. It is a mini-slide in some respects because it rarely broadens to more than 20 or 30 feet. But it becomes apparent as we progress that it is major in length, like the route up Macomb.

Eventually, it becomes so steep that we are forced to find paths around it. But until then, the footing is mostly solid rock instead of the loose debris on Macomb.

As we climb, the views behind us to the north are reward enough: first Ampersand Mountain and Ampersand Lake, then the jagged excitement of the Sawtooth Range.

Unlike last weekend, the weather cooperates. It's brisk and sunny with a speckle of lazy, fluffy clouds. Our blind date is turning out better than we expected. The only flaw shows up in the flies.

The views grow better as we climb. It's surprising that climbers haven't raved about Seymour; it can't be that they've been here on rotten days that all climbers have. The Marshalls rated its view 30th of the 46; I'd notch it up that scale.

I'd lower the rating, however, for that premier

Seymour slide *is best route to summit after initial half mile through a maze of herd paths. Slide path is narrow but steep most of the way.*

East from Seymour, high peaks parade their presence: MacIntyre Range at left, Marcy left center, then Skylight, Redfield and Allen. Duck Hole is in center below.

promoter of the Adirondacks in the middle of the last century, the Reverend William H. H. Murray. In Adventures in the Wilderness, *he wrote: "The black fly...like the Gorgon of old, is a myth — a monster existing only in men's feverish imagination."*

At 10:45 a.m., the black flies win out over imagination. Ben and I don head nets, and a half hour later top off on the ridge which, as usual, is not the summit we expected. The latter beckons like a close-cropped topnotch an eighth of a mile and a couple of hundred feet higher to the southwest. The spectacular facade of Seward and Donaldson frame it on the right.

A 15-minute stroll brings us to the summit cannister, which is shrouded by stunted trees. But a short walk beyond leads to glorious open views: busy peaks on the east clustered around those two big, brood hens, Marcy and Algonquin; the other three Sewards on the west; and to the south, Long Lake and other bodies of water which twinkle in the soft folds of the lower hills.

It is partly the great day, I suppose, but this peak is one of the loveliest either Jim or Ben and I have visited. It is like discovering that your suspect blind date is an absolute knockout.

It's nice for a change to find an Adirondack peak named for a New York state governor who actually visited the area. Verplanck Colvin said Horatio Seymour was an "explorer" because he ventured into the area in all seasons.

None of the other governors were familiar with the peaks which graced their names: Dix, Marcy, Seward and Wright. Also, the mountain we now know as Marshall was originally named by Colvin for Governor DeWitt Clinton, another no-show.

Even if Seymour Mtn. had not been named for him, the governor would have been remembered for tenacity. He was nominated for the top state office six times and elected twice. He ran for president in 1868, but lost to a more popular figure, Civil War hero Gen. Ulysses S. Grant.

Later, Seymour responded to Colvin's call to protect the Adirondacks, and was named head of a state commission to see if a public park was feasible. Colvin served as his secretary.

Ironically, Seymour is best known in Adirondack literature for escorting Amelia M. Murray, the maid of honor to Britain's Queen Victoria, on a tour from Elizabethtown to Boonville in 1855. When staying overnight at a place called Arnolds's Farm near the Fulton Chain of Lakes, the visiting Lady discovered that the Adirondacks were still primitive.

"There," as Lady Murray related in one of her letters, "we found Mrs. Arnold and six daughters. These girls, aged from twelve to twenty, were placed in a row against one wall of the shanty, with looks so expressive of astonishment, that I felt puzzled to account for their manner, till their mother informed us they had never before seen any other woman than herself!"

Seymour also had tenuous ties to one of the most extraordinary gatherings in the Adirondacks, some 10 miles to the west of Seymour Mtn. The man who guided him on the Murray trip, "Uncle Mart" Moody, later served at what came to be known as Philosophers Camp at Follensby Pond. It was so named because of the towering intellects of the visitors, including Ralph Waldo Emerson, Louis Agassiz and James Russell Lowell.

In the summer of 1858, the group canoed from Lower Saranac Lake to the south end of Upper Saranac Lake, and portaged down the Indian Carry to Stony Creek Ponds. From there, they headed west on the Raquette River and, some three miles beyond Axton Landing, headed south on

Long Lake peeps over the south shoulder of Emmons some eight miles to the southwest.

the outlet of Follensby Pond. The gathering might have been even more illustrious if the poet Henry Wadsworth Longfellow had accepted an invitation to join them.

But as the artist William James Stillman recounted of the occasion, Longfellow inquired, "Is it true that Emerson is going to take a gun?" When told that he was, the poet's rejoinder was, "Then someone will be shot!" And, said Stillman, Longfellow would talk no more of going.

You can't see Follensby Pond from Seymour Mtn. because Seward is in the way. Yet the image of the inquiring minds that descended on the pond is kept as fresh as ever through their literary and artistic works.

The woods on Seymour's summit block out the view to the north. But it's made up for by a fine, flat, open ledge a hundred yards or so back down the ridge — a "big, bare rock," Bob Marshall called it. On a clear day, the ledge magnifies by a hundred-fold the small-screen view one gets from the lowlands.

Dead ahead some three miles to the north of Seymour is Ampersand Mountain, while the Sawtooth Mountains live up to their name against the nearby sky. Peeping over the right shoulder of the latter range is Whiteface. And another three miles or so beyond Ampersand are the Saranac lakes, splattered across the checkerboard of farms which slope gently toward the St. Lawrence River and the Canadian borderlands.

Cradled near the Seymour side of Ampersand Mountain is its namesake lake. It was here that Stillman established in 1859 the Adirondack Club, on the shores of what Henry Van Dyke, author and educator of a later era, called "the wildest and most beautiful of all the Adirondack waters."

Ampersand Lake and mountain of the same name nestle to the north of open ledge below Seymour's summit. Head net keeps black flies at bay.

Stillman intended it to be a permanent gathering site for the eminent campers who had vacationed with him the year before at Follensby Pond. But the growing turmoil of the Civil War disrupted their plans, and the successor to the Philosophers Camp faded into oblivion in a couple of years.

One could hardly call any of their group veteran outdoorsmen. Instead, they sought the kind of freedom the Adirondack hiker gains today when, in the words of Emerson, "the knapsack of custom falls off his back with the first step he takes into these precincts."

Journal entry: Sunday, August 10, 1980. Too late, I realize that Ben and I would have had a great view of Follensby Pond last weekend when we topped off the Sewards, which are half again as close as Seymour. But even if we had thought of it then, I'm sure I would have been too tired to look and ruminate.

Those notable gents at the Philosophers Camp are long gone. But my guess is that they were just like the rest of us, who pack in habits that shape our characters.

It wouldn't surprise me, for example, if Emerson had tried to convert his campmates to one of his favorite intellectual concepts called Transcendentalism. God pervaded all nature, he believed, and could be discovered by anyone who devoted himself to plain living and high thinking.

Remote Follensby may have been a godsend for Emerson. It was the ideal place to vindicate his decision 14 years earlier to pass up an offer for a real-time test of Transcendentalism in a utopian New England community called Brook Farm. That endeavor failed within three years. The reason, according to the farm's founder, was "human selfishness and the lack of business capacity."

On the other hand, Emerson could have forgotten all about Transcendentalism at Follensby. A 20th century reviewer of his works concluded that, "sometimes, like Icarus, he approaches too close to the sun, and there is a crash, but the noise is drowned in his eloquence, and soon he is up again, soaring as though nothing had happened."

So who's perfect? We can still admire Emerson, whether or not we agree with what he said. His prose was graced with simplicity, economy and power.

I can also picture Agassiz, the famed geologist and teacher, pointing with excitement at the features of the peaks around him. They confirmed his discovery that glaciers once covered much of the planet, including the Adirondacks.

Son Ben, who's a serious student at 12 years of age, could benefit from the companionship of an Agassiz. Van Wyck Brooks called the

Saranac lakes *sparkle beyond low mountains to the west of Ampersand, at right. The open ledge on Seymour tempts hikers to laze and dream on perfect midsummer days.*

naturalist the "Johnny Appleseed of Science," who "shovelled into the minds of the young precisely what they did not learn in college."

I'm not quite sure where to place their companion, the poet James Russell Lowell. His great line, "What is so rare as a day in June," settles in nicely with Ben and me today, even though it's August. But nobody reads much of his other works any more because they glorify 19th century icons which are no longer relevant.

If it were up to me to invite the group back to Philosophers Camp, I'd replace Lowell with Dr. Edward Livingston Trudeau, who founded the first U.S. tuberculosis sanitarium 13 miles north of here at Saranac Lake. His Autobiography suggests that he was influenced by patients such as Robert Louis Stevenson and Alfred Donaldson, the Adirondack historian.

Trudeau captured perfectly my feelings as I loll with Ben on the sun-drenched rock ledge of Seymour: "Many a beautiful afternoon...I sat facing the ever-changing phases of light and shadow on the imposing mountain panorama at my feet, and dreamed the dreams of youth."

Ben brings me back to the present: "Dad, a girl's coming up the path."

A pretty young woman emerges from the forest on the trail we have just left. She has short blond hair, a short-sleeved shirt, short shorts, sturdy but shapely legs, and hiking boots. No pack.

We suggest she take in the view before moving on. But in one respect, she's like most hikers when she asks: "Where's the summit?" We describe the way, and she leaves.

In no time at all, she reappears. "I can't find the cannister," she says. So Ben and I lead her back to it and, since she has no supplies, offer her a packet of trail snacks.

She gobbles them eagerly, adding, "The bears got mine. I'm staying at Duck Hole. Next, I'm going to do the Sewards." We wonder as she leaves if she intends to try them today, and why she is alone.

Now, this is another Gretchen if I ever saw one. Like my daughter Gretchen, that is, who is about the same age, just beyond college, with similar blond hair and features. But she is not like my daughter in one way.

For years I have been trying to get Gretch to come along on one of our hikes in the high peaks. I keep telling her: that's where the boys are. But she is always busy flitting elsewhere. This blond girl, however, obviously got the word and that may be why she's here.

If so, it's a mismatch. Per the trailhead register, most of those who have signed in today are boys but they must be climbing other peaks. The only people she's seen here are Ben and me, and that's a shame. He's too young, and I'm already spoken for.

On our way down, Ben and I find double enjoyment in the slide and the day. It's a pity there aren't others to enjoy it. Both lean-tos are empty. And the five-mile trail ahead of us, while familiar, is still lonely.

Finally, near Blueberry Pond, a smiling, welcome figure charges into view. It is a hearty, young park ranger from Ray Brook headquarters, on his way to Duck Hole. My guess is he's about the same age as the girl.

We tell of meeting her on Seymour and of her plans to do the Sewards. I express my concern about a young girl being out alone. Maybe you ought to check her out, I suggest.

His eyes brighten and, with a smile he says, "I think I will."

No one else may pay attention to the glowing reports Ben and I plan to spread about Seymour. But today at least, we got someone's attention.

Mt. Marshall from Mt. Colden.

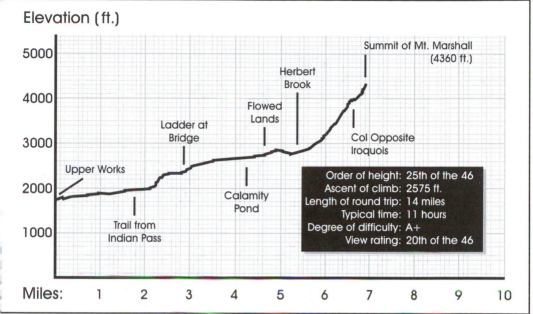

Elevation (ft.)

Summit of Mt. Marshall (4360 ft.)

Herbert Brook

Flowed Lands

Ladder at Bridge

Upper Works

Col Opposite Iroquois

Calamity Pond

Trail from Indian Pass

Order of height: 25th of the 46
Ascent of climb: 2575 ft.
Length of round trip: 14 miles
Typical time: 11 hours
Degree of difficulty: A+
View rating: 20th of the 46

Miles: 1 2 3 4 5 6 7 8 9 10

For contour trails, see U.S. Geological Survey map, pgs. 70-71.

43.
MARSHALL

Anyone who has climbed a half dozen Adirondack high peaks will tell you that they're all different.

And, it's possible in the pursuit of Marshall to find that just one peak can be different in a half dozen ways. Here's proof.

WHERE'S MARSHALL? (CHAPTER I)

Journal entry: Monday, August 2, 1971. *I have just learned that a trail was cut a few years back from Indian Pass trail near Scott Clearing to Lake Colden by way of Algonquin Pass, the defile between Iroquois Peak and Mt. Marshall. Son Jim and I decide to launch an assault by this new route since it's much shorter than the conventional approach from the Lake Colden/Flowed Land area. We'll be on our own in an unknown, trailless area, but that should be no problem: it would take a dunce to get lost on this short, wilderness hike.*

The Indian Pass trail snakes past busy lean-tos on the north shore of Heart Lake, then undulates at pleasant grades to the southwest.

At the Scott Clearing we are surprised to find that no one has occupied the lean-to. It nestles by a stream from the MacIntyre Range some four

Indian Pass comes into view at Scott Clearing, four miles southwest from the Loj. Wallface Mtn. on the right, a mile ahead, forms west wall of the pass.

miles from the Loj. The clearing, named for a man who lived in the area long ago, is a fifth of a mile beyond.

The Indian Pass trail passes the boulder walls of a crumbling dam from an old lumber camp, then dips toward a lush meadow interlaced with segments of Indian Pass Brook. The dizzying vertical bare face of Wallface Mtn. looms a mile ahead. One can appreciate what Richard Henry Dana wrote about it in 1849: "Before I had seen Yosemite Valley these cliffs satisfied my ideals of steep mountain walls."

During the fall and spring, the placid brook waters often turn into torrents. So hikers have the option of a high-water trail along the eastern bank or, in more placid times, a low-water trail through the clearing.

The junction with Algonquin Pass trail should be where the high-water and low-water trails meet, a quarter of a mile to the south. Jim and I search for it, then double back over a half-mile stretch to reconnoiter the major streams coming down from the east.

Finally, a quarter of a mile farther south, we find the missing junction sign. But by now, we have wasted an hour, and the humidity and bugs are rising for the kill. I decide we have had enough of Marshall for today.

As a consolation, I suggest we stroll up Indian Pass and see Wallface close-up. Jim groans, but I promote the prospect of a walk that is not much longer than an old Indian pack trail near home that climbs through sparse woods along the bank of a quiet stream.

How wrong can you get? Indian Pass may have been an easy walk eons ago, but no longer. Not far beyond the junction, the steep trail *rises over and through a fantastic jumble of huge stone blocks, some as big as houses, which have broken away from surrounding cliffs.*

A group of young boys and their leader who passed us earlier now return, tossing about whitish balls. "It's snow from the ice caves," one says. "They're all along the trail."

Snowballs in August? Jim and I poke into the dark crevices and, sure enough, find sizeable pockets of snow and ice, accompanied by drafts of gloriously frosty air. The formations are called talus caves; spelunkers say the ones in Indian Pass make up the largest such system in the world.

After a stiff climb of 400 feet in less than a half mile, the trail levels at a restful opening in a conifer grove that marks the top of Indian Pass. To the west, Wallface thrusts skyward more than a thousand feet from base to summit.

Jim and I had planned to go on to Sunset Rock, a promontory a half mile ahead, but what better spot than this for lunch in the wilderness? When the British actor W. C. Macready visited here a century and a half ago, he wrote to his wife that the "Notch," as it was then known, was a "wild scene of terrible beauty." Many think it still is: Time-Life book author Lincoln Barnett affirmed recently that Indian Pass is "the last, lost horizon of the Adirondacks."

New Yorkers must be on guard to see that it remains so. In 1924, the Essex County Board of Supervisors proposed to build a seven-mile road through the pass, linking North Elba with Newcomb. Eleanor Brown,

From the top of Indian Pass, *Wallface displays cliffs 500 feet high and 2,500 feet wide — the highest vertical rock wall in the eastern United States.*

who was appointed to the board of the Adirondack Park Association in 1995, noted in her book, The Forest Preserve, *that "further attempts to approve this route were rumored in the 1940s."*

Two tiny streams trickle from the top of Indian Pass on their way to the Atlantic Ocean. One, running south, initiates what David Henderson, manager of the McIntyre Iron Works in the last century, called the "infant murmurs of the giant Hudson River." The other, a fountainhead of the Ausable River, heads north to empty into the Atlantic more than 750 miles from the mouth of the Hudson.

For some reason, the monstrous facade of Wallface makes me think of the Apollo 15 astronauts who landed on the moon two days ago. It's the coincidence, I guess. Scott and Irwin are exploring an eerie world which few have ever seen first-hand. And while many others may have passed through Indian Pass, Jim and I have a similar feeling of exhilaration as we explore it for the first time.

Then it occurs to me why Wallface brought to mind the astronauts. Yesterday, while they were out prospecting in their lunar "bug," Commander Scott announced in a tone of great excitement, "We found what we came for... Oh, boy, I think we might have something close to an anorthosite!"

Scientists at the manned spacecraft center described anorthosite as a type of rock that is rare on earth. They dated grains of it found in soil from the Apollo 11 and 12 landing sites at 4.6 million years old. "Perhaps the material has been unchanged from the very first day our solar system was formed," said one.

During the lunar telecast, I thought the term "anorthosite" sounded familiar. Geologists say that the high peaks, among the oldest mountains on earth, are still standing because they are formed by a slab of anorthosite 1,200 square miles wide and a mile and a half thick. These so-called "basement rocks" of our continent are made of the material we see in the brightest areas of the moon.

What irony: Here we've spent billions of dollars putting these two men on the moon to bring back fist-sized chunks of the material, while surrounding Jim and me are billions of tons of the stuff for the taking. Their discovery may add missing pieces to the puzzle of the universe, but it seems like doing it the hard way.

WHERE'S MARSHALL: (CHAPTER II)

Journal entry: Sunday, August 8, 1971. *Three days ago, a good friend and business associate named Nat Boynton left on my desk at the office a cryptic note: "A Mountain Day Today."*

I knew just what he meant. He had told me of his wife's growing-up days in mountainous New Hampshire where her father practiced a puritanical discipline. Every day, he posted in the kitchen a list of chores for each member of the family.

Top of Algonquin Pass *greets the hiker less than two miles from Indian Pass trail. Huge rocks, corduroy lumber roads slow the way.*

Yet on days like the one today — crisp and cloudless — he skipped the list, asked his wife to pack a lunch, and said, simply: "Let's head for the hills."

Today is also a good "mountain day." I propose to my wife the same rationale naturalist John Muir used with his spouse almost exactly a hundred years ago: "The mountains are calling and I must go."

Jim and I hike from the Loj to Scott Clearing, then head east. The trail to the top of the pass is only a mile long, but many segments are badly eroded; others follow the remnants of old corduroy roads and rickety bridges used by loggers.

Topping off on Algonquin Pass is like climbing one of the 46 peaks — it lacks only 150 feet of being a 4,000-footer. In the center of the saddle is a rocky knob on the southern end of the Iroquois ridge that's supposed to be the place to begin the bushwhack. From there, hikers head south up the course of a tributary from Marshall. The ADK guidebook promises it leads "to gentler slopes" with "little blowdown."

Jim and I plow into the forest, and in five minutes conclude we have either chosen the wrong route or there have been bad storms since the book was printed nine years ago. Both the stream and its banks are littered with a fantastic clutter of fallen trees and huge, jumbled blocks of stone.

As we plod ahead, I think of another business associate, John Fitzgerald, who tells me he will launch this year a new magazine called

Bushwhack to Marshall *heads southwest from top of Algonquin Pass. Tangled blowdown, stifling heat and mosquitoes convince us to go back.*

Wilderness Camping.* *John, my friend, where are you when I need you?*

At streamside, there are faint traces of tracks. But it's not clear if they were made by animal or man; they soon disappear under barriers of blowdown. The going is hard and steamy work in the rotting under-brush. Mosquitoes abound in the stagnant pools, and flies join in to work us over.

Jim is frustrated and wor-ried. From above, he casts a questioning glance and gets the proper response: We'd better go back. It's a tough call because we can't be more than a half mile from the summit.

But we swallow our pride and along with it — an hour and three quarters later — a compensating lunch at Scott Clearing. Marshall will await another day.

Bob Marshall, who made the first recorded climb of his namesake peak with brother George and guide Herb Clark in 1921, observed that to reach it from Algonquin Pass, "you must tug, tussle, push and batter your way through as dense a mass of mountain balsam as ever grew." As a result, he said, "Progress is measured in inches."

Fifty years later, outdoor writer Fred Fraser agreed in the *Schenectady Gazette* that the bushwhack is "reserved for the most fanatical adventurers." The current book of the Adirondack Forty Sixers calls the trek, "one of the most exasperating in the mountains."

Younger son Ben and I returned to Scott Clearing on the day before Memorial Day in 1982 with other trail-clearing volunteers attending the Forty Sixer weekend at Adirondak Loj. Our crew removed downed

*The magazine later merged with Backpacker.

timber on the trails to Indian Pass and Wallface Ponds and constructed log walkways through a swamp prior to reaching the ponds.

The end of the trail near the ponds offered an intimidating close-up of MacNaughton Mtn., whose height was re-surveyed at 4,000 ft. Many Forty Sixers have added it to their want list of climbs, but it's not often at the top. MacNaughton has no herd paths and blowdown is severe over its broad summit.

The leader of our work crew was Jim Goodwin, a remarkable gentleman whom I suspect knows more about the Adirondack high peaks than anyone, including the early explorers and guides.

Goodwin, a retired Connecticut teacher, recorded his first climb of the 46 high peaks when he was nine years old, at a time when only 12 of the mountains had trails. He began guiding at age 12.

By the time he was 17, Goodwin had climbed Marcy 55 times. In 1985, when he was 75, he led an expedition commemorating the centennial of the Forest Preserve by the route of the original Marcy trail, cut by Old Mountain Phelps. That was Goodwin's 188th ascent. "It's embarrassing," he told the *Watertown Daily Times*. "It's the only mountain I've counted continually."

I called him in 1996 for an update. "Last year, when I turned 85," he told me, "I climbed Marcy again. That brought my total to 195. But I'm not sure if I'll hit 200."

Goodwin was the 24th to become a Forty Sixer. As of the Marcy excursion, he admitted reluctantly that he had climbed all of the peaks 15 times. "I don't like to think of climbing as a contest," he said.

Goodwin and his late sister, Peggy O'Brien, and son Tony (James A. Jr.), have long been active in high peak activities, including the Adirondack Mountain Club, the Forty Sixers, and the Adirondack Trail Improvement Society (ATIS). Tony is editor of the 11th and 12th editions of the *ADK High Peaks Region* guidebook.

WHERE'S MARSHALL? (CHAPTER III)

Journal entry: Saturday, August 5, 1972. *Challenging Marshall again after almost a year pumps me up for a couple of reasons.*

First, logic tells me that no Adirondack peak should be this hard, and I want to get it over with.

Second, I've just finished reading Arthur H. Masten's The Story of Adirondac, *which details the development and abandonment of the village by that name at the McIntyre mines near Tahawus. Just beyond the tiny settlement is one of the trailheads for Marshall.*

Up until 1850, most climbers approached the high peaks either from there or the southwest. Now, according to ranger Peter Fish, only seven per cent start from Adirondac. Good: that means Jim and I can

Deserted village *of Adirondac lies near end of the road to Calamity Brook trailhead. It's at the Upper Works, two and a half miles north of the open pit mine site.*

joust with our nemesis all by ourselves. It will also be refreshing to confront Marshall from another direction.

Adirondac is at the Upper Works, two and a half miles north of Tahawus, where the open pit mine is located. In its heyday, the little village not only had houses but a bank, a post office and a building with a cupola which served as both school and church.

The deteriorating buildings cling to a straight gravel road, leaving those who pass by with a fleeting impression. There are no signs of life — no shopkeepers leaning at their doorposts, no children engrossed with makeshift toys, no sleeping dogs or errant chickens...nothing to evoke the past but the vacant stares of empty windows.

During the 30 years of its active existence, Adirondac was a magnet for artists such as Henry Inman, Asher B. Durand and Thomas Cole. Writers who visited the site included Joel T. Headley, Richard Henry Dana and John Burroughs.

One visitor, the author Charles Dudley Warner, called the tiny village "The most melancholy spot in the Adirondacks."

Stark shadows cast by the simple structures reinforce the silence. Yet by half closing your eyes, you can capture the tableau described in 1863 by Burroughs, the famed naturalist:

"The barking of the dog brought the whole family [of the sole remaining occupant, the caretaker] into the street, and they stood till we came up. Strangers in that country were a novelty, and we were greeted like familiar acquaintances."

Fourteen years earlier, Richard Henry Dana wrote of his overnight stay at the then-bustling works:

"The agent lived in a house where it was plain that one room served for parlor, kitchen and nursery. He was a hard-worked, sore-pressed man. A chance to sleep on the floor in a house with ninety-six puddlers, with liberty to wash in the stream, was as fair a result as we had a right to expect in the one house into which strangers could be received."

The first leg of the trail follows the course of Calamity Brook to the Flowed Land and Lake Colden. The route was a favorite of David Henderson, who developed the original mine with his father-in-law, Archibald McIntyre, and Duncan McMartin, Jr.

Try as I may, with no help from color-blindness, I can find none of the colorful stones Henderson found in the stream.

Even if you've never heard of David Henderson, you'll never forget him after visiting a small pond, originally known as Duck Hole, a half mile before the trail reaches the Flowed Land.

Near the brook that flows from the pond is an ornate shaft with the inscription: "This monument erected by filial affection to the memory

Calamity Pond is named for David Henderson, a McIntyre mine developer, who was accidentally killed here. Monument commemorates the tragedy.

of our dear father, David Henderson, who accidentally lost his life on this spot. 3 September 1845."

Henderson was killed when his pistol discharged as it struck the ground when he lowered his pack.

The only previous view which Jim and I had of the Flowed Land, from Colden on a grey day in July a year ago, was indistinct. Today, it sparkles in the brilliant sunshine, lending hope to our search for Marshall.

Herbert Brook, named after the Marshall brother's guide, Herb Clark, is said to be the best route to the summit. When Jim and I reach it on the northwest shore of the Flowed Land, we head upward and plunge into a confusing maze of blowdown. After struggling for an hour and climbing no more than a half mile, herd paths follow tributaries. We guess the northern one is the right way.

Wrong as usual. Or we think so as the flow of the brook slows to a trickle and the paths peter out. It is the kind of predicament faced by T. Morris Longstreth when he explored the Adirondacks a half century earlier: "Of course we weren't lost. We were merely where we shouldn't have been, without knowing where that was."

It is now 2 p.m. and, as near as I can tell from the topographic map, we are at least a mile and a half from the summit. If we double back to the main brook and find that the route up is as rough as this, we will run out of daylight.

It's no contest, I tell Jim. We have to turn back.

What the English actor, William Macready, wrote to his wife when he visited Adirondac in 1844 still holds true: "We pushed, climbed, scrambled and tore our way through and over this wild and grand labyrinth. An European can have no idea of an American forest — indeed many Americans are as much abroad in forming any idea of its savage grandeur. I constantly pause to look around, above and all about me to feel the depth of loneliness, that it impresses on one."

Back at the Flowed Land campsite, a couple we greeted upon leaving Adirondac this morning ask with bright smiles: "Where's Marshall?"

Under my breath, I mutter: That's what I'd like to know. But Jim and I act as if we know what we were talking about, point down the trail toward Herbert Brook, and toss off some harmless generalities. They say they will undertake their assault tomorrow.

That's too soon for me. But the lure of Marshall endures. I know we'll return another day.

WHERE'S MARSHALL? (CHAPTER IV}

Journal entry: Saturday, June 9, 1973. This trip to the Adirondacks will be a milestone in one respect: Jim, now 16, has his learner's permit and will drive for the first time. Instead of his usual eloquent reluctance in early morning, he is cheerful and almost awake.

The timing is perfect, for I propose we again try Marshall. Jim winces when he thinks of a year ago, but allows he is ready to roll.

The prospect at Adirondac is not encouraging. Michael Mahrer, reporting in at the trailhead register for his party of five from New York City, told of his recent return from Marshall: "Back again. Blew it for the 4th time. Maybe I'll never be a 46er."

The skies hang low and gray. No one is in sight, but swarms of black flies match our cadence as we start out. The weeping clouds offer consolation.

At 12:45 p.m. the Flowed Land campsite is deserted, although packs and gear await the return of their owners. Nor do we see anyone to the east at the lean-to across the water on the spit of land near Livingston Pond.

The trail to Herbert Brook which skirts the west shore of the Flowed Land, was gloomy, wet and muddy on our last visit here during the August dry season. This year, two months earlier, nothing has changed except the depth of the mud and the tenacity with which it sucks at our boots. In a word, it is awful.

Jim and I think better of it after heading up the banks of Herbert Brook because the trailless jumble seems even worse. We

This is a trail? *Route along west shore of Flowed Land to mouth of Herbert Brook was once the worst section in the Adirondacks. It's been upgraded.*

struggle to a crook in the brook which turns like a wayward arrow toward the summit. The heat, bugs and ennui gang up on me.

To Jim, I suggest: let's go back.

He stares at me with incredulity. Here is his fearless leader, one who has always smiled at adversity as if he didn't know any better — admitting defeat?

True. But I'm tired. And, obviously out of shape after no serious hiking during the last 10 months. Jim, who is mindful of the prospective joy in driving home, agrees.

WHERE'S MARSHALL? (CHAPTER V)

Journal entry: Saturday, June 7, 1975. *Jim protests loudly. He says it is unfair to drag him out of bed like this. His mother interrupts: "This is your Father's Day gift. Get up and don't make him late."*

Jim says he is tempted to run away. With good reason: I want to try Marshall again. But this time I intend to do it right — with a Schenectady ADK group hike.

The clouds glower as we drive up, for there is a 60 per cent chance of rain. "Seventy per cent," says Jim, ears glued to the radio. The desolate buildings of Adirondac do nothing to lift his spirits. They remind me of Army boot camp.

Our new-found friends from the Nye-Street outing of last month, Bob Baldwin and his son Mark, will lead our contingent of 17. A half dozen from that jaunt are with us today.

Everyone but Jim and I don outer clothing as a gentle, steady rain begins to fall. Their sleek outfits contrast with those recommended by Benson L. Lossing, on a visit to Adirondac in 1859: "A man needs only a stout flannel hunting shirt, coarse and trustworthy trousers, woolen stockings, large heavy boots well saturated with a composition of beeswax and tallow, a soft felt hat or cap, and strong buckskin gloves."

Jim and I decide to start with only windbreakers, since it is fairly mild. All our clothing is cotton, but that should be no problem — it's almost summer.

The normally placid flow of Calamity Brook greets us with a roar. As the rain begins to fall in earnest, the accompanying trail, always wet, mimics the brook with a flow of its own. It's slow going; mostly we keep to the shoulders, clinging to branches to avoid dunking our feet.

Bob Baldwin agreed with me on Nye and Street that our pace was too strenuous. So he calls forward: "Tell Mark to slow down." But the younger ones in the pack charge on, and we have to struggle to keep up.

The wind freshens, so the heat of the march cannot compensate for the evaporative cooling effect. At the Henderson monument, I skip taking pictures because my hands are too numb.

Forecast: danger. *Enveloping clouds and rain warn hikers they should be prepared for anything if they plan to climb Marshall today.*

It is so wet that we all stay on our feet for lunch at Herbert Brook. The only bright spot is my Thermos of hot coffee. The others joke about it but envy me as the cup helps unbend my rigid fingers.

Finally, Jim and I put on our ponchos, but they don't help much because they stick to our wet clothes. Before long, I begin to shiver, first fitfully, then in earnest.

My guess is that the temperature is close to 40 degrees. But with the rain whistling in, a thermometer would read more like the one described by Robert Louis Stevenson during his winter at Saranac Lake: the mercury, he wrote, "curls up into the bulb like a hibernating bear."

Our climb soon degenerates into an erratic scramble. The usual routes, according to Bob Baldwin — herd paths and brook bed — are impassable because of white water. So we begin an endless crossing and re-crossing of the stream, poking through blowdown on an incline that seems to go straight up.

Baldwin, who has a lean frame like mine, allows that the cold is getting to him. "This is a tough hike in good weather," he says. "But this is terrible."

The six cold, wet hours on the trail are making it hard for me to grasp branches to pull myself upward. My feet, sloshing around in low boots, are also numb. And the only way I can step over logs when climbing is to lift my knees mechanically with my hands.

It occurs to me that I am in the early stages of hypothermia. This happens when you become chilled and your body temperature drops two or three degrees below normal. Your nervous system tries to restore heat by tensing muscles, and that brings on the shivers.

In the next stage, body temperature drops another five degress or so to as low as 91. Then, you begin to shiver violently and find it hard to speak or think, and become forgetful.

The latter cheers me. Granted, it is hard to talk while I'm shaking. But there's nothing wrong with my memory: I constantly think about getting this over with so I can get warmed up back in the car.

Other stragglers voice the same concerns as we try to catch up. It is 2:30 p.m., the enveloping clouds make it look like dusk, and we have a tough half mile before topping off, if we can find the top. A majority votes to head back while there is daylight.

Fog and rain have muted the Flowed Land. But the leaden surface looks as good to me as Charles Dudley Warner noted when he found himself lost a hundred years ago near Lower Ausable lake: "The 'rapture on the lonely shore' is agreeable only when you know you can at any moment go home."

Others keep to trail shoulders, but Jim and I slosh through the mud and puddles. It keeps the blood flowing to counteract a growing stiffness.

The high blast of the car heater on the way home is topped only by the prospect of a warm bed.

My wife apportions condolences according to her view. To Jim: "You poor boy, let me cook something hot to stop that shaking." And to me: "Do you mean to tell me you've hiked almost 14 miles up a mountain and now have to lift your legs to roll into bed?"

Cursed Marshall strikes again.

WHERE'S MARSHALL? (CHAPTER VI)

Journal entry: Saturday, August 16, 1980. *"We've had it," Tom Stanwood tells Ben and me. "There is no way we are going to make Gray and Skylight today. Or even our alternate target, Redfield."*

Ben and I have to agree, even though to this point we have done everything according to plan. We were up at 4 a.m., and marched out from Adirondac at 7:30 on the Calamity Brook trail to the Flowed Land and here to Herbert Brook. The topographic map shows that this route, coupled with the Opalescent River and Feldspar Brook trails on the east side of Lake Colden, is the shortest way to the three peaks Tom mentioned.

The rain, incidental when we left the parking lot this morning, became insistent on the trail. At the Flowed Land, and now here at the mouth of Herbert Brook, there is again no view of Mt. Colden or anything else — only enveloping clouds and rain. The excursion, chilled by a freshening breeze, is shaping up much like our attempt on Marshall five years ago. It was such a disaster that I quit hiking for three years.

Tom takes us by surprise: "I suggest we go back, or," and he hesitates a minute, "try Marshall."

Ben shudders at the thought. But on reflection, I point out there are two differences: The temperature today is in the '60s instead of the '40s. And we have wool clothing instead of cotton.

There's also a powerful incentive for me: I don't want to hike these miserable trails again; I have had enough calamities. Also, time is in our favor: if we go, we'll be starting three hours earlier than the last time.

Even so, says Ben, "It's not a good day for research on Mom's book." My wife is also a writer and has been thinking about doing a regency novel transplanted to 19th century North America. Ben told her the title I suggested: "Whoopee in the Adirondacks: a Campfire Classic."

She liked that about as much as I like our prospects today.

Marshall is not a good setting for a regency novel. In fact, it smacks more of Macbeth, but with a twist: Puddle, puddle, soil and trouble.

The herd path looks relatively easy to begin with. But when Tom plunges into blowdown, he loses his way, then gets back on track. Ben and I follow.

Then I see a familiar sight: the three tributaries of the brook, where Jim and I chose the northern one, going nowhere. But which of the other two?

"Confusion now hath made his masterpiece!"

Tom chooses the one in the middle, naturally the steepest. It loops over a sharp cliff on the right side of the main brook. Shortly, the path disintegrates and we assume the flat, exposed rock stream bed — though slippery with moss and drenched by a sheet of run-off — is our best course.

It is now somewhat cooler, with a quickening of the wind. Through a gap in the trees behind, we can see only whiteness. It makes Ben uneasy, and he asks, "Do you think we can make it?" I mumble some encouragement; it doesn't measure up to the pithiness of Shakespeare:

"But screw your courage to the sticking-place,
  and we'll not fail."

Herbert Brook lures hikers toward Marshall with cascades and limpid pools. Rain and freshening wind bring risk of hypothermia at higher elevations.

Tom offers no cheer: "This is my eighth try at Marshall. If we make it, this will be only my third time on top, and the first time from this direction." His successful ascents were made from Algonquin Pass. "I have a great deal of respect for this mountain," he adds.

The mountain has earned my respect, too. But in one way, it is like all the others: the ridge looming above us is surely not the top, but merely one more obstacle along the way.

> "Things at the worst will cease, or else climb upward/to what they were before."

The brook bed narrows and merges with a steep, muddy herd path which wends back and forth. Tom takes a fall on a slippery log; Ben, misjudging the muck, is slathered with it up to his ankles.

We are all beginning to get concerned because, though we have climbed a long way, the stream flow seems as strong as ever. Tom addresses our frustration: "Let's go on until one o'clock. If we're not at the col by then, we'll go back."

I heartily agree. The whipping winds form clouds around us, and the familiar chill of five years ago strikes again in my hands. I put them in my pockets to get warm, and promptly step off balance into a bog hole. When it comes to Marshall, I am

> "...weary with disaster, tugg'd with fortune..."

As on Allen, Tom charges up the trail and disappears. It is now 12:30 and the summit is nowhere in sight. In fact, we can see no more than a hundred feet in either direction: a slight depression to the north, and a modest rise to the south. Both are covered with stunted trees through which wind clouds whistle.

A shout by Stanwood from above on the west tells us we have reached the col and he is climbing the rise toward the true summit. Before Ben and I follow, a momentary void in the clouds exposes the false summit of Marshall to the north. Its bleak contour squats a couple of hundred feet above the col at Algonquin Pass.

> "Now o'er the one half-world
> Nature seems dead."

Then, as if someone has swept the sky with a dirty eraser, the clouds become an even, chalky gray, and Ben and I are again alone. It is the kind of strange landscape Bob Marshall loved to explore: "A blank place on the map."

Ben rubs his chilled hands, and asks: "Do you think there's danger of hypothermia?" Not yet, I assure him. But when we join Tom, where the wind whirls through the skeleton trees, he warns: "This summit is dangerous. It's enclosed, but there's no good shelter. With these wet clothes we'd better get up and off in a hurry."

> "If it were done when 'tis done, then 'twere well
> It were done quickly..."

On this summit, no curious bird appears to chirp a welcome. But my spirits are as high as the elevation. I have never been happier: I am through with my tormenter.

> "The heaven's breath smells wooingly here."

Soon, however, euphoria evaporates. I can only focus my camera if I guide my fingers by sight; the sense of touch is gone. In fact, I can barely grasp a pencil to sign the register. It shows that one recent climber was Dorothy Ann Pabst, who wrote: "#1 peak. It's a snap." She's probably a nice girl, but at this moment I hate her.

I try to zip up my jacket. But my numb fingers snag the catch on the fabric, so I let it flap. The battle is won, the war is almost over; who cares?

> "My little spirit, see,
> Sits in a foggy cloud, and stays with me."

At the first good stand of trees below — a swampy depression where Herbert Brook begins to appear — we lunch standing up. The food is the equivalent of dry clothes: a feeling of well-being returns.

As we decend to a warmer elevation, the path seems twice as slippery. First, Tom takes a nasty fall, his chest striking a protruding branch. Then it's Ben's turn. He slips and goes full length on the wide, flat rock of the stream bed. Fortunately, it hurts only his feelings.

Next, me. Coming last, I watch Tom and Ben negotiate an eight-foot drop through a crack in a cliff. I grab the outer remnant of a rotting tree

Wet feet are no concern to Ben and Tom Stanwood on decending Marshall. Rock under Herbert Brook is slick from moss and water action.

trunk on the upper lip of the cliff and swing out and down to a lower foot-hold. The sheath of wood lets go, and I plummet to the muddy base. With luck, I land feet first, my hand grasping empty air as the sheath goes flying.

We become more cautious but gain optimism as a shaft of sun spears Mt. Skylight to the southeast past the Flowed Land.

A quarter of a mile beyond the mouth of Herbert Brook, we meet a young couple. While we are wet and bedraggled, they seem to be out for a summer stroll: no hats, no jackets, no packs. They are from New Jersey and are heading for Lake Colden. From there, they will head over the col to Indian Pass, then climb back through it to their car at Adirondac. Their map of the high peaks has no contours.

It is now 3:45 p.m. and they are without flashlights. We advise against the trip. "It's stiff climbing," Tom admonishes. "You'll run out of daylight, and that's dangerous."

The young woman looks worried. But the man does not, and they continue on.

Soon, however, they rejoin us. The young man strides alongside and says: "I've been in the Adirondacks once before, at Lake Placid. I thought that was the Adirondacks. This is different." They fall in with us.

An emerging sun plus a quick change of socks at the Flowed Land campsite brightens our outlook. And when Mt. Colden shines a welcome, Ben becomes expansive: "That wasn't so bad. I don't know why you were so cautious about Marshall."

Tom and I do.

> "When our actions do not,
>   Our fears do make us traitors."

The sun remains brilliant for the four-mile hike out, even though lingering clouds from behind spit driblets at us. Marshall casts only a single glance through the retreating overcast.

At the car, Tom strips off his T-shirt and asks us to check for a bruise from his fall. There is none, but there is something else. Whereas there were few black flies on the harsh, upper regions, here in the short time Ben and I take to check him out, no-see-ums cover his upper body with red welts.

At home, Ben tells his mother of our triumph. She is suitably impressed and suggests that he report the good news in a letter to his brother Jim. Then she hustles him off to bath and bed.

Mt. Colden *is a welcome sight at Flowed Land on the return from Marshall. All that remains is a four and a half mile hike back to Adirondac.*

Sleep comes fitfully to me, and I sit bolt upright from a horrible dream: my wife asks why I failed for the sixth time to conquer Marshall.

> "Alack! I am afraid they have awak'd,
>   And 'tis not done. The attempt, and not the deed,
>   Confounds us."

But unlike Macbeth, the spectre of Marshall will haunt me no more. "I have done the deed."

I fall back into

> "Innocent sleep,
> Sleep that knits up the revell'd sleave of care,
> The death of each day's life, sore labour's bath,
> Balm of hurt minds, great nature's second course,
> Chief nourisher in life's feast."

Mt. Redfield from Cliff Mtn.

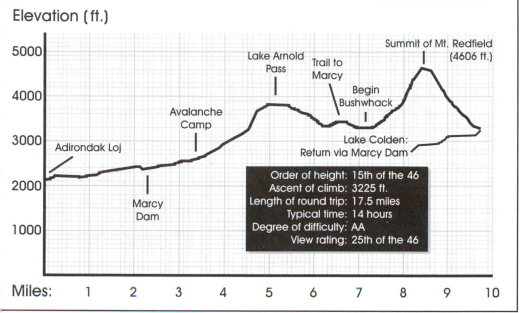

Elevation (ft.)

5000 — Lake Arnold Pass · Trail to Marcy · Summit of Mt. Redfield (4606 ft.)

4000 — Begin Bushwhack

Avalanche Camp

3000 — Adirondak Loj · Lake Colden: Return via Marcy Dam

2000 — Marcy Dam

Order of height: 15th of the 46
Ascent of climb: 3225 ft.
Length of round trip: 17.5 miles
Typical time: 14 hours
Degree of difficulty: AA
View rating: 25th of the 46

1000

Miles: 1 2 3 4 5 6 7 8 9 10

r contour trails, see U.S. Geological Survey map, pgs. 70-71.

44.
REDFIELD

People have long talked about how wonderful the trailless trek to Redfield used to be.

In their pioneering circuit of the high peaks in the 1920s, the Marshall brothers and guide Herb Clark reported they "tramped along through glorious, unmarred woods which covered the mountain." They started from the present site of Uphill Brook lean-to near the Opalescent River.

Such easy passage changed with the hurricane of 1950.

Others favored climbing the long ridge that led to the southeast from the col between Cliff and Redfield. But again, severe blowdown during the winter of 1969-70 leveled many of the "park-like trees" above the 3,600-foot level.

Some discovered that the trailless mile leading southwest from Lake Tear-of-the-Clouds to Redfield was, as the 1950 ADK guidebook described it, "easy and interesting." This brought the hiker past Moss Pond, one of four, genuine tarns in the high peaks — small lakes which formed in the bowl of glacial cirques.

The current ADK guidebook notes cryptically: "There is no continuous herd path on this route."

Earlier ADK guidebooks didn't shed much light on Redfield either. The first, in 1934, ignored the peak. Succeeding ones advised expansively, in a sentence or two, to start from either the Cliff/Redfield col or Uphill Brook, then "Return by same route." It wasn't until the sixth edition that hikers were warned there might be a problem "straying below the ridge to the south...a series of cliffs continually block one's progress."

Present-day hikers are not inclined to equivocate about Redfield. Stephanie and Stewart McConaughy told *Adirondack Peeks* in 1995 about their tough, three-hour search for the peak. The bushwhack, beginning with the multiple waterfalls of Uphill Brook, brought them not to Redfield but to Skylight.

In the Forty Sixers' *Of the Summits, of the Forests*, William Kozel related the problem Eugene Daxniell had when he hiked during the winter from Lake Tear to Redfield. While crossing Moss Pond, "Gene broke through the ice and was luckily stopped short by a second layer of ice three feet below."

Today, the accepted, feasible way to Redfield is via Uphill Brook. Before you begin, of course, you must first hike to the jumping-off point at Uphill Brook lean-to. That's 7.2 miles from Adirondak Loj by way of Lake Arnold, 7.5 miles from the Upper Works Parking lot, and 7.9 miles from the Loj via Lake Colden.

Journal entry: Thursday, August 28, 1980. This hike is shaping up as a question mark for me, since it will chew up a day of vacation. There are too many negative signs.

The weather is supposed to be cloudy with the chance of rain ranging from 30 to 60 per cent.

And then there's Ben. The prospect of Redfield alone is bad enough, but he wants to climb Gray and Skylight. Tom Stanwood didn't help much with his advice: "Hike in from Tahawus for an overnight at Twin Brook lean-to; then climb all three the next day."

No way. I keep thinking of those onerous packs from our circuit of the Sewards. They made me a confirmed day-tripper.

As Ben and I head west on Rt. 73 toward the turnoff for Adirondak Loj, the buildings on top of Whiteface, like the sultan's turret in Omar Kháyyám's Rubáiyat, *have been "caught in a noose of light." The clouds, however, are unimpressed; they choke off the lone sliver of sun.*

I am ready to go home. Only Ben's urging keeps me going.

The parking lot at the Loj is full of cars, the hikers' hut closed. No one is in sight.

A quarter of a mile along the trail to Marcy Dam, a dozen young people stir from an overnight under the dubious shelter of flimsy plastic sheets. There is little chance that the clothes they wring and hang will dry in the cool sogginess. They are unconcerned.

George Bernard Shaw substantiated the obvious: "Youth is a wonderful thing. What a crime to waste it on children."

Eight boy scouts, wet hair plastered to faces and hastily-tied packs bouncing on their backs, stagger on under the urging of their leader. "Beautiful day!" he booms in a voice dripping with sarcasm.

Just beyond the junction to Algonquin, a heavy-set couple with a lad of about seven in tow seems intent on escape. Their blank stares mirror exhaustion bordering on panic. Street clothes are bedraggled under plastic coats, their belongings dangling over shoulders in laundry bags. The boy is buffeted by the large canvas suitcase he carries with both hands.

They neither look at us nor speak. Their faces tell it all: up from the city for their first time in the wilderness. And all they can think is, "No one told us it would be like this!"

No ranger is in sight at Marcy Dam. Nor are there many campers. Those who are up are intent on getting out.

My pace is sluggish because I would like to join them; mentally, I have already turned back. Ben notices: "You always tell me I'm pessimistic. Why are you today?"

I cobble up a comparison with Verplanck Colvin, who always seemed to run out of daylight or good weather on his Adirondack surveys during the last century. Ben and I have experienced both all year. With the exception of Seymour, we've been dogged by rain on every excursion. Not to mention bugs, humidity and late homecomings.

At the Avalanche Camp lean-tos, only one soul is up and around, even though it is 9:05 a.m. "We were drenched last night," mutters the camper as he fumbles while trying to start a fire, with no success.

We begin the steep haul up to Lake Arnold and meet a young couple on their way down, who report a further tale of woe. They have just returned via the Crossover trail from Indian Falls, where bears ransacked their food last night. The young woman brandishes a whistle: "This scared them off, but only till we went to sleep again. They ripped the bottoms of our packs even though they were suspended from trees."

Cheer up, I tell them: help is on the way. This summer, New York's Department of Environmental Conservation says it will set up experimental bear-proof poles at campgrounds so people can safely hang up food. Next year, ENCON plans to install bear-proof food lockers at every state campsite.

The thought of it depresses me as much as the recent permit system for groups camping at Lake Colden.

There goes the neighborhood.

As if to lend encouragment, a momentary rip in the clouds reveals a patch of blue. The sun beams through a spotlight which races up the north flank of Mt. Colden.

Lake Arnold is the same, dull, jade green that son Jim and I saw on our first visit. Today, however, the bullfrogs are silent.

The cutoff trail around the west side of the lake, which Ben and I take by mistake, is worse than I remembered — a swampy wasteland. The main trail, on the other side, is not much better, but passable. It mounts a gentle rise a quarter of a mile to the top of the pass between Mt. Colden and the enormous ridge extending to the northwest from Marcy.

At this point, we are less than a hundred feet below the height of Cliff Mtn., which is some two miles ahead to the southwest. Ben is not only encouraged, but excited. "If we've come this far by mid-morning, we can surely do Gray and Skylight," he says.

There's only one word to describe the trail from Lake Arnold to Feldspar Brook: terrible. It has had no obvious maintenance, and consists mainly of herd paths which lead around blowdown and marshy areas while meandering back and forth across a watercourse.

After about a mile, the trail levels off and joins the Opalescent River flowing from Marcy on the east. It then winds through wet areas which, if anything, are worse than those on the upper trail. In my mind, it typifies that vast area north of the Mohawk River which Lewis Evans described in a 1755 General Map of the Middle British Colonies in America: *"This Country by Reason of Mountain Swamps and drowned Land is impassable and uninhabited."*

Numerous collegians at the lean-to where Feldspar Brook joins the Opalescent seem to have a similar opinion of the area: they are all moving out.

We meet another couple, decked out for a stroll on the boardwalk — sport shirts, Bermuda shorts, black socks and black street shoes. They say they are off to climb Marcy; their current challenge is to round up their young son and two dogs, scampering about the area.

They are camped at Lake Colden, and the father advises us we should go that way in returning to Marcy Dam. The trail is "dead level," he affirms, then elaborates: "There are a lot of side trails on the way out which have great views and don't take much climbing. One goes over Algonquin."

How's that again? We thank them, and wish them the luck they'll need.

By this time, Ben knows that my heart is not into going for Gray and Skylight today. So we take the 20-minute jaunt that leads to Uphill Brook lean-to to consider Redfield. That lean-to is tucked into a lovely campsite. There, the brook joins forces with the Opalescent River for a race to Lake Colden, the Hudson River and eventually the Atlantic Ocean.

Correction: the area may have been lovely at one time, but it is now despoiled. A stubble of chopped tree stumps suggests a morning-after that will take more than after-shave to correct.

Professor William C. Redfield never climbed his namesake mountain. But he did pass through here in 1837 with the first party to climb Mt. Marcy.

The noted meteorologist and his group came from the McIntyre mine at Tahawus by way of Lake Colden. From there they followed the Opalescent River east to its "South Elbow," formed where it joins Uphill Brook. The explorers then turned north past the confluence of Feldspar Brook with the Opalescent, entering what they called the "High Valley" between Marcy and Mt. Colden. That is the marshy, level area traversed by the trail from Lake Arnold.

At the north end of the level land, Redfield and party turned to follow the Opalescent to the east through a pass between Marcy and a major ridge to the north. The next day, on their way to the summit, they crossed the modest meadow between Little Marcy and Marcy. It spawns the headwaters of two streams, one flowing to the Hudson, the other to the Ausable.

Neither they nor anyone else got around to climbing Mt. Redfield until nearly 60 years after their pioneering trip to Marcy. That put Mt. Redfield in exalted company: the third and fourth highest Adirondack peaks were not climbed also until years after the first ascent of Marcy — 12 years later for Haystack, and 36 for Skylight.

The trail leading through the High Valley from Lake Arnold toward Redfield has been improved during the last few years. Log and plank walkways now ease the way along the course of the Opalescent to Feldspar Brook. The old Feldspar lean-to was torn down in 1992 and and a new one moved farther away from the river to avoid further despoliation.

One thing has not changed, however. Once you head up the brook from Uphill Brook lean-to, you realize that the Adirondack wilderness is as challenging as ever.

Journal entry: Thursday, August 28, 1980. Ben and I are unable to find a main herd path behind the lean-to. But near the brook, I spot two people who look like professional explorers. The older man, with neatly-trimmed beard and meticulous hiking outfit, gestures vigorously at a topographic map for the benefit of his younger companion. I ask him about Redfield.

"I haven't the foggiest," he replies. "But maybe you can tell me how to find the yellow trail." You're on it, I tell him, pointing at the yellow marker on the tree next to him. His eyes float skyward.

After 15 minutes of thrashing through the maze of paths behind the lean-to, I decide we had better bushwhack to the brook and head up. Sure enough, a faint path on the bank merges with a major herd path coming in from the west. We are on our way.

An enormous feeling of relief engulfs me. We have, I believe, unlocked the key to our conquest of the 46. Assuming we conquer Redfield today, all of the tough trailless peaks will be out of the way. There is still Gray, of course, the highest of all the trailless ones. But trail veterans say it is an easy, half-hour climb from Lake Tear. Assuming you make it up there.

My relief is soon tempered with doubt, for the herd path toward Redfield is erratic and difficult. It laces over and under blowdown, teeters perilously on steep, slippery cliffs, and forces us often to rock-hop pools in the brook.

A fall discourages Ben because, as he reminds me, he would rather be going after the big ones. We think we spot Skylight; the darkening clouds emit no light on the question.

It is also now one p.m., when I estimated we would top off. Yet I believe we have not gone even a half mile since leaving Uphill Brook lean-to. The going is slower than on any of our hikes this year.

At a steep and slippery ledge, I yank myself upward and bang my kneecap squarely on an exposed rock. Blood immediately seeps through my pantleg. It makes me lightheaded, so I sit down and apply a bandage.

Of course, Ben is worried. But I suggest a rest is all that's needed. The gash pulsates with pain and turns an ugly black and blue.

Is this it, I wonder? Trying the leg, I find that it still works. So we push on.

A little more than a half mile from the lean-to, the herd path skirts a stunning, 60-foot-high waterfall, then leaves the brook to turn south. The path parallels a tributary which shoots upward before shrink-

ing to seepage. It is not as steep as the paths on Seward, Seymour or Marshall, but it seems interminable.

We look for guidelines which will mark our progess. First Colden, then Algonquin and Iroquois come into sight, followed by Skylight and, finally, Wright. With the exception of the latter, all are only a few hundred feet higher than Redfield. And that's the problem — they all look much higher than where we are.

It is 2:30 p.m. and both Ben and I are very tired. But stunted trees and a freshening breeze offer the unmistakable promise of a summit. We decide to keep going.

MacIntyre Range *appears on way to Redfield, above 60-foot waterfall on Uphill Brook, a half mile south of lean-to. Iroquois is at left, Algonquin right, and Boundary center.*

As we surmount a high ridge, I decide that if we find the summit is still a long distance away, we'll go back.

Ben senses triumph, however, and scrambles ahead. His shout demolishes my pessimism. "We're here! It's the cannister!"

Redfield's summit, as on so many Adirondack high peaks, is heavily wooded, except for a 10 by 20 foot corridor leading to an expansive overlook to the south. Ben perches atop a car-size boulder near the edge, pointing and shouting: "There's Allen! There's Dix and Nippletop! And isn't that Moss Pond down there?"

The topo map indicates that the sizeable body of water in Skylight Brook Valley is not Moss Pond, but instead is just another gem in the Adirondack jewel box. It glistens with a dull sheen; the overcast sky threatens but as yet has brought no rain.

Experts say we should be able to spot Marcy and other high peaks to the north and west from here. But that would mean fighting our way through the jumbled trees on the summit ridge. And, anyway, who cares? Neither Ben nor I really wanted to attempt Redfield, nor did we believe at times we could actually conquer it. But we made it, so we congratulate each other and slump to the ground for a rest.

From Redfield, *tiny unnamed pond struggles for attention through the murky overcast. Allen Mtn. rises beyond it, two miles to the south.*

Prof. Redfield is not a household name with hikers today. He is remembered mostly for his reports on pioneering scientific work. He did pique the interest of the general public when *Family Magazine* published his "Some Account of Two Visits to the Mountains in Essex County, New York, in the Years 1836 and 1837." It detailed his discovery of Mt. Marcy, and the role he played in that first ascent. The story is acknowledged as one of the first to open the floodgates for an enormous outpouring of words and pictures about the Adirondacks.

Prior to that, the meteorologist published a classic theory on the path of storms. Redfield based it upon a study of trees felled during a great windstorm in Connecticut, concluding that the damage was progressive rather than haphazard.

The poor professor — born a hundred years too soon. If he had been around to witness the aftermath of the damage caused in the Adirondack high peaks by the 1950 hurricane, or by the 1995 storm which caused so much havoc in the Five Ponds Wilderness area, he would have been pleased to see his theory ratified on a grand scale.

Journal entry: Thursday, August 28, 1980. Ben wants to stay awhile, and so do I. But we know without telling each other that we must have a quick bite, record our names, and go. It is now three p.m., and our return will cover more than nine miles.

We have no concern about reaching our car before dark. The only question is: how long will we be hiking in darkness. The descent offers no relief. Redfield's herd path is as bad going down as up.

We see no one, even at Uphill Brook lean-to. In that respect, Redfield is like most of the other trailless peaks. Of the 11 which Ben and I have climbed this year, we met only seven people on four of them.

The thought of trudging up 600 feet on the return trail via Lake Arnold, even though it is the shortest route to the Loj, is too much for Ben and me. The couple on their way to Marcy were right in their advice, even though the particulars were wrong. We decide to descend to Lake Colden, and head for Marcy Dam via Avalanche Pass.

The ADK guidebook tells us the trail from Uphill Brook lean-to to Lake Colden is a bit more than a mile and a half. To me, it is the longest such short distance in the Adirondacks.

One sees a succession of dazzling sights along the way: waterfalls, flumes, deep pools and restful glades. But the trail is badly eroded, with much brush slashed and trampled underfoot. It helps explain why restrictions have been placed on camping in the Colden area.

The guidebook also tells us that three of the 16 lean-tos in the Colden-Flowed Land area lie just beyond the suspension

Boisterous Opalescent *roars through flume a mile down the river from Uphill lean-to. Sparkling waterfalls brighten the trail to Lake Colden.*

Others came before us on the lower segment of trail from Uphill lean-to to Lake Colden. Area is one of most heavily used in the high peaks.

bridge crossing the Opalescent near Lake Colden. But in the dusk we see only one, which is vacant.

Two people in a boat on Lake Colden do not return our waves. The looming masses of Mt. Colden and Algonquin on either side accentuate the dusk, even though it is only 5:30 p.m. The clouds are still threatening.

We are encouraged by the cheery greetings of four young people at Caribou lean-to,* a short distance beyond the north end of Lake Colden. They have brought along a puppy, a fluff-ball of white, which wags its affection. We ask directions, for there are no markers in the aimless pattern of paths.

"Where are you going, and where did you come from?" one of the girls asks. They seem surprised when we tell them. They have never heard of Redfield.

I assume in the growing gloom that the shortest course to Marcy Dam is to ignore the trail and follow the telephone poles which lead to the dam from the ranger station at Lake Colden. A dead end at a swamp proves me wrong. We backtrack and soon welcome a fresh breeze blowing the length of Avalanche Lake.

The trail to Avalanche Pass, confounding the city folks who advised us at Feldspar, is anything but level. However, from the top of the divide, the rest of the hike is generally downhill. I tell Ben that we have it made.

I hope so, for he is both skittish and exhausted. I try to comfort him by pointing to the shapeless masses that should be Old Nameless on our right and the MacIntyres on the left. He perks up only when we spot

* Removed in the early 1980s.

the glow of campfires at the Avalanche lean-tos. The occupants have had a partial change of mind: they are not leaving, but are again in their sleeping bags. It is only 8:30 p.m.; we unlimber our flashlights.

Marcy Dam is a similar sight — lots of lights but no activity, even at the ranger hut.

On the way out, Ben is listless but game. He takes the lead, fluttering his flashlight through the pitch black. Every once in a while, he gains assurance with a glance back and a searching "Hi."

As we get in the car, I reaffirm my optimism about completing the 46. Ben and I arose at 4 a.m. It's now almost 10 o'clock and while I have

Secure walkways replace floating log bridges which plagued hikers along Avalanche Lake. ENCON completed the work in 1976.

a gimpy knee and three hours of driving ahead of me, I feel great. I see no reason why we can't conquer any high peak in the Adirondacks at any time.

Don't you agree? I ask Ben, who sits silently upright as we drive away from the Loj.

He is sound asleep. But the oblivious smile on his face is confirmation enough.

Gray Peak, left center, and Mt. Skylight, at right, from Algonquin Peak.

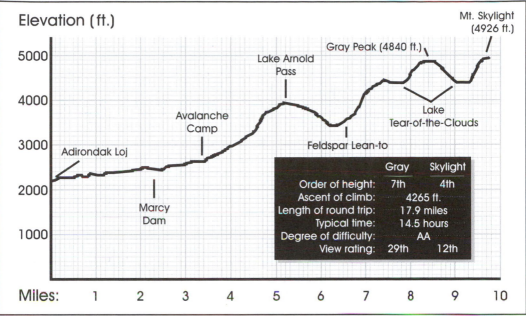

Elevation (ft.)

Mt. Skylight (4926 ft.)

Gray Peak (4840 ft.)

Lake Arnold Pass

Avalanche Camp

Adirondak Loj

Feldspar Lean-to

Lake Tear-of-the-Clouds

Marcy Dam

	Gray	Skylight
Order of height:	7th	4th
Ascent of climb:	4265 ft.	
Length of round trip:	17.9 miles	
Typical time:	14.5 hours	
Degree of difficulty:	AA	
View rating:	29th	12th

Miles: 1 2 3 4 5 6 7 8 9 10

For contour trails, see U.S. Geological Survey map, pgs. 70-71.

45, 46.
GRAY, SKYLIGHT

Journal entry: Monday, August 17, 1981. Ben keeps pestering me to choose my favorite among the 46 high peaks of the Adirondacks.

I can't select one, I tell him; I like them all. And, my favorite keeps changing, per my field notes.

On Gothics, it was: "This is my favorite hike for viewing in all of the Adirondacks." The Dial and Nippletop climb, I noted, was perhaps "the most interesting." And, each time I climbed Rocky Peak Ridge, I agreed with the experts: it was "probably the best." Even Blake, which most people put near the bottom of their list, was transformed on a sprightly summer day into "one of my favorite mountains."

My feelings will probably change again when I conquer these last two...if I ever do. At this point, it's almost as if I were just along for the ride, trying to keep up.

Ben urges me on, so he can finish his tour of the 46. Our good hiking friend, Tom Stanwood, senses victory and wants to bring along friends for a party, as he did when finishing on Colden. Wife Elizabeth cheers us on, too; there were times when she thought I'd never make it.

Another prime motivator for me is the prospect of exploring fabled Lake Tear-of-the-Clouds. Verplanck Colvin described his excitement in discovering that glacial tarn in the col between Marcy and Skylight in his report to the New York state legislature in 1873:

"...At an elevation of 4,293 feet...is a minute, unpretending tear of the clouds...a lovely pool shivering in the breezes of the mountains, and sending its limpid surplus through Feldspar Brook and to the Opalescent River, the wellspring of the Hudson."

My only regret is that older son Jim, who now lives in Florida, won't be along for the great adventure.

The occasion has been a long time in coming. Ben and I have mentally wrestled for a year now on how to meet the challenge. Last year we failed three times in the attempt.

In August, Ben and Tom and I aborted the first excursion because of bad weather, and climbed Marshall instead. A month later, Ben and I again diverted from our mission because of bad weather, and took the easier jaunt to Mt. Colden. A week later, Ben and Tom and I tried once more. That time, we were turned back at the junction of the Opalescent River and Feldspar Brook by snow, ice and premature blasts of winter.

When we do try again, Ben and I have decided upon two criteria: good weather, and no camping out. If that makes us Fair Weather Hikers, so be it. It's also obvious that we're not great party-goers.

A superb weather forecast for today and tomorrow — fair skies coupled with a zero chance of rain — makes up my mind. I call Mrs. Biesemeyer in Keene and tell her Ben and I will be on our way to stay at the Mountain House tonight. My good wife urges us on, even though it will use up our last vacation days.

Not today. *Late in September 1980, son Ben, left, and Tom Stanwood and I decided we did not have the proper snow gear to climb Skylight.*

We pull in late on East Hill Road to find a note of welcome from Mrs. Biesemeyer on the night stand in our Alpine Lodge cabin. I turn off the porch light as she instructed, and Ben and I are enveloped by intense blackness. But it is softened by the glorious stars of our galaxy wheeling through the heavens.

Under three blankets on my bed, the excitement builds. I have had real doubts I would make it this far. In fact, I have fantasized about completing my journal without actually going on this last hike.

Through the window, a shooting star sputters into nothingness, snuffing out my musings in the process.

Journal entry: Tuesday, August 18, 1981. Incredibly, no one is up at the Loj to take advantage of this incredible weather. The air is brisk, almost cold, the sky empty of clouds. Ben and I put on heavy sweaters as we move out at 6:30 a.m.

Only a few wisps of smoke and disheveled heads wobble up at the Marcy Dam and Avalanche Camp lean-tos. Most of the lumpy sleeping bags are still.

If I do complete the 46 today, I'll be prepared: I have a folding camera tripod for self-portraits of Ben and me and a small bottle of champagne. Ben lugs a huge jug of iced tea. He pats it lovingly: "I would have given $20 for this last month when it was so hot on Bear Den."

We move up the dull trail to Lake Arnold one more time. Today, my pace is slow and deliberate. I recall the ancient hiker who moved in this manner around Jim and me on my first climb to Colden. I disdained his pace then; I know better now.

Ben interrupts my thoughts: "How about doing the Crows tomorrow? It'll be a sentimental celebration of our first warm-up hike before we started on the 46. Then we can have four celebrations — one for today's hike, one for the Crows, one with Tom, and one for doing Yard."

Yard Mtn.? He hasn't seen my champagne and he's already tipsy.

Lake Arnold at 9:35 a.m. is as serene as the lily pads. Then a young couple appears from Avalanche Camp, looking for the Indian Falls crossover trail. They intend to follow it to Tahawus via Marcy and Haystack. We direct them to where they missed the trail and suggest they keep moving. They, too, have a long way to go.

Ben takes a cue from them: "How about coming back over Marcy from Skylight? It's no farther and adds only 400 feet of climbing."

I groan an answer: Maybe.

He's thinking, I know, of the revulsion we both have for the swampy trail to Feldspar we must traverse again if we return that way. But as we move along that trail today, we find that while it is still very wet, it is very beautiful. Modest trail work has eased most of the obstacles we encountered on our three hikes here last August and September.

We find no one at the Feldspar trail junction. Surprisingly, we have shortened by an hour the time it took us to come here a year ago with Tom Stanwood.

Ben announces: "We're a mile and a quarter from being 45ers, and less than two hours from becoming 46ers." It dawns on me that we just might achieve our goal.

The beginning of the trail, which heads up toward the southeast along the course of Feldspar Brook, reminds me of the route from Avalanche Camp to Lake Arnold. It ascends steeply on its way to Lake Tear, gaining a thousand feet in a little over a mile. Near the end, it becomes more attractive as it winds through conifers, then moderates in grade.

Lake Tear-of-the-Clouds *nestles serenely in the col between Gray and Skylight, both out of picture at left and right. Huge dome of Marcy peers over intervening mountain slopes.*

At first, we think we see Gray on the left. But it becomes obvious it is but a secondary ridge when the towering superstructure of the true peak comes into view.

The trail, now almost level, enters the plateau between Gray and Skylight. We climb one last rise, then descend to the elusive Lake Tear-of-the-Clouds, which we first saw two years ago from Marcy. Beyond the pond, to the northeast, the huge snout of Marcy cleaves the sky.

Verplanck Colvin spotted the small pond while he was on Marcy, conducting his Adirondack survey during the last century. Guides of that era told him that the waters from the pond flowed to the Ausable and St. Lawrence rivers. But, as Colvin noted, none of them could be sure because they had not explored the valley to see the pond up close.

In mid-September of 1872, after sinking his survey's copper bolt No. 1 on Marcy's summit, Colvin resolved to search out the pond. Along the way, he decided to explore Gray, the seventh highest Adirondack peak, which bulges from a ridge on the west side of Marcy. There was no record that Gray had been climbed.

Today's guidebooks warn that it is difficult to sort out a definitive herd path from the summit of Marcy to Gray. Of course, there were no herd paths when Colvin and his veteran guide from North Elba, William B. Nye, set off on their exploration. And they faced an even more daunting obstacle: dense fog.

However, they discovered a unique solution when they called after their hound, which had bounded off in search of some wild creature. As related by Russell M. L. Carson in *Peaks and People of the Adirondacks*, echoes from their voices identified "the deep, near answer of old Marcy" behind them, and Skylight to the south. This told them that Gray must lie in between them to the southwest, "the dull, no-echo way."

Colvin and Nye fought their way to the summit of Gray through what Colvin described as a pygmy forest of balsams, prickling with "dead boughs like bayonets." Again with the aid of echoes, they descended to the bottom of the valley separating Gray from Skylight, battling chaparral, steep ledges and slippery rocks.

Along the way, they cut into one tree to determine its age. As testament to the severe climate above 4,000 feet in the Adirondacks, they counted, according to Colvin, "a hundred annual rings of woody growth," though the tree was no more than five feet high.

Through the trees from the west end of the valley, they saw the sheet of water they had observed from Marcy. Colvin, who was the first to record visiting the little pond, named it Lake Tear-of-the-Clouds, because as he wrote, it was "dripping with the moisture of the heavens." According to local custom, Colvin and Nye cut a broad blaze upon a tree near the shore to make it "the register and proof of our visit."

Today, Lake Tear appears to be much like it was when Colvin described it in his 1879 report to the New York state legislature:

"On either side the dwarfed forest of spruces, with here and there a birch contorted in its efforts to maintain existence, margined the dark pool. At the upper or eastern end of the lake extended a singular open marsh or wild meadow, covered with a sort of sedge and the familiar 'blue-joint' grass, the marsh broken here and there by cavities, showing subterranean streams, the feeders of the lakelet.

"At the northern side a channel of shallow water, which ceased suddenly a few rods from the lake, seemed to represent the inlet, shallow in water but deep in mud. This and the shallow between us and the marsh island, swarmed with embryo frogs...I noticed and collected a few minute shells. Besides these, a couple of snipe,* which seemed to make their summer home by the shores of this elevated water, were the only other living creatures noticed."

Lake Tear is shaped something like an eye, perhaps 500 feet across. C. A. Siegfried predicts in a New York State Museum publication that like other small Adirondack bodies of water, it eventually may fill with sediment and plant remains to become a bog.

Walter Kretser, Project Manager of the Adirondack Lake Survey, says that the last water samples taken at Lake Tear in the 1970s were highly acidic, so it is almost certain to be sterile today. That hasn't bothered beavers, according to various reports, which have established a dam at the outlet of the pond.

In his report, Colvin revealed what he considered one of the most important discoveries of his Adirondack explorations: "Near the outlet some large rocks clustered in the shallow water and, farther on, the lake contracted to a narrow stream, which soon went plunging down its rocky bed to join the other branches of the Opalescent." He confirmed that Lake Tear-of-the-Clouds did not flow to the Ausable, but into Feldspar Brook and on to the Hudson. He had found the highest source of that river, a good half century after the discovery of the headwaters of another mighty river, the Columbia, on the American west coast.

As with Lake Tear, there are no fish in Feldspar Brook — its steep and rushing waters are hostile to the aquatic insect life which brook trout feed upon. No matter: the flow continues for 310 miles before the Hudson empties into the Atlantic Ocean at New York City. Much of the first 156 miles pass through wilderness, seldom seen and seldom visited — ideal for fishing. The southern 154 miles, from the city of Troy on

* *Long-billed, brownish wading birds.*

down, offers good fishing in its own way — the river is below sea level and floods with the ocean tides.

Journal entry: Tuesday, August 18, 1981. Nineteenth century historian Benson J. Lossing told of starting on the long journey to the Atlantic from Marcy and then to Lake Tear-of-the-Clouds in his book of the 1860s, The Hudson, from the wilderness to the sea. The trip may have been inspired by his first Sunday in the Adirondack wilderness, when he exclaimed: "It was a perfect summer day, and all around us were freshness and beauty. We were alone with God and his works."

That matches my mood at Lake Tear today. But our timetable has almost no slack. Ben and I must get up and down Gray before we earn the luxury of philosophical loafing. It is 1:45 p.m.

Before we leave, Ben straddles the rivulet that marks the beginning of the Hudson River. It boggles the mind to think that this trickle will be almost four and a half miles wide when it flows under the New York State Thruway bridge at Tappan Zee, 10 miles north of New York City. Even that span is nearly a mile less than the river's widest point at Croton-on-Hudson, 10 miles north of the bridge.

We look for the blaze which marked Colvin and Nye's descent from Gray, but find no trace of it.

At first, we follow a false herd path. The real one, exactly where the ADK guidebook indicates, leads due north from the outlet of Tear. It's easy to follow, but the ascent takes three quarters of an hour instead of the half hour predicted by our

The Hudson River? *Ben straddles the highest source of the mighty river. At Lake Tear, it begins a 310-mile journey to the Atlantic at New York City.*

friends from the little Dixes, the Seagles. No wonder: the herd path rises 500 feet above Lake Tear; Gray is the highest of the trailless Adirondack peaks.

Veterans paint discouraging images of Gray's summit — heavily wooded, poor views, etc. All wrong. Gray, on this day at least, is spectacular on all four sides, from Skylight on the south to Colden and the MacIntyres on the northwest.

The blunt summit of Marcy seems to be within throwing distance on the east, although it's a strong half-mile throw. We're close enough to spot various stick figures moving around on the summit.

On descending, we introduce ourselves to a lone hiker on the way up. He is Leif Savery of Yonkers, New York, who is about to become a Forty Sixer. "I just came over from Redfield, so this will be a piece of cake," he says. He reports that he will have completed all of the 46 in two years, all by himself. "I had to tell someone," he exclaims.

Skylight from Gray. *The 500 feet of descent from Gray, highest of the trailless peaks, gives the hiker a good grasp of the route up Skylight.*

Back at Lake Tear, Ben and I conclude that we will return via Lake Colden. I tell him I'm not physically up to adding on the 1,000-ft. climb up Marcy today; he confides that psychologically he's not up to squishing through the Feldspar trail to Lake Arnold again.

We are both relieved. We face no more real climbing today. Except, of course, for one small detail — Skylight.

People are now pressing into the area. Since our packs are loaded for any contingencies, we hide them, wolf down half a sandwich, and head east along the trail, which skirts the boggy shoreline of Lake Tear. In 10 minutes, we cover the fifth of a mile leading to Four Corners. This is where our *trail from Feldspar joins with others coming from Marcy on the north, Skylight on the south, and from the trail heading west over Bartlett Ridge from Upper Ausable Lake.*

A lone figure slumps in the small clearing. "My children are going up Skylight," the middle-aged man tells me. "They want to do the 46, but not me. I did Dix with them and got this far today. That's enough."

I follow Ben up the soggy trail and resume my deliberate pace. A dozen or so young people bound down the trail. Mountain goats.

The trail soon becomes drier and the balsams more sparse and gnarled. Which prompts a momentous decision for Ben and me: who should finish

***Four corners** is the crossroads of four major trails in the central high peaks. The state removed lean-tos here and at Lake Tear in 1976.*

first? "You deserve it, Dad," says Ben. "Go on ahead." No, I tell him. Without you I wouldn't be here. So you go first.

At the tree line, the spirit of a mountain goat takes over Ben, too, and makes the decision for him. We each grab a rock to place on the summit cairn — a sure palliative to prevent rain, according to a hiking legend created in 1936 by Ernest R. Ryder of Troy, NY, the seventh Forty Sixer to climb all of the high peaks.

Ben scrambles up and out of sight.

Surmounting Skylight, for the hiker, is anti-climactic. Most of the highest Adirondack summits, like those of Marcy, Algonquin and Haystack, give up only after you've climbed a long expanse of bare rock. Not here. I can hardly believe that what I see from timberline is actually the top. But it's confirmed by the huge cairn formed of stones hauled up by hikers.

Ben is adding his good-sized rock as I arrive, and I do the same. Only mine is more like a marble. I'll risk a few drops of rain — I'm exhausted. It is three p.m.

Ben races to record the 360-degree vision on film. Not me. I don't care about photos or champagne. I just want to sit and savor.

I review all of the difficult things I've attempted — jobs, dreams, projects, the Army, etc. Nothing has been so hard or as satisfying.

Most times when we've viewed Skylight from the surrounding peaks, it's been crawling with hikers. At this moment, no one is here with us. Good thing: they'd wonder who that goof is, slumped by the artificial rock pile with a silly grin on his face.

I couldn't care less. This is Nirvana.

Skylight's summit, said Old Mountain Phelps, is broad and clear — "smooth enough for a school children's playground."

Not quite.

The summit does expose several acres of open rock, the widest such area on any of the high peaks. In places, the gentle summit curvature does look almost horizontal. And, it's spotted with large, bucolic patches of alpine meadow.

But the topmost surface of Skylight can only be described as dynamic. Fissures zigzag across bare bedrock. Boulder erratics sprawl where glaciers dumped them ages ago. And around the perimiter, dwarf trees and shrubs form an intimidating barricade. They crouch in shallow ravines as if waiting to pounce on alpine azaleas and other rare plants that have been able to withstand the killing winds.

The surrounding mountains enhance the dynamism, in particular to the north. Pioneering hiker Robert Marshall noted that they form "a wall of virgin summits...including all twelve of the highest peaks in the Adirondacks." It gave him, he said, "a feeling of massiveness" which he did not recall from the summit of any other Adirondack mountain. In all, one can gorge from an incredible visual menu of 30 of the 46 high peaks.

The huge cairn on Skylight positions hikers to view one of the premier sights on the peak. Sandwiched between Marcy and Haystack is Panther Gorge, a deep chasm scoured by glaciers. With good-sized red spruce trees on its precipitous slopes and a dancing waterfall, it is at once beautiful and awesome — the Forty Sixers' Jim Goodwin calls it "sort of a miniature Yosemite Valley."

Verplanck Colvin named Panther Gorge in 1877 after shooting a "monstrous creature, cooly defiant, standing at the brow of a precipice on some dead timber." The animal made its home, he observed, in an "abode of plenty." While in the area a couple of years earlier, his aim was not so good, fortunately. He reported to the state legislature, "Two eagles, rising from the gulf at the east, soared past us majestically, unmindful of revolver shots."

All of the panthers and many of the eagles are gone from the Adirondacks. But hikers still come face to face with other

From Skylight, Haystack looms at right, beyond Panther Gorge. Giant is at center; then to left, Gothics and Basin.

esoteric creatures. In 1995, one group reported to the Forty Sixers' *Adirondack Peeks* that "coyotes followed us off Skylight at midnight."

Old Mountain Phelps was a member of the Colvin survey group which made the first ascent of Skylight in 1873. On that outing, Colvin could not claim the right to christen the mountain as he had done on so many other summits. Old Mountain Phelps had already named Skylight in 1857 while on Marcy with Frederick S. Perkins, an amateur painter. The two of them decided on the name because a rock projection on Skylight's summit looked like a dormer window on a roof.

Colvin confirmed that Haystack and Skylight were the third and fourth highest peaks in the Adirondacks. As the Watermans noted in *Forest and Crag*, Skylight was "the last really major virgin summit" in the northeast.

Skylight preserves several legacies of Colvin from the 1870s. His survey bolt No. 17 is embedded in bedrock. Also, his survey report is as pertinent today as it was when he climbed there:

"Skylight, so recently the untrodden summit, with its barrier of dwarf forest, is now from this new pass by a new trail an ascent of only so many minutes." Colvin lamented that "the first romance is gone forever." But he took the long view, which hikers would do well to remember today:

"While these changes have opened to travel many of the most interesting nooks among our mountains, they have only rendered more marked, by contrast, the wildness of the remainder, and the unvisited wilderness centres or cores are still left in all their sylvan purity..."

Come and explore, again and again, Colvin seemed to be telling us. For, as he concluded, few will ever "fully understand what the

Adirondack wilderness really is. It is a mystery even to those who have crossed and recrossed it...on foot through its vast and silent recesses."

Journal entry: Tuesday, August 18, 1981. Now that my breathing has slowed to a crawl, I haul out the champagne near the summit cairn. It tastes — well, different. Ben and I decide we like Adirondack water better. Anyway, we take a sip and toast each other, Ben's mother, Jim and Ben's sisters Judy and Gretchen, Tom, and anybody else who today may be on Marcy, Haystack, Redfield, Allen, Basin, and the rest.

I tell Ben that this climb has answered his incessant query: today, Skylight is my favorite mountain. I give it a better view rating than the 13th awarded by the Marshall brothers and their guide, Herb Clark.

Ben nudges me. Two hikers are emerging from the treeline. Ben also points out that it is 3:30 p.m.; we have nine miles to go, and he is tired. So am I.

Even so, I hate to leave. It is the feeling one gets at the end of an exceptional movie or concert. But in the same way, we will carry away enduring memories.

Marcy beams approval as 14-year quest to climb and explore the 46 high peaks ends on Skylight. *Glacial erratics litter the summit; man-made rock-pile — "rain insurance" — is at right.*

We reach Four Corners in 15 minutes, as opposed to the 40 we took in ascending. Backpacks are resting there, but without their owners.

Hikers can no longer camp in the col between Skylight and Marcy because it is above 4,000 feet. But as late as the early 1970s, the area provided a welcome respite for those out prowling the peaks.

The state's old Conservation Department constructed its first lean-to in 1919, at Lake Tear-of-the-Clouds. It boasted a magnificent view of Mt. Marcy — a fitting complement to Colvin's "lovely pool [which] lifted on its granite pedestal toward heaven the loftiest water-mirror of the stars."

Later, a second lean-to was built at Four Corners. But overuse even at this high altitude led to despoilment of the surroundings. DEC removed them both in 1976.

Theodore Roosevelt was indisputably the best known person to lunch at Lake Tear when he vacationed in the high peaks in September 1901.

Roosevelt, vice president at the time, had just spent a tense four days at the bedside of President William McKinley, who had been shot by an anarchist in Buffalo, New York. When McKinley's condition improved, the vice president headed for the Adirondacks.

Originally, he and his family stayed at the Tahawus Club, which had been initiated for sportsmen near the site of the old mining community. Roosevelt, remembered as much as an outdoorsman and conservationist as a politician, immediately organized a party to climb Marcy.

Stormy weather convinced other family members to return to base camp after an overnight at Lake Colden. But Theodore Roosevelt urged his guides to press on. He felt, as he later wrote, "There is delight in the hardy life in the open."

After climbing Marcy, clouds rolled in so they descended the 1,000 feet to Lake Tear. They had no more begun eating their lunch shortly after noon when a ranger appeared, clutching a telegram. The vice president, as Edmund Morris wrote in *The Rise of Theodore Roosevelt*, instinctively "knew what message the man was bringing."

The president had taken a turn for the worse. It was Friday the 13th.

On arriving late at the Tahawus Club, Roosevelt insisted that he be driven immediately by horse-drawn wagon over dangerous roads to the railhead at North Creek. A state marker on Rt. 28N, some six miles north of Minerva, indicates a stop where his driver changed horses.

Somewhere while en route that night, Roosevelt became President of the United States, at the moment William McKinley passed away.

Journal entry: Tuesday, August 18, 1981. *Ben and I retrieve our packs at Lake Tear and gaze at Mt. Marcy while polishing off the remaining half of our sandwiches. It's a strange feeling: we may b sitting on the exact spot where Teddy Roosevelt and his guid lunched almost a hundred years ago.*

True or not, our thoughts match those expressed by Roosevelt: "There are no words that can tell of the hidden spirit of the wilderness, that can reveal its mystery, its melancholy, and its charm."

Before starting back, Ben and I take a last look at Lake Tear-of-the-Clouds. We note that — sterile or not — something is nibbling at the surface. Bugs, I conclude.

A short distance down the trail leading to Feldspar, we chat with two young men at a rivulet coming down from nowhere. They ask: "Is it safe for drinking?" When we assure them it is, one adds: "We're new here, and don't know the territory."

Both are from New York state originally, but one now attends college in Burlington, Vermont, and the other in Chapel Hill, North Carolina. They say Adirondack trails are far steeper than the kind of ridge hiking they're used to in the Green and Blue Ridge mountains. "There are more rocks and exposed roots here," says the one from North Carolina.

I know what he means. I've hiked segments of the 2,100-mile Appalachian Trail — in the Virginia segment of the Blue Ridge, along the Hudson River in downstate New York, on Mt. Greylock in the Berkshires of Massachusetts, and on parts of the Long Trail in the Green Mountains of Vermont.

Those mountains are caressed more closely by civilization. As an example, Ben Rolston, a former business associate and former president of Vermont's Green Mountain Club, told me how one can climb the 265 miles of the Long Trail from Massachusetts to Canada, as he often did, without leaving the marked path for supplies.

The Long Trail, unlike remote paths in the Adirondacks, is bisected by highways 19 times as it traces a tortuous route along the spine of the Green Mountains. Rolson's wife, with her husband's schedule in hand, preceded him a day or so at various crossings to leave buried rations at predetermined locations.

Our new friends say they have come over from climbing Marcy after sleeping last night on the truck route close to Marcy Dam. The temperature was in the 30s and there was a half inch of frost on their sleeping bags when they awoke. "I only got a half hour's sleep," says the same young man. "I'm beat."

It's five p.m. when the four of us reach the junction where Feldspar Brook joins the Opalescent River. Our new friends had planned to return by the trail along Lake Colden and Avalanche Lake. But I warn them they're sure to run out of daylight. They have no flashlights, so we decide to go with them on the shorter trail to Lake Arnold and out.

Ben surges with them down into the swamp, and the three disappear ahead of me. Ben, I know, is agonizing over conflicting desires: to keep up and chat with ones closer to his age, or to fall back and keep me in sight. Fortunately, they stop to rest at Lake Arnold. It gives me time to drag up and join them.

Dusk is descending, so we tell them they can take one of our flash-lights if they want to go ahead; they can mail it back. Or, they can accompany us to the Loj and we'll drive them to their car. Instead, they decide to stay with us until Marcy Dam. They should have no trouble from there; the road is smooth and cuts a wide swath through the trees to let the twilight shine in.

As we swing down the long, rocky gully from Lake Arnold, the young man from North Carolina grimaces: "My legs are like jelly and my toes feel like they're sticking out a half inch." He shakes his head as he points to boots he had "shined brown for this trip." They are black from the mud.

"No sleeping out for us tonight," his partner chimes in. "We're going to find a motel with hot showers and HBO."

"Count me out on HBO," replies the tired one, who obviously has sleep in mind.

His partner seems to be getting a second wind. "We planned to stay at the Loj tonight. I thought it would be like the hikers' huts in Vermont. You can stay there for a dollar and a half a night, or a dollar if you belong to the Green Mountain Club. But," and he gestures now, "the Loj charges eight dollars. Outrageous!"

A dollar a night? Those huts must be state-supported, or they've found another Nirvana. And it's wise they didn't try the White Mountains in New Hampshire. An overnight stay in one of the Appalachian Mountain Club huts, with supper and breakfast, can cost 50 times that much.

Campers at Avalanche Camp and Marcy Dam are preparing to bed down. I note disturbing signs at the latter: a couple with a German Shepherd and another with a pair of bag-toting Dobermans. They seem well-trained, but growl at each other.

Striving for perfect safety, I suppose. It reminds me of a business maxim: the closer an organization is to perfection, the closer it is to collapse. If that relates to the Adirondacks' camping system, we stand to lose the wild and free spirit which hikers treasure.

Ben and I bid our friends goodbye and head out on the last leg of our journey. It is eight p.m. now, and very murky. I haul out my flash-light and — it won't turn on. Ben pulls his out and — it won't work either. No problem this time. We carry spare batteries, so we're back in business in no time.

I can't help but notice that Ben is a very different hiker than the one who joined me on this great adventure four years ago. Then, he was only a boy, burdened by adolescent weariness as we neared the end of most hikes.

Not now. He is a strong young man who, although only 13 and gangly, strides confidently ahead into the darkness, pausing only to make sure I'm OK and still coming.

That's the only jarring note upon my completion of the 46. Ben and I did them together, of course. But for me, it was with great difficulty. Now that the challenge has been overcome, there is doubt in my mind that Ben or Jim will want to keep hiking with someone so slow.

Ben rescues me from that depressing thought. "Just think, Dad. We'll do the Crows tomorrow and Yard soon. Then let's try Mansfield and Camel's Hump in Vermont like our friends suggested. And there's lots more in the Catskills and the White Mountains. Isn't that great!"

EPILOGUE

Journal entry: Tuesday, May 31, 1996. Climbing the 46 Adirondack high peaks is a mystical experience. Upon reaching the last summit, some people are so overcome with emotion they have trouble expressing their feelings.

But they try, as in these reports to Adirondack Peeks, *magazine of the Forty Sixers:*

"It's beyond comparison," says John D. Ryan, Jr. "Tears came to my eyes, and I could hardly say a word. I've never experienced such elation and joy at reaching a goal at any other time of my life."

William A. Stowe compares the achievement to winning an Olympic gold medal for the United States, as he did for stroking the fastest eight-oared shell in the world. He never again expected, he said, to have "that same rush of adrenaline, known only to winners."

As of mid-1995, Stowe and his wife were half way to becoming Forty Sixers. But, he said, "that same wonderful feeling of Olympic accomplishment follows me up every mountain, and over every obstacle and task I set out to achieve."

Completion of the 46 was so overpowering to Kirk Luchtenberg that, on nearing his final summit, he felt the need to be by himself. His partners sensed it, he said, so "without a word continued on to let me...finish alone."

Grace Hudowalski, long-time historian for the Forty Sixers, wrote recently that "one should never underestimate the power of the mountains." In spite of adverse conditions, she says, hikers always return. Why?

I can see her smiling as she tapped out the answer on her typewriter: "One doesn't try to explain the mountains."

I did, in this book. Reaching Skylight's summit brought for me a kaleidoscope of emotions: exhilaration, exhaustion, triumph, contentment, pride, and so on. But the only legible reference I can find in my field notes is: "Never been happier."

The day after Ben and I completed our last climb of the 46 Adirondack high peaks, we sought to sustain the emotional high. So we re-climbed Little Crow and Big Crow mountains, a couple of miles east of Keene. It was a sentimental journey, since they were the first Adirondack peaks Ben climbed with me prior to our exploration of the 46.

Journey's end. *But not really. The 46 high peaks are but a prologue to exploring the other wonders of the Adirondacks.*

When I think back to that time, staring at the beckoning peaks, it rekindles early emotions from the great adventure.

Emerson hinted at my feelings when he wrote, "The universe is a more amazing puzzle than ever." But that's too grand a sentiment for the sliver of universe Ben and I gazed on that day. The artist Bill Watterson came closer in his final cartoon for Calvin and Hobbes, *on the last day of last year.*

Calvin, the irrepressible six-year old, looked into the woods at the back of his house and enthused to his best friend, a stuffed tiger: "It's a magical world, Hobbes, ol' buddy...Let's go exploring!"

Sons Jim and Ben and I concluded several things from our explorations.

I know the two boys found that conquering the high peaks made it easier for them to face new challenges elsewhere. Eventually, each moved out on his own to begin college far away from home — Jim in Florida, Ben in Arizona.

In a way, they emulated John Wesley Powell, the one-armed Civil War hero, who headed the Adirondack Survey prior to Verplanck Colvin and later became director of the U.S. Geological Survey. Before that, Powell led the first expedition down the Colorado River through the Grand Canyon. His report on that journey began with this bold statement: "We are now ready to start our way down the Great Unknown."

I discovered in a hurry that mountain climbing is good for what ails you. It not only corrected my back problem, but helped keep me trim. I lost five pounds on the Redfield expedition. After climbing Gray and Skylight, my belt tightened two notches; I had shed six pounds.

Climbing the high peaks is good for the soul, too. Explorer and environmental activist John Muir expressed it well: "Nature's peace will flow into you as the sunshine into the trees. The winds will blow their freshness into you, and the storms their energy, while cares will drop off like autumn leaves."

Off on his own. *On a re-visit to Cascade, I watch gangly son Ben climb to the summit. Conquest of the 46 prepped him and son Jim for other challenges in life.*

Above all, exploring the 46 Adirondack high peaks broadens your perspective on life. From both a historical and literary point-of-view, it gives one the rare privilege, as the late William Chapman White wrote, to be "part of a time that was and time yet to come."

My final conclusion offers practical guidance to those interested in doing what we did:

BURNSIDE'S LAW OF HIKING

- *If there is a remote chance that it will rain or snow in the Adirondacks, it will.*
- *Adirondack trails are three times as long and hard as they appear on the map.*
- *That knob you think is the summit is a mile short of your goal.*
- *As heat and humidity go up on a linear scale, the number of black flies goes up logarithmically.*

And finally:

- *The best way to count to 46 is slowly.*

ACKNOWLEDGEMENTS

In preparing this book, I strove to fulfill Ernest Hemingway's philosophy: "The writer must know something better than anyone else does."

That's a tall order — the "principle of the iceberg," Hemingway called it. "There are seven-eighths of it underwater for every part that shows. Anything you know, you can eliminate, and it only strengthens your iceberg. It is the part that doesn't show. If the writer omits something because he does not know it, then there is a hole."

If there are holes in this book, it isn't the fault of those who gave me such good advice and encouragement. I'm grateful to all of them.

My thanks go first to members of the Adirondack Mountain Club and the Adirondack Forty Sixers who helped me in my quest: ex-ADK President Dave Newhouse, who advised me on how to get started; Robert Ringlee, another ex-ADK head whose enthusiasm for the high peaks is contagious; trip leaders such as John Winkler, Bruce Wadsworth, Eugene Brousseau, Bob Baldwin and, in particular, Tom Stanwood, who more than anyone saw to it that I completed my exploration of the 46; and those who provided helpful guidance during hikes, such as Pete and Dodie Seagle on the Little Dixes and Mindaugus Jatulis on the Sewards.

And to Grace Hudowalski, long-time historian of the Forty Sixers, this book is a delayed response to her request of 15 years ago: "Write us something about your climbs so we can attach it to your file."

I'm grateful also to the Adirondackers who were so gracious and generous in checking facts: Mary MacKenzie, historian for the village of Lake Placid and the town of North Elba; Mildred Dobie, former Supervisor of the town of North Hudson; Jim Goodwin, probably the most knowledgeable of current high peak explorers; Adrian Edmonds, Adirondack oral historian and founder of Keene Valley Adirondack Realty; and Pete Sanders, former manager of Elk Lake Lodge.

My thanks also go to those who welcomed me to the archives of the Adirondack Research Library, a unit of the Association for the Protection of the Adirondacks in Schenectady, New York — the Association's Executive Director, David Gibson, steering committee members Edith Pilcher and Bill Healy, and others among their many volunteers. I received a similar warm welcome at the New York State

Library in Albany, at the Schenectady County Public Library, and the Keene Valley Public Library.

Where does one start and stop in thanking those who have written with such feelings about the high peaks? The early days bring to mind Alfred L. Donaldson and Verplanck Colvin, preceded and followed by countless others. The late Dorothy Plum deserves a special blessing for preserving their output in the *Adirondack Bibliography* for the Adirondack Mountain Club.

A few contemporary writers whose influence shines through in this book: Paul Jamieson, who first piqued my interest in the high peaks with *An Adirondack Reader*; Fred Fraser, who wrote an excellent series of columns on climbing the peaks in the '60s for *The Schenectady Gazette*, now the *Daily Gazette*; Eleanor Brown, a member of the Adirondack Park Agency, who wrote a definitive ADK handbook for conservationists, *The Forest Preserve of New York State*, in 1985; Tony Goodwin, who edited the superb *Guide to Adirondack Trails, High Peaks Region* for the ADK; Laura and Guy Waterman, with their *Forest and Crag* for the Appalachian Mountain Club; and Mike Hendricks, who regularly reports on goings-on in the high peaks through articles in newspapers served by the Associated Press.

I've read Adirondack magazines so thoroughly for so long I feel like I know the editors — from Stuart Ludlum and Lionel Atwill from the early days of *Adirondack Life* to its current editor, Elizabeth Folwell; from Trudy Healy, a co-founder of the Forty Sixers' *Adirondack Peeks* in 1963 to the present co-editors, David W. and Suzanne E. Lance; and from those who guided the Adirondack Mountain Club's early monthly magazine, *High Spots*, to Neal Burdick, who now edits its successor periodical, *Adirondac*.

The crisp appearance of the book is due in large part to the designer, Deborah Keats, to graphic artist and compositor Gretchen F. Bradley, and to the creator of the mountain profiles, Eric Swanzey, aided by his former business associate, Marianne Barber.

I am deeply grateful to those who reviewed my manuscript: Pewilla Dick of Boston, a former editor with Little, Brown & Co.; son Benjamin; and my favorite writer of them all, wife Elizabeth.

Finally, it goes without saying that I owe a huge debt to my partners who accompanied me on the great adventure: sons James C. and Benjamin J.

James R. Burnside
Schenectady, New York

BIBLIOGRAPHY

Abbott, Henry. *The Birch Bark Books*. Harrison, NY: Harbor Hill Books, 1980 (reprint).

Avery, Myron H. *Guide to the Appalachian Trail in New England*. Washington, DC: The Appalachian Trail Conference, Inc., 1952.

Barnett, Lincoln. *The Ancient Adirondacks*. New York: Time-Life Books, 1974.

Bartlett, John. *Familiar Quotations*. Boston: Little Brown & Co., 1980.

Beckey, Fred. *Mountains of North America*. San Francisco: Sierra Club Books in association with the American Alpine Club, 1982.

Berry, Wendell. *Recollected Essays, 1965-1980*. San Francisco: North Point Press, 1981.

Brooks, Van Wyck. *The Confident Years 1985-1915*. New York: E. P. Dutton & Co. Inc., 1952.

Brown, Eleanor. *The Forest Preserve of New York State: A Handbook for Conservationists*. Glens Falls, NY: The Adirondack Mountain Club, 1985.

Bull, John; Farrand, John, Jr. *Field Guide to North American Birds, Eastern Region*. New York: Borzoi Books (Alfred A. Knopf, Inc.), 1977.

Burdick, Neal S., Ed., *A Century Wild: Essays Commemorating the Centennial of the Adirondack Forest Preserve*. Saranac Lake, NY: The Chauncy Press, 1985.

Burroughs, John. *Time and Change*. Boston: Houghton Mifflin, 1912.

Carson, Russell M. L. *Peaks and People of the Adirondacks*. Garden City, NY: Doubleday, Doran & Co., Inc., 1928.

Chapman, William K. *Mammals of the Adirondacks*. Utica, NY: North Country Books, Inc., 1991.

Colvin, Sidney, Ed. *The Letters of Robert Louis Stevenson*. New York: Charles Scribner's Sons, 1923.

Colvin, Verplanck. *Report of the Topographical Survey of the Adirondack Wilderness of New York for the Year 1873*. Albany, NY: State of New York, 1874.

Colvin, Verplanck. *Seventh Annual Report on the Progress of the Topographical Survey of the Adirondack Region of New York, to the Year 1879*. Albany, NY: Weed, Parsons & Co., 1880. Includes condensed reports for 1874-1878.

Cooper, James Fenimore. *The Last of the Mohicans*. New York: The Limited Editions Club, 1932.

Cotter, Lawrence E., Ed. *Guide to Adirondack Trails*. Glens Falls, NY: Adirondack Mountain Club, ninth edition, 1979.

DeSormo, Maitland C. *Noah John Rondeau: Adirondack Hermit*. Utica, NY: North Country Books, 1969.

DeSormo, Maitland C. *The Heydays of the Adirondacks*. Saranac Lake, NY: Adirondack Yesteryears, Inc., 1974.

Dillard, Annie. *Pilgrim at Tinker Creek*. New York: Harper & Row, 1974.

Donaldson, Alfred L. *A History of the Adirondacks*. New York: Century Co., 1921 (two volumes).

Doughty, Howard. *Francis Parkman*. New York: The Macmillan Co., 1962.

Eiseley, Loren. *The Immense Journey*. New York: Random House, 1957.

Emerson, Ralph Waldo. *The Essays of Ralph Waldo Emerson*. New York: The Limited Editions Club, 1934.

Famighetti, Robert, Ed. *The World Almanac*. Mahway, NJ: Funk & Wagnalls, 1993.

Finch, Robert; Elder, John. *Nature Writing*. New York: W. W. Norton & Company, 1990.

Fitzgerald, Bryan T. *Guide Book of the Long Trail*. Montpelier, VT: The Green Mountain Club, 1990.

Fosburgh, Hugh. *One Man's Pleasure*. New York: William Morrow & Company, Inc., 1960.

Fowler, Barney. *Adirondack Albums*. Schenectady, NY: Outdoor Associates, Vol. I, 1974; Vol. II, 1980; Vol. III, 1982.

Franklin, Benjamin. *Poor Richard's Almanacks, Etc*. New York: The Heritage Press, 1964.

Goodwin, Tony, Ed. *Guide to Adirondack Trails, High Peaks Region*. Series editor, Neal S. Burdick. Glens Falls, NY: eleventh edition, 1985. Lake George, NY: twelfth edition, 1992.

Haines, Paul. *Problems in Prose*. New York, Evanston and London: Harper & Row, 1963.

Hammond, Samuel H. *Hills, Lakes, and Forest Streams; Or, A Tramp in the Woods*. New York: J. C. Darby, 1854.

Hammond, Samuel H. *Wild Northern Scenes; or Sporting Adventures with the Rifle and Rod*. New York: Darby & Jackson, 1857.

Headley, Joel Tyler. *The Adirondacks; or, Life in the Woods*. New York: Baker & Scribner, 1849.

Healy, Bill. *The High Peaks of Essex*. Fleischmanns, NY: Purple Mountain Press, 1992.

Heller, Murray. *Call Me Adirondack*. Saranac Lake, NY: The Chauncey Press, 1989.

Hoagland, Edward. *Walking the Dead Diamond River*. New York: Random House, 1973.

Hoffman, Charles Fenno. *Wild Scenes in the Forest and Prairie*. New York: Colyer, 1843.

Holland, W.J. *The Butterfly Guide*. Garden City, NY: Doubleday, Page & Co., 1923

Horse Trails in New York State. Albany, NY: New York State Department of Environmental Conservation, 1992.

Hudowalski, Grace L., Ed. *The Adirondack High Peaks*. Adirondack, NY: The Adirondack Forty Sixers, 1970.

James, Henry. *The Letters of William James*. Boston: The Atlantic Monthly Press, 1920.

Jamieson, Paul F. *Adirondack Pilgrimage*. Glens Falls, NY: The Adirondack Mountain Club, Inc., 1986.

Jamieson, Paul F., Ed. *The Adirondack Reader*. New York: The Macmillan Co., 1964.

Jamieson, Paul F., Ed. *The Adirondack Reader* (second edition). Glens Falls, NY: The Adirondack Mountain Club, Inc., 1982.

Kelley, Brooks Mather. *Yale. A History*. New Haven and London: Yale University Press, 1974.

Kent, Rockwell. *N by E*. New York: Random House, 1930.

Khayyám, Omar. *Rubáiyát*. New York: The Heritage Press, 1946.

Kirschenbaum, Howard; Schafstall, Susan; Stuchin, Janine. *The Adirondack Guide*. Raquette Lake, NY: The Sagamore Institute, 1983.

LaBastille, Anne. *Woodswoman*. New York: E. P. Dutton, 1978.

Longstreth, T. Morris. *The Adirondacks*. New York: The Century Co., 1917.

Longstreth, T. Morris. *The Catskills*. New York: The Century Co., 1918.

Leopold, Aldo. *A Sand County Almanac*. New York: Oxford University Press, 1949.

Lossing, Benson, J. *The Hudson, from the wilderness to the sea*. New York: Virtue and Yorston, 1866.

Marshall, Robert. *Alaska Wilderness*. Berkeley, Calif: University of California Press, 1970.

Marshall, Robert. *The High Peaks of the Adirondacks*. Albany, NY: The Adirondack Mountain Club, Inc., 1922.

Masten, Arthur H. *The Story of Adirondac* (reprint). Syracuse, NY: Syracuse University Press, 1968.

McLaughlin, Donald W., Ed. *Guide to Adirondack Trails*. Glens Falls, NY: Adirondack Mountain Club, eighth edition, 1972.

McMartin, Barbara. *Discover the Adirondack High Peaks*. Woodstock, VT: Backcountry Publications, 1993.

Merton, Thomas. *Raids on the Unspeakable*. New York: New Directions, 1964.

Morris, Edmund. *The Rise of Theodore Roosevelt*. New York: Ballantine Books, 1979.

Mowat, Farley. *People of the Deer*. Boston: Little, Brown, 1952.

Murray, William H. H. *Adventures in the Wilderness*. Boston: Fields, Osgood, & Co., 1869.

Nash, Ogden. *The Pocket Book of Ogden Nash*. New York: Pocket Books, a Simon & Schuster Division, 1962.

Nash, Roderick. *Wilderness and the American Mind*. New Haven and London: Yale University Press, 1967.

Nelson, E. W. *Wild Animals of North America*. Washington, DC: The National Geographic Society, 1930.

O'Kane, Walter Collins. *Trails and Summits of the Adirondacks*. Houghton Mifflin Co., 1928.

Peattie, Donald Culross. *An Almanac for Moderns*. New York: Putnam, 1935.

Peattie, Roderick. *The Friendly Mountains*. New York: The Vanguard Press, 1942.

Phelps, Dr. Orra A., Ed. *Guide to Adirondack Trails*. Albany, NY: Adirondack Mountain Club, first edition, 1934; New York: second edition, 1941.

Pilcher, Edith. *Up the Lake Road: The First Hundred Years of the Adirondack Mountain Reserve*. Keene Valley, NY: The Adirondack Mountain Reserve, 1987.

Plum, Dorothy A., Ed. *Adirondack Bibliography*. Gabriels, NY: Adirondack Mountain Club, 1958.

Plum, Dorothy A., Ed. *Adirondack Bibliography Supplement 1956-1965*. Blue Mountain Lake, NY: The Adirondack Museum, 1973.

Plum, Dorothy A., Ed. *Adirondack Bibliography. Supplement: 1966-1968*. Glens Falls, NY: Adirondack Mountain Club, 1970.

Porte, Joel, Ed. *Emerson and his Journals*. Cambridge, MA: Harvard University Press, 1982.

Porter, Eliot. *Forever Wild*. Blue Mountain Lake, NY: The Adirondack Museum. New York and London: Harper & Row (undated).

Porter, L. Morgan, Ed. *Guide to Adirondack Trails*. Gabriels, NY: Adirondack Mountain Club, sixth edition, 1957; seventh edition, 1962.

Powell, John Wesley. *Exploration of the Colorado River of the West and Its Tributaries*. Washington, DC: U.S. Government, 1875.

Pownall, Thomas. *Topographical Description of the Dominions of the United States of America*. Lois Mulkearn, Ed. Pittsburgh: University of Pittsburgh Press, 1949.

Roosevelt, Theodore. *African Game Trails*. New York: Charles Scribner's Sons, 1910.

Ruskin, John. *Modern Painters of Truth and Theoretic Faculties*. London: Smith, Alder and Co., 5 vol., 1846-1860.

Shorey, A.T., Ed. *Guide to Adirondack Trails*. Albany, NY: Adirondack Mountain Club — third edition, 1945, fourth edition, 1947, and fifth edition, 1950.

Slack, Nancy G. and Bell, Allison W. *85 Acres*. Lake George, NY: The Adirondack Mountain Club, Inc., 1993.

Smith, Vivian Green, Ed. *With Hand and Heart: The Courtship Letters of Franklin B. Hough and Mariah Kilhan*. Utica, NY: North Country Books, 199

Stevenson, Robert L. *A Child's Garden of Verses*. Chicago: Charles Scribner's — the Book House for Children, 1950.

Stevenson, Robert L. *Letters of Stevenson*. New York: Charles Scribner's, 1923.

Stoddard, Seneca Ray. *The Adirondacks: Illustrate*d. Albany, NY: Weed, Parsons & Co., 1874.

Stoddard, Seneca Ray. *Old Times in the Adirondacks*. (Reprint). Burlington, VT: George Little Press, Inc., 1971.

Street, Alfred B. *The Indian Pass*. New York: Hurd and Houghton, 1869.

Tefft, Tim. Ed., *Of the Summits, of the Forests*. Morrisonville, NY: the Adirondack Forty Sixers, 1991.

Terrie, Philip G. *Forever Wild: Environmental Aesthetics and the Adirondack Forest Preserve*. Philadelphia: Temple University Press, 1985.

Terrie, Philip G. Terrie, Ed. Reprint of *Peaks and People of the Adirondacks*. Glens Falls, NY: The Adirondack Mountain Club, 1973.

Thoreau, Henry David. *Walden, or Life in the Woods*. New York: The Heritage Press, 1939.

Todd, John. *Long Lake*. Reprint of 1845 edition. Harrison, NY: Harbor Hill Books, 1983.

Twain, Mark, *The Adventures of Colonel Sellers*. Charles Neider, Ed. London: Chatto and Windus, 1966.

Wadsworth, Bruce. *An Adirondack Sampler*. Glens Falls, NY: Adirondack Mountain Club, 1979.

Wallace, E. R. *Guide to the Adirondacks*. Published with H. Harry Smith, *Modern Babes in the Woods*. Syracuse: Watson Gill, 1872.

Warner, Charles Dudley. *In the Wilderness*. New York: Houghton, Mifflin & Co./ Cambridge, MA: The Riverside Press, 1905.

Warren, Michael. *Appalachian Trail*. Portland, OR: Graphic Arts Center Publishing Co., 1979.

Waterman, Laura and Guy. *Forest and Crag: A History of Hiking, Trail Blazing, and Adventure in the Northeast Mountains*. Boston: Appalachian Mountain Club, 1989.

Watson, Winslow C. *The Military and Civil History of the County of Essex, New York*. Albany, NY: J. Munsell, 1869.

Weston, Harold. *Freedom in the Wilds*. St. Huberts, NY: Adirondack Trail Improvement Society, 1971.

White, William Chapman. *Adirondack Country*. New York: Alfred Knopf, 1968.

World Book Encyclopedia, The. Chicago: World Book, Inc., 1984.

Wyckoff, Jerome. *The Adirondack Landscape: A Hiker's Guide*. Gabriels, NY: Adirondack Mountain Club, 1967.

PERIODICALS

Adirondac. Lake George, NY: Adirondack Mountain Club, Inc.

Adirondack Council Newsletter. Elizabethtown, NY: Adirondack Council.

Adirondack Life. Jay, NY: Adirondack Life, Inc.

Adirondack Mountain Club, The. Lake George, NY: Adirondack Mountain Club, Inc.

Adirondack Peeks. Morrisonville, NY: Adirondack Forty Sixers, Inc.

Backpacker. Emmanus, PA: Rodale Press, Inc.

Book Talk. Syracuse, NY: Syracuse University Press.

Business Week. New York: The McGraw-Hill Companies.

Conservationist. Albany, NY: New York State Department of Environmental Conservation.

Daytona Beach News-Journal. Daytona Beach, FL.

Flightline. Dallas, TX: American Airlines, Inc.

Gazette, Daily and Sunday. Schenectady, NY: The Gazette Newspapers, Inc.

High Spots. Early monthly magazine of the Adirondack Mountain Club.

Knickerbocker News. Schenectady, NY: Capital Newspapers, Inc. (Now incorporated into the *Albany Times-Union*).

Lake Placid News. Lake Placid, NY.

Lookout, The. Schenectady, NY: Schenectady Chapter, Adirondack Mountain Club.

National Geographic. Washington, DC: The National Geographic Society.

Natural History. New York: American Museum of Natural History.

Newsweek. New York: The Washington Post Co.

New York Observer. (Now defunct).

New York Times, The. New York: The New York Times Company.

Placid Pioneer, The. Lake Placid, NY: North Elba Historical Society.

Republican. Keeseville, NY. (Now incorporated into the *Valley News* of Elizabethtown, NY).

TIME. New York: Time, Inc.

Times-Union, Albany. Albany, NY: Capital Newspapers Division of the Hearst Corporation.

Wall Street Journal, The. New York: Dow Jones & Co.

Watertown Daily Times. Watertown, NY.

Welcome to Whiteface Mountain. Albany, NY: New York State Department of Environmental Conservation.

World of Whiteface, The. Albany, NY: New York State Department of Environmental Conservation.

INDEX

Boldface numbers indicate major coverage by chapter.

D

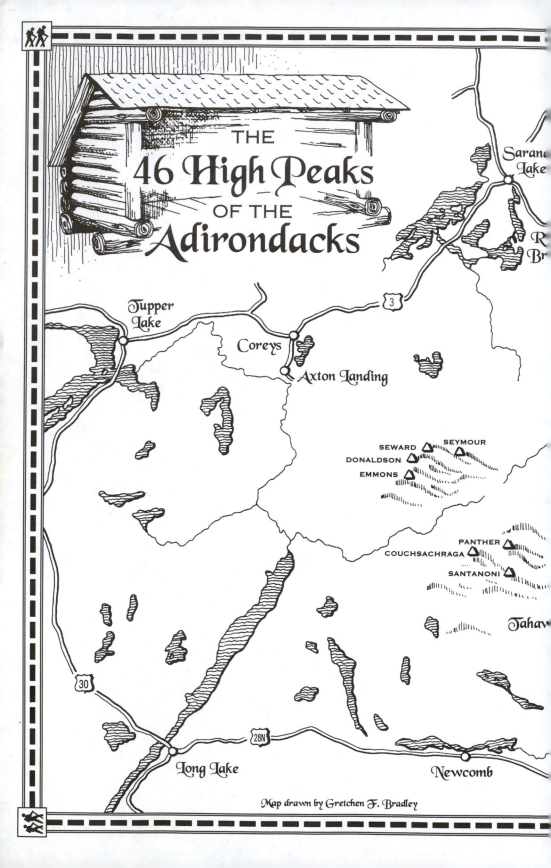

THE
46 High Peaks
OF THE
Adirondacks

Saran
Lake

R
Br

Tupper
Lake

3

Coreys

Axton Landing

SEWARD ▲ SEYMOUR ▲
DONALDSON ▲
EMMONS ▲

PANTHER ▲
COUCHSACHRAGA ▲
SANTANONI ▲

Tahaw

30

28N

Long Lake

Newcomb

Map drawn by Gretchen F. Bradley